INTRODUCTION TO LATIN

Second Edition

INTRODUCTION TO LATIN

Second Edition

Susan C. Shelmerdine

Focus Publishing
Newburyport, Massachusetts

In memory of
Gerda M. Seligson and Glenn M. Knudsvig,
teachers, scholars, friends

Introduction To Latin Second Edition
© 2013 Susan C. Shelmerdine

Focus Publishing/R. Pullins Company
PO Box 369
Newburyport, MA 01950
www.pullins.com

ISBN: 978-1-58510-390-4
CIP information is available.
To see available ebook versions, visit www.pullins.com.

Library of Congress Cataloging-in-Publication Data

Shelmerdine, Susan Chadwick.
  Introduction to Latin / Susan C. Shelmerdine. -- Second edition.
      pages. cm.
  ISBN 978-1-58510-390-4
  1. Latin language--Grammar. I. Title.
  PA2080.2.S47 2013
  478.2'421--dc23
                          2013002909

Printed in the United States of America

10 9 8 7 6 5 4 3 2 1

0213H

Introduction to Latin

List of Illustrations xii

Preface xiii

Preface to the Second Edition.. xv

The Latin Alphabet and Pronunciation..1

Chapter One 5
    The Sentence   5
        Parts of Speech   5
        What Words Do (Function)   6
        Sentence Patterns: 6
            Intransitive   7
            Transitive   7
    The Verb   7
        Present Active Indicative   8
        Present Active Infinitive   8
        Principal Parts   9
        Indicative Uses: Statements and Questions   9
        Infinitive Use: Complementary   9

Chapter Two 13
    Latin Cases   13
        Nominative and Accusative Case Uses   13
    The Noun   14
        Gender   14
        Dictionary Entry   15
        First Declension   15
        Second Declension: Masculine   16
        Second Declension: Neuter   17
    The Conjunction   18
    Reading Latin: Using Expectations   18

Chapter Three 23
    Imperative: Commands   23
    Vocative Case: Direct Address   24
    Genitive Case   24
        Possession   24
        Of the Whole (Partitive)   24
    Dative Case   25
        Indirect Object   25
        Reference (Interest)   25
    Expectations   25

Chapter Four..29
   The Adverb   29
   The Preposition   29
   Ablative Case   30
      Means (Instrument)   30
   Expressions of Place   30
      Place to Which   30
      Place Where   31
      Place from Which   31
   Adverbial Modification (Summary)   31
   Word Order   32
   Reading Skills   32

Chapter Five..37
   The Adjective: First and Second Declensions   37
      Agreement   39
      Substantive Use   40
   More Uses of the Genitive   40
      Explanatory   41
      Objective   41
      Subjective   41
   Adjectival Modification (Summary)   41
   Sum: Present Indicative and Infinitive   41
   Sentence Pattern: Linking   41
   More Uses of the Ablative   42
      Accompaniment   42
      Manner   42

Reading Chapter I..47
   Narrative Reading I: Fall of Troy   47
   Dictionary Practice/Form Identification   48
   Review of the Sentence and its Parts   48
   Question Words for Extra Practice   48
   Word Derivations   49
   English Abbreviations   50

Chapter Six 51
   Imperfect Active Indicative: First and Second Conjugations   51
   Future Active Indicative: First and Second Conjugations   52
   Sum: Imperfect and Future Indicative   52
   The Gap   53
   Infinitive Use: As a Noun   54
   Dative of Possession   54

Chapter Seven 59
   Third Declension Nouns: Consonant Stem   59
      Third Declension: Masculine and Feminine   59

Third Declension: Neuter   60
Gender Patterns   61
The Pronoun: Personal (1)   62
ego; tū   62
Possum: Present, Imperfect and Future Indicative   63
Sentence Pattern: Special Intransitive   63

Chapter Eight 69
Third and Fourth Conjugations   69
Present Active Indicative and Infinitive   69
Present Active Imperative   70
The Pronoun: Personal (2)   71
is, ea, id as a Personal Pronoun   71
Sentence Pattern: Factitive   71

Chapter Nine 77
Imperfect Active Indicative: Third and Fourth Conjugations   77
Future Active Indicative: Third and Fourth Conjugations   77
The Pronoun: Demonstrative   78
hic, haec, hoc   79
ille, illa, illud   79
is, ea, id   79
Adjectival Use   80

Chapter Ten 85
Third Declension Nouns: i-Stem   85
Third Declension Adjectives   86
Expressions of Cause   89

Reading Chapter II..93
Narrative Reading II: Aeneas in Italy   93
Dictionary Practice/Form Identification   94
Review of the Sentence and its Parts   95
Questions Words for Extra Practice   95
Word Building   95
Roots   95
Vowel Weakening   96
English Abbreviations and Phrases   96

Chapter Eleven...97
Perfect Active Indicative   97
Pluperfect Active Indicative   99
Future Perfect Active Indicative   100
Special Adjectives in –**īus**   101
Numerals   102
Expressions of Time   103

Chapter Twelve 109
   Dependent Clauses   109
      Adverbial Use   109
      Word Order   111
   Accusative of Extent and Degree   111
   Dative with Adjectives   112

Chapter Thirteen...117
   The Pronoun: Relative   117
   Adjectival Use: Relative Clause   118
   The Pronoun: Reflexive   119

Chapter Fourteen 125
   Passive Voice (1)   125
      Present Passive Indicative   126
      Imperfect Passive Indicative   127
      Future Passive Indicative   127
      Present Passive Infinitive   128
   Sentence Pattern: Passive   129
   Ablative of Agent   129

Chapter Fifteen 135
   Passive Voice (2)   135
      Perfect Passive Indicative   135
      Pluperfect Passive Indicative   136
      Future Perfect Passive Indicative   136
      Perfect Passive Infinitive   137
   Linking Sentence Pattern Revisited   137
   Possessive Adjectives and Possession Using **eius**   138
   Ablative of Specification (Respect)   139

Chapter Sixteen...143
   Fourth Declension   143
   Fifth Declension   144
   Locative Case   145
   Other Place Expressions   145

Reading Chapter III 151
   Narrative Reading III: Numa   151
   Dictionary Practice/Form Identification   152
   Review of the Sentence and its Parts   153
   Question Words for Extra Practice   153
   Word Building   153
      Families of Words   153
      Consonant Changes   154
   English Abbreviations and Phrases   154

Chapter Seventeen..155
   Participles   155

Tenses of the Participle   157
Participle Uses   158
Ablative Absolute   159

Chapter Eighteen 165
Dependent Clauses: Noun Use – Relative Clause   165
The Interrogative Pronoun: **quis, quid**   166
The Interrogative Adjective: **quī, quae, quod**   166
Intensive Pronouns: **ipse; īdem**   167

Chapter Nineteen..173
Infinitive Forms   173
Perfect Active Infinitive   173
Future Active Infinitive   173
Review of all Infinitive Forms   174
Noun Clause: Indirect Statement   175
Tenses of the Infinitive in Indirect Statement   176

Chapter Twenty...183
Irregular Verbs: **volō, nōlō, mālō**   183
Negative Commands with **nōlō**   183
Noun Clauses: Objective Infinitive   184

Chapter Twenty-One..189
Comparison of Adjectives   189
Declension of Comparatives   190
Irregular Comparison   191
Comparison with **quam** and Ablative of Comparison   192
Indefinite Pronoun: **quīdam, quaedam, quoddam**   192

Reading Chapter IV 197
Narrative Reading IV: Tullus and the Treachery of Mettius   197
Dictionary Practice/Form Identification   199
Review of the Sentence and its Parts   200
Question Words for Extra Practice   200
Word Building: Compounds   201
English Abbreviations and Phrases   202

Chapter Twenty-Two..203
Comparison of Adverbs   203
More on **quam**   204
Deponent Verbs   204
Special Intransitive: Deponent Verbs used with an Ablative Object   206

Chapter Twenty-Three...211
Irregular Verbs   211
eō, īre, iī (īvī), itūrus (to go)   211
Compounds of **eō**   212
ferō, ferre, tulī, lātus (to carry, bear)   212

Compounds of **ferō**   213
Paradigm of **vīs, vīs,** *f.*   213

Chapter Twenty-Four 219
Present Active Subjunctive   219
Present Passive Subjunctive   220
Present Subjunctive of **sum, possum** and **volō**   221
Independent Uses of the Subjunctive   221
Exhortation/Command   221
Wish   222
Doubt   222
Possibility   222

Chapter Twenty-Five 227
Imperfect Active Subjunctive   227
Imperfect Passive Subjunctive   227
Imperfect Subjunctive of **sum, possum** and **volō**   228
Dependent Uses of the Subjunctive: Adverbial Clauses   228
Purpose   228
Result   229

Chapter Twenty-Six 235
Perfect Active Subjunctive   235
Pluperfect Active Subjunctive   236
Perfect and Pluperfect Subjunctive of **sum** and **possum**   236
Tenses in Independent Uses of the Subjunctive   237
Tenses in Dependent Uses of the Subjunctive: Sequence of Tenses   238
Dependent Uses of the Subjunctive: Adverbial Clauses   239
Circumstances, Cause, Concession   239
Time, with anticipation   239

Chapter Twenty-Seven 245
Perfect and Pluperfect Passive Subjunctive   245
Adverbial Clauses: Conditions   246
Simple conditions   246
Subjunctive conditions   246

Chapter Twenty-Eight 253
Irregular Verbs: **fīō, fierī, factus sum**   253
Dependent Uses of the Subjunctive: Noun Clauses   253
Noun Result   254
Indirect Question   254
Indirect Command   255
Clauses of Fearing   256

Chapter Twenty-Nine 261
The Gerund   261
The Gerundive   263
Passive Periphrastic and Dative of Agent   265

Chapter Thirty 271
    More on Relative Pronouns   271
        Connecting Relative   271
        Clauses of Characteristic   272
        Clauses of Purpose   273
    Review of Cases   273
        Nominative   273
        Vocative   273
        Accusative   274
    Dictionary Practice/Form Identification   274

Chapter Thirty-One 281
    Subordinate Clauses in Indirect Speech   281
    Impersonal Constructions   282
    More on the Dative   283
        Dative with Compound Verbs   283
        Dative of Purpose   284
    Review of Cases   285
        Genitive   285
        Dative   285
    Dictionary Practice/Form Identification   286

Chapter Thirty-Two 291
    The Supine   291
    Ut + Indicative   292
    More on the Ablative   293
        Description (Quality)   293
        Degree of Difference   293
    Review of Cases   294
        Ablative   294
        Locative   294
    Dictionary Practice/Form Identification   295

List of Latin Sources 301

Morphology Reference Section 307

Vocabulary by Chapter 323

English-Latin Vocabulary 341

Latin-English Vocabulary 353

List of Intransitive Verbs 367

Index 369

LIST OF ILLUSTRATIONS

Maps

Italy xiv

Troy and the Aegean.. 46

Caesar's Gaul... 134

Illustrations

Amphitrite on a Sea Horse. Mosaic from Ostia, 2nd c. A.D. 4

Altar in the Forum. Pompeii, 1st c. A.D. 22

Chariot and Triton (sea-god). Mosaic from Ostia, 2nd c. A.D. 68

Snack Bar. Pompeii, 1st c. A.D. 108

Mosaics outside Merchant's Office Complex, Ostia, end 2nd c. A.D. 182

Street. Pompeii, 1st c. A.D. 234

Neptune on his Chariot and Sea Creatures. Mosaic from Ostia, 2nd c. A.D. 260

Forum with Mt. Vesuvius in the distance. Pompeii, 1st c. A.D. 290

PREFACE

There are many textbooks for learning Latin, and different approaches have worked for different students over the years. This book is primarily intended for college level students who do not have the luxury of time to explore the language through a true "reading" method and still gain exposure to the ancient authors. The aims of this book can be stated briefly:

- to provide a streamlined text that can be completed in one year, even for courses which meet only three days a week

- to provide brief explanations of English grammar as needed within the text itself so students will have an easy reference point for the Latin material

- to provide "real Latin" readings early and often, in the form of both sentences and short passages. In all but one or two cases the Readings in each chapter are unconnected to those in the previous chapter, so they can be easily used or skipped as each instructor wishes

- to offer a variety of different kinds of exercises, especially in the early chapters

- to get out of the way of the instructor. Rather than trying to explain every nuance of the grammar in detail, this text offers concise explanations and allows the instructor to expand those explanations as he or she wishes

- not to overwhelm the student. Some texts provide so much explanation, study hints, cultural sidebars, and the like that students have trouble distinguishing between the "need to know" and the "nice to know" material. This text tries to focus on the "need to know" material.

A few words of explanation about the style of the text and the presentation of vocabulary may also be in order. The writing is intentionally informal because college students have said they prefer this. Chapter Vocabulary is placed at the end of each chapter where it can be found easily, although students should be encouraged to memorize it before doing the chapter exercises. This vocabulary provides a core of common words for students to memorize and has been limited to a manageable 20-25 words in most cases, with the total number of words indicated in parentheses. Full listings of all forms are given in the Chapter Vocabulary and in the Latin to English Vocabulary at the end of the book. Intransitive verbs, with the exception of **sum** and **eo** with its compounds in Chapter 23, are listed without a fourth principal part to help students distinguish them from transitive verbs. A complete list of the intransitive verbs with the future active participle in the fourth principal part slot is included at the end of the Latin to English Vocabulary. Vocabulary help for Readings and Practice Sentences uses abbreviated listings of the kind students are likely to see in dictionaries and notes accompanying upper level texts. It is important that students learn basic vocabulary meanings and practice the skill of deciding what meaning is appropriate in different contexts. Therefore this book does not annotate many idioms or include many specialized meanings for Latin words. Words which can reasonably be guessed in the Readings and Practice Sentences are printed in bold to encourage students to make informed guesses.

This book uses traditional terms for the most part and avoids jargon wherever possible, but it also tries to incorporate advances in language pedagogy pioneered by several generations of scholars at the University of Michigan. So readers will occasionally see an unfamiliar but very useful term, such as Gap or Expectations, and will benefit from several types of exercises developed at Michigan, such as the Dictionary Practice exercises in the Reading Chapters. My debt to my own teachers and colleagues, Gerda M. Seligson and Glenn M. Knudsvig, will be obvious to many and is an honor to acknowledge here, even though this is not a book they would have written.

My colleagues at The University of North Carolina, Greensboro offered kind and helpful comments on many drafts of this text. My grateful thanks go to them, as well as colleagues at Bowdoin College, Virginia Polytechnic Institute and State University and Wake Forest University, and students at all four institutions for their willingness to try the text in its early stages. They have all helped to make the book better, as have colleagues elsewhere who offered suggestions along the way. John Traupman provided invaluable help with his careful reading of the final draft. Special thanks also go to Cynthia Shelmerdine for her help on the index, to Maura Heyn for the pictures and to Jeffrey Patton for creating the maps.

Note: The short narrative used in exercise 103 was adapted from part of a now defunct web page, so I am unable to give proper credit to the original author.

Italy

PREFACE TO THE SECOND EDITION

I am most grateful to colleagues, readers, students, and instructors who were generous enough to offer constructive criticism of the 1st edition and suggestions to improve the book. As before, I have put the needs of a beginning learner ahead of elegantly written Latin and strict adherence to all rules of usage. (In Reading Chapter I, for example, *bellum pugnant* appears in place of *bellum gerunt*, because the 3rd conjugation has not yet been taught.) Students who go on to read more Latin will absorb these things as they go, but no first year student should be expected to master all the details at once.

Thanks to my colleagues at The University of North Carolina, Greensboro who were willing to talk over specific issues as I tried to chart a course between the different approaches of traditional classicists and linguists. Special thanks to Maura Heyn and Sarah Wright for reading so many drafts and providing feedback that was at the same time helpful and humane. Thanks also to Sarah Wright for heroic efforts in helping with proofs and the index.

Most of the changes in this edition are in response to student and colleague comments. They aim to spread material out more evenly between the first and second halves of the book, and to afford additional time for the more complex syntax in the second half of the book. In a college course meeting 3 days a week, it should be possible to cover Ch. 1-15 (or 16) in the first semester. Major changes are detailed below:

- A Derivatives exercise has been added after each Chapter Vocabulary through Chapter 29, asking students to define English words and link them with the Chapter Vocabulary to which they are related. These exercises can be assigned at the beginning of each chapter to encourage students to learn the vocabulary first.

- Chapters 1-5 are substantially the same, with two changes in the order of material presented. Imperatives and Vocatives have been moved from Ch. 6 to Ch. 3 and, in Ch. 4 the Preposition is introduced before the Ablative case. For those wanting more formal explication of syntax, Ch. 4 and 5 have short summaries of Adverbial and Adjectival Modification. Ch. 5 has added an explanation of three Genitive uses which were not included in the previous edition, but were used in readings and practice sentences; instructors can decide if they want their students to learn these uses at this early stage. Principal parts have been handled as in the 1st edition (see p. xiii).

- Four Reading Chapters are included, with narrative readings accompanied by comprehension questions in Latin. (The "question words for extra practice" can be used with the material in the regular chapters as well.)

These chapters also include a review of material in the preceding chapters, and a short list of English abbreviations and phrases derived from Latin.

- Personal and Demonstrative pronouns have been spread among 3 chapters (Ch. 7-9), and Interrogative and Reflexive pronouns appear in separate chapters later on.

- Introduction of 3rd and 4th conjugation verbs has been consolidated and is presented in Ch. 8 and 9, before the Perfect system which is now presented for all conjugations at once in Ch. 11.

- 3rd declension i-stem nouns have been separated from consonant stems and are now introduced with 3rd declension adjectives in Ch. 10. These nouns are marked in the vocabulary with an asterisk.

- Adverbial and Adjectival dependent clauses have been moved to Ch. 12-13 (from Ch. 18-19).

- The Passive verb system has been moved to Ch. 14-15 (from Ch. 17 and 20).

- Participles are introduced early in the second half of the book, Ch. 17 (instead of Ch. 24), and Indirect Statement has been moved to Ch. 19 (from Ch. 22).

- The Subjunctive material has been rearranged and spread out. The most common uses are now covered in Ch. 24-28.

- Ch. 30-32 are intended as a bridge to the next level of Latin; they concentrate on reading and do not have English to Latin exercises. They introduce some constructions likely to be found at the next level of Latin, provide a review of case uses, and include a variety of readings with minimal editing.

- Long marks (macrons) have been a constant battle to correct and, in some cases, different dictionaries handle them differently. I have done my best to standardize the usage in this book, but apologize in advance for the errors that remain.

Susan C. Shelmerdine
December, 2012

The Latin Alphabet and Pronunciation

A. The Alphabet

The Latin alphabet has 24 letters, the same letters as in the English alphabet, but without **j** and **w**. Latin vowels are the same as in English: **a, e, i, o, u** and **y**. The letter **i** was used as both a vowel and a consonant; before another vowel in the same syllable, it is the consonant and is written as a **j** in some books: **Iūlius** = *Julius* (yule-ee-us), *adiuvō* (ad-you-woh).

Pronunciation

B. Vowels

Vowels in Latin are either long or short by nature. Long vowels are marked with a macron (a long mark - so called from the Greek for "long," *makros*).

Long		Short	
ā	father	a	alike
ē	they	e	pet
ī	unique	i	it
ō	obey	o	off
ū	rude	u	put

y occurs in words borrowed from Greek and is pronounced like French **tu**, a sound that doesn't occur in English dialects, but can be produced by putting your lips in place to say "ooo," and saying "eee" instead.

C. Diphthongs

Two vowels pronounced as one sound are called diphthongs. Latin has six diphthongs, which are pronounced as follows:

ae	like the **ai** in a**i**sle	haec, aequor
au	like the **ou** in **ou**t	laudō, **au**t
ei	like the **ei** in w**ei**gh	deinde
eu	**eh-oo** as in feud	heu
oe	like the **oi** in s**oi**l	proelium, coepit
ui	**oo-ee** as in t**wee**d	cui, huic

D. Consonants

Most Latin consonants are pronounced like their English counterparts. Note the following additional points:

1

c is always a hard sound like the **c** in **c**at, never as in **c**ent	**c**ēna, **c**um
g is always a hard sound like the **g** in **g**oat, never as in **g**entle	**g**lōria, **g**ēns
i (**j**) as a consonant is always like the **y** in **y**ellow	**i**am
r is produced by tapping the tip of the tongue against the roof of the mouth, and probably sounded like the **r** in pea**r**l pronounced with a Scottish accent	**R**ōma, fortūna
s is always like the **s** in **s**ea, never as in plea**s**e	**s**enātus, puellā**s**
t is always like the **t** in **t**ime, never as in na**t**ion	ra**t**iō
v sounds like English **w** in **w**ine (not **v**ine)	**v**īnum, **v**ēritās
x sounds like English **ks**; like the **x** in e**x**tinct (not e**x**ert)	e**x**

Combinations

bs is pronounced like **ps** in ecli**ps**e	a**bs**tulit, ur**bs**
gu, qu sound like **gw, qw** and the **u** is not counted as a vowel	lin**gu**a; in**qu**it, **qu**ī
ch sounds like English **k** in bac**kh**and, (not **ch**eese)	**ch**orus, pul**ch**er
ph originally sounded like the **ph** in she**ph**erd (not **ph**iloso**ph**y) - but over time came to be pronounced like our **f**.	**ph**iloso**ph**ia
th sounds like the **th** in ho**th**ouse (not **th**eater)	**th**eātrum
double consonants were pronounced as two distinct sounds with a slight pause between the two: (e.g.) ou**t-t**ake	e**cc**e, pue**ll**a, te**rr**a, mi**tt**ō

E. Syllables

There are no silent letters in Latin, so a Latin word has as many syllables as it has vowels and/or diphthongs:

vē-ri-tā-te, con-ci-li-um	4
for-tū-na, pu-el-la	3
lau-dō, er-rat	2
mē, quī	1

Words are divided as follows:

1. between two vowels, or a vowel and a diphthong:
   ā-ēr, vi-ae

2. between double consonants (usually):
   an-nus, mag-nus

3. a single consonant between two vowels goes with the second vowel:
   a-mor, me-mo-ri-a

Syllable Quantity

Knowing the quantity of a syllable is important for accenting a word properly and for understanding verses in poetry later on.

A syllable is long by nature if it contains a long vowel or a diphthong:

> Rō-ma, lau-dem

A syllable is usually long by position if it has a short vowel followed by **x** or **z** or by two (or more) consonants:

> **o**p-tō, sa-pi-**e**n-ti-a

The letter **h** is not counted as a consonant when determining the quantity of a syllable.

F. Accent

A Latin word is accented either on the second or third syllable from the end of the word.

Words of two syllables are accented on the next to last syllable:

> a´-mor
> du´-cem

Words of more than two syllables are accented on the next to last syllable if it is long:

> mo-nē´-mus
> for-tū´-na

otherwise on the third to last syllable:

> re´-gi-tur
> a-gri´-co-la

Some little words, called *enclitics* (from the Greek because they "lean on" the preceding word), are added to and pronounced with other words. The most common enclitics are: **-que, -ve, -ne**. When one of these is added to another word, the accent is always on the syllable before the enclitic: po-pu-lus´-que, de-a´-ve.

Amphitrite on a Sea Horse. Mosaic from Ostia, 2nd c. A.D.

CHAPTER 1

The Sentence
    Parts of Speech
    What Words Do (Function)
    Sentence Patterns
        Intransitive
        Transitive
The Verb
    Present Active Indicative
    Present Active Infinitive
    Principal Parts
    Indicative Uses: Statements and Questions
    Infinitive Use: Complementary

1. The Sentence

A sentence in Latin, as in English, is made up of words that express a complete thought. The simplest form of a sentence includes only a subject and a verb:

    The farmer works.   They walk.

In order to understand sentences in English, we depend on knowing some rules of word order, for example: subjects come before verbs. Latin, however, uses a system that adds different endings onto certain words to make their function and meaning clear, so you will need to learn those endings before you can read Latin. You will also need to understand the different types of words that make up a sentence and what each of those words does.

2. Parts of Speech

Latin does not have an article (*the, a, an*), but otherwise has the same parts of speech as English:

Part of Speech	Definition	English Examples
• **verb**	a **verb** expresses existence, action, occurrence	is, hits, teaches, happens
• **noun**	a **noun** names a *person, place,* or *thing* (including an *idea* or a *quality*)	farmer, house, truth, Frank
• **adjective**	an **adjective** adds to (modifies) the meaning of a noun or pronoun to specify a quality	large, old, good, true

Part of Speech	Definition	English Examples
• adverb	an **adverb** usually modifies a verb, giving information about time, place, manner or degree	today, often, here, well
• preposition	a **preposition** connects a noun or pronoun to another word in the sentence and shows a relationship between the two	from, into, with, by
• pronoun	a **pronoun** substitutes for a noun, referring to something without naming it	he, who, it, this, that
• conjunction	a **conjunction** connects words or groups of words	and, but, if, when
• interjection	an **interjection** is an exclamation	oh!, alas, huh?

Each of the different parts of speech just listed has a function in the sentence, which will be the focus of this and future chapters. Chapter vocabulary will be listed by part of speech. This chapter includes only verbs and nouns.

3. **What Words Do (Function)**

The **subject** of a sentence is the person or thing the sentence is about. To identify the subject, use the verb of the sentence and ask "who/what _____s?" – the answer will be the subject. It is usually a noun or pronoun.

> The woman praises the boy. > who praises? > <u>woman</u> = subject

The **verb** of a sentence expresses an action or occurrence. The same term, "verb," names both the part of speech and its function.

> The woman praises the boy. > what is happening? > someone <u>praises</u> = verb

The **direct object** of a sentence is the person or thing that receives the action of the verb directly. Like the subject, it is usually a noun or pronoun.

> The woman praises the boy. > who receives praise? > the <u>boy</u> = direct object

4. **Sentence Patterns**

Reading Latin (or any language) becomes easier if you know what to expect in a sentence. It is therefore very useful to recognize certain common sentence patterns and their core parts. The verb sets the pattern for a sentence. The meaning of the verb determines what items are necessary to complete the action it expresses, and this allows you to know what other core items to expect. This chapter began with a sentence pattern that included only a subject and a verb (*The farmer works*), but other sentences also include a direct object (*The woman praises the boy*).

This chapter will teach you the two common patterns just mentioned, and future chapters will add four more. While you don't need to know the names of these patterns to read Latin, it will be easier to talk about them if you learn the terms in bold below.

1) **Intransitive**
   • subject
   • verb

The **intransitive** pattern requires only a subject and a verb to express a complete thought:

| The farmer works. | Subject = farmer | Verb = works |
| They walk. | Subject = they | Verb = walk |

Verbs that do not take a direct object are called **intransitive verbs**.

2) **Transitive**
   • subject
   • verb
   • direct object - in the accusative case

The **transitive** pattern requires a direct object to complete the action of the verb:

| The woman has a rose. | Subject = woman | Verb = has | D.O. = rose |
| We call the farmer. | Subject = we | Verb = call | D.O. = farmer |

Verbs that take a direct object are called **transitive verbs**.

5. **The Verb**

Verbs in Latin fall into four regular groups, called **conjugations**. Each conjugation has a common set of endings, which are added to the **stem** of the verb. The verb stem carries the meaning of the verb and a characteristic vowel:

1st Conjugation [-ā-]		**2nd Conjugation [-ē-]**	
amā-	love	**monē-**	advise
laudā-	praise	**vidē-**	see

The endings are called **personal endings** because they carry information about who the subject of the verb is. These endings are traditionally identified by **person** (first, second, or third) and **number** (singular or plural) as follows:

	SINGULAR		PLURAL	
1st person	**-ō**	I	**-mus**	we
2nd person	**-s**	you	**-tis**	you, you all
3rd person	**-t**	he, she, it	**-nt**	they

Verb forms with personal endings are called **finite** forms (from the Latin for "limit," *finis*) because they are limited by identifying the subject.

Verbs are also identified by

   • Tense - when an action happens (e.g., present, future)

   • Voice - whether the subject is doing the action (active) or receiving the action (passive)

   • Mood - whether the verb is a simple statement or question (indicative), or a command (imperative), etc.

These items will be discussed in future chapters.

Present Active Indicative

This chapter introduces **present active indicative** verb forms of the first and second conjugations:

	1st Conjugation		**2nd Conjugation**	
1st sg.	amō	I love	moneō	I advise
2nd sg.	amās	You love	monēs	You advise
3rd sg.	amat	He, she, it loves	monet	He, she, it advises
1st pl.	amā**mus**	We love	monē**mus**	We advise
2nd pl.	amā**tis**	You (all) love	monē**tis**	You (all) advise
3rd pl.	ama**nt**	They love	mone**nt**	They advise

Notice that the personal endings are the same for both conjugations and are added directly to the stem of the verb in each form. In the "I" form (first person singular) of the first conjugation, the stem vowel -**a**- contracts with the personal ending to produce the form **amō** rather than **amaō**.

Two important points should be noted here:

- The present tense can be translated "I love," "I am loving," or "I do love."

- Because the ending on the verb tells you who the subject is, Latin does not have to use a separate word for the subject as we do in English: **vident** = *they see*

Exercise 1. Identify the person of each singular verb form. Then change each form to plural.

Example: amō   1st person; amāmus

1. terreō
2. laudat
3. habet
4. vocās
5. timēs
6. superō

Present Active Infinitive

The **infinitive** is a verbal noun, a form of the verb that is not limited (*infinitus*) by a personal ending. Here are the present active infinitive verb forms of the first and second conjugations:

1st Conjugation		**2nd Conjugation**	
amāre	to love	monēre	to advise
laudāre	to praise	vidēre	to see

To find the present stem of a verb, drop the -**re** from the present active infinitive. The vowel on the verb stem will show what conjugation the verb belongs to:

amā (re) - first conjugation
monē (re) - second conjugation

Exercise 2. Identify the conjugation of each verb by looking at the stem vowel.

1. laudāre
2. terrēre
3. timēre
4. iuvāre
5. habēre
6. vocāre

6. **Principal Parts**

The dictionary entry for a verb includes the first person singular indicative form (*I love*) and the present infinitive form (*to love*), along with two other forms, which will be introduced in future chapters. These forms are called **principal parts** because they contain the verb stems on which all other forms are built. Because it is not always possible to predict these stems, it is important to memorize all the principal parts for each verb. Here are some examples for the first and second conjugations:

1st Conjugation			
amō	**amāre**	**amāvī**	**amātus**
I love	to love	I have loved	having been loved
laudō	**laudāre**	**laudāvī**	**laudātus**
I praise	to praise	I have praised	having been praised
2nd Conjugation			
moneō	**monēre**	**monuī**	**monitus**
I advise	to advise	I have advised	having been advised
videō	**vidēre**	**vīdī**	**vīsus**
I see	to see	I have seen	having been seen

Some verbs do not have all four principal parts (and are often called "defective" because they are missing forms). You will notice this in the dictionary listing when it happens. This book also uses **-ūrus** for the fourth principal part of most intransitive verbs: **tacitūrus** "about to be silent".

7a. **Indicative Uses: Statements and Questions**

Indicative verb forms are used to **make simple statements** and to **ask simple questions**:

Fēmina labōrat.	The woman works.
Fēminane labōrat? Labōratne fēmina?	Is the woman working? Does the woman work?

Notice that Latin does not require any change of word order to signal a question. Often the enclitic **-ne** (§F) is added on the end of the first word of a question.

7b. **Infinitive Use: Complementary**

Infinitives have properties of both verbs and nouns, and have several different uses. One of the most common is to **complete the meaning of another verb**. This use of the infinitive is called the **complementary infinitive**:

Labōrāre dēbeō.	I ought **to work**.
Optatne **tacēre**?	Does he desire **to be silent**?

For now when you see an infinitive, it should lead you to expect either **dēbeō** or **optō**;

future chapters will add to the list of verbs which can be completed by a complementary infinitive. Uses of the infinitive as a noun will be introduced in Chapter 6 and later chapters.

Exercise 3. Identify the person and number of each verb, then translate into English in 3 different ways.

Example: amant   third person, plural; "they love," "they are loving," "they do love"

1.	optat	6.	vocās
2.	vident	7.	terrēs
3.	habēmus	8.	iacētis
4.	labōrātis	9.	superant
5.	timeō	10.	iuvāmus

Exercise 4. Identify the person and number of each English verb, then translate into Latin. Make sure to use the proper stem vowel for each Latin form.

Example: they are afraid   third person, plural; timent

1.	he is working	6.	am I silent?
2.	do they love?	7.	she warns
3.	it scares	8.	you (pl.) call
4.	you (sg.) desire	9.	they are seeing
5.	we owe	10.	do you (sg.) have?

Exercise 5. Using the stem meanings given below, translate each of the following into English. Then, paying attention to the stem vowel in each form, see if you can write the first two principal parts, which would appear in the dictionary for each verb.

Example: errant (wander) "they wander"; errō, errāre

1.	pugnās (fight)	6.	nāvigāmus (sail)
2.	miscet (mix)	7.	tenēs (hold)
3.	volant (fly)	8.	servātis (save)
4.	dolētis (grieve)	9.	rīdēmus (laugh)
5.	audent (dare)	10.	stat (stand)

Exercise 6. Some of the following sentences contain nouns that will be explained in Chapter 2. For now, if the noun ends in **-a**, it is the subject; if it ends in **-am**, it is the direct object. Note that if you see the **-am** ending, it should lead you to expect a transitive sentence pattern with a transitive verb; absence of this form should lead you to expect an intransitive pattern and an intransitive verb. Translate each of the following sentences into English.

1.	Agricola labōrat.	6.	Aquane nautam terret?
2.	Fēminam laudant.	7.	Optāsne labōrāre?
3.	Fēmina rosam habet.	8.	Fortūna nautam iuvat.
4.	Timētis.	9.	Tacēre dēbeō.
5.	Videtne nauta aquam?	10.	Pecūniam amāmus.

Chapter 1 Vocabulary

Nouns (these forms will be explained in Chapter 2)

agricola, agricolae *m.*	farmer
aqua, aquae *f.*	water
fēmina, fēminae *f.*	woman
fortūna, fortūnae *f.*	chance, luck, fortune
nauta, nautae *m.*	sailor
pecūnia, pecūniae *f.*	money, property
rosa, rosae *f.*	rose

Verbs (English translations will be given in the infinitive form)

amō, amāre, amāvī, amātus	to love
dēbeō, dēbēre, dēbuī, dēbitus	"ought to, should"; to owe; to be obligated to
habeō, habēre, habuī, habitus	to have; consider
iaceō, iacēre, iacuī, iacitūrus	to lie (e.g., on the ground)
iuvō, iuvāre, iūvī, iūtus	to help; please
labōrō, labōrāre, labōrāvī, labōrātus	to work, strive
laudō, laudāre, laudāvī, laudātus	to praise
moneō, monēre, monuī, monitus	to advise, warn, remind
optō, optāre, optāvī, optātus	to choose, desire, wish for
superō, superāre, superāvī, superātus	to overcome, conquer, surpass
taceō, tacēre, tacuī, tacitūrus	to be silent ("I am silent")
terreō, terrēre, terruī, territus	to terrify, scare
timeō, timēre, timuī	to fear, be afraid (of)
videō, vidēre, vīdī, vīsus	to see
vocō, vocāre, vocāvī, vocātus	to call, summon

Other

-ne *(attached to the end of the first word in the sentence, usually the most important word in the question)*	signals a yes-no question *(no English translation)*

(23)

Derivatives: One way to help learn new Latin words is to connect them with English words that are derived from the Latin roots. For each English word below, give the Latin word from the Chapter 1 Vocabulary to which it is related and the English word's meaning.

Example: adopt   Latin word: **optō**; Meaning of adopt: to take by choice

1. labor
2. fortunate
3. terrify
4. laudable
5. habit
6. aquarium
7. adjutant
8. rosette
9. vocal
10. admonition
11. timid
12. nautical
13. tacit
14. adjacent
15. agriculture
16. debt
17. feminine
18. insuperable
19. impecunious
20. amorous

CHAPTER 2

Latin Cases:
 Nominative and Accusative Case Uses
The Noun
 Gender
 Dictionary Entry
 First Declension
 Second Declension: Masculine
 Second Declension: Neuter
The Conjunction
Reading Latin: Using Expectations

8a. **Latin Cases**

Instead of using word order to identify subjects and other elements in a sentence, Latin uses forms, called **cases**, which provide information about what each noun, pronoun, or adjective is doing in a sentence. Sometimes the function is equivalent to an English subject or direct object (as you saw in the sentences in Chapter 1), but sometimes the case must be translated with an English preposition in addition to the noun. Latin has six common cases (and a seventh less common one). Each case may signal more than one function, but the most common uses are these:

Case Name	Common Use
Nominative	**subject of a finite verb**
genitive	possession; "of ___"
dative	indirect object; "to ___," or "for ___"
Accusative	**direct object**
ablative	"by, with, from, in _____" (often with a preposition)
vocative	direct address
locative	place

This chapter includes only the **nominative** and **accusative** case uses. The other cases will be introduced in Chapters 3, 4 and 16. Sample paradigms will typically list only the first five cases.

8b. **Nominative and Accusative Case Uses**

Nominative

- Subject of a finite verb (a verb with a personal ending - §5)

  Agricola labōrat. The **farmer** works.

Accusative

- Direct Object

    Fēminam amant. They love the **woman.**

9. **The Noun**

Nouns in Latin fall into five regular groups, called **declensions** according to the vowel that originally appeared at the end of the noun stem. Sound changes over time have made this vowel disappear in many of the forms. The easiest way to identify the declension of a noun is to look at the genitive singular case ending, which is unique to each declension:

Declension	Genitive singular ending	Characteristic vowel
1	-ae	ā
2	-ī	o
3	-is	ī (or a consonant)
4	-ūs	u
5	-ēī, eī	ē

The stem carries the meaning of the noun and the case endings indicate its function in the sentence. To find the stem of a noun, drop the genitive singular ending:

agricol -ae   first declension
amīc -ī   second declension

In addition to being marked for **case**, the endings on a noun, like the personal endings on verbs, are also marked for **number** (singular or plural).

Exercise 7. Identify the declension of each noun from its genitive singular ending.

1.	aquae	4.	bellī	7.	senātūs
2.	amīcī	5.	ignis	8.	cōnsiliī
3.	nautae	6.	diēī	9.	puellae

10. **Gender**

Latin nouns are also identified by **gender** (masculine, feminine or neuter). Grammatical gender does not necessarily correspond to biological gender; it can be predicted for some words but not for others. You will need to memorize the gender of each noun when you learn it. Some general patterns, however, are useful to remember:

- Most first declension nouns are feminine. The common exceptions are often remembered as the "PAIN" words, which are all masculine:

Poēta	poet
Agricola	farmer
Incola	inhabitant
Nauta	sailor

- Most second declension nouns with a nominative in **-us** or **-er** are masculine. The most common exceptions are:

humus	ground	feminine
vulgus	crowd	neuter (sometimes masculine)
pelagus	sea	neuter

  Names of trees, towns and islands (e.g., quercus "oak") are feminine.

- Second declension nouns with a nominative in **-um** are neuter.

11. Dictionary Entry

The **dictionary entry** for a noun lists the nominative singular form, the genitive singular form, and the gender of the noun. The genitive singular form identifies the noun's declension:

puella, puellae *f.*	girl	Gen. **-ae**	=	first declension
amīcus, amīcī *m.*	friend	Gen. **-ī**	=	second declension
rēgnum, rēgnī *n.*	kingdom	Gen. **-ī**	=	second declension

Here are sample nouns for the first and second declensions, with the case endings listed separately to the right.

12. First Declension

Singular	Noun	English meaning	Endings
Nominative	fēmina	a woman _____s	**-a**
Genitive	fēminae	of a woman	**-ae**
Dative	fēminae	to/for a woman	**-ae**
Accusative	fēminam	____ ____s a woman	**-am**
Ablative	fēminā	(by, with, from) a woman	**-ā**
Plural			
Nominative	fēminae	women_____	**-ae**
Genitive	fēminārum	of women	**-ārum**
Dative	fēminīs	to/for women	**-īs**
Accusative	fēminās	____ ____s women	**-ās**
Ablative	fēminīs	(by, with, from) women	**-īs**

Notice the following:

- The long -**ā** of the ablative singular ending distinguishes it from the nominative singular, so it should be memorized from the outset.

- The dative and ablative plural have the same ending, -**īs**. In a sentence, the context will usually make the identification of the case clear. The same is true for the genitive and dative singular and the nominative plural endings (-**ae**).

Exercise 8. Identify each of the following first declension nouns by case and number. If the ending is ambiguous, include all possibilities.

Example: nautam   accusative singular

1.	lūnā	4.	fortūnae
2.	nātūra	5.	agricolārum
3.	aquīs	6.	puellās

Exercise 9. Following the pattern of **fēmina**, decline **nauta** and **aqua** in all cases, singular and plural.

Exercise 10. Identify the case of each singular noun form. Then change each form to plural. (Some forms will have more than one answer.)

Example: fortūnā   ablative; fortūnīs

1.	casam	4.	aquā
2.	agricola	5.	nātūrae
3.	pecūniae	6.	puellā

13a. **Second Declension: Masculine**

Singular	**Noun**	**Noun**	**Endings**
Nominative	anim**us**	puer	**-us** or **-er**
Genitive	anim**ī**	puer**ī**	**-ī**
Dative	anim**ō**	puer**ō**	**-ō**
Accusative	anim**um**	puer**um**	**-um**
Ablative	anim**ō**	puer**ō**	**-ō**
Plural			
Nominative	anim**ī**	puer**ī**	**-ī**
Genitive	anim**ōrum**	puer**ōrum**	**-ōrum**
Dative	anim**īs**	puer**īs**	**-īs**
Accusative	anim**ōs**	puer**ōs**	**-ōs**
Ablative	anim**īs**	puer**īs**	**-īs**

Notice the following:

- As in the first declension, the dative and ablative plural have the ending **-īs**. The dative and ablative singular of the second declension also have the same ending, **-ō**.

- Also as in the first declension, the genitive singular and nominative plural endings (**-ī**) are the same. Once again, the context will usually make the identification of the case clear.

- Some words in **-er** drop the **-e-** from the stem in all but the nominative singular. Compare **puer, puerī** with **ager, agrī**. The genitive singular shows you the stem that will be used for the remaining forms.

13b. **Second Declension: Neuter**

Singular	Noun	Endings
Nominative	rēgn**um**	-um
Genitive	rēgn**ī**	-ī
Dative	rēgn**ō**	-ō
Accusative	rēgn**um**	-um
Ablative	rēgn**ō**	-ō
Plural		
Nominative	rēgn**a**	-a
Genitive	rēgn**ōrum**	-ōrum
Dative	rēgn**īs**	-īs
Accusative	rēgn**a**	-a
Ablative	rēgn**īs**	-īs

Notice the following:

- In the neuter pattern, the nominative and accusative case endings are **always** the same, both in the singular and the plural. Use the context of the sentence to decide which case is being used.

- All other endings are the same as those for the masculine pattern.

Exercise 11. Given the gender indicated, identify each of the following second declension nouns by case and number. If the ending is ambiguous, include all possibilities.

Example: dominōs   accusative plural

1. amīcum (*m.*)
2. bellum (*n.*)
3. locōrum (*m.*)
4. dōna (*n.*)
5. animī (*m.*)
6. virīs (*m.*)

Exercise 12. Following the second declension patterns above, decline **amīcus**, **ager** and **bellum** in all cases, singular and plural.

Exercise 13. In each of the following sentences, replace the underlined word with the correct form of the word in parentheses; if the subject changes, make sure the verb agrees with the new number. Write out the whole sentence.

Example: Fēmina puellās amat. (puer pl.) > **Puerī** puellās ama**nt**.

1. Rosās habeō. (ager pl.)
2. Puellam vocāmus. (vir)
3. Vidēsne lūnam? (rēgnum)
4. Puer timet. (agricola pl.)
5. Dominus puerōs ridet. (puella pl.)
6. Dominī consilium habent. (dōnum pl.)

Exercise 14. Identify the case of each noun and the person and number of each verb. Remember that the nominative case marks the subject and the accusative marks the direct object; translate each of the following sentences into English.

1. Virī clāmant.
2. Agricola agrum videt.
3. Monēsne puellās?
4. Dōnum amīcī amant.
5. Animum bellum terret.
6. Nautae clāmāre audent.
7. Cōnsilium laudāmus.
8. Fēmina dōna optat.
9. Iuvātisne dominōs?
10. Rēgna superāre dubitant.

Exercise 15. Identify the function of each English noun or pronoun as Subject or Direct Object and list the Latin case needed to express that function; ignore the article ("the"). Identify the person and number of each English verb. Then translate into Latin.

1. I see the gifts.
2. Are the boys scaring (their) friends?
3. We ought to help (our) friend.
4. The woman loves the man.
5. The sailors are accustomed to working.
6. You (sg.) are afraid.

14. **The Conjunction**

Latin uses "coordinating" **conjunctions** (words like *and, but, or*) just as English does, to connect words, phrases and sentences. The most important thing to notice is that **the words being connected always have the same function** (e.g., 2 subjects, 2 verbs; never a subject and a verb, or a subject and direct object):

The sailor helps and works.	2 verbs: help + work
The woman and the man hesitate.	2 subjects: woman + man
The boy shouts but the man is silent.	2 sentences: boy shouts + man is silent

As in English, conjunctions in Latin are commonly placed between the words or phrases they connect. An exception to this is the enclitic **-que,** which is added to the *second* item of those being connected:

puer et puella	boy and girl
et puer et puella	both the boy and the girl
puer puellaque	boy and girl
rīdēmus clāmāmusque	we are laughing and shouting

A coordinating conjunction should lead you to expect another word or phrase with the same function as that in the first item. If two subjects are joined by a conjunction, the verb will usually be plural:

Agricola et puer labōrant. The farmer and the boy are working.

Exercise 16. In the following sentences, identify the two items being connected and their function; then translate the sentence into English.

Example: Puerī labōrant et clāmant.   labōrant + clāmant: verbs
                                        The boys are working and shouting.

1. Puer puellaque labōrant.
2. Pecūniam videt sed tacet.
3. Habēmusne aquam et rosās?
4. Timent virī et fēminae amīcōs vocant.
5. Bellum et puerōs et puellās terret.
6. Agricola nautaque dōna laudant.

15. **Reading Latin: Using Expectations**

In order to read successfully (in any language), it is necessary to have a sense of what makes a complete sentence. In English we expect a simple statement to appear in the order subject + verb + direct object ("the woman praises the boy"), and we become so accustomed to this pattern that we don't think about it as we read. Similarly, if we see the verb "hit," we know the sentence is not complete without a direct object (§4). Since Latin does not use the same word order as English, it is more difficult to know at first when a sentence is complete. Once you learn to notice certain clues, however, you will find that you can predict what will come next even in a Latin sentence and you will be able to read sentences from left to right in the Latin word order.

Chapter 1 introduced two common sentence patterns and some endings that help you to identify verbs. This chapter has introduced endings that help you identify the case of a noun and therefore its use in a sentence. With these tools, you should be able to predict what to expect as you read a Latin sentence.

Intransitive: **agricola labōrat.**   The farmer works.

- subject   nominative case ending
- verb   verb ending

Transitive: **fēmina rosam habet.**   The woman has a rose.

- subject   nominative case ending
- verb   verb ending
- direct object   accusative case ending

Because conjunctions connect items with the same function (§14), you should also be able to predict what form is coming next when you see a phrase such as "**puella et _____**" (*another nominative*). If you pay close attention to the endings on words and practice the art of expecting what is likely to come next in a sentence, you will soon find yourself reading Latin successfully.

Exercise 17. In the following sentences, use your knowledge of sentence patterns, verb and noun endings, vocabulary, and how conjunctions work to fill in the blank with the form needed to complete each sentence.

Example: Puer iuva___.   Puer iuvat.
            (Puer is nominative singular, so the verb needs a third singular ending)

1. Fēmina iace___.
2. Habetne puell___ rosās?
3. Vir amīc___ (sg.) amat.
4. Dominī dōn___ (pl.) optant.
5. Vir___ clāmant.
6. Naut___ agricolaeque locum laudant.
7. Terretne puerōs bell___ ?
8. Virum vidē___ et vocāmus.
9. Amīc___ pecūniam habent.
10. Vir labōrā___ solet.

Exercise 18. Identify the function of each word as you read it (Subject, Object, Verb, Complementary Infinitive, Connector), then translate the following sentences.

1. Vir puerque casam vident.
2. Puella clāmat et fēmina timet.
3. Nauta iacet sed amīcus labōrat.
4. Vidēsne dōna?
5. Cōnsilium habētis.
6. Agricolam iuvāre solent.
7. He desires to see the gift.
8. The woman praises the fields.
9. Is she laughing at the boy?
10. They ought to see the place.
11. We conquer the kingdoms.
12. Both the farmer and the lord are calling the sailors.

Narrative A

A short description of Italy before wars with neighbors and with foreigners interrupted the peaceful life of the people:

> Ītalia agrōs et agricolās habet. Nātūra aquam cibumque dat et bellum puerōs puellāsque nōn terret. Locum virī fēminaeque laudant. Iuvat fortūna populum!

Vocabulary:

Ītalia, Ītaliae *f.*	Italy	dō, dare	to give
cibus, cibī *m.*	food	populus, populī *m.*	the people

Chapter 2 Vocabulary

Nouns

ager, agrī *m.*	(cultivated) field; countryside
amīcus, amīcī *m.*	friend
animus, animī *m.*	mind, spirit, courage; soul
bellum, bellī *n.*	war
casa, casae *f.*	house, hut
cōnsilium, cōnsiliī *n.*	plan, advice
dominus, dominī *m.*	master, lord
dōnum, dōnī *n.*	gift, present
locus, locī *m.*	place, position
(in pl. sometimes also neuter)	
lūna, lūnae *f.*	moon
nātūra, nātūrae *f.*	nature
puer, puerī *m.*	boy
puella, puellae *f.*	girl
rēgnum, rēgnī *n.*	kingdom, royal power
vir, virī *m.*	man; occasionally "husband"

Verbs

audeō, audēre, ausus sum	to dare
clāmō, clāmāre, clāmāvī, clāmātus	to shout
dubitō, dubitāre, dubitāvī, dubitātus	to hesitate, doubt
rīdeō, rīdēre, rīsī, rīsus	to laugh, laugh at
soleō, solēre, solitus sum	to be accustomed

Coordinating Conjunctions

et	and
et ... et	both ... and
-que	and
sed	but

(23)

Derivatives: For each English word below, give the Latin word from the Chapter 2 Vocabulary to which it is related and the English word's meaning.

1.	dominate	9.	audacious
2.	puerile	10.	donate
3.	virile	11.	clamorous
4.	counselor	12.	dubious
5.	risible	13.	lunar
6.	amicable	14.	bellicose
7.	locale	15.	casino
8.	obsolete	16.	animosity

Altar in the Forum. Pompeii, 1st c. A.D.

CHAPTER 3

Imperative: Commands
Vocative Case: Direct Address
Genitive Case
      Possession
      Of the Whole (Partitive)
Dative Case
      Indirect Object
      Reference (Interest)
Expectations

So far you have learned the core items of a sentence: the subject (nominative case), the verb, and the direct object (accusative case). This chapter introduces a new verb form used to give commands and three new cases, two of which are used most often as modifiers of these core items.

16. **Imperative: Commands**

In Chapter 1 you learned that Latin expresses simple statements and simple questions by using the indicative mood (§7 A). To indicate a direct command, Latin uses a mood called the **imperative** (from the Latin verb **imperō**, *to command*), which usually appears in the second person (singular or plural) and present tense:

	1st Conjugation		**2nd Conjugation**	
2nd sg.	amā	(you) love!	monē	(you) advise!
2nd pl.	amā**te**	(you all) love!	monē**te**	(you all) advise!

Notice that

- The singular form is usually the same as the present stem, found by dropping **-re** from the present active infinitive (§5).
- The plural form adds **-te** to the present stem.

Negative commands will be introduced in a future lesson.

Exercise 19. Identify each of the following singular verbs as indicative or imperative. Then change each form to plural and translate.

Example: amat   Indicative; amant; they love

1. rideō
2. vocā
3. implet
4. iuvās
5. tacē
6. nārrō

17. **Vocative Case: Direct Address**

The **vocative** case in Latin is used to address a person (or thing) directly. Its form is identical to the nominative in both the singular and the plural of all declensions, except for the singular of 2nd declension nouns ending in **-us** or **-ius.** 2nd declension nouns in **-us** use the vocative singular ending **-e**; those ending in **-ius** use the ending **-ī**:

	1st Declension		2nd Declension	
singular	fēmina	amīc**e**	fil**ī**	vir
plural	fēmin**ae**	amīc**ī**	fili**ī**	vir**ī**

Sometimes the vocative is preceded by **ō** and, in modern texts, it is often set off from the rest of the sentence by commas. The vocative can appear in statements and questions, but it is especially common in commands:

statement:	Agricola, ō **amīcī**, semper labōrat.	(Oh) friends, the farmer is always working.
question:	Nārrāsne, **nauta**, fābulam?	Sailor, are you telling a story?
command:	**Amīce**, puerīs fābulam nārrā!	Friend, tell the boys a story!

Exercise 20. Identify each of the following sentences as statements or commands, then translate.

1. Puellae cēnam parant.
2. Puellae cēnam parāte.
3. Puer amīcōs vocat.
4. Puer amīcōs vocā.
5. Amīcus tacet.
6. Amīce tacē.

18. **Genitive Case**

Remember that the genitive singular is the second form listed in the dictionary entry for nouns and helps identify the declension of the noun (§11):

	1st Declension	2nd Declension
Gen. sg.	puell**ae**	loc**ī**
Gen. pl.	puell**ārum**	loc**ōrum**

The **genitive** case is usually best translated "of _____" and can indicate several different relationships between a noun and another word. Two of the most common uses of the genitive are to show:

- **Possession**
  liber **puellae**   the book **of the girl** (the girl**'s** book)
  animus **virī**   the spirit **of the man** (the man**'s** spirit)
- **Of the Whole (Partitive)** - the genitive expresses the whole of which a part is mentioned
  turba **virōrum**   a crowd **of men**
  nēmō **fēminārum**   no one **of the women** (none **of the women**)

Exercise 21. Change each genitive form to the plural, then translate the new sentence.

1. Amīcus fēminae tacet.
2. Habēsne dominī librōs?
3. Arma virī habet.
4. Templum deī vidēmus.

19. **Dative Case**

The dative singular forms have different endings in the first and second declensions, but the dative plural forms are the same in both declensions:

	1st Declension	**2nd Declension**
Dat. sg.	puell**ae**	loc**ō**
Dat. pl.	puell**īs**	loc**īs**

The **dative** case is usually best translated "to _____" or "for _____" and, like the genitive, has a number of different uses. Two of the most common uses are to show:

- **Indirect Object** - the person to whom something is given, said or done

  Puellae dōnum dat.   He gives a gift **to the girl**.
                                                                 (= he gives **the girl** a gift)
  Virō fābulās nārrāmus.   We tell stories **to the man**.
                                                                 (= we tell **the man** stories)

  Notice that, in the translations in parentheses above, a shift of English word order replaces the word "to" before the indirect object.

- **Reference (Interest)** - the person to whom a statement refers or is of interest

  Dominō labōrat.   He is working **for the master.**
  Puerīs dōnum habet.   He has a gift **for the boys**.
  Nautae pontus est pulcher.   **To a sailor (in the eyes of a
                                                                 sailor)** the ocean is beautiful.
  (est and pulcher will be taught in Chapter 5)

Exercise 22. Change each dative form from singular to plural, then translate the new sentence.

1. Turba rēgnō labōrat.
2. Nautae fābulam nārrat.
3. Habēsne puellae librōs?
4. Arma dominī puerō parāmus.
5. Fīlius virō pecūniam dēbēre solet.
6. Nēmō aquam agricolae portat.

Exercise 23. In each of the following English sentences, identify the words that Latin would express with a genitive or dative form, and say how they are used.

Example: We give the girl the man's book.   girl = dative - indirect object
                                                                         man's = genitive - possession

1. Some of the men destroyed the house of the king.
2. Tell the king this.
3. The prince's army is fighting for the king.
4. I will show the king part of the treasure.

20. **Expectations**

With the addition of the genitive and dative cases, reading Latin becomes more complicated, and it becomes even more important to pay attention to the context of the sentence. The first declension ending **-ae** can signal either a nominative plural, or a genitive or dative singular, and the second declension ending **-ī** can signal either a nominative plural or a genitive singular. However the number of the verb (singular or plural) will help you resolve these ambiguities since a nominative plural noun should be accompanied by a plural verb.

Similarly, in the first two chapters, an accusative noun led you to expect a transitive verb. Now, verbs with the meanings "show," "tell," and "give" regularly occur not only with an accusative direct object, but also a dative indirect object:

dō	I give a gift **to him**.	(= I give **him** a gift.)
nārrō	We tell a story **to her**.	(= We tell **her** a story.)
mōnstrō	They show a book **to us**.	(= They show **us** a book.)

Since Latin often places the verb at the end of a sentence, the presence of both an accusative and a dative should lead you to expect one of these verbs. Practicing the fine art of expecting what might come next will make you a better (and faster) reader.

Exercise 24. Identify the case and use of the underlined form and then translate the sentence.

Example: Rosās fēminae puellīs dant.   fēminae = Nominative, plural, feminine
The women give roses to the girls. *or*
The women give the girls roses.

1. Mōnstrāsne silvam filiīs?
2. Templum dīs aedificant.
3. Turba virōrum caelum videt.
4. Puerī, fābulam nārrāte.
5. Fēmina puellae virōque cēnam parat.
6. Arma virumque laudō.
7. Agrōs agricolae laudāre solēmus.
8. Imperium dominī filium terret.

Exercise 25. Translate each of the following sentences.

1. Puerī puellaeque clāmāre solent.
2. Templum deārum implēte!
3. Habēsne rēgnō cōnsilium, ō Rōmule?
4. Amīcōs iuvāre dēbēmus.
5. Dī turbae imperium mōnstrant.
6. Silva virum fēminamque terret.
7. Animum virō nātūra dat.
8. Vocāte, ō puellae, agricolās.

Exercise 26. Translate into Latin. Remember to identify the function of each English word first and decide what Latin case and number is needed for each noun, and what person and number is needed for each verb.

1. They are building the man's house.
2. The girls desire to see the forest and ocean.
3. O gods, winds fill up the sky.
4. Are you (pl.) telling stories to the boys?
5. A man is bringing weapons for the farmers.
6. We ought to have gifts for the women.
7. Does the ocean's water scare the sailors?
8. She hesitates to laugh.

Narrative B

Sometimes we learn about early wars from the accounts of poets. The war here is fictional.

Poētae fābulās nārrant et mōnstrant animum virōrum: Advenae ad terram Ītaliae nāvigant. Pugnāre solent et bellum portant. Puerī puellaeque timent. Populus templum aedificat et dīs dōna dat. Sed virī Ītaliae imperium habent et nautās superant. Turba virōs laudat et populus gaudet.

Vocabulary:

poēta, -ae *m.*	poet	Ītalia, Ītaliae *f.*	Italy
advena, advenae *m.*	foreigner	populus, populī *m.*	the people
ad terram	"to the land"	gaudeō, gaudēre	to rejoice
nāvigō, nāvigāre	to sail		

Practice Sentences

Identify the case and use of the underlined words, then translate.

Example: Amīcus puerō librum dat.　　　dative - indirect object of dat
　　　　　　　　　　　　　　　　　　A friend gives a book to the boy.

1. Mūsa, virō causās bellī memorā. (Vergil - adapted; *the poet asks the Muse to help him with his poem*)

2. Bella parat Mīnōs. (Ovid; *the city of Athens is about to be attacked*)

3. Dēbēmus vidēre templa deōrum. (Sallust – adapted; *urging people to consider the simple buildings constructed by their ancestors*)

Vocabulary:

Mūsa, -ae *f.*	Muse	Mīnōs (nom.)	Minos, legendary king of Crete
causa, -ae *f.*	cause, reason		
memorō, -āre	recall, tell		

Chapter 3 Vocabulary

Nouns

arma, armōrum *n.* (pl.)	arms, weapons
caelum, caelī *n.*	sky, heavens
cēna, cēnae *f.*	dinner
dea, deae *f.*	goddess
dat. pl. and abl. pl. = deābus	
deus, deī *m.*	god
nom. pl. = dī; *dat. pl. and abl. pl.* = dīs	
fābula, fābulae *f.*	story
filius, filiī *m.* (*voc. sg.* = filī)	son
imperium, imperiī *n.*	command, (military) power
liber, librī *m.*	book
nēmō *m.*	no one
acc. sg. = nēminem	
pontus, pontī *m.*	sea, ocean
Rōmulus, Rōmulī *m.*	Romulus (legendary founder of Rome)
silva, silvae *f.*	forest, wood
templum, templī *n.*	temple, shrine
turba, turbae *f.*	crowd
ventus, ventī *m.*	wind, breeze

Verbs

aedificō, aedificāre, aedificāvī, aedificātus	to build
dō, dare, dedī, datus	to give
impleō, implēre, implēvī, implētus	to fill, fill up; complete
mōnstrō, mōnstrāre, mōnstrāvī, mōnstrātus	to show, demonstrate
nārrō, nārrāre, nārrāvī, nārrātus	to tell (a story)
parō, parāre, parāvī, parātus	to prepare
portō, portāre, portāvī, portātus	to carry, bring
pugnō, pugnāre, pugnāvī, pugnātus	to fight

(24)

Derivatives: For each English word below, give the Latin word from the Chapter 3 Vocabulary to which it is related and the English word's meaning.

1.	edifice	9.	celestial
2.	fabulous	10.	deify
3.	narrative	11.	ventilate
4.	turbulence	12.	pugnacious
5.	armory	13.	library
6.	data	14.	apparatus
7.	filial	15.	monstrosity
8.	sylvan	16.	imperious

CHAPTER 4

The Adverb
The Preposition
Ablative Case
      Means (Instrument)
Expressions of Place
      Place to Which
      Place Where
      Place From Which
Adverbial Modification (Summary)
Word Order
      Reading Skills

This chapter introduces two new parts of speech (adverb and preposition) commonly involved in modifying the action of the verb. It also introduces the ablative case.

21. The Adverb

Adverbs give information about time, place, manner or degree, and answer questions such as when?, where?, how?, how much?, to what extent? They usually modify verbs, although they may also modify adjectives, other adverbs, or even a whole sentence:

They live **there**.
He is **almost** seven.
They work **very quickly**.
This is **indeed** an interesting topic.

Unlike nouns, adverbs in Latin are not declined. Many adverbs end in **-ter** or **-ē**, but the form of others must be memorized:

fortiter	bravely
hodiē	today
facile	easily
ibi	there
tandem	finally

22. The Preposition

Like adverbs, Latin **prepositions** are not declined. In Latin as in English, *a preposition never appears alone in a sentence*. It occurs with a noun (or pronoun) called the **object of the preposition**, which is either in the **accusative** or the **ablative** case. Like adverbs, prepositional phrases give information about (e.g.) where, with whom, or why the action of the verb occurs:

Agricola **trāns agrum** ambulat.	The farmer walks **across the field**.
Puer **in casā** sedet.	The boy is sitting **in the house**.

The dictionary entry for a preposition will indicate which case it is used with, and this case should be memorized when you learn each new preposition. Note that some prepositions can be used with either case and will have different meanings with each case:

in (+ abl.)	in, on
in (+ acc.)	into, onto, against

A preposition usually comes before its object. Chapter 2 introduced the idea of using expectations as you read Latin (§20). Remember, when you see a preposition in Latin it should lead you to expect a noun in either the accusative or ablative.

23. **Ablative Case**

The ablative singular always ends in a vowel, usually long. In the first and second declensions the ablative plural forms are the same and are also identical to the dative plural:

	1st Declension	2nd Declension
Abl. sg.	puellā	locō
Abl. pl.	puellīs	locīs

Remember that in the first declension, the long **-ā** of the ablative singular ending distinguishes it from the nominative singular, which ends in a short **-a**.

The **ablative** case has been called the "junk case" by students over the years because it seems to have so many meanings. This is not far from the truth, since the ablative case in Latin combines three distinct cases from an earlier language. As a result, there is no single way to translate the ablative, although using a phrase with the English prepositions *by, with, from, in,* or *at* will cover most of the common uses.

One important use of the ablative *without a preposition* is to show:

- **Means (Instrument)** — the thing by or with which something is done

Oculīs videō.	I see **with my eyes**.
Armīs pugnant.	They fight **with weapons**.
Verbīs mōnstrāmus.	We show [this] **by (means of) words**.

24. **Expressions of Place**

Latin regularly uses prepositional phrases to indicate where or in what direction an action happens:

- Preposition with **Accusative**

  Place to Which (Motion Towards)

Portāsne aquam **ad virōs**?	Are you carrying water **to the men**?
In templum ambulat.	She walks **into the temple**.

- Preposition with **Ablative**

    Place Where

Agricola **in agrō** labōrat.	The farmer works **in the field**.
Prō templīs sedent.	They sit **in front of the shrines**.

    Place from Which (Motion From)

Puella **ā turbā** errat.	The girl wanders **away from the crowd**.
Puerī **ē pontō** festīnant.	The boys hurry **out of the ocean**.

Notice that with either place from which or place to which, you should expect a verb of motion in the sentence.

Exercise 27. Choose the verb that best meets the expectation raised by the prepositional phrase, then translate the phrase.

1. in silvam _____   A) iacet   B) festīnant
2. in casā _____   A) labōrātis   B) errās
3. ab agrō _____   A) clāmat   B) ambulant
4. ad agrum _____   A) rīdēmus   B) festīnāmus
5. ex templō _____   A) ambulō   B) sedeō

Exercise 28. Identify the case and use of each of the underlined words, then translate the sentence.

Example: Virī in <u>agrīs</u> pugnant.   ablative - place where; object of prep. **in**
                                                The men are fighting in the fields.

1. Puella, ad <u>fēminam</u> librum portā.   5.   Ad templum <u>deō</u> dōna semper
2. In <u>viā</u> dominus iacet.   portāmus.
3. Superātisne <u>armīs</u> virōs?   6.   Vir fēminaque ē <u>turbā</u> ambulant.
4. Nautae in <u>pontō</u> nāvigant.   7.   Prō <u>casīs</u> fābulās nārrāre solēmus.
                                            8.   Virī prō <u>rēgnō</u> pugnant.

You have now learned three different Latin forms that can be translated into English with the preposition "to." Be careful as you read to distinguish among these very different uses:

- **laudāre**   to praise   infinitive
- **puerō**   to the boy   dative indirect object
- **ad locum**   to the place   preposition + accusative (motion towards)

Exercise 29. For the following sentences, indicate how you would express the underlined phrase in Latin. Do not translate the phrases.

Example: We give a gift <u>to the girls</u>.   dative indirect object

1. They are walking <u>to the forest</u>.   4.   He delivered your letter <u>to us</u>.
2. We want <u>to learn</u> Latin!   5.   Will you come <u>to the city</u>?
3. She told a story <u>to the children</u>. 6.   I ought <u>to stay</u> with them.

25. **Adverbial Modification (Summary)**

Adverbial modifiers modify a verb, adverb, or adjective (§27), but not a noun. The new items you have just learned (adverbs, prepositional phrases, ablative of means) and the dative of reference from the last chapter (§19) function as adverbial modifiers. These modifiers are *not* part of the core of a sentence. While the "core" items (subject, verb and, sometimes, direct object) are required for a sentence to be complete, adverbial modifiers are not required, but can be added to provide extra information about what is going on in the sentence. It is useful to note that the following underlined modifiers are all equivalent in function:

simple sentence (core only):	The boy runs.
plus adverbial modifier (adverb):	The boy runs <u>quickly</u>.
plus adverbial modifier (prep. phrase):	The boy runs <u>into the house</u>.
plus adverbial modifier (abl. of means):	The boy runs <u>on his feet</u>.

26. **Word Order**

Word order in Latin is much more variable than in English, which has strict word order rules. In general, the first and last words of the sentence in Latin are the most important, so an author may put in those places whatever words he wants to emphasize. If no special emphasis is intended, usually the subject will appear first and the verb last. Word order in poetry and in highly rhetorical works, however, may be quite different from "normal" word order in a prose narrative. With these cautions, and an extra warning not to take the following as any kind of "rule," here is a "normal" word order pattern for a Latin sentence in which no particular emphasis is intended:

Amīcus virī puerō in agrō aquam saepe dat.
The man's friend often gives water to the boy in the field.

subject	**amīcus**	nominative
modifier of the subject	**virī**	genitive
indirect object	**puerō**	dative
modifier of the verb (e.g. place)	**in agrō**	prep. phrase
direct object	**aquam**	accusative
adverb	**saepe**	adverb
verb	**dat**	verb

Reading Skills

As you continue to build expectations in reading Latin, one of the best skills to practice is that of recognizing words and phrases that naturally go together. Good readers do not read a sentence one word at a time, but automatically group portions of text into short, meaningful phrases. Linguists call these word groups "chunks." The more words we can group together into meaningful "chunks," the faster we read. This is true in Latin as well as English, but it takes practice. Different readers will identify chunks of different lengths. In the sentence above, for instance, there are at least two chunks:

amīcus virī	the man's friend	subject plus modifier
in agrō	in the field	prepositional phrase

Some readers will also see a third chunk:

| **saepe dat** | (he) often gives | adverb plus verb |

And others will automatically see the direct object with the verb in this third chunk:

aquam saepe dat   (he) often gives water

Notice that **puerō in agrō** is not a meaningful phrase, despite the similarity of the endings on **agrō** and **puerō**.

Exercise 30. In the following sentences, copy each chunk you see and identify its function as in the examples above.

1. Puellīs fābulam nārrāre nōn solet.
2. Vir fēminaque ex agrō festīnant.
3. Nēmō puerōrum in silvam ambulāre audet.
4. Pontum et caelum oculīs facile vidēmus.
5. Vidētisne saepe lūnam in caelō?

Exercise 31. Identify the sentence pattern(s) in each of the following sentences and then translate each of the following.

1. In saxō post casam, ō puerī, sedēte.
2. Ventus aquaque caelum implent.
3. Agricola trāns agrum tandem festīnat.
4. Fēmina puerōs ad cēnam vocat et in casam festīnant.
5. Turbae viam monstrā.
6. Dāsne amīcīs Rōmulōque cōnsilia?
7. Nēmō saxa ē silvā portat.
8. Dominus virōs verbīs facile terret, sed amīcī rīdent.

Exercise 32. Translate into Latin.

1. A stone is lying in the road.
2. Do the sons desire to see the money?
3. Fight on behalf of (your) friends!
4. The farmer is finally building a house for his friend.
5. We often praise the achievements of the sailors.
6. They give the crowd of men weapons.
7. The gods always fill the sky with winds.
8. Boys and men hurry out of the crowd and toward the temple of the goddess.

Reading 1 *(adapted)*

The early Latin poet Ennius (239-169 B.C.) tells how the god Neptune got his domain from Jupiter:

Iuppiter Neptūnō imperium dat
pontī et Neptūnus īnsulās et loca prope pontum rēgnat.

Vocabulary:

īnsula, īnsulae *f.*	island	pontī – *this use of the gen. at §30*	
Iuppiter (nom.)	Jupiter (a god)	prope (+ acc.)	near
Neptūnus, -ī *m.*	Neptune (a god)	rēgnō, rēgnāre	to rule over

Practice Sentences

Identify the case and use of the underlined word, then translate.

Example: Turba <u>virōrum</u> in viā errat.   genitive - partitive (of the whole)
                                                A crowd of men wanders in the road.

1. In <u>oculīs</u> animus habitat.   (Pliny the Elder)
2. In terrīs <u>imperium</u> Caelum habet.   (Ennius – adapted; *talking about the order of the universe*)
3. Neptūnus <u>ventīs</u> implet vēla.   (Vergil – adapted; *Neptune helps the Trojans on their sea voyage*)

Vocabulary:

habitō, habitāre	to live	vēlum, vēlī *n.*	sail
terra, terrae *f.*	land, earth		

Chapter 4 Vocabulary

Nouns

factum, factī *n.*	deed, act, exploit, achievement
oculus, oculī *m.*	eye
saxum, saxī *n.*	rock, stone; cliff
verbum, verbī *n.*	word
via, viae *f.*	road; way

Verbs

ambulō, ambulāre, ambulāvī, ambulātūrus	to walk
errō, errāre, errāvī, errātus	to wander; err
festīnō, festīnāre, festīnāvī, festīnātus	to hurry, hasten
nāvigō, nāvigāre, nāvigāvī, nāvigātus	to sail, sail over (across), navigate
sedeō, sedēre, sēdī, sessūrus	to sit

Adverbs

facile	easily
nōn	not
saepe	often
semper	always
tandem	finally
tum	then, at that time; next

Prepositions

ā, ab (+ abl.)	away from
ad (+ acc.)	to, toward
ē, ex (+ abl.)	out of, from
in (+ abl.)	in, on
in (+ acc.)	into, onto, against
post (+ acc)	behind; after
prō (+ abl.)	in front of; on behalf of; instead of
trāns (+ acc.)	across, beyond

(23)

Derivatives: For each English word below, give the Latin word from the Chapter 4 Vocabulary to which it is related and the English word's meaning.

1. verbose
2. erratic
3. sedentary
4. binoculars
5. absent
6. perambulate
7. transport
8. postscript
9. viaduct
10. sempiternal

CHAPTER 5

The Adjective: First and Second Declensions
      Agreement
      Substantive Use
More Uses of the Genitive
      Explanatory
      Objective
      Subjective
Adjectival Modification (Summary)
Sum: Present Indicative and Infinitive
Sentence Pattern: Linking
More Uses of the Ablative
      Accompaniment
      Manner

So far, you have learned about the core of a sentence (§3, 4) and adverbial modifiers (§25). This chapter introduces a new part of speech (adjective) that modifies nouns. It also introduces a new sentence pattern and additional uses of the genitive and ablative cases.

27. **The Adjective: First and Second Declensions**

Adjectives in Latin look like nouns and use most of the same endings. Unlike nouns, which have only one gender, adjectives have masculine, feminine and neuter forms. The dictionary entry for an adjective lists the nominative singular form of each gender: **bonus, bona, bonum**. Adjectives fall into two groups; one uses the endings of the first and second declensions, and the other uses endings of the third declension. There are no fourth or fifth declension adjectives.

This chapter introduces adjectives of the first and second declensions, which follow the patterns for nouns that you have already seen (§12, 13). Adjectives of the third declension will be introduced in Chapter 10.

Here is a sample adjective of the first and second declension:

bonus, bona, bonum   **good**

Singular	Masculine	Feminine	Neuter
Nominative	bonus	bona	bonum
Genitive	bonī	bonae	bonī
Dative	bonō	bonae	bonō
Accusative	bonum	bonam	bonum
Ablative	bonō	bonā	bonō
Plural			
Nominative	bonī	bonae	bona
Genitive	bonōrum	bonārum	bonōrum
Dative	bonīs	bonīs	bonīs
Accusative	bonōs	bonās	bona
Ablative	bonīs	bonīs	bonīs

Some adjectives follow the pattern of **puer** (§13):

līber	lībera	līberum
līberī	līberae	līberī
etc.		

Some follow the pattern of **ager** (§13):

noster	nostra	nostrum
nostrī	nostrae	nostrī
etc.		

Note that the stem of these adjectives can be determined by dropping the nominative feminine or neuter singular ending:

līber (a)   **līber** (um)
nostr (a)   **nostr** (um)

Exercise 33. Given the dictionary entries below, identify each of the following forms by part of speech (adjective or noun), case, number and gender. If the ending is ambiguous, include all possibilities.

altus, alta, altum   pontus, pontī *m.*
imperium, imperiī *n.*   pulcher, pulchra, pulchrum
parvus, parva, parvum   rosa, rosae *f.*

	Item	Part of Speech	Case	Number	Gender
Example:					
	rosam	noun	accusative	singular	feminine
	parvōrum	adjective	genitive	plural	masc. or neuter

1. pontōs
2. parvō
3. pontī
4. rosīs
5. altīs
6. pulchrā
7. imperia
8. altum

28. **Agreement**

Adjectives agree with the nouns they modify in case, number and gender. This does *not* mean that they belong to the same declension or that their endings always look the same:

pulchra puella	(nominative, singular, feminine)	beautiful girl
pulcher amīcus	(nominative, singular, masculine)	handsome friend
bonum agricolam	(accusative, singular, masculine)	good farmer
malus vir	(nominative, singular, masculine)	evil man

For a while you will only see first and second declension nouns and adjectives. Beginning in Chapter 7 you will begin to see combinations of nouns and adjectives from different declensions.

When one adjective modifies two or more nouns of different genders, it often agrees with the nearest noun.

ager et casa tua   your field and house

See also §33 below for adjectives in the "predicate position."

Because Latin uses agreement in case, number and gender to indicate what noun an adjective modifies, the adjective and noun do not have to appear next to each other, or in a particular order, as they usually do in English. This is especially true in poetry, but you should expect that a noun and its adjective may be separated in any text that you are reading. Often an adjective will precede the word it modifies and help to resolve the form of that word if it is otherwise ambiguous.

Exercise 34. Identify each of the following nouns by case, number and gender, then say which adjective(s) could modify the noun listed with them. Be prepared to say why the others could *not* modify the noun.

Example: pontus: alta, magnus, pulcher, parvī
pontus (nom. sg. m.)   magnus, pulcher (also nom. sg. m.)
(alta is not m., parvī can be nom. m., but not sg., or m. sg., but not nom.)

1.	vir:	magnus	malum	pulcher	bonī
2.	puellā:	parva	pulchrā	tuās	līberā
3.	pontōs:	altus	parvās	multōs	pulchrum
4.	rēgnīs:	tuī	aegrā	meās	pulchrīs
5.	locō:	altā	magnus	parvō	bonōs
6.	dōnum:	pulchrum	parvus	meum	magnōrum
7.	nauta:	bona	bonus	līber	malae
8.	nātūra:	bona	prīmus	dīvīnā	tua

Exercise 35. Translate each of the following noun-adjective pairs into the Latin case indicated.

1.   good sailor (nom.)
2.   large gifts (acc.)
3.   small field (nom.)
4.   beautiful roses (acc.)
5.   bad fortune (dat.)
6.   our places (nom.)

29. **Substantive Use**

In Latin, as in English, an adjective can be used without an accompanying noun (this is called the "substantive" use), as in the following:

the land of the free and the home of the brave

In this use, the adjective functions as a noun, and the meaning is understood from the context (the land of the free people...). In Latin, the gender and number of the adjective give you extra help at filling in the missing noun. If the adjective has a masculine ending, it usually indicates men (or people in general); if it is feminine, women; if neuter, things:

bonus	a good man
bonī (nom. pl.)	good men; good people
aegra (nom. sg.)	sick woman
magnum (neuter)	large thing
mala (nom. pl.)	bad things

Exercise 36. Translate the underlined word or phrase in the context of the sentence given.

1.   <u>Multa</u> vidēmus.
2.   <u>Altum</u> nāvigant.
3.   <u>Malī</u> puellae aquam nōn dant.
4.   Do you like <u>beautiful things</u>?
5.   The <u>free man</u> is not afraid.
6.   We help the <u>good women</u>.

30. **More Uses of the Genitive**

In Chapter 3 you learned that the genitive case can indicate possession or the whole of which a part is mentioned (§18). The genitive can also indicate other relationships between two nouns, although it may still be translated into English with "of _____." Here are three common uses:

- **Explanatory** — the genitive explains more about the noun

  deus **pontī**   god **of the sea**

- **Objective** — the genitive would be the object if the other noun were a verb

  imperium **pontī**   command **of the sea**   (he commands **the sea**)

- **Subjective** — the genitive would be the subject if the other noun were a verb

  cōnsilium **turbae**   the advice **of the crowd**   (**the crowd** advises)

Without context, it can sometimes be hard to distinguish between the objective and subjective uses: "fear of the enemy" could mean either *someone fears the enemy* (objective) or *the enemy fears someone or thing* (subjective).

31. **Adjectival Modification (Summary)**

Adjectival modifiers modify nouns. The adjective and the uses of the Genitive case that you have learned so far function as adjectival modifiers. Like adverbial modifiers, they are not part of the sentence core and, thus, are not required elements in a sentence. Adjectival modifiers provide extra information about a noun in the sentence. It is useful to note that the following underlined modifiers are equivalent in function:

simple sentence (core only):   The boy sees the temple.

plus adjectival modifier (adjective):   The boy sees the <u>large</u> temple.
plus adjectival modifier (genitive):   The boy sees the temple <u>of the gods</u>.
plus adjectival modifier (genitive):   The boy sees a crowd <u>of people</u>.

32. **Sum: Present Indicative and Infinitive**

In Latin, as in most languages, the verb *to be* is irregular and must be memorized. Here is the **present indicative** of **sum**:

1st sg.	sum	I am
2nd sg.	es	you are
3rd sg.	est	he, she, it, there is
1st pl.	su**mus**	we are
2nd pl.	es**tis**	you (all) are
3rd pl.	su**nt**	they, there are
Infinitive	**esse**	to be

33. **Sentence Pattern: Linking**

So far you have had two regular sentence patterns (§4):

  1) Intransitive   **Agricola labōrat.**   The farmer works.

    - subject
    - verb

2) Transitive   **Fēmina rosam habet.**   The woman has a rose.

- subject
- verb
- direct object - in the accusative

A third common pattern is called **linking**. In this pattern the verb functions like an equal sign, linking the subject to an adjective or noun that describes the subject: the man is (=) good. The adjective or noun that completes the picture of the subject is commonly called the **subject complement**. Since the subject of a finite verb is always nominative, the subject complement is also nominative: **vir** est **bonus**. = The man *is* good. Here are the elements of this sentence pattern:

3) **Linking**

- subject
- linking verb
- subject complement (= predicate nominative)

Future chapters will introduce other verbs that can occur in a linking pattern, but **sum** is one of the most common. Note that **sum** may occur in both a linking and an intransitive pattern:

Linking:	**Virī sunt līberī.**	The men are free.
	Virī sunt.	They are men.
Intransitive:	**Sum.**	I am.
	Sunt virī.	Men exist. (or) There are men.

When this verb appears as the *first word* in the sentence, it is frequently a signal of the intransitive pattern: *there is, there are*. Sometimes, as in the second and fourth examples (**virī sunt / sunt virī**), you will need to use the context of the sentence to decide the meaning.

When an adjective in the subject complement or "predicate" modifies multiple nouns of different genders, it is regularly plural and, if the nouns refer to people, it is usually masculine:

Vir et fēmina sunt bonī.   The man and woman are good.

34. **More Uses of the Ablative**

In Chapter 4 you learned that the ablative case could be used *without a preposition* to indicate the means or instrument by which something is done (§23), and *with a preposition* to indicate place where or place from which (§24). With the preposition **cum** the ablative can indicate two different things, depending whether the noun is animate (a person) or inanimate (not a person):

- **Accompaniment** — the person/people with whom something is done

    Cum amīcīs labōrat.   She works **with her friends**.

- **Manner** — the way in which something is done

    Cum cūrā labōrat.   She works with care.

When the noun is modified by an adjective in an ablative of manner, the adjective regularly comes first and the preposition may be omitted. If it is included, it often appears between the two words:

Magnā cum cūrā labōrat.   She works **with great care.**

These uses of the ablative, like the earlier ones, function as Adverbial Modifiers.

Exercise 37. Fill in the blank(s) with the form(s) needed to complete each sentence. Remember to use your knowledge of sentence patterns, noun and verb endings, chunks (§26) etc. to help you know what to expect (§15, 20).

1. Fīliī ad silv_____ festīnant.
2. Nautae cum amīc_____ nāvig_____ solent.
3. Me_____ liber nōn magn_____ est.
4. Esne bon_____?
5. Agricola magn_____ sapienti_____ habet.
6. Nēmō vir_____ saxum iact_____ audet.
7. Amīce, animum hab_____!
8. Puerī puellaeque parv_____ sunt.

Exercise 38. Identify the sentence pattern(s) in each of the following sentences and then translate.

1. Multī in nostrā terrā multa nōn habent.
2. Pontus magnus aquā viās silvāsque implet.
3. Bonus tacet sed malus saepe clāmat.
4. Facta bonōrum virōrum sunt bona.
5. Dominus virōs puerōsque ad bellum vocāre parat.
6. Sunt in meīs agrīs bonī agricolae.
7. Aegrae prō templō sedēre solent.
8. Fēmina multōs amīcōs nautae iuvat.
9. Iactāsne post casam tuās rosās?
10. Pontus est altus.

Exercise 39. Translate into Latin.

1. There are many gods of the winds.
2. I do not hesitate to wander in the forest.
3. No one wishes to set [*use a form of* **dō**] a bad example.
4. He is hurrying to the divine temple of the gods.
5. The man's kingdom lies across the sea.
6. He finally gives the girl beautiful gifts.
7. They are preparing a plan with great care.
8. The men often work in the field with (their) sons.
9. The rose is beautiful.
10. Girls, call the farmers out of the fields.

In the Readings and Practice Sentences from now on, try to guess the meanings of the words in bold before looking for them in the accompanying vocabulary.

Reading 2 *(adapted)*

Ennius describes a calm crossing from Italy to Africa.

Mundus caelī **vastus** tacet
et Neptūnus saevus undīs asperīs **pausam** dat.

Vocabulary:

mundus, -ī *m.*	universe, firmament	unda, -ae *f.*	wave
		asper, -a, -um	rough
vastus, -a, -um	vast, huge	pausa, -ae *f.*	rest, pause
saevus, -a, -um	savage		

Reading 3 *(adapted) (practice guessing words in bold)*

Lucius Annaeus Florus (c. 120 A.D.) wrote an abridged version of Roman history, from the founding of Rome to the time of Augustus. The following passage is adapted from the beginning of his account. The story begins with Romulus and Remus, twin sons of a priestess, Rhea Silvia, and the Roman god, Mars. These twins were born during the reign of Amulius.

> **Note:** The Romans did not use capital letters to signal the beginning of a sentence, and some modern Latin texts also follow this practice. Some of the narrative readings in this book will only use capitals for proper names and the beginning of paragraphs and some quotations.

Prīmus et **Rōmae** et imperiī conditor **Rōmulus** est, filius deī, Martis, et Rhēae Silviae. **Rōmulum** cum **Remō** frātre in Tiberīnum rēx, Amulius, iactat. sed **īnfantēs** clāmant et lupa puerōs iuvat. tum sub **arbore** Faustulus pāstor parvōs puerōs videt et portat **īnfantēs** in casam et puerōs ēducat.

Vocabulary:

Rōma, -ae *f.*	Rome	rēx (nom.)	king
conditor (nom.)	founder	īnfantēs (nom. pl.)	infants
Martis (gen.)	Mars (a god)	lupa, -ae *f.*	she-wolf
Rhea Silvia, -ae *f.*	Rhea Silvia (a priestess)	pāstor (nom.)	shepherd
		arbore (abl.)	tree
Remus, -ī *m.*	Remus	ēducō, -āre	to bring up, rear
frātre (abl.)	brother		
Tiberīnus, -ī *m.*	Tiber (river in Rome)		

Practice Sentences

Identify the case and use of the underlined words, then translate.

1. Nēmō ad altum ambulat <u>locum</u> sī timet. (Publilius Syrus - adapted)
2. Sī virum <u>multī</u> timent, multōs timēre dēbet. (Publilius Syrus - adapted)
3. Nec vīta nec fortūna propria est <u>virīs</u>. (Publilius Syrus - adapted)
4. Fortūna <u>caeca</u> est. (Cicero)
5. Cogitō cum meō <u>animō</u>. (Plautus)
6. Hīc <u>dea</u> silvārum solet nāre. (Ovid – adapted; *describing the goddess, Diana*)

Vocabulary:

sī	if	caecus, -a, -um	blind
nec ... nec	neither ... nor	cogitō, -āre	to think, ponder
vīta, -ae *f.*	life		
proprius, -a, -um	one's own; permanent	hīc (adv.)	here
		nō, nāre	to bathe

Chapter 5 Vocabulary

Nouns

cūra, cūrae *f.*	care, anxiety
exemplum, exemplī *n.*	example, model
sapientia, sapientiae *f.*	wisdom
silva, silvae *f.*	forest, wood
terra, terrae *f.*	land, earth, soil; country

Verbs

iactō, iactāre, iactāvī, iactātus	to throw
sum, esse, fuī, futūrus	to be, exist

Adjectives

aeger, aegra, aegrum	sick, weak
altus, alta, altum	high, deep
bonus, bona, bonum	good
dīvīnus, dīvīna, dīvīnum	divine, of the gods; prophetic
līber, lībera, līberum	free
longus, longa, longum	long
magnus, magna, magnum	large, great
malus, mala, malum	bad
meus, mea, meum	my, mine
multus, multa, multum	much; many (pl.)
noster, nostra, nostrum	our, ours
parvus, parva, parvum	small

prīmus, prīma, prīmum	first
pulcher, pulchra, pulchrum	beautiful, handsome; fine
tuus, tua, tuum	your, yours, your own (sg.)
vester, vestra, vestrum	your, yours (pl.)

Prepositions

cum (+ abl.)	with
sub (+ abl.)	under, beneath
sub (+ acc.)	to the foot/base of, along under *(implying motion)*

(23)

Derivatives: For each English word below, give the Latin word from the Chapter 5 Vocabulary to which it is related and the English word's meaning.

1.	liberate	7.	primordial
2.	eject	8.	multitude
3.	malice	9.	essential
4.	altimeter	10.	submarine
5.	curator	11.	territory
6.	magnificent	12.	pulchritude

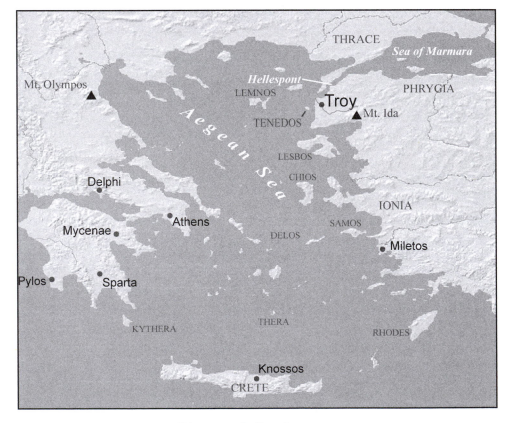

Troy and the Aegean

READING CHAPTER I

Narrative Reading I: Fall of Troy
Dictionary Practice / Form Identification
Review of the Sentence and its Parts
Question Words for Extra Practice
Word Derivations
English Abbreviations

The first five chapters have introduced you to the basics of Latin verbs, nouns, adjectives, prepositions and conjunctions. This chapter and the reading chapters that occur periodically throughout the book will include review material for extra practice.

Narrative Reading I: Fall of Troy *(practice guessing words in bold)*

This passage describes how the Trojan War came to an end after ten years of fighting between the Greeks and Trojans.

Graecī et **Trōiānī** bellum **longum** pugnant. tandem aliī **Graecōrum** ad īnsulam Tenedum nāvigant et aliī in ligneō equō latent. ignārī dolī **Trōiānī** in **Trōiam** equum portant. laetī sunt et multa convīvia multō cum **vīnō** parant. tum somnus **Trōiānōs** habet. **Graecī** ab īnsulā ad terram **Trōiae** nāvigant; amīcī ex equō festīnant et portās **Trōiae** reserant. ūnus **Trōiānus** ex somnō aliōs excitat, "ō amīcī, ad arma festīnāte!" sed **Graecī** **Trōiānōs** dolō armīsque superant.

Vocabulary:

Graecus, -a, -um	Greek	dolus, -ī *m.*	trick, deceit
Trōiānus, -a, -um	Trojan	Trōia, -ae *f.*	Troy
longus, -a, -um	long	laetus, -a, -um	happy
aliī ... aliī	some ... others	convīvium, -ī *n.*	feast
alius, -a, -um	other	vīnum, -ī *n.*	wine
īnsula, -ae *f.*	island (Tenedos)	somnus, -ī *m.*	sleep
ligneus, -a, -um	wooden, of wood	porta, -ae *f.*	gate
equus, -ī *m.*	horse	reserō, -āre	to open,
lateō, -ēre	to lie hidden		unlock
ignārus, -a, -um	unaware of, not	ūnus, -a, -um	one
(+ gen.)	knowing	excitō, -āre	wake up, rouse

* See map of Troy and the Aegean.

Dictionary Practice/Form Identification

Identify the words below based on the dictionary entries given. Be sure to indicate the **entry from which each is taken**, and the **part of speech** and to *give all possibilities for ambiguous forms.*

For **nouns** and **adjectives**: give case, number, and gender

For **verbs**: give person, number and mood (Indicative)
*all verb forms so far are Present and Active

    A.   doleō, dolēre, doluī: to grieve, suffer pain
    B.   dolō, dolāre, dolāvī, dolātus: to chop with an ax
    C.   dolus, dolī *m.*: trick, device
    D.   dolōsus, dolōsa, dolōsum: crafty, deceitful

		Entry	*Part of Speech*	*Form ID*
1.	dolat	B	verb	third person singular indicative
2.	dolent			
3.	dolīs			
4.	dolōsārum			
5.	dolōs			
6.	dolātis			
7.	dolēs			
8.	dolōsum			
9.	dolō			
10.	dolāmus			

Review of the Sentence and its Parts

One way to review old material, and to place new material in the context of what has already been introduced, is to organize the information graphically. Here is one example of how you could map out the parts of a sentence covered so far:

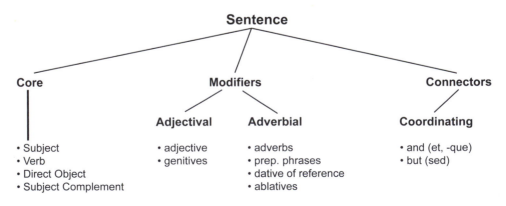

Question Words for Extra Practice

In Chapters 1-5 you have seen "yes-no" questions signalled by the placement of **-ne** at the end of the first word in the sentence. Later in the book you will learn the details of how Latin asks other questions but, for now, learning a few "question words" will allow you to study and review in a very useful way, and to work orally if you want. Here are some basic question words/phrases:

Quis (sg.)/Quī (pl.)	who?	asks for an animate subject
Quem (sg.)/Quōs (pl.)	whom?	asks for an animate direct object
Quid (sg.)	what?	asks for an inanimate subject or direct object
Ubi	where?	
Unde	from where?	
Quō	to where?	
Quōcum	with whom?	
Quō modō	in what manner?	

A)   Underline any answer that makes sense for each of the following questions.

1. Quis in agrō labōrat?   saepe   puerum   agricola   ā casā
2. Quem dominus laudat?   puer   virum   puellās   locum
3. Quō filiī festīnant?   in silvam   in viā   ad templum ab agrō
4. Quōcum ambulāmus?   cum cūrā   facile   prō fēminā   cum amīcīs
5. Quid puerōs terret?   bellum   pontus   dominus   trāns aquam
6. Quō modō labōrant?   facile   in agrō   cum cūrā   longī

B) Based on the narrative reading at the beginning of this chapter, answer the following questions in Latin.

1. Quī pugnant?   6. Quid Trōiānōs habet?
2. Quō aliī Graecōrum nāvigant?   7. Unde Graecī nāvigant?
3. Ubi aliī Graecōrum latent?   8. Unde amīcī festīnant?
4. Quid Trōiānī in Trōiam portant? 9. Quis clāmat, "ad arma festīnāte!"?
5. Quī laetī sunt?   10. Quōs Graecī superant?

These kinds of questions can be used for any of the readings and many of the sentences in each chapter.

Word Derivations

Each Chapter Vocabulary has included a Derivatives exercise asking you to look at English words and connect them with the new Latin vocabulary in that chapter. Another way to build your knowledge of Latin (and English) vocabulary is to look at Latin words and stems and see if you can collect English words that are derived from them. For each of the following Latin words, write down as many English derivatives as you can.

Example: fortūna: fortune, fortunate, unfortunate (etc.)

1. ab   7. imperium
2. ager   8. magnus
3. ambulō   9. nauta
4. clāmō   10. taceō
5. dominus   11. terreō
6. errō   12. vocō

English Abbreviations

Many common abbreviations in English come from Latin words. Note the following (n.b.):

- cp.   **comparā**   compare
- et al.   **et aliī**   and others
- etc.   **et cetera**   and the rest
- n.b.   **notā bene**   note well
- pro   **prō**   in favor (of)

CHAPTER 6

Imperfect Active Indicative: First and Second Conjugations
Future Active Indicative: First and Second Conjugations
Sum: Imperfect and Future Indicative
The Gap
Infinitive Use: As a Noun
Dative of Possession

Chapter 1 introduced the present tense of first and second conjugation verbs and showed how finite verbs in Latin have a set of personal endings that are added to the stem of the verb. In the Latin system, the stem carries the meaning of the verb, and the endings carry information about the subject. This chapter introduces two new tenses that indicate action in the past and in the future. These tenses are marked by a tense sign, which appears between the verb stem and the personal ending. It also introduces a new use of the infinitive and a use of the dative with the verb *to be*.

35. **Imperfect Active Indicative: First and Second Conjugations**

The **imperfect** is one of three past tenses in Latin and is easily recognized by the tense sign **-bā-** between the verb stem and the personal endings:

	1st Conjugation		**2nd Conjugation**	
1st sg.	amā**bam**	I was loving, etc.	monē**bam**	I was advising, etc.
2nd sg.	amā**bās**	You were loving	monē**bās**	You were advising
3rd sg.	amā**bat**	He/she was loving	monē**bat**	He/she was advising
1st pl.	amā**bāmus**	We were loving	monē**bāmus**	We were advising
2nd pl.	amā**bātis**	You (all) were loving	monē**bātis**	You (all) were advising
3rd pl.	amā**bant**	They were loving	monē**bant**	They were advising

Notice that:

- The personal endings are the same as those used in the present tense (§5) except for the first person singular where **-m** replaces **-ō**.

- A long vowel (here in **-bā-**) shortens before final **-m, -t, -nt**. This is a general rule, which you have already seen in the present tense (§5 - notice the third person singular and plural forms of **amō** and **moneō**) and will see again in other verb forms.

The **imperfect** tense in Latin usually indicates an action *going on in the past but not completed*. It can be translated into English in a variety of ways, depending on the context of the sentence:

	Continuous action	he was advising *or* he kept advising
	Repeated or Habitual action	he used to advise *or* he advised every year
	Attempted action	he tried to advise
	Beginning of an action	he began to advise

36. Future Active Indicative: First and Second Conjugations

The **future** of first and second conjugation verbs can be recognized by the tense sign -**bi**- between the verb stem and the personal endings:

	1st Conjugation		2nd Conjugation	
1st sg.	amā**bō**	I shall love	monē**bō**	I shall advise
2nd sg.	amā**bis**	You will love	monē**bis**	You will advise
3rd sg.	amā**bit**	He/she will love	monē**bit**	He/she will mix
1st pl.	amā**bimus**	We shall love	monē**bimus**	We shall advise
2nd pl.	amā**bitis**	You (all) will love	monē**bitis**	You (all) will advise
3rd pl.	amā**bunt**	They will love	monē**bunt**	They will advise

Again, the personal endings are the same as those used in the present tense. Notice two points here:

- In the first person singular, the ending -**bō** is contracted from -**biō**.
- In the third person plural, -**bu**- replaces -**bi**-.

Exercise 40. Using the stem meanings given below, translate each of the following into English. Then, paying attention to the stem vowel in each form, see if you can write the first two principal parts as they would appear in the dictionary for each verb.

Example: errant (wander) "they wander"; errō, errāre

1. explōrābās (investigate)
2. pārēbō (obey)
3. intrābunt (enter)
4. turbāmus (disturb)
5. miscēbis (mix)
6. praebēbant (offer)
7. exspectābit (wait for)
8. sustinēbam (support)
9. favēbat (support)
10. mūtābātis (change)

Exercise 41. Identify each of the following forms by person, number, tense (present, imperfect or future) and mood (indicative or imperative), then translate into English.

Example: amābant   third person, plural, imperfect, indicative; "they used to love"

1. iactābit
2. iacēbat
3. superābimus
4. movēbō
5. errā
6. tenēbam
7. pugnāte
8. nūntiātis
9. sedē
10. manēbunt

37. Sum: Imperfect and Future Indicative

Like the present tense of **sum** (§32), the imperfect and future tenses are irregular and must be memorized. These forms, like the present tense forms, will be used to form other tenses of regular verbs, so you will see them frequently as you read Latin.

	Imperfect		Future	
1st sg.	eram	I was, used to be, etc.	erō	I shall be
2nd sg.	erās	You were	eris	You will be
3rd sg.	erat	He, she, it, there was	erit	He, she, it, there will be
1st pl.	erāmus	We were	erimus	We shall be
2nd pl.	erātis	You (all) were	eritis	You (all) will be
3rd pl.	erant	They, there were	erunt	They, there will be

Notice that

- The endings for each tense are regular.

- The imperfect has **era-** (**erā-**) throughout.

- The future has **eri-** throughout except in the first singular and third plural forms.

Remember that the imperfect tense can be translated into English in a variety of ways, depending on the context of the sentence (§35):

Continuous action	he was *or* he kept being
Repeated or Habitual action	he used to be *or* he (always) was
Attempted action	he tried to be
Beginning of an action	he began to be

Exercise 42. Translate each of the verbs into the correct Latin form of **sum**. Do not translate the whole sentence.

Example: She is good.   est

1. The man was unhappy.
2. Will they be our friends?
3. We are in the house.
4. I used to be sick.
5. You (pl.) are free men.
6. The queen will be angry.
7. Were they being bad?
8. I will be brave.

38. **The Gap**

Latin can leave out ("gap") words in a sentence that are expected. This is especially common when a coordinating conjunction (§14) is present, but can occur without a conjunction too. When a gap is present it is important to pay close attention to the case of each word and to make use of your skill at expecting what should be present in the sentence. In Latin identical subjects, verbs or direct objects can be gapped in either the first or second coordinate clause; in the example below, **laudat** (verb) is gapped in the first clause, and **virum** (direct object) is gapped in the second:

Puer virum sed nōn puella laudat.   The boy praises the man, but the girl does not.
or The boy praises the man, but the girl does not praise the man.

Rules for gapping in English are more strict than those for Latin, so care must be taken if you are translating. Note that *the boy praises the man, but not the girl* would have been an ambiguous translation of the above sentence. Why?

Exercise 43. Translate each of the following sentences in which one or more items are gapped. Be ready to identify the function of the gapped word(s).

Example: Nauta ventōs nōn aquam timet.   A sailor fears winds, not water.
A sailor fears winds, (he does) not (fear) water.
timet - verb is gapped in 1st Latin clause

1. Rosās optāmus, bellum nōn.
2. Dōna ad templum portābāmus et rēgīna dīs dabit.
3. Agricola agrum, nauta pontum amat.
4. Via ad pontum bona sed longa est.

39. **Infinitive Use: As a Noun**

The infinitive in Latin, just as in English, is a verbal noun, which retains properties of both verbs and nouns. When used as a complementary infinitive (§7b), it functions to complete the meaning of another verb. When used as a noun, the infinitive is considered neuter and singular, but retains its ability to govern an object and is modified by an adverb (not an adjective). This use of the infinitive is particularly common as the subject or subject complement of **sum** and with certain impersonal verbs.

Amāre est bonum.   **To love** is good; **Loving** is a good thing.
Vidēre loca bella iuvat.   **To see** beautiful places is pleasing; **Seeing** beautiful places is pleasing; It is pleasing **to see** beautiful places.

Note that in both examples, the Latin infinitive can be translated with either an infinitive or a gerund (*loving, seeing*).

Exercise 44. Translate the sentences below into Latin.

1. To be afraid is not good.
2. Laughing pleases the boys.
3. To sail will be strange for the girls.
4. Owing money is bad.

40. **Dative of Possession**

In Chapter 3 you learned two common uses of the dative case (§19): to show the indirect object and for more general reference. Another common use is the dative with a form of **sum** to show possession:

- **Possession** - the person who possesses

    Virō est liber.   **The man** has a book.
    (the book belongs **to the man**)
    Puerīs pecūnia erat.   **The boys** used to have money.

In expressing possession, the Dative with **sum** emphasizes the fact of possession, while the Genitive signals the possessor as a subordinate point in the sentence.

Does the man have a book?   **Virō** est liber.   **The man** has a book.
Whose book is it?   **Virī** est liber.   The book is **the man's.**

Exercise 45. Using the Dative of Possession, translate the sentences below into Latin.

1. The master has fame.
2. The sailors used to have money.
3. The unhappy crowd does not have courage.
4. The good men will have wisdom.

Exercise 46. Translate each of the following sentences.

1. Templum novum sine exemplō aedificāre malum erit.
2. Nunc caelum pulchrum est et lūna magna.
3. Dē viā in silvam turba multa saxa movēbat.
4. Fīliō vestrō multī amīcī erunt.
5. Vir bonam vītam habēre solēbit?
6. Fīlia mea rēgīnae dōna pulchra dabat.
7. Puer agricolam aquam saepe ōrābat.
8. Manēbisne, fīlī, in silvīs cum amīcīs tuīs?
9. Terra laeta est sed propter bellum agricolae labōrāre nōn optant.
10. In casā fēminae puellaeque cēnam parābunt et amīcīs multās fābulās nārrābunt.

Exercise 47. Translate into Latin.

1. Friends, your house is small, but beautiful.
2. The daughter used to have a good reputation. [*use* **sum**]
3. The girls kept throwing rocks without a care.
4. The master's son used to give money to men in front of the temple.
5. We will praise the Romans, for their fame is great.
6. Will the sick women be happy after the war?
7. Report the new rumor to the sailors now.
8. For a long time, the queen did not desire to give her kingdom to her son.
9. They will beg the gods for great wisdom and a long life.
10. Boys and girls, be quiet and I will tell the people a strange story.

Reading 4 *(loosely modeled) (practice guessing words in bold)*

Florus continues the story of Romulus and Remus (review Reading 3). Usually the eldest brother was king, but since these brothers were twins, they asked the gods for help in deciding who should rule.

Rōmulus et Remus nunc virī erant. Alba tunc erat Latiō caput et Amulius **rēgnābat**. sed Rōmulus urbem novam aedificāre optābat et **rēgnāre**. Rōmulus et Remus deōs cōnsilium ōrābant; **geminī** enim erant. dī **ōrāculum** dabant: vulturiōs exspectāte! Remus prīmus paucōs vulturiōs, tum Rōmulus multōs vulturiōs vidēbat. Rōmulus igitur **geminum** superābat et Remus miser erat. Rōmulus moenia aedificābat sed propter **magnitūdinem** parvam Remus rīdēbat et facile trāns moenia ambulābat. Rōmulus magnā cum īrā clāmābat et **geminum** necābat.

Vocabulary:

Remus, -ī *m.*	Remus	ōrāculum, -ī *n.*	oracle
Alba, -ae, *f.*	Alba (a city)	exspectō, -āre	watch for
Latium, -iī, *n.*	Latium (an area of Italy)	vulturius, -ī, *m.*	vulture
		paucī, -ae, -a (pl.)	few
caput (nom.)	"chief city"	igitur (adv.)	so, therefore
Amulius, -iī *m.*	Amulius (a king)	moenia (acc. pl.)	(city) walls
rēgnō, -āre	to rule, be king	magnitūdinem (acc. *f.*)	size
urbem (acc. *f.*)	city	necō, -āre	to kill
geminus, -a, -um	twin		

Practice Sentences *(practice guessing words in bold)*

Identify the case and use of the underlined words, then translate.

1. Errāre est **hūmānum**.   (attributed to St. Jerome)
2. Sum **pius** Aenēās et fāma super caelum est.   (Vergil - adapted; *the hero, Aeneas, introduces himself*)
3. **Avāritia** enim sine poenā nōn est.   (Seneca - adapted)
4. Animīs deōrum tanta īra est?   (Vergil - adapted; *the poet wonders at the anger of the goddess Juno*)
5. Magnam pecūniam dēbēbat.   (Sallust – adapted; *describing Caesar, whose generosity leads to difficulties for him*)
6. Dolēre malum est.   (Cicero)

Vocabulary:

hūmānus, -a, -um	human	avāritia, -ae *f.*	greed, avarice
pius, -a, -um	pious	poena, -ae *f.*	penalty, punishment
Aenēās (nom. sg.)	Aeneas (a Trojan hero)	tantus, -a, -um	such great

Chapter 6 Vocabulary

Nouns

fāma, fāmae *f.*	fame, report, reputation; rumor
fīlia, fīliae *f.*	daughter
dat. pl. and abl. pl. = fīliābus	
īra, īrae *f.*	anger
Ītalia, Ītaliae *f.*	Italy
populus, populī *m.*	the people, a people, nation
rēgīna, rēgīnae *f.*	queen
vīta, vītae *f.*	life

Verbs

doleō, dolēre, doluī, dolitūrus	to grieve, mourn, suffer pain
maneō, manēre, mānsī, mānsūrus	to remain, stay
moveō, movēre, mōvī, mōtus	to move; excite; affect
nūntiō, nūntiāre, nūntiāvī, nūntiātus	to announce, report
ōrō, ōrāre, ōrāvī, ōrātus	to pray, beg, beg for (*often with 2 accusatives, one of the person, the other of the thing*: **dōnum virum** ōrant. "they are asking the **man** for a **present.**")
teneō, tenēre, tenuī, tentus	to hold, possess, keep; restrain

Adjectives

laetus, laeta, laetum	happy; fertile
miser, misera, miserum	miserable, unhappy
novus, nova, novum	new; strange
Rōmānus, Rōmāna, Rōmānum;	Roman
Rōmānī, Rōmānōrum *m.* (pl.)	the Romans
(as a noun)	

Adverbs

diū	for a long time
nunc	now, at present
tunc	then

Prepositions

dē (+ abl.)	down from; about, concerning
propter (+ acc.)	because of, on account of
sine (+ abl.)	without

Coordinating Conjunction

enim *(never appears as the first word in a sentence - "postpositive")*	for; in fact; yes, truly

(24)

Derivatives: For each English word below, give the Latin word from the Chapter 6 Vocabulary to which it is related and the English word's meaning.

1. tenacious
2. descent
3. commiserate
4. irascible
5. novice
6. vitamin
7. affiliation
8. mansion
9. famous
10. emotion
11. populous
12. sinecure

CHAPTER 7

Third Declension Nouns: Consonant Stem
     Masculine and Feminine
     Neuter
     Gender Patterns
The Pronoun: Personal (1)
     ego; tū
Forms of Possum
Sentence Pattern: Special Intransitive

So far all the nouns you have learned have been in either the first or the second declension. This chapter introduces nouns in the third declension, with a new set of case endings that must be memorized. It also introduces the personal pronouns *I*, *you*, *we* and *you* (pl.), forms of an irregular verb that resemble the forms of **sum** you have already learned (§32 and §37) and a few verbs whose objects are in the Dative or Ablative case.

41. **Third Declension Nouns: Consonant Stem**

Nouns of the third declension fall into two general categories: those whose stems end in a consonant, and those whose stems end in -i- (these will be introduced in Chapter 10). Consonant stem nouns can be divided into two groups: those that have no distinct ending in the nominative singular, and those that add -s to form the nominative singular. In either consonant group, you can always identify the stem by removing the case ending from the genitive singular form. Masculine and feminine nouns in the third declension use the same set of endings. The Vocative is identical to the Nominative in the singular and plural.

41a. **Third Declension: Masculine and Feminine**

Singular	[—]	[-s]	Endings
Nominative	cōnsul	rēx	—, -s
Genitive	cōnsul**is**	rēg**is**	-is
Dative	cōnsul**ī**	rēg**ī**	-ī
Accusative	cōnsul**em**	rēg**em**	-em
Ablative	cōnsul**e**	rēg**e**	-e
Plural			
Nominative	cōnsul**ēs**	rēg**ēs**	-ēs
Genitive	cōnsul**um**	rēg**um**	-um
Dative	cōnsul**ibus**	rēg**ibus**	-ibus
Accusative	cōnsul**ēs**	rēg**ēs**	-ēs
Ablative	cōnsul**ibus**	rēg**ibus**	-ibus

Note the following:

- The consonant of the stem may combine with the **-s** ending of the nominative singular to produce a different spelling; try pronouncing the combined form aloud to predict the result:

  rēg + s > rēx

  noct + s > nox

- In the plural, the nominative and accusative endings are the same, **-ēs**, and the dative and ablative endings are the same, **-ibus**. As in the first and second declensions, the context of the sentence should help you determine what case the noun is in.

Exercise 48. Identify each of the following third declension nouns by case and number. If the ending is ambiguous, include all possibilities.

Example: hominī   dative singular

1. pāce
2. lēgēs
3. ducibus
4. virtūtem

5. patrum
6. hominis
7. frātrī
8. cīvitās

Exercise 49. Following the third declension consonant patterns above, decline **virtūs**, **dux** and **frāter** in all cases, singular and plural. Be sure to check the genitive singular forms in the Chapter Vocabulary in order to learn what stem to use for each noun.

41b. **Third Declension: Neuter**

Singular		Endings
Nominative	caput	——
Genitive	capit**is**	**-is**
Dative	capit**ī**	**-ī**
Accusative	caput	——
Ablative	capit**e**	**-e**
Plural		
Nominative	capit**a**	**-a**
Genitive	capit**um**	**-um**
Dative	capit**ibus**	**-ibus**
Accusative	capit**a**	**-a**
Ablative	capit**ibus**	**-ibus**

Like the first group of masculine and feminine nouns in this declension (e.g. **cōnsul**), neuter nouns add no ending to the nominative singular. Because the nominative and accusative case endings are **always** the same for all neuter nouns, this means the accusative singular will also lack a distinct ending. Neuter plural nouns in the nominative and accusative always end in **–a**; this is true in all declensions.

Gender Patterns

The gender of a noun in the third declension may be masculine, feminine or neuter and must be memorized when you learn the word. As in the first and second declensions (§10), however, some general patterns are very useful to remember:

- **Masculine**

Words Ending	Examples
-tor, -tōris	victor, victōris; gladiātor, gladiātōris

- **Feminine**

Words Ending	Examples
-tās, -tātis	cīvitās, cīvitātis; vēritās, vēritātis; libertās, libertātis
-tūs, -tūtis	virtūs, virtūtis; senectūs, senectūtis
-tūdō, -tūdinis	multitūdō, multitūdinis; necessitūdō, necessitūdinis
-tiō, -tiōnis	ōrātiō, ōrātiōnis; imitātiō, imitātiōnis; ratiō, ratiōnis

- **Neuter**

Words Ending	Examples
-al, ālis	animal, animālis; capital, capitālis
-us, -oris	tempus, temporis; corpus, corporis; lītus, lītoris
-men, -minis	flūmen, flūminis; nōmen, nōminis; carmen, carminis
-e, -is	mare, maris; cubīle, cubīlis

Exercise 50. Identify each of the following third declension nouns by case, number and gender, then say which adjectives could modify the noun listed with them. Be prepared to say why the others could NOT modify the noun.

Example: rēx: nova, Rōmānus, līber, parvī
           rēx (nom. sg. m.)   Rōmānus, līber (also nom. sg. m.)

1.	cīvitās:	magnās	parva	pulchrīs	līberā
2.	luce:	parva	pulchrā	multīs	novō
3.	homō:	bonus	Rōmānō	miser	multōs
4.	ducum:	nostrum	aegrōs	meī	novōrum
5.	māter:	mea	vester	laetae	bonā
6.	corporī:	pulchrī	parvus	meō	magnīs
7.	frātris:	tuīs	bonī	laeta	malae
8.	lībertāte:	novā	nostrō	magna	prīmī
9.	pācem:	novum	longam	prīma	bonārum
10.	virtūs:	vestra	meus	magnās	bonī

Exercise 51. Translate each of the following noun-adjective pairs into the Latin case indicated.

1.	great states (nom.)	4.	good king (dat.)
2.	happy mother (acc.)	5.	our father (gen.)
3.	small head (abl.)	6.	strange rights (abl.)

42. **The Pronoun: Personal (1)**

While a noun is a name (**nōmen**) for something, a **pronoun** is a word that can be used instead of a noun (**prō nōmine**) to refer to it without naming it (§2). Latin, like English, has different kinds of pronouns. This chapter will introduce one important group of pronouns, and the rest will be introduced in future chapters.

Personal pronouns in Latin, like nouns (and adjectives), have case and number, but they do not fit into regular declensions and are differentiated by person rather than gender: first person (*I, we*) and second person (*you, y'all*). For third person (*he, she, it, they*) Latin uses another pronoun, which you will learn in Chapter 8. Because a Latin finite verb identified the subject by means of its ending, the nominative forms of the personal pronouns were generally used only for *emphasis*, *contrast* or *clarity*.

Personal Pronouns: ego; tū

Singular	1st Person		2nd Person	
Nominative	ego	I	tū	you
Genitive	meī	of me	tuī	of you
Dative	mihi	to/for me	tibi	to/for you
Accusative	mē	me	tē	you
Ablative	mē	(by/with...) me	tē	(by/with...) you
Plural				
Nominative	nōs	we	vōs	you
Genitive	nostrum, nostrī	of us	vestrum, vestrī	of you
Dative	nōbīs	to/for us	vōbīs	to/for you
Accusative	nōs	us	vōs	you
Ablative	nōbīs	(by/with...) us	vōbīs	(by/with...) you

Note the following:

- In the plural, the nominative and accusative forms end with **-ōs**, and the dative and ablative endings with **-ōbīs**. As with nouns, the context of the sentence should help you determine what case the pronoun is in.

- In the genitive plural, the forms **nostrum** and **vestrum** are used as partitive genitives; **nostrī** and **vestrī**, like **meī** and **tuī**, are used objectively (§30; e.g., "love of you," "fear of us")

- When the ablative of these pronouns is used with **cum**, the preposition is written after the pronoun in one word: **mēcum, tēcum, nōbīscum, vōbīscum.**

Exercise 52. Translate the underlined word(s) in each sentence with the correct Latin form.

1. She was walking <u>with us</u>.
2. <u>I</u> like him, but <u>you</u> (pl.) don't.
3. Who gave <u>you</u> (sg.) that book?
4. A few <u>of us</u> will stay.
5. Tell <u>me</u> a story!
6. He is conquering <u>you</u> (pl.).
7. They led <u>you</u> (sg.) and <u>me</u> home.
8. Did she run away <u>from you</u> (sg.)?

43. **Possum: Present, Imperfect and Future Indicative**

Possum is an irregular verb that comes from the combination of the verb **sum** with **potis**, an old adjective meaning *able*. The **-t-** of the adjective's stem changes to **-s-** when followed by a form of **sum** beginning with **s**, and the resulting forms all follow the conjugation of **sum**, which you have already learned.

Indicative

	Present		Imperfect	Future
1st sg.	pos**sum**	I am able, I can	pot**eram**	pot**erō**
2nd sg.	pot**es**	You are able, can	pot**erās**	pot**eris**
3rd sg.	pot**est**	He, she, it is able, can	pot**erat**	pot**erit**
1st pl.	pos**sumus**	We are able, can	pot**erāmus**	pot**erimus**
2nd pl.	pot**estis**	You (all) are able, can	pot**erātis**	pot**eritis**
3rd pl.	pos**sunt**	They are able, can	pot**erant**	pot**erunt**
Infinitive	**posse**	to be able		

As with certain other verbs you have learned (**dēbeō, dubitō, optō, soleō**), **possum** very often occurs with a complementary infinitive (§7b). When you see an infinitive, therefore, you might expect to see a form of **possum** in the same sentence.

Nēmō ventum **vidēre potest.**   No one **can see** (**is able to see**) the wind.

44. **Sentence Pattern: Special Intransitive**

So far you have learned three sentence patterns 1) **Transitive** (§4), 2) **Intransitive** (§4), and 3) **Linking** (§33).

In a fourth, less common, sentence pattern, certain intransitive verbs take their object in the **dative** or **ablative** instead of the accusative case; (a very few verbs take a genitive object, but they are not included in the Chapter Vocabulary for this book). In this pattern the dative or ablative is a necessary core item in the sentence, just as the accusative direct object is with other verbs. The previous uses of the dative and ablative you have learned have all been as modifiers, which give extra information in the sentence.

4) **Special Intransitive**
   • subject
   • verb
   • object - in the dative or ablative

The special intransitive pattern only occurs with a small group of special verbs, so it is best to memorize the case of the object when you learn the verb. The dictionary listing for verbs that take a dative object or an ablative object will indicate this as follows:

careō, carēre, caruī, caritūrus (+ abl.)	to be without, free from; need, miss
noceō, nocēre, nocuī (+ dat.)	to harm, be harmful to
pāreō, pārēre, pāruī (+ dat.)	to obey, be obedient to
placeō, placēre, placuī, placitūrus (+ dat.)	to please, be pleasing to

Notice that when sentences with one of these special verbs are translated into English, the object often sounds just like a direct object:

careō —	**Vir Ītaliā caret.**	The man misses Italy.
noceō —	**Arma virīs nocent.**	The weapons harm the men.
		The weapons are harmful to the men.
pāreō —	**Dominō pārent.**	They obey the master.
		They are obedient to the master.
placeō —	**Rosa fēminae placet.**	The rose pleases the woman.
		The rose is pleasing to the woman.

Exercise 53. Identify the sentence pattern in each of the following, then translate.

Example: Bellum cīvitātī nocet.   Special Intransitive; "war harms the state"

1. Nōbīs fābulam nārrāte.
2. Fīlius pecūniā caret.
3. Virtūs tua erit magna.
4. Templum dīs placet.
5. Terrentne ventī pontusque tē?
6. Nēmō deō pārēre dubitat.
7. Turba puerōrum puellārumque timet.
8. Turba corpus terret.

Exercise 54. Fill in the blank(s) with the form(s) needed to complete each sentence.

1. Ducēs cōnsilium parā_____. (future)
2. Lūx magn____ et pulch_____ erat.
3. Dī virtūt____ hominibus dant.
4. Tum cōnsul____ pārēbāmus.
5. Māter pat____que laetī erant.
6. Popul____ magna sapientia ____.
   (*use present tense of* **sum**)

Exercise 55. Identify obvious chunks and then translate each of the following sentences.

1. Frātribus virtūs magna erit.
2. Lūcem lūnae in caelō vidēre poterās?
3. Nōs rīdēbāmus sed nōn tū.
4. Corpus miserī rēgis in viā iacēbat et Rōmānī caput in urbem portābant.
5. Ducēs populum Rōmānum ad arma vocābunt.
6. Malane fortūna tuō patrī semper erat?
7. Rēx rēgīnaque bonī esse optant.
8. Ventus aquaque agrīs nocent.
9. Frāter, patrī nostrō nunc pārē!
10. Cōnsulibus magnum imperium erat.

Exercise 56. Translate into Latin.

1. The Roman temples were pleasing to the god of war.
2. To see the ocean will be pleasing to you.
3. The men were obeying their leader but were not able to work without light.
4. Brother, announce the freedom of your king to the people now.
5. Italy always needs good consuls.
6. Will the men be able to be happy in the new state?
7. The summit was high.
8. Our leader has many sons. [*use* **sum**]
9. The Roman farmer was praising the courage and reputation of his brothers.
10. Your (pl.) mother will prepare many gifts for you and me.

Reading 5 *(loosely modeled) (practice guessing words in bold)*

The poet Ovid (43 B.C.-17 A.D.) tells a story about the only man (Deucalion) and woman (Pyrrha) to survive a great flood sent by Jupiter. In this passage, the couple asks the goddess Themis what they should do to repopulate the earth and they get a surprising answer.

Deucaliōn Pyrrhae dīcēbat: "nōs **duo** turba sumus; habet cētera pontus. hominumque sōla exempla manēmus." diū dolēbant sed tandem dīs ōrāre placēbat. īram deōrum timēbant sed ad templum deae ambulābant. humī iacēbant gelidōque ōscula saxō templī dabant et ōrābant: "Ō dea, nōs iuvā et tuō imperiō pārēbimus!" dea **ōrāculum** dabat: "movēte vōs ā templō et vēlāte caput ossaque post tergum iactāte magnae mātris!" diū tacēbant et imperiīs deae pārēre dubitābant. tandem Deucaliōn: "magna māter terra est; saxa in corpore terrae ossa sunt." tum pārēbant et iactābant post tergum multa saxa. **formae** saxōrum subitō **formae** virōrum fēminārumque erant!

Vocabulary:

dīcō, dīcere	to say, speak	ōrāculum, -ī *n.*	oracle
duo (adj.)	two	vēlō, -āre	to cover
cētera (acc. pl. *n.*)	"the rest"	os, ossis *n.*	bone
sōlus,-a, -um	only	tergum, -ī *n.*	back
humī	"on the ground"	forma, -ae *f.*	shape
gelidus, -a, -um	cold	subitō (adv.)	suddenly
ōsculum, -ī *n.*	kiss		

Reading 6 *(adapted) (practice guessing words in bold)*

Ennius tells how Jupiter forbade the eating of human flesh.

Sāturnus et Ops cēterīque tunc
hominēs **hūmānam** carnem solēbant edere;
sed prīmus Iuppiter lēgēs hominibus
mōrēsque dabat et ēdictō **prohibēbat**
hūmānam carnem.

Vocabulary:

Sāturnus (nom.)	early Roman god	edere (inf.)	to eat
Ops (nom.)	goddess of plenty	Iuppiter (nom.)	Jupiter
cēterī, -ae, -a	other	mōs, mōris *m.*	custom
hūmānus, -a, -um	human	ēdictum, -ī *n.*	edict
carō, carnis *f.*	flesh	prohibeō, -ēre	to prohibit

Practice Sentences *(practice guessing words in bold)*

Identify the case and use of the underlined words, then translate.

1. Dōnā <u>nōbīs</u> pācem, Domine.   (traditional hymn)
2. Bona fāma in <u>tenebrīs</u> proprium **splendōrem** tenet.   (Publilius Syrus)
3. Iūra dabat <u>lēgēs</u>que <u>virīs</u>.   (Vergil; *describing Queen Dido ruling her people*)
4. Virum bonum et magnum <u>hominem</u> dolēmus.   (Cicero – adapted; *on the death of Lentulus*)
5. "Egō sum lūx mundī; <u>mē</u>cum homō habēbit lūcem vītae."   (Vulgate – adapted; *Jesus speaks to the Pharisees*)
6. <u>Deō</u> placēre nōn possunt.   (Vulgate; *St. Paul describes people who live by their desires, not believing in Jesus*)
7. <u>Corpus</u> animus sempiternus movet.   (Cicero)
8. <u>Dux</u> fēmina factī.   (Vergil; *describing Dido's role in the founding of Carthage*)

Vocabulary:

dōnō, -āre	to give	splendor, -ōris *m.*	splendor
tenebrae, -ārum *f.* (pl.)	the lower world; darkness	sempiternus, -a, -um	eternal
proprius, -a, -um	one's own; permanent		

Chapter 7 Vocabulary

Nouns

caput, capitis *n.*	head; summit
cīvitās, cīvitātis *f.*	state; citizenship
cōnsul, cōnsulis *m.*	consul (one of two supreme magistrates elected annually in the Roman Republic)
corpus, corporis *n.*	body, corpse
dux, ducis *m.*	(military) leader, commander
frāter, frātris *m.*	brother
homō, hominis *m.*	human being, man
iūs, iūris *n.*	right, law; justice
lex, lēgis *f.*	law
lībertās, lībertātis *f.*	freedom, liberty
lūx, lūcis *f.*	light
māter, mātris *f.*	mother
nōmen, nōminis *n.*	name
pater, patris *m.*	father; senator
pāx, pācis *f.*	peace
rēx, rēgis *m.*	king
virtūs, virtūtis *f.*	courage, excellence, virtue

Pronouns

ego, nōs	I, we
tū, vōs	you, you (pl.)

Verbs

careō, carēre, caruī, caritūrus (+ abl.)	to be without, free from; need, miss
noceō, nocēre, nocuī (+ dat.)	to harm, be harmful to
pāreō, pārēre, pāruī (+ dat.)	to obey, be obedient to
placeō, placēre, placuī, placitūrus (+ dat.)	to please, be pleasing to
possum, posse, potuī	to be able, "I can"

(24)

Derivatives: For each English word below, give the Latin word from the Chapter 7 Vocabulary to which it is related and the English word's meaning.

1. regal
2. homicide
3. translucent
4. decapitate
5. innocent
6. fraternity
7. incorporate
8. paternity
9. legislator
10. plea
11. jury
12. virtuous
13. matrimony
14. pacifist
15. possible
16. egocentric

Chariot and Triton (sea-god). Mosaic from Ostia, 2nd c. A.D.

CHAPTER **8**

Third and Fourth Conjugations
> **Present Active Indicative and Infinitive**
> **Present Active Imperative**

The Pronoun: Personal (2)
> **is, ea, id as a Personal Pronoun**

Sentence Pattern: Factitive

So far all the verbs you have seen, with the exceptions of **sum** and **possum**, have been in the first or second conjugation. This chapter introduces verbs in the third and fourth conjugations. It also introduces a pronoun often used for the third person (*he, she, it, they*), and introduces a new sentence pattern.

45. **Third and Fourth Conjugations**

Verbs in the third and fourth conjugations use the same personal endings you learned for the first and second conjugations (§5). **3rd conjugation verbs** are characterized by having a short **-e-** on their stem; the short **-e-** becomes **-u-** in the third person plural and a short **-i-** in the other forms. This is the same pattern you have already seen in the future tense of **sum** (§37).

A few common verbs in this conjugation also have an **-i-** in their stem, which is visible in the first singular and third plural forms, but usually disappears before another **-i-** or short **-e**. These verbs are typically called **third conjugation -iō** verbs from their first singular form. **4th conjugation verbs** have a stem that ends in **-ī-**. This **-i** shortens before a vowel or final **-t** but is visible in all the forms.

Present Active Indicative and Infinitive

	Third Conjugation Indicative [-e-]		Fourth Conjugation Indicative [-ī-]
	3rd Regular	**3rd –iō**	**4th**
1st sg.	regō I rule	capiō	audiō
2nd sg.	regis You rule	capis	audīs
3rd sg.	regit He, she it rules	capit	audit
1st pl.	regimus We rule	capimus	audīmus
2nd pl.	regitis You (all) rule	capitis	audītis
3rd pl.	regunt They rule	capiunt	audiunt

The **Present Active Infinitive**, as in the first and second conjugations, adds **-re** to the verb stem:

Stem	Infinitive	Meaning	Stem	Infinitive	Meaning
rege-	reg**ere**	to rule	audī-	audīre	to hear
cape-	cap**ere**	to take	venī-	venīre	to come

Remember that the infinitive of the second conjugation has a long **-ē-**, while that of the third conjugation has a short **-e**:

2nd Conjugation	3rd Conjugation
docēre	regere
vidēre	capere

Present Active Imperative

The **Present Active Imperative**, as in the first and second conjugations (§16), uses the present verb stem for the second singular form and adds **-te** to present stem for the second plural; 3rd conjugation has short **-i-** in the plural

	3rd Regular		3rd –iō		4th	
2nd sg.	rege	(you) rule!	cape	(you) take!	audī	(you) listen!
2nd pl.	reg**ite**	(you all) rule!	cap**ite**	(you all) take!	aud**īte**	(you all) listen!

Three common third conjugation verbs, and an irregular verb you will learn in Chapter 23 (**ferō**), form their second singular imperatives without the stem vowel:

Verb	2nd sg. Imperative	2nd pl. Imperative
dīcō	dīc	dīcite
dūcō	dūc	dūcite
faciō	fac	facite
ferō	fer	ferte

Students through the ages have remembered these forms with the following rhyme:

dīc, dūc, fac, and **fer**
Should have an **-e**, but it isn't there.

Exercise 57. Identify each of the following verbs by person, number and mood (indicative or imperative), then translate into English. All forms are present tense.

1.	scrībit	7.	dīcis	13.	regitis
2.	sedent	8.	dormīs	14.	creat
3.	agunt	9.	capimus	15.	audīte
4.	faciunt	10.	audī	16.	iūdicant
5.	rege	11.	dūc	17.	veniunt
6.	mittimus	12.	docētis	18.	valēs

Exercise 58. Following the model verbs above, conjugate **dūcō**, **faciō** and **veniō** in the present active indicative, singular and plural, and give the infinitive form.

46. **The Pronoun: Personal (2)**

Is, ea, id as a Personal Pronoun

You have already learned the personal pronouns for the first person (*I, we*) and second person (*you, y'all*) (§42). In the next chapter (§50) you will learn about demonstrative pronouns (*this, that*). The most common demonstrative pronoun in Latin is often used as a personal pronoun for the third person. In this chapter it will only be used to mean *he, she, it, they.*

Is, ea, id   he, she, it, they; (this, that)

Singular	Masculine	Feminine	Neuter
Nominative	is	ea	id
Genitive	eius	eius	eius
Dative	eī	eī	eī
Accusative	eum	eam	id
Ablative	eō	eā	eō
Plural			
Nominative	eī	eae	ea
Genitive	eōrum	eārum	eōrum
Dative	eīs	eīs	eīs
Accusative	eōs	eās	ea
Ablative	eīs	eīs	eīs

Notice that this pronoun has regular first and second declension forms in the plural, but some irregular singular forms. Note especially the genitive and dative singular forms, which are the same for all three genders.

Exercise 59. Identify each of the following pronouns by case, number and gender. If the ending is ambiguous, include all possibilities.

1. eius
2. eīs
3. eae
4. id
5. eōrum
6. eī
7. eā
8. ea

Exercise 60. Translate the underlined word(s) in each sentence with the correct Latin form.

1. She was walking <u>with him</u>.
2. We like <u>him</u>, but <u>they</u> (fem.) don't.
3. Who gave <u>her</u> (sg.) that book?
4. A few <u>of them</u> will stay.
5. Do you see <u>it</u>?
6. <u>He</u> and <u>she</u> are friends.
7. We do not know <u>them</u>.
8. He is working <u>for her</u>.

47. **Sentence Pattern: Factitive**

So far you have seen four sentence patterns 1) **Transitive** (§4), 2) **Intransitive** (§4), 3) **Linking** (§33), and 4) **Special Intransitive** (§44).

A fifth pattern, called **factitive** (from **faciō**, *to make*), occurs with verbs that require both a direct object and a second accusative that indicates the effect or consequence of the verb's action on the direct object: **Is mē laetam facit.** = He makes me happy. The second accusative is commonly called the **object complement** because it is necessary to complete the sense of the verb's action. Here are some other examples of factitive sentences in English with the direct object in bold and the object complement underlined; notice that the underlined word is required to complete the meaning of each sentence:

You are painting the **house** <u>purple</u>.
He considers **her** a <u>friend</u>.
They call the **philosopher** <u>wise</u>.
We elected **him** <u>senator</u>.

The elements of this sentence pattern are as follows:

Factitive (uses a special verb with two accusatives)

- subject
- factitive verb
- direct object
- object complement (predicate accusative)

Here are some verbs that commonly take two accusatives in this pattern:

appellō, appellāre, appellāvī, appellātus	to call, name
creō, creāre, creāvī, creātus	to choose, elect
faciō, facere, fēcī, factus	to make
habeō, habēre, habuī, habitus	to consider
iūdicō, iūdicāre, iūdicāvī, iūdicātus	to judge
vocō, vocāre, vocāvī, vocātus	to call

Note that the verbs that take two accusatives in this sentence pattern can also occur in a transitive pattern:

transitive:	**Amīcōs vocābit.**	He will call his friends.
factitive:	**Cīvitātem Rōmam vocābit.**	He will call the state Rome.
transitive:	**Pācem faciunt.**	They make peace.
factitive:	**Eum cōnsulem faciunt.**	They make him consul.

When the second accusative is an adjective it can be difficult to tell which pattern is being used:

Cōnsilium bonum facit.	He is making a good plan. *or*
	He is making the plan good.

When this happens, depend on the context to help you make your best guess.

You have learned two other verbs (**doceō, ōrō**) that can take two accusative objects, but these do *not* establish a factitive pattern since the second accusative does not refer to the direct object:

dōnum virum ōrant.	they are asking the **man** for a **present**.
litterās puerōs docēs.	you are teaching the **boys literature**.

These are transitive sentences with a regular direct object (the person) and a secondary object (the thing asked for or taught).

Exercise 61. Identify each of the following as a transitive or factitive sentence pattern (and be prepared to say why), then translate.

1. Nēmō mē vocābit.
2. Nēmō mē amīcum vocābit.
3. Is eōs novās lēgēs docēbat.
4. Virum ducem creāmus.
5. Cēnam nōbīs facit.
6. Bellum fēminās miserās facit.
7. Eius librum habeō.
8. Eius facta mala habēmus.
9. Dūc nōs ad templum.
10. Eam pulchram iūdicābam.

Exercise 62. Translate each of the following sentences.

1. Eī nihil de iūre lēgibusque sentiunt.
2. In tuā casā dormīre solēbam.
3. Frātrem eius vidēre nōn poterāmus.
4. Docēsne eōs vēritātem?
5. Hominēs veniunt et arma Rōmānōrum capiunt.
6. Tū, rege imperiō populōs, Rōmāne.
7. Rōmānī Rōmulum deum habēbant.
8. Dux litterās dē cīvitāte ad eum mittit.
9. Eratne is sapientiā plēnus?
10. Nōs lībertātem bonam iudicābāmus.

Exercise 63. Translate into Latin.

1. Show (sg.) me the money!
2. We are grieving, for the angry king rules without wisdom.
3. Your (sg.) brother was shouting very angrily ("with great anger").
4. Many of them hesitate to tell us about the war in Italy.
5. We were sitting in the house, but you (sg.) were not able to stay with us.
6. My mother and father teach me courage.
7. They always consider the sea deep.
8. Will they walk with her into the forest and will they be afraid?
9. There is nothing new under the sky.
10. You (pl.) hear many things, but I do not.

Reading 7 *(adapted)*

Pliny the Younger (A.D. 61-112), a senator during the Roman Empire, wrote many letters to friends. In this one, he describes his life and hints that he wants his friend to write.

> Quid agis? Ego vītam laetam – id est, ōtiōsissimam – vīvō. Epistulās ergō longās nōn scrībō, sed legere optō. Vale.

Vocabulary:

id	"that"	epistula, -ae *f.*	letter
ōtiōsissimus, -a, -um	very idle	ergō (adv.)	therefore
vīvō, -ere	to live		

Reading 8 *(adapted)*

The poet Ovid begins his poem, the Metamorphoses, *by announcing his theme and asking the gods for inspiration. He begins with the origins of the universe.*

Before translating, draw an arrow from each adjectival modifier (adjective or genitive noun) to the noun it modifies:

> In nova optō mūtātās dīcere fōrmās corpora; dī, (vōs enim mūtātis illās) adspīrāte meō carminī prīmāque ab orīgine mundī ad mea dūcite tempora carmen!
>
> Ante pontum et terrās et caelum ūnus erat tōtō nātūrae vultus in orbe; virī eum dīcunt "chaos." erat et terra et pontus et caelum, sed erant īnstabilēs et illōrum fōrma nōn manēbat.

Vocabulary:

mūtātus, -a, -um	changed	ante (+ acc.)	before
fōrma, -ae *f.*	form, shape	ūnus, -a, -um	one
mūtō, -āre	to change	tōtus, -a, -um	the whole
illās	"them" (the forms)	vultus (nom. sg. *m.*)	face, appearance
adspīrō, -āre (+ dat.)	help, favor	orbis, -is *m.*	earth, world
carmen, -inis *n.*	song	eum	"it" (the
orīgō, -inis *f.*	beginning, origin		appearance)
mundus, -ī *m.*	world, universe	īnstabilēs (adj.)	unstable
tempus, -oris *n.*	time, period of time	illōrum	"of these" (earth, sea, etc.)

Practice Sentences

Identify the case and use of the underlined words, then translate.

1. Magna dī cūrant, <u>parva</u> **neglegunt**. (Cicero)
2. Vītam regit fortūna, nōn <u>sapientia</u>. (Cicero)
3. Virum <u>bonum</u> nātūra, nōn ōrdō facit. (Publilius Syrus)
4. Lex videt īrātum, īrātus <u>lēgem</u> nōn videt. (Publilius Syrus)
5. Tū <u>nōbīs</u> carēs. (Cicero; *writing a friend who hasn't seen him in too long*)
6. Monet amīcus meus <u>tē</u>. (Cicero)
7. Ego tamen frūgālitātem, id est modestiam et temperantiam, <u>virtūtem</u> maximam iūdicō. (Cicero; *on virtue*)
8. <u>Ars</u> est enim **philosophia** vītae. (Cicero)

Vocabulary:

cūrō, -āre	to care about	temperantia, -ae *f.*	moderation
neglegō, -ere	to neglect	maximus, -a, -um	greatest
ōrdō, -inis *m.*	rank, class, station	ars, artis *f.*	art
frūgālitās, -tātis *f.*	frugality, economy	philosophia, -ae *f.*	philosophy
modestia, -ae *f.*	restraint, freedom from excess		

Chapter 8 Vocabulary

Nouns

moenia, moenium *n.* (pl.)	walls; fortifications
littera, litterae *f.*	letter (of the alphabet); pl. letter, literature
nihil *n. (indeclinable)* nil *(contracted form)*	nothing
vēritās, vēritātis *f.*	truth

Verbs

agō, agere, ēgī, actus quid agis?	to do, perform; drive how are you (doing)?
audiō, audīre, audīvī, audītus	to hear, listen (to)
capiō, capere, cēpī, captus	to take, seize, capture
creō, creāre, creāvī, creātus	to create; elect, choose
dīcō, dīcere, dīxī, dictus	to say, speak, tell
doceō, docēre, docuī, doctus	to teach (*often with 2 accusatives, one of the person, the other of the thing taught*)
dormiō, dormīre, dormīvī, dormitūrus	to sleep
dūcō, dūcere, dūxī, ductus	to lead
faciō, facere, fēcī, factus	to do; make
iūdicō, iūdicāre, iūdicāvī, iūdicātus	to judge; to decide
legō, legere, lēgī, lēctus	to read; choose, select
mittō, mittere, mīsī, missus	to send
regō, regere, rēxī, rēctus	to rule
scrībō, scrībere, scrīpsī, scrīptus	to write
sentiō, sentīre, sēnsī, sēnsus	to feel, perceive
valeō, valēre, valuī, valitūrus valē, valēte *(imperative)*	to be well, healthy; to be strong goodbye, farewell
veniō, venīre, vēnī, ventūrus	to come

Adjective

īrātus, īrāta, īrātum	angry
plēnus, plēna, plēnum (+ gen. or abl.)	full (of), filled (with)

Pronoun

is, ea, id	he, she, it [Ch. 8]; this, that [Ch.9]

(24)

Derivatives: For each English word below, give the Latin word from the Chapter 8 Vocabulary to which it is related and the English word's meaning.

1. irate
2. sentient
3. induce
4. plentiful
5. regime
6. dormitory
7. prevail
8. factory
9. adjudicate
10. scribble
11. annihilate
12. auditorium
13. verdict
14. missile
15. event
16. document

Imperfect Active Indicative: Third and Fourth Conjugations
Future Active Indicative: Third and Fourth Conjugations
The Pronoun: Demonstrative
    hic, haec, hoc
    ille, illa, illud
    is, ea, id
    Adjectival Use

So far, you have learned the personal pronouns for the first and second persons **ego/nōs** and **tū/vōs** (§42), and a third, demonstrative, pronoun often used to mean *he, she, it, they* (§46). This chapter introduces two additional demonstrative pronouns and their uses. It also introduces the imperfect and future tenses of third and fourth conjugation verbs.

48. **Imperfect Active Indicative: Third and Fourth Conjugations**

The **imperfect** of the third and fourth conjugations is formed exactly like that of the first and second conjugations (§35), with the tense sign **-ba-** between the verb stem and the personal endings:

	3rd Regular		**3rd –iō**	**4th**
1st sg.	regēbam	I was ruling, etc.	capiēbam	audiēbam
2nd sg.	regēbās	You were ruling	capiēbās	audiēbās
3rd sg.	regēbat	He / she was ruling	capiēbat	audiēbat
1st pl.	regēbāmus	We were ruling	capiēbāmus	audiēbāmus
2nd pl.	regēbātis	You (all) were ruling	capiēbātis	audiēbātis
3rd pl.	regēbant	They were ruling	capiēbant	audiēbant

Note that the stem vowel **-i-** of third **-iō** verbs is visible in these forms. While this **-i-** usually disappears before a short **-e** (**capiō, capere**) (§45), it remains before a long **-ē**.

49. **Future Active Indicative: Third and Fourth Conjugations**

The **future** of the third and fourth conjugations uses the vowel **-e-** (**-a-** in the first singular form) before the ending, instead of the tense sign **-bi-** that appeared in the first two conjugations:

	3rd Regular		3rd –iō	4th
1st sg.	regam	I shall rule	capiam	audiam
2nd sg.	regēs	You will rule	capiēs	audiēs
3rd sg.	reget	He / she will rule	capiet	audiet
1st pl.	regēmus	We shall rule	capiēmus	audiēmus
2nd pl.	regētis	You (all) will rule	capiētis	audiētis
3rd pl.	regent	They will rule	capient	audient

The personal endings are again the same as those used in the present tense except in the 1st. sg., which ends with **-m** instead of **-ō**. The stem vowel **-i-** of third **-iō** verbs is visible in all the forms.

Exercise 64. Identify each of the following verbs by person, number, tense (present, imperfect or future) and mood (indicative or imperative), then translate into English.

1.	fugiēbātis	6.	serviētis	11.	dīc (§45)
2.	dūcet	7.	scrībam	12.	venient
3.	agēbam	8.	crēdite	13.	audī
4.	mittēs	9.	sentiēbāmus	14.	finiet
5.	praebēs	10.	incipiunt	15.	dormiēbātis

Exercise 65. Write the indicated form of each verb, then translate into English.

Example: discō, discere (third sg. imperfect):   discēbat; he/she/it was learning

1. dormiō, dormīre (third pl. present)
2. legō, legere (first sg. future)
3. veniō, venīre (second sg. pres. imperative)
4. crēdō, crēdere (first pl. imperfect)
5. scrībō, scrībere (third sg. future)
6. sedeō, sedēre (third sg. future)
7. relinquō, relinquere (third pl. imperfect)
8. serviō, servīre (third pl. future)
9. petō, petere (first sg. imperfect)
10. incipiō, incipere (second pl. future)

50. The Pronoun: Demonstrative

Demonstrative pronouns are used to point out (**dēmōnstrāre**) a specific person or thing: *did you hear* **that**?; *he likes* **those**. As in English, these pronouns can also be used as adjectives, modifying a noun: *did you see* **that** *man?*; *he likes* **those** *books*. Like **is, ea, id** (§46), the other two demonstrative pronouns in this chapter have regular first and second declension forms in the plural, but some irregular singular forms. Note again the genitive and dative singular forms, which are the same for all three genders. The pronouns in this chapter are very common and should be memorized carefully and drilled regularly.

hic, haec, hoc   this, these; the latter

Singular	Masculine	Feminine	Neuter
Nominative	hic	haec	hoc
Genitive	huius	huius	huius
Dative	huic	huic	huic
Accusative	hunc	hanc	hoc
Ablative	hōc	hāc	hōc
Plural			
Nominative	hī	hae	haec
Genitive	hōrum	hārum	hōrum
Dative	hīs	hīs	hīs
Accusative	hōs	hās	haec
Ablative	hīs	hīs	hīs

ille, illa, illud   that, those; the famous; the former

Singular	Masculine	Feminine	Neuter
Nominative	ille	illa	illud
Genitive	illīus	illīus	illīus
Dative	illī	illī	illī
Accusative	illum	illam	illud
Ablative	illō	illā	illō
Plural			
Nominative	illī	illae	illa
Genitive	illōrum	illārum	illōrum
Dative	illīs	illīs	illīs
Accusative	illōs	illās	illa
Ablative	illīs	illīs	illīs

is, ea, id   this, that (see §46)

Note the following:

- **Hic** and **ille** are more emphatic than **is**, which is used when no emphasis is intended.

- **Hic** points out someone or something near in space or time: *this man* (right here), and often refers to the latter (second) of two people or things already mentioned.

- **Ille** points out someone or something further away in space or time: *that man* (over there), and often refers to the former (first) of two people or things already mentioned.

Adjectival Use

When used as adjectives, these demonstratives agree in case, number and gender with a noun in the sentence. Compare the following uses of **is, ea, id**:

as a pronoun:	**Is** est amīcus.	**He** is a friend.
	Amābam **eam**.	I used to love **her**.
	Vidēmus **ea**.	We see **those (things)**.
as an adjective:	**Is** amīcus est bonus.	**This** friend is good.
	Amābam **eam** fēminam.	I used to love **that** woman.
	Vidēmus **ea** loca.	We see **those places.**

When **ille** is used as an adjective, it may indicate a well-known or famous person or thing. When it does this, it usually follows the noun it modifies:

Rōmulus ille urbem aedificābat.   **That (famous) Romulus** was building a city.

Exercise 66. Identify each of the following pronouns by case, number and gender. If the ending is ambiguous, include all possibilities.

1. haec
2. illae
3. huius
4. id
5. hās
6. illārum
7. eī
8. illud
9. huic
10. hanc

Exercise 67. Fill in the blank to complete each sentence and translate.

1. Ill_____ cōnsulem faciēmus.
2. Ex silv_____ fugiunt.
3. E_____ (= his) coniugī serviam.
4. Coniūnx h_____ (= this) nōs petit.
5. Vēritātī crēd_____ bonum est.
6. Multa bona ill_____ dabās.
7. Ego patrī sed nōn frātr_____ pāreō.
8. Mīles plēnus timōr_____ erat.

Exercise 68. Identify the obvious chunks and then translate each of the following sentences.

1. Inter līberōs virtūs semper erit bona.
2. Dē huius coniuge multa dīcam.
3. Tūne ea iūra fugere audēs?
4. Verba illīus audiēbāmus, sed dormiēbās.
5. Multīs cum lacrimīs filius filiaque ante casam patrem relinquēbant.
6. In illō agrō corpus sine capite iacēbat.
7. Ea mātrī iam servit.
8. Crēdēsne huic? Praebēbisne eī tuam dextram?
9. Ille dux ad Ītaliam cum patre filiōque veniet.
10. Hic homō nōs factīs dūcere incipit.
11. Placēbantne carmina brevia illīus poētae vōbīs?
12. Rēx hanc turbam īrātam facere nōn optat.

Exercise 69. Translate into Latin.

1. You (pl.) are Romans, but I am not.
2. Obey the divine law and tell us the truth now!
3. We were not able to see their tears.
4. This plan will please these (men), but will not restrain those angry (men).
5. The state used to praise the wisdom of our leaders.
6. Boys, either listen or read those books.
7. Do you (pl.) judge his life good?
8. The brothers were fighting about the fertile land of that (man).
9. They are coming from the right (side) in front of the forest.
10. Are you (sg.) beginning to trust these soldiers?

Reading 9 *(adapted)*

Pliny chides a friend for not writing him.

Ōlim mihi epistulās nōn mittis. 'nihil est,' dīcis, 'quod scrībere possum.' sed hoc scrībe, aut, 'sī valēs, bene est; egō valeō.' hoc mihi sufficit; est enim bonum. nōn lūdō, **sērius** sum. quid agis? sine sollicitūdine magnā **ignārus** esse nōn possum. Valē.

Vocabulary:

ōlim (adv.)	for a while now	sufficit	is enough
epistula, -ae *f.*	letter	lūdō, -ere	to joke, play
quod	which (*refers to* nihil)	sērius, -a, -um	serious
		sollicitūdō, -inis *f.*	anxiety, uneasiness
sī	if	ignārus, -a, -um	ignorant, unaware
bene (adv.)	well (good)		

Reading 10 *(adapted)*

Plautus (c. 254 -184 B.C.) was a Roman dramatist who wrote comedies. In his Pseudolus, *two slaves (Harpax and Pseudolus) have met and one lies about his name before the other cuts the conversation off so they can conduct their business.*

HARPAX. Tū servus es aut līber?

PSEUDOLUS. Nunc serviō.

HARP. Esne tū ab illō mīlite Macedoniō, servus eius?

PS. Sum.

HARP. Sed quid est tibi nomen?

PS. Surus sum.

HARP. Surus?

PS. Id est nomen mihi.

HARP. Verba multa facimus.

Vocabulary:

servus, -ī *m.*	slave	quid	What?
Macedonius, -a, -um	Macedonian	Surus, -ī *m.*	Surus

Practice Sentences

Identify the case and use of the underlined words, then translate.

1. Cūra mihi pāx est ..., <u>frātrī</u> fera bella placēbant. (Ovid; *Ceyx mourns his brother who was not like him*)
2. **Silent** enim lēgēs inter <u>arma</u>. (Cicero)
3. Facta mea, nōn **dicta**, <u>mīlitēs</u>, sequiminī et exemplum ā mē petite. (Livy – adapted; *a consul encourages his men before battle*)
4. Hōc **vōcem** carmine movet: "Ab Iove, **Mūsa**, ... <u>carmina</u> nostra movē!" (Ovid – adapted; *Orpheus <the subject of* movet> *begins a song*)
5. Forsan et <u>haec</u> ōlim meminisse iuvābit. (Vergil; *Aeneas tries to encourage his men*)
6. <u>Vōs</u> vērō patriae fīliōs iūdicō. (Cicero – adapted; *honoring men fallen in battle*)
7. Ego <u>hoc</u> tibi dēbeō. (Terence)
8. Eī vōbīs labōrant, <u>vōbīs</u> serviunt. (Cicero – adapted)

Vocabulary:

ferus, -a, -um	fierce, savage	Mūsa, -ae *f.*	Muse
sileō, -ēre	to be silent	Iuppiter, Iovis, *m.*	Jupiter
dictum, -ī *n.*	word	forsan (adv.)	perhaps
sequiminī = 2 pl. imperative	"follow"	meminisse	to remember
vōx, vōcis *f.*	voice	vērō (adv.)	in fact, truly

Chapter 9 Vocabulary

Nouns

carmen, carminis *n.*	song, poem
coniūnx, coniugis *m.* or *f.*	wife; husband; spouse
lacrima, lacrimae *f.*	tear
mīles, mīlitis *m.*	soldier
patria, patriae *f.*	country, fatherland
poēta, poētae *m.*	poet
timor, timōris *m.*	fear, terror

Verbs

crēdō, crēdere, crēdidī, crēditus	to believe, trust (+ dat. of *person believed*; + acc. *of thing believed*)
finiō, finīre, finīvī, finītus	to end, finish; limit; die
fugiō, fugere, fūgī, fugitūrus	to flee (from), escape, avoid
incipiō, incipere, incēpī, inceptus	to begin
petō, petere, petīvī *or* petiī, petītus	to seek, go after; ask; attack
praebeō, praebēre, praebuī, praebitus	to show; offer, provide
relinquō, relinquere, relīquī, relictus	to leave, abandon
serviō, servīre, servīvī *or* serviī, servītūrus (+ dat.)	to serve

Adjective

clārus, clāra, clārum	clear, bright; famous; loud
dexter, dextra, dextrum	right (side); right hand; pledge (of friendship)

Pronouns

hic, haec, hoc	this
ille, illa, illud	that

Adverbs

ōlim	once (upon a time), one day (in the future)
tamen	however, nevertheless, yet
et	even; also

Prepositions

ante (+ acc.)	before, in front of
inter (+ acc.)	between, among

Coordinating Conjunction

aut	or
aut ... aut	either ... or

(25)

Derivatives: For each English word below, give the Latin word from the Chapter 9 Vocabulary to which it is related and the English word's meaning.

1.	relinquish	6.	timorous
2.	military	7.	antebellum
3.	fugitive	8.	charm
4.	conjugal	9.	incredible
5.	petition	10.	lacrimose

CHAPTER 10

Third Declension Nouns: i-Stem
Third Declension Adjectives
Expressions of Cause

So far, all the third declension nouns you have seen have had consonant stems and all the adjectives you have seen have used endings taken from the first and second declensions. This chapter introduces nouns with **i**-stems and adjectives, which both use third declension endings. It also introduces different ways to express cause in Latin.

51. Third Declension Nouns: i-Stem

I-stem nouns originally showed an -**i**- in most of their endings (so, for example, Acc. sg. -**im**, Acc. pl. -**īs**) but, over time, some of these endings were replaced by those you learned in §41 (e.g. Acc. sg. -**em**, Acc. pl. -**ēs**). The usual pattern of **i**-stems is illustrated by the following:

Singular	Masc./Fem.	Neuter	Endings
Nominative	urbs	mare	*(variable)*
Genitive	urb**is**	mar**is**	-**is**
Dative	urb**ī**	mar**ī**	-**ī**
Accusative	urb**em**	mare	-**em**, ——
Ablative	urbe	mar**ī**	-**e**, -**ī**
Plural			
Nominative	urb**ēs**	mar**ia**	-**ēs**, -**ia**
Genitive	urb**ium**	mar**ium**	-**ium**
Dative	urb**ibus**	mar**ibus**	-**ibus**
Accusative	urb**ēs**	mar**ia**	-**ēs**, -**ia**
Ablative	urb**ibus**	mar**ibus**	-**ibus**

With the exception of the ablative singular neuter, the endings of **i**-stem nouns are not significantly different from those of regular consonant stem nouns (for example, Gen. pl. -**um** and -**ium**). Below are some general rules for determining what nouns are **i**-stems. All **i**-stem nouns in this book are marked with an asterisk in the Chapter Vocabulary lists.

Masculine and Feminine

- nouns that have the same number of syllables in the nominative and genitive singular; these usually have a nominative singular in **-is** (sometimes **-ēs**). For example:

auris, auris *f.*	ear	fīnis, fīnis *m.*	end
caedēs, caedis *f.*	murder, slaughter	hostis, hostis *m.*	enemy
cīvis, cīvis *m.* or *f.*	citizen	ignis, ignis *m.*	fire
classis, classis *f.*	fleet (of ships)	mōlēs, mōlis *f.*	mass, structure
collis, collis *m.*	hill	nāvis, nāvis *f.*	ship

Two common exceptions are: **canis, canis** (dog) and **iuvenis, iuvenis** (young person).

- monosyllables in **-s** or **-x** preceded by a consonant. For example:

ars, artis *f.*	skill, art	mors, mortis *f.*	death
arx, arcis *f.*	citadel, summit	nox, noctis *f.*	night
dēns, dentis *m.*	tooth	pars, partis *f.*	part
gēns, gentis *f.*	nation	pōns, pontis *m.*	bridge
mēns, mentis *f.*	mind, judgment	urbs, urbis *f.*	city

Note that **nox, noctis** has two consonants in its stem (cf. **dux, ducis**) and is counted as an **-i** stem.

Neuter

- nouns that end in **-al**, **-ar**, or **-e**. For example:

-al		**-ar**		**-e**	
animal, animālis	animal	exemplar, -āris	model	mare, maris	sea
capital, capitālis	capital crime			cubīle, cubīlis	couch

52. **Third Declension Adjectives**

Adjectives in the third declension follow the declension of **i**-stem nouns, with the Ablative sg. in **-ī** and the Genitive pl. in **-ium**. Third declension adjectives are characterized by their nominative singular endings: some use a different ending for each gender (as the first and second declension adjectives did, §27); others use one ending for masculine and feminine and a second for neuter; a third group uses one set of endings for all three genders. An example from each group is given below.

The dictionary listing for each of these adjectives will indicate which group they belong in as follows:

3-ending:	**ācer, ācris, ācre**	(nom. sg. masc. + fem. + neuter forms)
2-ending:	**omnis, omne**	(nom. sg. masc./fem. + nom. sg. n. forms)
1-ending:	**ingēns, ingentis**	(nom. sg. + gen. sg. forms)

Three-Ending Adjectives

Singular	Masculine	Feminine	Neuter
Nominative	ācer	ācris	ācre
Genitive	ācris	ācris	ācris
Dative	ācrī	ācrī	ācrī
Accusative	ācrem	ācrem	ācre
Ablative	ācrī	ācrī	ācrī
Plural			
Nominative	ācrēs	ācrēs	ācria
Genitive	ācrium	ācrium	ācrium
Dative	ācribus	ācribus	ācribus
Accusative	ācrēs	ācrēs	ācria
Ablative	ācribus	ācribus	ācribus

Note:

- An exception to this pattern is **celer**, **celeris**, **celere** (swift), which keeps the stem **-er** throughout. **Celer** uses the genitive plural ending **-um**, but that form only appears as a substantive signifying a military rank.

Two-Ending Adjectives

Singular	Masc./Fem.	Neuter
Nominative	omnis	omne
Genitive	omnis	omnis
Dative	omnī	omnī
Accusative	omnem	omne
Ablative	omnī	omnī
Plural		
Nominative	omnēs	omnia
Genitive	omnium	omnium
Dative	omnibus	omnibus
Accusative	omnēs	omnia
Ablative	omnibus	omnibus

One-Ending Adjectives

Singular	Masc./Fem.	Neuter
Nominative	ingēns	ingēns
Genitive	ingentis	ingentis
Dative	ingentī	ingentī
Accusative	ingentem	ingēns
Ablative	ingentī	ingentī
Plural		
Nominative	ingentēs	ingentia
Genitive	ingentium	ingentium
Dative	ingentibus	ingentibus
Accusative	ingentēs	ingentia
Ablative	ingentibus	ingentibus

Exercise 70. Identify each of the following third declension adjectives by case, number and gender. If the ending is ambiguous, include all possibilities.

Example: difficilem   Accusative singular masculine or feminine

1. forte
2. potentium
3. facilī

4. celeribus
5. omnia
6. difficilēs

Exercise 71. Identify each of the following nouns by case, number and gender, then say which adjectives could modify the noun listed with them. Be prepared to say why the others could NOT modify the noun.

Example: caput: pulcher, magna, omne, ingēns
         caput (nom. or acc. sg. n.)
         omne, ingēns (also nom. or acc. sg. n.)

1.	arte:	dulcī	pulchrum	bonā	difficilia
2.	hōrīs:	brevis	fēlīcibus	prīmī	omnēs
3.	tempus:	celer	omne	fēlīx	longus
4.	dominus:	fēlīx	fortēs	noster	potēns
5.	nūminis:	magnā	potentia	clārī	parvīs
6.	mēns:	pulchra	īrātā	ācris	omne
7.	liber:	magnus	parvum	ingentem	omnis
8.	vītā:	facile	omnī	laeta	novō

Exercise 72. Translate each of the following noun-adjective pairs into the Latin case indicated.

1. short life (gen.)
2. every mother (nom.)
3. huge fields (dat.)
4. strange truth (nom.)
5. easy times (acc.)

6. powerful leader (abl.)
7. new laws (gen.)
8. pleasant dinner (acc.)
9. lucky daughter (abl.)
10. mighty masters (nom.)

53. **Expressions of Cause**

Latin, like English, has a variety of ways to express **cause**:

- **Ablative** (without a preposition)

    Dux **cūrīs** aeger erat.   The leader was sick **with worry (because of cares)**.
    Multa bellī **timōre** faciunt.   They do many things **out of a fear** of war.

It is sometimes hard to distinguish this use of the ablative from an ablative of means (§23) or ablative of manner (§34). If you aren't sure, try translating "because of ____," "by means of ____" and "with ____" to see which suits the context best.

- **Preposition + accusative** or **ablative**

    dē or **ex** with the **ablative**

    Dux **ex vulnere** aeger erat.   The leader was sick **from a wound**.
    Certīs **dē causīs** agit.   He is acting **for** definite **reasons**.

    ob and **propter** with the **accusative**

    Laetī sumus **propter pācem**.   We are happy **because of the peace**.
    Ob iniūriam nōn pugnābit.   **Because of his injury**, he will not fight.

- **Causā** and **grātiā** with the **genitive**

    Cīvitātis causā pugnāte!   Fight **for the sake of the state!**
    Exemplī grātiā ūnum dīcō.   I mention one thing **for example**.

    The genitive precedes these words, as in the examples above.

Exercise 73. In the following paragraph identify those phrases that indicate **means**, **manner**, **accompaniment** and **cause**. (Do not translate into Latin.)

The leader marched with his men through the mountains and with great speed they attacked the city with their weapons. The citizens, terrified by the attack, ran with their wives and children to the river. But it was swollen with rain, and they refused to cross through fear. With difficulty they moved along the banks of the river and finally escaped by a path through the forest.

Exercise 74. Where possible draw an arrow from each adjective (or pronoun used as an adjective) to the noun it modifies, and then translate each of the following sentences.

1. Bellum breve sed difficile populō erat.
2. Rēgī nostrō pācis grātiā dōna saepe praebēmus.
3. Omnēs propter artem poētae dīs grātiās agunt.
4. Mīlitēs ācrēs patriam timōris causā nōn relinquent.
5. Tibi vīta dulcis longaque erit.
6. Mihi aut lībertātem aut mortem date!
7. Ōlim amīcī potentēs illīus ad urbem venient.
8. Rōmānīs pugnāre prō patriā bonum erat.
9. Ille dux ē timōre ad Ītaliam cum patre filiōque fugit.
10. Habēbantne Rōmānī omnēs Rōmulum deum?

Exercise 75. Translate into Latin.

1. His (*use* gen. of **is**) wife had many skills, but no virtue. (*use a form of* **sum** + dat.)
2. Is it easy to seek the truth?
3. We are attacking part of the city with fire.
4. That soldier leaves weapons on the field and escapes death.
5. Because of the deeds of those men, our fatherland is strong (*use a form of* **valeō**).
6. Good leaders always act with justice.
7. Fortune helps the brave.
8. One day the songs of these poets will be famous.
9. They kept fighting against these soldiers for the sake of your (pl.) freedom
10. Everyone desires a quick and easy death.

Reading 11 *(adapted)*

Tacitus (c. A.D. 56 – after A.D. 113) describes the Germans' way of ruling and doing battle. Among other differences, the Germans organized their battle groups by families and clans, and encouraged the women to cheer from the sidelines.

Germānī rēgēs ex **nōbilitāte**, ducēs ex virtūte legunt. Nec rēgibus **īnfīnīta** aut lībera potestās, et ducēs exemplō potius quam imperiō agunt; sī ante aciem pugnant, **admīrātiōne** praesunt. Effigiāsque et **signa** ex silvīs **sacrīs** in proelium portant. Ad mātrēs, ad coniugēs vulnera praebent; nec illae **numerāre** aut exigere plāgās timent, cibōsque et hortāmina mīlitibus dant.

Vocabulary:

nōbilitās, -tātis *f.*	noble birth, nobility	signum, -ī *n.*	token, sign
īnfīnītus, -a, -um	unlimited	proelium, -ī *n.*	battle
potestās, -tātis *f.*	power	sacer, -cra, -crum	sacred
potius quam	"rather than"	vulnus, -eris *n.*	wound
sī	if	numerō, -āre	to count
aciem (acc.)	line of battle	exigō, -ere	to demand to see
admīrātiō, -iōnis *f.*	admiration	plāga, -ae *f.*	wound, blow
praesum	to lead	cibus, -ī *m.*	food
effigia, -ae *f.*	image (of an animal)	hortāmen, -inis *n.*	encouragement

Reading 12 *(adapted)*

Cicero (106-43 B.C.) talks about the importance of the laws to the Roman state.

Lex est fundāmentum lībertātis; mēns et animus et cōnsilium et sententia cīvitātis est in lēgibus. ut corpora nostra sine mente, sīc cīvitās sine lēge partēs adhibēre nōn potest. lēgum ministrī sunt **magistrātūs**, lēgum **interpretēs** iūdicēs, et tandem lēgum **servī** sumus itaque līberī esse possumus.

Vocabulary:

fundāmentum, -ī *n.*	foundation	magistrātūs (nom. pl.)	magistrates
sententia, -ae *f.*	purpose, will	interpres, -etis *m.*	interpreter
ut (conjunction)	just as	iūdex, -icis *m.*	judge
sīc (adv.)	thus	servus, -ī *m.*	servant
adhibeō, -ēre	to use	itaque	and so, therefore
minister, -trī *m.*	administrator		

Practice Sentences

Identify the case and use of the underlined words, then translate.

1. Terra corpus est sed mēns <u>ignis</u> est. (Ennius - adapted; *discussing the nature of the universe*)

2. Per ego hās <u>lacrimās</u> dextramque tuam tē ōrō. (Vergil; *Dido begs Aeneas to listen to her*)

3. Īra **necessaria** est, nec sine <u>illā</u> superāre potest, nisi illa implet animum. (Seneca – adapted; *quoting Aristotle, and will go on to disagree with this view*)

4. Mēns latet in animīs <u>hominum</u> et pars animī est. (Cicero - adapted)

5. Ars grātia <u>artis</u>. (MGM motto)

6. Ars est cēlāre <u>artem</u>. (Anonymous)

7. Iuvābit hoc <u>tē</u>; mē certē iuvat …. Igitur et laudō et grātiās agō. (Pliny; *writing to a friend who took his advice and pardoned his freedman*)

8. Dēbēs agere <u>dīs</u> grātiās. (Pliny)

Vocabulary:

necessaria, -ae *f.*	necessary	lateō, -ēre	to lie hidden
nisi	"unless"	certē (adv.)	surely
cēlō, -āre	to hide, conceal	igitur (adv.)	therefore

Chapter 10 Vocabulary

Nouns

*ars, artis *f.*	skill, art
causa, causae *f.*	cause, reason
causā (+ gen.)	for the sake of, because of
grātia, grātiae *f.*	grace; favor, kindness; gratitude
grātiā (+ gen.)	for the sake of, because of
grātiās agere (+ dat.)	to thank
*ignis, ignis *m.*	fire
*mare, maris *n.*	sea
abl. sg. = mare *and* marī	
*mēns, mentis *f.*	mind, judgment, reason

*mors, mortis *f.*	death
*pars, partis *f.*	part, share, direction
*urbs, urbis *f.*	city

Adjectives

ācer, ācris, ācre	sharp, fierce; eager
brevis, breve	brief, short
celer, celeris, celere	swift, quick, rapid
difficilis, difficile	difficult
dulcis, dulce	sweet; pleasant
facilis, facile	easy
fēlīx, fēlīcis	fortunate, lucky
fortis, forte	brave; strong
ingēns, ingentis	huge; mighty
omnis, omne	all, every
potēns, potentis	powerful; able

Prepositions

ob (+ acc.)	because of
per (+ acc.)	through, along; because of; by (*in oaths and prayers*)

Coordinating Conjunctions

atque, ac	and
nec *or* neque	and not, and … not
nec … nec; neque … neque	neither … nor

(24)

Derivatives: For each English word below, give the Latin word from the Chapter 10 Vocabulary to which it is related and the English word's meaning.

1.	dulcit	7.	potential
2.	ignition	8.	maritime
3.	omniscient	9.	fortitude
4.	acerbic	10.	abridge
5.	demented	11.	partition
6.	celerity	12.	urban

READING CHAPTER II

Narrative Reading II: Aeneas in Italy
Dictionary Practice / Form Identification
Review of the Sentence and its Parts
Question Words for Extra Practice
Word Building
    Roots
    Vowel Weakening
English Abbreviations and Phrases

Narrative Reading II: Aeneas in Italy

Adapted from Livy 1.1

*This passage picks up the story of what happens after the end of the Trojan War.
Although the Trojans are defeated by the Greeks, one of their leaders (Aeneas) leads
a group of survivors out of the burning city and travels to found a new city in Italy.*

Tandem **Graecī Trōiam** longum post bellum superant. Aenēās,
fīlius Anchīsae, ex urbe fugit et multīs cum sociīs ad partem
Ītaliae nāvigat. Trōia et huic locō nōmen est. ibi **Trōiānī**
praedam ex agrīs agere incipiēbant. Latīnus rēx Aborīginēsque,
quī tum ea tenēbant loca, cum armīs ex urbe atque agrīs
concurrunt. **Trōiānī** arma ad proelium parant, sed ante bellum
Latīnus ducem advenārum vocat ad conloquium. 'Quī estis?'
rēx dīcit. Aenēās miseram fābulam **Trōiae** nārrat:

(continued)

Vocabulary:

Graecus, -a, -um	Greek	Latīnus (nom.)	Latinus (an
Trōia, -ae *f.*	Troy		early king in Italy)
Aenēās, Aenēae *m.*	Aeneas,	Aborīginēs	original
	Anchises' son	(nom. pl.)	inhabitants
Anchīsēs, Anchīsae *m.*	Anchises	quī (nom. sg. & pl.)	who; who?
socius, -ī *m.* (pl.)	comrades	concurrō, -ere	to charge, rush
ibi (adv.)	there	proelium, -ī *n.*	battle
praeda, -ae *f.*	plunder	advena, -ae *m.*	foreigner, stranger
	(e.g. cattle)	conloquium, -ī *n.*	conference

Narrative Reading II *(continued)*

'**Trōiānī** sumus; ego sum Aenēās, fīlius Anchīsae et Veneris deae; Penātēs mēcum portō; in hōc locō novam urbem aedificāre optāmus.' rēx Latīnus **nōbilitātem** gentis virīque et Aenēae animum aut bellō aut pācī parātum videt. huic dextram dat, fidem **futūrae amīcitiae**, et ducēs foedus faciunt. tum Latīnus fīliam, **Lāvīniam**, Aenēae in **mātrimōnium** dat. **Trōiānī** novam urbem aedificābunt et Aenēās ab nōmine coniugis "Lāvīnium" hanc urbem appellābit.

Vocabulary:

Venus, Veneris *f.*	Venus	fidem (acc.)	pledge
Penātēs, -ium *m.* (pl.)	household gods	futūrus, -a, -um	future
nōbilitās, -tātis *f.*	nobility	amīcitia, -ae *f.*	friendship
gēns, gentis *f.*	race, people, nation	foedus, -eris *n.*	treaty
		mātrimōnium, -i *n.*	marriage
parātus, -a, -um	prepared	Lāvīnium, -iī *n.*	Lavinium
Lāvīnia, -ae *f.*	Lavinia	appellō, -āre, -āvī	to name, call

Dictionary Practice/Form Identification

Identify the words below based on the dictionary entries given. Be sure to indicate the **entry from which each is taken** and the **part of speech**, and to *give all possibilities for ambiguous forms.*

For **nouns** and **adjectives**: give case, number, and gender

For **verbs**: give person, number, tense (present, imperfect, future) and mood (indicative or imperative). *All forms so far are active.

A. amor, amōris *m.*: love
B. amō, amāre, amāvī, amātus: to love
C. amīcus, amīcī *m.*: friend
D. amīcitia, amīcitiae *f.*: friendship

		Entry	Part of Speech	Form ID
1.	amābunt			
2.	amōrī			
3.	amīcitiās			
4.	amābās			
5.	amīcīs			
6.	amāte			
7.	amōrēs			
8.	amāmus			
9.	amīcō			
10.	amōre			

Review of the Sentence and its Parts

If you are using a "graphic organizer," you can update it to add new material or refocus your review items. Here is the chart from Reading Chapter I, with core items replaced by sentence patterns, and additional coordinating conjunctions from the vocabulary for chapters 6-10:

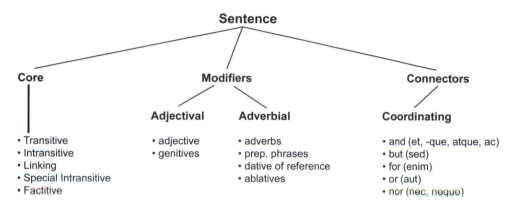

Question Words for Extra Practice

Quis (sg.)/Quī (pl.)	who?	asks for an animate subject
Quem (sg.)/Quōs (pl.)	whom?	asks for an animate direct object
Quid (sg.)	what?	asks for an inanimate subject or direct object
Ubi	where?	
Unde	from where?	
Quō	to where?	
Quōcum (sg.)/Quibuscum (pl.)	with whom?	
Quō modō	in what manner?	

Based on the narrative reading at the beginning of this chapter, answer the following questions in Latin.

1. Quis est Aenēās?
2. Unde fugit?
3. Quibuscum nāvigat?
4. Quō nāvigat?
5. Quī tum erat rēx huius partis Ītaliae?
6. Unde Aborīginēs concurrunt?
7. Quid Aenēās nārrat?
8. Ubi Trōiānī urbem aedificāre optant?
9. Quid Latīnus videt?
10. Quem Latīnus Aenēae dat?

Word Building

Roots

You have now learned enough vocabulary to begin recognizing families of words that use the same root. Look, for example, at the following set of words, which use the root **am-**:

amor, amōris *m.*: love
amō, amāre, amāvī, amātus: to love
amīcus, amīcī *m.*: friend
amīcitia, amīcitiae *f.*: friendship

The root meaning for **am-** is "love." By learning some of the common roots and root meanings in Latin, you can simplify your work at building a usable Latin vocabulary.

Vowel Weakening

As you begin to learn Latin roots, you should also be aware of a feature common to all languages, the tendency for some vowels to weaken. This is especially common with compound words:

- short **a** before a single consonant weakens to short **i**

  ca**p**iō > inc**i**piō
  amīcus > in**im**īcus

- short **a** before two consonants weakens to short **e**

  ca**p**tus > inc**e**ptus

For each of the following words, identify the root, guess at its meaning, and list as many words from the Chapter Vocabulary as you can that use the same root:

Example: capiō   Root = CAP, Meaning = "take," Other words: incipiō

1. faciō   3   rēgnum
2. dūcō   4. timor

Based on the Latin words you have already learned, see if you can guess the meaning of each of the following:

1. fuga, -ae *f.*   3   locō, -āre, -āvī, -ātus
2. iūdex, iūdicis *m.*   4. tacitus, -a, -um

English Abbreviations and Phrases

- e.g.   **exemplī grātiā**   for example
- i.e.   **id est**   that is

- **ad hoc**   for this (purpose)
- **in locō parentis**   in place of a parent
- **inter alia**   among other things
- **prō bonō (pūblicō)**   for the public good

CHAPTER 11

Perfect Active System
    Perfect Active Indicative
    Pluperfect Active Indicative
    Future Perfect Active Indicative
Special Adjectives in -īus
Numerals
Expressions of Time

So far you have learned three tenses of Latin verbs, all built on the present stem (§5): present, imperfect, and future. This chapter introduces three new tenses, all built on the perfect stem, which is found in the third principal part (§6). It also introduces numerals, and different ways to express time in Latin.

54. **Perfect Active Indicative**

The **perfect** is a past tense in Latin that must be distinguished from the imperfect tense (§35). The perfect is formed by adding personal endings to the stem of the third principal part. To find the stem, remove the **-i-** from the third principal part:

    amō, amāre, **amāv (ī)** – first conjugation
    moneō, monēre, **monu (ī)** – second conjugation
    regō, regere, **rēx (ī)** – third conjugation
    capiō, capere, **cēp (ī)** – third conjugation **-iō**
    audiō, audīre, **audīv (ī)** – fourth conjugation
    sum, esse, **fu (ī)** – **sum** (the perfect forms of this verb, and of **possum**, are regular)

Note that some verbs with a **-v** in the stem may drop the **-v**:

    petō, petere, **petīvī** *or* **petiī**
    audiō, audīre, **audīvī** *or* **audiī**

The personal endings for the **perfect active indicative** are the same for all conjugations:

	Singular		Plural	
1st person	-ī	I	-imus	we
2nd person	-istī	you	-istis	you, you all
3rd person	-it	he, she, it	-ērunt, -ēre	they

Note that in the third person pl. form, the ending has a long -ē-, and that sometimes (particularly in poetry) the ending is shortened to **-ēre**. This means you will need to pay close attention to the verb stem and the context of the sentence to determine whether the form is an indicative or an infinitive.

Here are the **perfect active indicative** verb forms of the each regular conjugation:

	1st Conjugation		Endings
1st sg.	amāvī	I loved, I have loved	-ī
2nd sg.	amāvistī	You loved	-istī
3rd sg.	amāvit	He, she, it loved	-it
1st pl.	amāvimus	We loved	-imus
2nd pl.	amāvistis	You (all) loved	-istis
3rd pl.	amāvērunt, amāvēre	They loved	-ērunt, -ēre

	2nd Conj.	3rd Conj.	4th Conj.	Sum, esse, fuī
1st sg.	monuī	rēxī	audīvī	fuī
2nd sg.	monuistī	rēxistī	audīvistī	fuistī
3rd sg.	monuit	rēxit	audīvit	fuit
1st pl.	monuimus	rēximus	audīvimus	fuimus
2nd pl.	monuistis	rēxistis	audīvistis	fuistis
3rd pl.	monuērunt, monuēre	rēxērunt, rēxēre	audīvērunt, audīvēre	fuērunt, fuēre

The **perfect** tense in Latin has two distinct meanings:

- The **historical perfect** corresponds to the simple past tense in English, and has been described as "the tense of *narration* (as opposed to the Imperfect, the tense of *description*)."

    I *traveled* [**perfect**] to Italy one summer and, while I *was walking* [**imperfect**] around Rome, I *saw* [**perfect**] the Roman Forum.

One way to think about the historical perfect in contrast to the imperfect is to imagine the historical perfect as a snapshot or digital image, and the imperfect as a video tape or digital stream.

- The **present perfect** also refers to an action that happened in the past, but stresses the present result of that completed action.

    I **have finished** my homework (so I can do something else now).
    I **have climbed** this tree (and am now perched at the top).
    I **have learned** to swim (and don't need lessons any more).

The context of the sentence will usually make clear how to understand the perfect tense, and your own competence in English will help you decide which translation "sounds better."

Exercise 76. Identify each of the following verbs by person, number and tense, then translate giving two English translations where possible.

Example: amāvī   first person, singular, perfect; "I have loved," "I loved"

1.	errābit	9.	tenuērunt	17.	dormiēs
2.	fūgimus	10.	erunt	18.	miscēs
3.	venit	11.	fuī	19.	relīquistis
4.	vēnit	12.	ambulābunt	20.	duxērunt
5.	carēbās	13.	scrībis	21.	dīxēre
6.	potuit	14.	nūntiāvit	22.	discessimus
7.	cēpī	15.	ēgistī	23.	sēnsī
8.	pāruistī	16.	petiī	24.	fīniēbant

Exercise 77. Following the model verbs above, conjugate **pugnō, doleō** and **relinquō** in the perfect active indicative, singular and plural. Be sure to check the principal parts in the Chapter Vocabulary in order to learn what stem to use for each verb.

Exercise 78. Translate the underlined words into Latin.

1. The sailors <u>heard</u> many stories.
2. Father, <u>have</u> you <u>been</u> sick?
3. We <u>missed</u> our children.
4. They <u>were sleeping</u> in the house.
5. At that time, I <u>feared</u> the danger.
6. He <u>was</u> a free man for a long time.
7. I <u>used to praise</u> the king.
8. <u>Has</u> he <u>written</u> the letter?

55. Pluperfect Active Indicative

The **pluperfect** tense is sometimes called the past perfect because it refers to an action completed in the past. The pluperfect is formed by adding **-era-** + the regular endings (**-m, -s, -t, -mus, -tis, -nt**) to the perfect stem. Many students remember these forms as a combination of the perfect stem + the imperfect of **sum** (§37):

	1st Conjugation		Endings
1st sg.	amāveram	I had loved	-era m
2nd sg.	amāverās	You had loved	-erā s
3rd sg.	amāverat	He, she, it had loved	-era t
1st pl.	amāverāmus	We had loved	-erā mus
2nd pl.	amāverātis	You (all) had loved	-erā tis
3rd pl.	amāverant	They had loved	-era nt

	2nd Conj.	3rd Conj.	4th Conj.	Sum, esse, fuī
1st sg.	monueram	rēxeram	audīveram	fueram
2nd sg.	monuerās	rēxerās	audīverās	fuerās
3rd sg.	monuerat	rēxerat	audīverat	fuerat
1st pl.	monuerāmus	rēxerāmus	audīverāmus	fuerāmus
2nd pl.	monuerātis	rēxerātis	audīverātis	fuerātis
3rd pl.	monuerant	rēxerant	audīverant	fuerant

Exercise 79. Change each perfect verb form to the pluperfect and translate the new form.

Example: rēximus   rēxerāmus: "we had ruled"

1.	sēdistī	7.	dūxit
2.	pugnāvimus	8.	fēcistī
3.	ēgī	9.	fīnīvistis
4.	tenuit	10.	miscuēre
5.	vēnistis	11.	petiī
6.	mānsērunt	12.	fuit

Exercise 80. Translate into Latin.

1.	I reported.	10.	It began.
2.	I was reporting.	11.	It had begun.
3.	I had reported.	12.	It was beginning.
4.	They kept speaking.	13.	You (sg.) had mourned.
5.	They spoke.	14.	You (sg.) mourned.
6.	They had spoken.	15.	You (sg.) were mourning.
7.	We slept.	16.	You (pl.) seized.
8.	We used to sleep.	17.	You (pl.) tried to seize.
9.	We had slept.	18.	You (pl.) had seized.

56. Future Perfect Active Indicative

The **future perfect tense** (which is rarely used in English) refers to an action completed in the future. It is formed by adding -**eri**- (-**er**- in the first sg.) + the present endings (-**o**, -**s**, -**t**, -**mus**, -**tis**, -**nt**) to the perfect stem. Except in the third plural form, these endings are identical to the future of **sum** (§37):

	1st Conjugation		Endings
1st sg.	amāverō	I shall have loved	-er ō
2nd sg.	amāveris	You will have loved	-eri s
3rd sg.	amāverit	He, she, it will have loved	-eri t
1st pl.	amāverimus	We shall have loved	-eri mus
2nd pl.	amāveritis	You (all) will have loved	-eri tis
3rd pl.	amāverint	They will have loved	-eri nt

	2nd Conj.	3rd Conj.	4th Conj.	Sum, esse, fuī
1st sg.	monuerō	rēxerō	audīverō	fuerō
2nd sg.	monueris	rēxeris	audīveris	fueris
3rd sg.	monuerit	rēxerit	audīverit	fuerit
1st pl.	monuerimus	rēxerimus	audīverimus	fuerimus
2nd pl.	monueritis	rēxeritis	audīveritis	fueritis
3rd pl.	monuerint	rēxerint	audīverint	fuerint

Exercise 81. Change each perfect verb form to the future perfect and translate the new form.

Example: rēximus   rēxerimus: "we shall have ruled"

1.	mīsī	6.	dēbuit
2.	dīxērunt	7.	fīnīvimus
3.	creāvistī	8.	dedī
4.	incēpistis	9.	iactāvērunt
5.	fēcēre	10.	vīdistī

Exercise 82. Translate into Latin.

1.	I will write.	6.	You (sg.) will have taught.
2.	I will have written.	7.	She came.
3.	They will judge.	8.	She will have come.
4.	They will have judged.	9.	You (pl.) will read.
5.	You (sg.) will teach.	10.	You (pl.) will have read.

Exercise 83. Identify each of the following verbs by person, number and tense, then translate. Can you write the principal parts of these verbs from memory?

Example: valueram   first singular pluperfect of valeō: "I had been well"

1.	eram	7.	potuerint
2.	fuistī	8.	ēgerāmus
3.	fuerō	9.	ēgeris
4.	poterant	10.	dederant
5.	poterunt	11.	gessistis
6.	potuērunt	12.	mōvērunt

57. **Special Adjectives in -īus**

There are nine irregular first and second declension adjectives in Latin, which follow the same pattern for the genitive and dative singular that you have seen in the demonstrative pronouns (§50):

	Masculine	Feminine	Neuter
Gen. sg.	-īus	-īus	-īus
Dat. sg.	-ī	-ī	-ī

With the exception of the genitive and dative singular forms shown above, these adjectives are declined like **bonus, bona, bonum**. (See §58 below for **ūnus, ūna, ūnum** as a model.)

alius, alia, aliud	other, another	**tōtus, tōta, tōtum**	whole
alter, altera, alterum	the one (of two)	**ūllus, ūlla, ūllum**	any
neuter, neutra, neutrum	neither (of two)	**ūnus, ūna, ūnum**	one
nūllus, nūlla, nūllum	none	**uter, utra, utrum**	which?
sōlus, sōla, sōlum	alone		(of two)

Exercise 84. Identify each of the following nouns by case, number and gender, then say which adjectives could modify the noun listed with them. Be prepared to say why the others could NOT modify the noun.

1.	mortis:	meae	celer	ūllīus	facilibus
2.	ratiō:	celer	nūllus	omnis	ūna
3.	populō:	aliī	huic	potēns	laeta
4.	poētam:	fēlīx	alterum	bonā	sōlam
5.	aetāte:	hōc	omnī	tōtā	dulce
6.	nūminis:	potentī	utrīus	hoc	magnī

58. Numerals

	Cardinal		Ordinal	
1	ūnus, -a, -um	I	prīmus, -a, -um	first
2	duo, duae, duo	II	secundus, -a, -um	second
3	trēs, tria	III	tertius, -a, -um	third
4	quattuor	IV	quārtus, -a, -um	fourth
5	quīnque	V	quīntus, -a, -um	fifth
6	sex	VI	sextus, -a, -um	sixth
7	septem	VII	septimus, -a, -um	seventh
8	octō	VIII	octāvus, -a, -um	eighth
9	novem	IX	nōnus, -a, -um	ninth
10	decem	X	decimus, -a, -um	tenth
11	ūndecim	XI	ūndecimus, -a, -um	eleventh
12	duodecim	XII	duodecimus, -a, -um	twelfth
20	vīgintī	XX		
30	trīgintā	XXX		
40	quadrāgintā	XL		
50	quīnquāgintā	L		
100	centum	C		
500	quīngentī, -ae,-a	D		
1,000	mīlle	M		

> ***Note: mīlle** in the plural is a neuter noun (**mīlia, mīlium**) and is often followed by a partitive genitive: **duo mīlia hominum**   two thousand men (literally: "two thousands of men")

So far all the adjectives you have learned have been declinable. Latin adjectives representing numerals fall into two groups. All the ordinals are declined like **bonus, -a, -um**. The cardinals, except for the first three, are indeclinable. Note the following paradigms for the first three cardinals.

ūnus, -a, -um

Singular	Masculine	Feminine	Neuter
Nominative	ūnus	ūna	ūnum
Genitive	ūnīus	ūnīus	ūnīus
Dative	ūnī	ūnī	ūnī
Accusative	ūnum	ūnam	ūnum
Ablative	ūnō	ūnā	ūnō

duo, duae, duo   **trēs, tria**

Plural	Masculine	Feminine	Neuter	M. & F.	Neuter
Nominative	duo	duae	duo	trēs	tria
Genitive	duōrum	duārum	duōrum	trium	trium
Dative	duōbus	duābus	duōbus	tribus	tribus
Accusative	duōs	duās	duo	trēs	tria
Ablative	duōbus	duābus	duōbus	tribus	tribus

With numerals, Latin often uses **ē/ex** or **dē** plus the ablative instead of a partitive genitive (§18):

duae ex fēminīs	two **of the women**
ūnus dē virīs	one **of the men**
turba **virōrum**	a crowd **of men**

Exercise 85. Translate each of the following into Latin in the case and number indicated.

Example: two women (nom.)   duae fēminae

1. the other song (gen.)
2. the whole truth (nom.)
3. any soldier (dat.)
4. one hundred tears (acc.)
5. three poets (abl.)
6. second wife (acc.)

59. **Expressions of Time**

Latin expresses time using the accusative or ablative without a preposition, as follows.

- with **Accusative**

  Length of Time

Trēs annōs manēbāmus.	We stayed **for three years.**
Haec **partem** aetātis faciēbat.	He was doing this **for part** of his life.

  Note: Length of time is sometimes emphasized with the preposition **per**:

Per annum labōrābam.	I worked **throughout the year**.

- with **Ablative**

  Time When – indicating a point in time

Agricola **prīmā lūce** labōrat.	The farmer works **at first light** (= dawn).
Discessitne **sextā hōrā**?	Did he depart **at the sixth hour** (= noon)?
Vēnērunt **tertiā nocte**.	They came **on the third night**.

Time Within Which – indicating a range of time

Mīlitēs **tribus annīs** discēdent.	The soldiers will depart **within three years.**
Tertiō annō templum aedificāvērunt.	They built the temple **during the third year.**

Exercise 86. For the following sentences, copy each chunk you see and be prepared to identify it; then translate the full sentence.

Example: Fīlius agricolae multīs cum amīcīs in agrum errābat

fīlius agricolae	(subject with modifier in the genitive)
multīs cum amīcīs	(prepositional phrase: accompaniment)
in agrum	(prepositional phrase: place to which)

1. Hic homō nōs nōn sōlum verbīs sed etiam factīs dūcere incēpit.
2. Ille multōs annōs fēlīx potēnsque fuerat.
3. Deditne fīlius meus tibi pecūniam ūllam?
4. Puerī brevī tempore labōrāre incipient.
5. Pater frāterque meus īrae grātiā hāc hōrā discēdent.
6. Trēs aut quattuor amīcōs in urbe magnā petīvimus.
7. Omnēs verbīs rēgis rēgīnaeque pāruērunt.
8. Nōs ūnīus fēminae causā bellum facimus.
9. Ea neque vīderāmus neque audierāmus.
10. Decem hōrās manēbimus, tum in urbem veniēmus.

Exercise 87. Translate into Latin.

1. The angry men had suddenly attacked the others at the tenth hour.
2. At that time everyone [*use a form of* **omnis**] elected him leader of the city.
3. Nine men built that new temple.
4. Life was sweet for the lucky daughter of the second consul.
5. In one year our powerful leader has harmed many men.
6. Will your (sg.) third book be short?
7. They taught your (sg.) two sons the truth.
8. Five of the women were looking for water at noon.
9. The Romans waged war in Italy for seven years.
10. The whole state will thank our great leader.

Reading 13 *(adapted)*

Cicero, in his writings about the nature of the gods, talks about the ideas of previous philosophers, including the Greek Xenocrates.

Xenocratēs scrīpsit librōs dē nātūrā deōrum sed nūllam speciem dīvīnam **dēscrīpsit**. dīxit enim: "Deī octō sunt, quīnque ex eīs in stellīs vagīs sunt, ūnus in sīderibus caelī est." ille septimum sōlem adiungit octāvamque lūnam.

Vocabulary:

speciem (acc.)	form	sīdus, sīderis *n.*	star
dēscrībō, -ere, dēscrīpsī	to describe	sōl, sōlis *m.*	sun
		adiungō, -ere	"to add *x* as *y*"
stellīs vagīs (abl.)	planets		*factitive here*

Reading 14 *(adapted)*

Cicero writes from Athens to his wife Terentia about his recent trip and the mail he has received. The Cicero mentioned in the letter is his and Terentia's son; Tullia is their daughter.

Sī tū et Tullia, lūx nostra, valētis, ego et Cicerō valēmus. ad **Athēnās** tardē et incommodē vēnimus, **adversī** enim ventī erant. dē nāve ambulāvimus et nōbīs Acastus cum litterīs praestō fuit illō tempore. **accēpī** tuās litterās et ex multīs amīcīs litterās.

Vocabulary:

sī	if	nāvis, nāvis *f.*	ship
Athēnās	"Athens"	Acastus, -ī *m.*	a friend of Cicero's
tardē	slowly	praestō (adv.)	present, here
incommodē	inconveniently	accipiō, -ere, accēpī	to receive
adversus, -a, -um	contrary (blowing the wrong way)		

Practice Sentences

Identify the case and use of the underlined words, then translate.

1. Nec tōtā tristis locus ūllus in urbe est.
   (Ovid; *all Athens rejoices when Theseus is saved from death*)

2. Tullus magnā **glōriā** bellī **rēgnāvit** annōs duōs et trīgintā.
   (Livy; *talking about the Roman king, Tullus, who destroyed Alba Longa*)

3. Iam caelum terramque meō sine nūmine, ventī, mīscēre audētis?
   (Vergil; *Neptune, god of the sea, scolds the winds*)

4. Maria omnia caelō miscuit.
   (Vergil; *describing a storm the goddess, Juno, has engineered*)

5. Aliās terrās petunt; iūra, lēgēs, agrōs, lībertātem nōbīs relinquunt.
   (Caesar; *A Gaul is describing what previous conquerors had done*)

6. Habuī noctem plēnam timōris ac **miseriae**.
   (Cicero; *a friend's late arrival caused him to worry*)

7. Ūnīus ob īram in pontō mānsimus.
   (Vergil – adapted; *Juno's anger keeps the Trojans at sea*)

8. Hunc ego patris causā vocāvī ad cēnam.
   (Cicero; *Cicero treats the badly -behaved son of a friend well*)

Vocabulary:

tristis, -e	sad	rēgnō, -āre, -āvī	to rule
Tullus, -ī *m.*	Tullus	miseria, -ae *f.*	misery, unhappiness
glōria, -ae *f.*	glory, fame		

Chapter 11 Vocabulary

Nouns

aetās, aetātis *f.*	age, life
annus, annī *m.*	year
hōra, hōrae *f.*	hour, season
*nox, noctis *f.*	night
nūmen, nūminis *n.*	divine will, divine power
ratiō, ratiōnis *f.*	reason, judgment; method
tempus, temporis *n.*	time, period of time (e.g. a season); opportunity

Verbs

discēdō, discēdere, discessī, discessūrus	to depart, go away; separate
misceō, miscēre, miscuī, mixtus	to mix, mingle; stir up, disturb

Adjectives

alius, alia, aliud	other, another
(alterīus *is commonly used for* gen. sg.)	
aliud ... aliud	one thing ... another (thing)
aliī ... aliī	some ... others
alter, altera, alterum	the one, the other (of two); next, second
neuter, neutra, neutrum	neither (of two)
nūllus, nūlla, nūllum	not any, no
secundus, secunda, secundum	second; favorable
sōlus, sōla, sōlum	alone, only
nōn sōlum ... sed etiam	not only ... but also
tōtus, tōta, tōtum	whole, entire
ūllus, ūlla, ūllum	any
ūnus, ūna, ūnum	one
uter, utra, utrum	which? (of two)
numerals in §58 as assigned by your instructor	

Adverbs

etiam	also; even
iam	now; already
sīc	thus, so
subitō	suddenly

(23)

Derivatives: For each English word below, give the Latin word from the Chapter 11 Vocabulary to which it is related and the English word's meaning.

1.	nocturnal	7.	ratio
2.	neuter	8.	solitary
3.	annul	9.	miscellaneous
4.	centennial	10.	unite
5.	temporary	11.	horoscope
6.	alias	12.	total

Snack bar. Pompeii, 1st c. A.D.

CHAPTER 12

Dependent Clauses (1)
　　　Adverbial Use
　　　Word Order
Accusative of Extent and Degree
Dative with Adjectives

So far you have been reading simple and compound sentences. These have sometimes included coordinating conjunctions, which connect either words or phrases with the same function, or independent sentences (§14). This chapter introduces complex sentences and subordinating conjunctions, which connect a dependent clause to the main clause. It also introduces another use of the accusative case and a new use of the dative case with certain adjectives.

60.　Dependent Clauses

A **dependent (subordinate) clause** is one that can not stand alone as a complete sentence. Compare the following:

Dependent clause	Complete sentence
When we go to Rome, ...	We go to Rome.
If it is raining, ...	It is raining.

A sentence that has a dependent clause is called a complex sentence. In such sentences, the main (independent) clause carries the most important information, and the dependent clause adds extra information. Dependent clauses use exactly the same sentence patterns as main clauses.

Adverbial Use

The dependent clauses in this chapter are **adverbial modifiers** (§25), which add information that answers the questions When?, Why?, Where?, and which usually modify the verb in the main sentence.

The conjunctions you have seen so far are called **coordinating conjunctions** because they connect items on the same level in a sentence. New in this chapter are **subordinating conjunctions,** which do NOT connect sames, but instead connect dependent clauses to main clauses. This book will call these subordinating conjunctions "**clause markers**" because they help to mark the beginning of a dependent clause. Be careful, because although clause markers come first in English word order, they may not be the first word in a Latin clause.

The clause markers in this chapter are indeclinables and carry essential information about the category of information contained in the dependent clause. Memorize completely the following clause markers for clauses in this chapter:

Adverbial Clause Marker	English Meaning	Category
antequam	before	time
cum	when	time
dum	while, as long as	time
postquam	after	time
quia	because	cause
quod	because	cause
sī	if	condition
ubi	when	time
ubi	where	place

Note:

- **Cum** can appear as a preposition with an ablative (§34), so be careful to distinguish this use from that of **cum** as a clause marker.

- **Dum** ("while") regularly appears with a present tense in Latin to show continued action in the past. When translating into English, use the **imperfect tense.**

Exercise 88. In the following passage, circle each clause marker, and bracket the entire dependent clause. Be ready to explain how you decided where each dependent clause begins and ends.

Once upon a time after he had established his worship in Greece, the god, Bacchus, was traveling with his companion, Silenus, in Phrygia. Shepherds in the area did not recognize Silenus when they found him drunk in their fields and so took him to King Midas. Since Midas had accepted the rites of Bacchus, however, he recognized the god's friend and after he threw a big party he sent him back to Bacchus. Because he was grateful, Bacchus granted Midas one wish, and Midas said, "May everything I touch turn to gold." Although Bacchus was sorry the monarch had not chosen better, he granted this wish. Now when Midas touched a leaf, it turned to gold! And if he picked up a stone, it turned to gold! While this gift was new, Midas rejoiced in his luck, but soon he came to regret his wish. For although he became very rich, he found he could not even eat or drink. When he picked up bread, it also turned to gold, and when he tried to drink fresh water, it hardened as soon as his lips touched the liquid. Finally he begged Bacchus for help and the god told him to go where he could wash away his "magic touch."

Word Order

In Latin, as in English, a dependent clause may come anywhere in the main sentence:

- **If you don't memorize the clause markers**, you will have trouble reading Latin.

- You may still have trouble **although you work hard,** but you will succeed in the end.

- Do it **because I said so**!

Notice in the examples above (and in those from Ex. 88) that once a dependent clause starts, the main clause does not interrupt it. Even if one dependent clause interrupts another in a sentence, the clause that interrupts must finish before the interrupted clause can continue:

[**If the weather** <when we leave on our trip> **is unpleasant**] we will be sorry.

This is also true in Latin. So, as you begin to read complex sentences, a good practice is to mark each dependent clause as you read the sentence from left to right. Then concentrate on what the **main** clause means, before you try to fit the adverbial dependent clause into your translation.

Exercise 89. Identify the **dependent** clauses in each of the following sentences and then translate the **main** clauses only.

1. Poēta tibi hoc carmen dedit dum in tuā casā sumus.
2. Cum in urbem mīlitēs vēnērunt, omnēs magnō cum timōre fūgimus.
3. Sī potēns cīvitās vestra est omnēs laetī estis.
4. Propter bellum fēminae puellaeque dum virī pugnant Ītaliam relinquēbant.
5. Carēbāsne amīcīs frātribusque, postquam ex patriā nocte discessistī?
6. Illī nōn crēdidī quod multa facta mala fēcerat.

Exercise 90. Now add the dependent clauses to your translations of the sentences in Exercise 89.

Exercise 91. Identify the **dependent** clauses in each of the following sentences.

1. When we walked into the forest we saw the huge fire.
2. He fought with courage as long as he was strong.
3. While the house was full of soldiers, our sons and daughters slept in the field.
4. Stay where the gods' great temples are.
5. Because the king loved him my brother always desired to be good.
6. If you (all) trust that leader, he will easily lead you to the sea.

Exercise 92. Translate each of the sentences from Exercise 91 into Latin.

61. Accusative of Extent and Degree

Just as Latin expresses extent (length) of time by using the accusative *without a preposition* (§59), it also expresses extent of space and degree with the accusative *without a preposition*. These uses only occur with a few vocabulary words (indicating measures of space or degree – "miles," "feet," "very much," "not at all," etc.), and are not as common as the other uses of the accusative you have seen so far.

- **Extent of Space**

Arborēs octō **pedēs** altae erant.	The trees were eight **feet** high.
Flūmen **iter** abest.	The river is a **day's march** away.

- **Degree**

Tē **tantum** amō.	I love you **so much**.
Agricola **multum** in agrō labōrat.	The farmer works **a lot ("much")** in the field.

Exercise 93. In the following paragraph identify those phrases that indicate length of time, extent of space and degree. (Do not translate into Latin.)

> On the second day after the king's death, the soldiers left the city at dawn and marched for many hours. They grieved greatly and cared nothing for the difficulty of the journey. Having covered fifty miles in a few days, they set up camp a few paces from a small river and stayed there one month. During the night of the next full moon, they returned to the city and found a new wall nine feet high around the town.

62. **Dative with Adjectives**

The dative is often used with adjectives meaning *friendly, unfriendly, similar, dissimilar, faithful, suitable, fit, equal, near,* etc. This use corresponds to the English idiom in most cases.

Cōnsulēs **nōbīs** sunt amīcī.	The consuls are friendly **to us**.
Locus aptus erat **templō**.	The place was suitable **for a temple**.
Rōmānī dissimilēs **aliīs** erant.	The Romans were unlike **others**.

Exercise 94. Bracket each dependent clause where one exists, identify the sentence pattern in all clauses, then translate the following sentences.

1. Sī id aedificāveris, venient.
2. Nec ducēs nec mīlitēs trāns flūmen fugere audēbunt, quod aqua duodecim pedēs alta est.
3. Amīcus rēgīnae inimīcus mihi erat.
4. Prīmā lūce Rōmānī nōbīs ignī saxīsque nocēre facile poterant.
5. Ille arbor ā flūmine vīgintī pedēs āfuit.
6. Postquam iter difficile per silvam fēcerant, nūllus mīles tōtam noctem dormīre potuit.
7. Hic in agrīs per tōtam aetātem labōrābat, sed pecūniā semper caruit.
8. Bonās lēgēs scrībere malīs difficile semper est.
9. Dum bellum gerimus, nostrī ducēs nova cōnsilia cēpērunt.
10. Sī fidēlis nōbīs nōn eris, amīcī tuī esse nōn poterimus.

Exercise 95. Translate into Latin.

1. That sea had been 20 feet deep in this place.
2. In two nights they will have finished the long journey.
3. Soldiers ought to be faithful to the leaders.
4. Because the boy was dear to (his) mother, she taught him many skills.
5. If they are unfriendly to you (pl.), should you be friendly to these nations?

6. Doing these things will be easy for me.
7. Before they came to the city, they had a lot of money.
8. Our laws were equal to those of our fathers.
9. While you (pl.) slept under that tree, another person left the body of the consul in the field.
10. For three years no part of these cities was free from fear.

Reading 15 *(adapted)*

Livy was a Roman historian who lived from 59 B.C. to A.D. 17. In this excerpt he talks about Romulus, the founder and first king of Rome. He describes Romulus' success as a leader and his miraculous end in the Campus Martius in Rome.

Rōmulus trecentōsque mīlitēs ad custōdiam nōn in bellō sōlum sed etiam in pāce habuit. ob Rōmulum urbs Rōma valuit et quadrāgintā annōs pācem habuit postquam ille discessit. Titus Livius fābulam dē "morti" Rōmulī nārrāvit. Cum Rōmulus cōntiōnem in Campō Mārtiō habēbat, subitō fuit tempestās cum magnō fragōre et **densō** rēgem cēlāvit nimbō, et populus timuit. ubi post tempestātem lūx erat, Rōmānī Rōmulum nōn vīdērunt; nec deinde in terrīs Rōmulus fuit. populus in campō mānsit, diū enim dolēbat. tandem omnēs Rōmulum deum habuērunt.

Vocabulary:

trecentōs	300	fragor, -ōris *m.*	crash (of thunder)
ad custōdiam	"as a body guard"	densus, -a, -um	thick, dense
Rōma, -ae *f.*	Rome	cēlō, -āre, -āvī	to hide
cōntiō, -iōnis *f.*	meeting, assembly	nimbus, -ī *m.*	cloud,
campus, -ī *m.*	plain		storm cloud
Mārtius, -a, -um	of Mars	deinde (adv.)	then, afterwards
tempestās, -tātis *f.*	storm		

Reading 16 *(adapted)*

Varro was a Roman scholar who lived from 116-27 B.C. Called "most learned of the Romans" by Quintilian, he wrote many books, including surviving works on the Latin language and on agriculture, the latter begun when he was 80. Here he talks about two different ways men live and which is older.

Duae vītae sunt hominibus, rustica et urbāna, sed tempore **dīversam orīginem** habent. antīquior enim rustica, quod fuit tempus, cum agrōs colēbant hominēs neque urbem habēbant. Immānī **numerō** annōrum **urbānōs** agricolae praestant. nec mīrum, quod dīvīna nātūra dat agrōs, ars **hūmāna** aedificat urbēs, quia artēs omnēs in **Graeciā** intrā mille annōrum fuerant, sed agrī semper erant. itaque nōn sine causā maiōrēs nostrī ex urbe in agrōs rēvēnērunt, quod et in pāce rusticī Rōmānī eōs alēbant et in bellō adiuvābant. nec sine causā terram appellābant mātrem.

Vocabulary:

rusticus, -a, -um	rural, in the country	hūmānus, -a, -um	human
urbānus, -a, -um	urban, in the city	Graecia, -ae, *f.*	Greece
dīversus, -a, -um	different, separate	intrā	within
orīgō, -inis *f.*	origin, beginning	maiōrēs, -ōrum	ancestors
antīquior (nom. adj.)	older, more ancient	*m.* (pl.)	
colō, -ere	inhabit; cultivate	rēveniō, -īre, -vēnī	to return,
immānis, -e	huge, enormous		go back
numerus, -ī *m.*	number	alō, -ere	to feed
praestō, -āre	*here* "pre-date"	adiuvō, -āre	to help,
mīrus, -a, -um	surprising		support
		appellō, -āre	to call

Practice Sentences

Identify the case and use of the underlined words, then translate.

1. "Uter nostrum tandem, Labiēne, populāris est, tūne … an ego?" (Cicero; *arguing that he has the best interests of the people at heart*)

2. Tōtam urbem īrā implēvēre. (Livy; *speaking of men wanting vengeance against the enemy for plundering their fields*)

3. Hoc dum [ea] nārrat, forte audīvī. (Terence; *of eavesdropping*)

4. Aliud est male dīcere, aliud **accūsāre**. (Cicero)

5. Sī ratiō dīvīna est, nūllum autem bonum sine ratiōne est, bonum omne dīvīnum est. (Seneca)

6. Sīc tōtus mundus deōrum est **immortālium** templum. (Seneca – adapted)

7. Ūnā cum gente tōt annōs bella gerō. (Vergil; *the goddess, Juno, talks of her hatred for the Trojans*)

8. Is ūnum Deiotarum in tōtō orbe terrārum ex animō amīcum, ūnum fidēlem populō Rōmānō iūdicāvit. (Cicero; *describing Pompey's regard for Deiotarus, an ally of the Romans*)

Vocabulary:

populāris, -e	devoted to the people	mundus, -ī, *m.*	world, universe
Labiēnus, -ī *m.*	Labienus (an opponent)	immortālis, -e	immortal
		ūnum	*here* = sōlum
autem (coord. conj.)	however	Deiotarus, -ī *m.*	Deiotarus, a foreign king
male dīcō, -ere	to denounce	orbis (*m.*) terrārum	the world
accūsō, -āre	to accuse		

Chapter 12 Vocabulary

Nouns

arbor, arboris *f.*	tree
flūmen, flūminis *n.*	river
*gēns, gentis *f.*	clan, tribe, family; nation; people
iter, itineris *n.*	journey, path, route; a day's march
pēs, pedis *m.*	foot

Verbs

absum, abesse, āfuī, āfutūrus	to be absent, away, distant
gerō, gerere, gessī, gestus	to bear, carry on; wear
bellum gerō	to wage war

Adjectives

amīcus, amīca, amīcum	friendly (to)
aptus, apta, aptum	fit, suitable (for)
cārus, cāra, cārum	dear (to)
fidēlis, fidēle	faithful, loyal (to)
inimīcus, inimīca, inimīcum	unfriendly, hostile (to)
pār, paris	equal (to)
similis, simile	similar (to), like

Adverb

forte	by chance

Coordinating Conjunction

itaque	and so, therefore

Subordinating Conjunctions

antequam	before
cum	when
dum	while, as long as
postquam	after; when
quia	because
quod	because; since
sī	if
ubi	when; where

(24)

Derivatives: For each English word below, give the Latin word from the Chapter 12 Vocabulary to which it is related and the English word's meaning.

1. inimical
2. verisimilitude
3. impede
4. adapt
5. arboreal
6. gerund
7. itinerant
8. infidel
9. parity
10. ubiquitous

CHAPTER 13

The Pronoun: Relative
Dependent Clauses (2)
      Adjectival Use: Relative Clause
The Pronoun: Reflexive

The last chapter introduced dependent clauses that were adverbial modifiers (used like adverbs) and marked by indeclinable words such as **cum**, **dum** and **ubi**. This chapter introduces dependent clauses that are adjectival modifiers (used like adjectives) and whose clause markers do decline. These clause markers are **relative pronouns**. The chapter also introduces a fourth type of pronoun.

63. **The Pronoun: Relative**

The **relative pronouns** in English are: *who, which, that; whom* is the objective (accusative) case of *who*, and *whose* is the possessive. In Latin the relative pronoun is declined as follows:

Singular	Masculine	Feminine	Neuter
Nominative	quī	quae	quod
Genitive	cuius	cuius	cuius
Dative	cui	cuī	cuī
Accusative	quem	quam	quod
Ablative	quō	quā	quō
Plural			
Nominative	quī	quae	quae
Genitive	quōrum	quārum	quōrum
Dative	quibus	quibus	quibus
Accusative	quōs	quās	quae
Ablative	quibus	quibus	quibus

Note:

- When the ablative of these pronouns is used with **cum**, the preposition is regularly written after the pronoun in one word: **quōcum**, **quācum**, **quibuscum**.

64. **Adjectival Use: Relative Clause**

Most relative clauses modify a noun in the main clause, playing the same role a simple adjective plays. Compare the following English examples:

Big monsters scare me.   Monsters *that are big* scare me.

Exercise 96. Rewrite the following sentences replacing the first adjective with a relative clause.

1. Big monsters are often green.
2. The claws of green monsters are huge.
3. I like purple monsters better.
4. Once I gave my supper to a purple monster.

In English, the relative clause comes immediately after the noun it modifies — this noun is often called its *antecedent*. In Latin this is not necessarily true, but the **antecedent will *always* have the same gender and number as the relative pronoun**. Because the case of a word identifies its function in its own clause, and because a relative pronoun is in a different clause from its antecedent, the cases of the two words are likely to be different. Compare the following examples and identify the case and use of the relative pronoun in each example:

Virum **quī fugit** vidēmus.	We see the man **who is escaping**.
Vir **cuius librum puer āmīsit** īrātus est.	The man **whose book the boy lost** is angry.
Vir **cui librum dedī** mē laudat.	The man **to whom I gave the book** praises me.
Virum **quem monuērunt** vidēmus.	We see the man **whom they advised**.

As with the dependent clauses you learned in the last chapter, once the relative clause starts, the main clause does not interrupt it. Even if one dependent clause interrupts another in a sentence, the interrupting clause must finish before the interrupted clause can continue:

We elected the man [**who saved the state** <that Romulus founded>] consul.

It remains a good practice, therefore, to bracket each dependent clause as you read the sentence from left to right. Then concentrate on what the **main** clause means, before you try to fit the relative clause into your translation. In time, you should be able to read the sentence just as it appears in Latin.

Exercise 97. Bracket all the **dependent** clauses in the following passage, and then translate the core items of the **main** clause only.

Intereā eā legiōne, quam sēcum habēbat, mīlitibusque, quī ex prōvinciā convēnerant, ā lacū Lemannō, quī in flūmen Rhodānum īnfluit, ad montem Iūram, quī fīnēs Sequanōrum ab Helvetiīs dīvidit, mīlia passuum XIX mūrum in altitūdinem pedum XVI fossamque perdūcit.

Vocabulary:

intereā (adv.)	meanwhile	mūrum, -ī *n.*	wall
legiō, -iōnis *f.*	legion	fossa, -ae *f.*	ditch
conveniō, -īre, -vēnī	to gather	perdūcō, -ere	to construct, extend
lacus, -ūs *m.*	lake	mīlia passuum	"miles" (= "thousands
īnfluō, -ere	to flow into		of paces")

Exercise 98. Draw an arrow from the **dependent** clause at the right to the noun in the main clause that it modifies. Then translate the whole sentence.

1. Epistulam virō dedī.   [quī ad rēgem vēnit]
2. Epistulam virō dedī.   [quam ad rēgem mīsistī]
3. Epistulam virō dedī.   [quem ad rēgem mīsistī]
4. Nautae ā nāvibus discēdēbant.   [quōs amāmus.]
5. Nautae ā nāvibus ambulābant.   [quī eās aedificāverant]
6. Nautae ā nāvibus discēdēbant.   [quae celerēs erant]

Exercise 99. Translate the underlined words into Latin.

1. The laws <u>that this man wrote</u> are good.
2. We left the city <u>in which many people were working</u>.
3. I know a man <u>whose name is Romulus</u>.
4. The woman <u>whom the boys saw</u> was making dinner.
5. The girl <u>to whom I used to give roses</u> was pretty.
6. He sees the soldiers <u>who are fighting</u>.
7. You <u>who are my mother</u> are beautiful.
8. I <u>who am your father</u> will always love you.

65. **The Pronoun: Reflexive**

The **reflexive pronoun** is used to refer back to the subject of the sentence (or clause) in which it occurs: "I see **myself**," "you persuade **yourself**." Because it refers back to the subject, this pronoun does not occur in the nominative case.

In Latin, the reflexive pronouns for the first and second persons are the same as the personal pronouns (§42). The third person reflexive pronoun is different and uses the same forms for the singular and plural.

Reflexive Pronoun

Singular	**3rd person**	
Genitive	suī	of himself, herself, itself
Dative	sibi	to/for himself, herself, itself
Accusative	sē, sēsē	himself, herself, itself
Ablative	sē, sēsē	(by/with...) himself, herself, itself
Plural		
Genitive	suī	of themselves
Dative	sibi	to/for themselves
Accusative	sē, sēsē	themselves
Ablative	sē, sēsē	(by/with...) themselves

- **sēsē** is sometimes used for emphasis, with no difference in meaning from **sē**.

Examples:

Mē laudō.	I praise **myself**.
Tibi persuādēs.	You persuade **yourself**.
Ille **sē** videt.	That man sees **himself**.
Illa **sē** videt.	That woman sees **herself**.
Ille **eum** videt.	That man sees **him** (another person).

Exercise 100. Translate each of the following sentences, which have either a personal or a reflexive pronoun in them.

1. tē videō.
2. mē videō.
3. eum videō.
4. sē videt.
5. nōs videt.
6. nōs vidēmus.
7. eōs vidēmus.
8. sē vident.
9. audītisne eōs?
10. audītisne vōs?
11. audiuntne ea?
12. eīs servīmus.
13. eī servīmus.
14. tibi servīmus.
15. mihi servit.
16. sibi servit.

Exercise 101. Bracket any dependent clauses, identify the sentence pattern in each clause, and then translate the following sentences.

1. Paucī omnia quae incipiunt fīniunt.
2. Potēns ad sē uxōrem omnēsque amīcōs vocāvit.
3. Mīlitēs quī hōc tempore pedibus pugnābant fessī saepe fuērunt.
4. Hic quī Rōmam relīquit nec cōnsulibus nec sibi crēdidit.
5. Iter ingēns inter duo flūmina et montem altum fēcimus.
6. Fīne ūnīus annī cōnsulēs quōs Rōmānī creāvērunt discēdent.
7. Vīdistīne forte fēminam cui reliquam pecūniam dedī in mediā urbe?
8. Nāvēs in quibus rēx rēgīnaque trāns mare cum aliīs nāvigāvērunt spectāvimus.
9. Ille poēta cuius epistulam hodiē accēpimus eam partem Ītaliae incolit.
10. Dux quī ratiōnem vertit tōtam gentem quae nōbīs inimīca erat vīcit.

Exercise 102. Translate into Latin.

1. Did you watch the powerful man who said, "I came, I saw, I conquered"?
2. He put a huge rock in the middle of the field that my father had (possessed).
3. Our leaders began to wage war when they discovered new tribes across the mountains.
4. We will find the boy who did this before he runs to the master.
5. Have you sent the letter that you wrote to the soldier?
6. They will learn many difficult things if they work for a long time.
7. Rome is a huge city, which is dear to the people.
8. I used to love the man who was speaking.

Reading 17 *(adapted)*

Eutropius summarizes the accomplishments of Rome's last king, Lucius Tarquinius Superbus, called "superbus" ("proud") for his arrogance. According to this account, his son brought about the end of Rome's rule by kings when he raped Lucretia, another man's wife. She demanded that her husband and father avenge this outrage, and then killed herself, triggering a revolution that led to the Roman Republic. Lucretia became a famous symbol of chastity and faithfulness for the Romans.

> L. Tarquinius Superbus, septimus atque ultimus rēgum, Volscōs, gentem quae nōn longē ab urbe est, vīcit, cum Tuscīs pācem fēcit et templum Iovis in Capitōliō aedificāvit. Posteā dum Ardeam oppugnat, imperium perdidit. Nam cum fīlius eius, Tarquinius iunior, nobilissimam fēminam Lucrētiam, Collātīnī uxōrem, stūprāvit, postquam eā dē iniūriā coniugī et patrī et amīcīs nārrāvit, in omnium cōnspectū sē occidit. Propter hanc causam Brūtus, populum concitāvit et Tarquiniō adēmit imperium.

continued

Vocabulary:

ultimus, -a, -um	last	nobilissimus, -a, -um	most noble
		potestās, -tātis, *f.*	power
Volscī, -ōrum *m.* (pl.)	Volscans (Italian tribe)	coerceō, -ēre	to restrain
in apposition to gentem		Lucrētia, -ae *f.*	Lucretia (proper
longē (adv.)	far, distant		name)
Tuscī, -ōrum *m.* (pl.)	Tuscans (a neighboring	Collātīnus, -ī *m.*	Collatinus (proper
	Italian tribe)		name)
Iuppiter, Iovis *m.*	Jupiter	stūprō, -āre, -āvī	to rape
Capitōlium, -iī *n.*	Capitoline (one of the	iniūria, -ae *f.*	injury, violence
	seven hills of Rome)	cōnspectū (abl.)	sight, view
posteā (adv.)	after this, afterwards	occīdō, -ere, -īdī	to kill
Ardea, -ae *f.*	Ardea (a neighboring	Brūtus, -ī *m.*	Brutus, nephew of
	town)		king Tarquinius
oppugnō, -āre	to attack	concitō, -āre, -āvī	to incite, stir up
perdō, -ere, -didī	to destroy, lose	adimō, -ere, adēmī	to deprive, take
iunior (nom.)	"junior," the younger	(+ acc. *and* dat.)	away from

continued

Mox mīlitēs, quī cīvitātem Ardeam cum rēge oppugnābant, eum relīquērunt, et cum vēnit ad urbem rēx portae clausae erant. quamquam rēxerat annōs quattuor et vīgintī, cum uxōre et līberīs fūgit. Ita Rōma rēcta est per septem rēgēs annōs duo centum et quadrāgintā trēs. Hinc Rōmānī cōnsulēs, prō ūnō rēge, duo hāc causā creāvērunt: sī ūnus malus esse optāvit, alter, quī habēbat potestātem similem, eum coercēre potuit.

Vocabulary:

mox (adv.)	soon	līberī, -ōrum, *m.* (pl.)	children
porta, -ae *f.*	gate	rēcta est	"was ruled"
clausus, -a, -um	shut, closed	hinc (adv.)	after this (time)

Practice Sentences

Identify the case and use of the underlined words, then translate.

1. Nōn omnēs <u>quī</u> habent citharam sunt citharoedī. (Varro)

2. <u>Hominēs</u>, dum docent, discunt. (Seneca)

3. Nōn caret is <u>quī</u> nōn **dēsīderat**. (Cicero)

4. Per trepidam turbam <u>sibi</u> fēcerat viam. (Livy – adapted; *an assassin tries to escape in a crowd*)

5. Rīsī tē hodiē <u>multum</u>. (Plautus; *one character mocks another*)

6. Omnēs, quī tum eōs agrōs, ubi hodiē est haec urbs, incolēbant, aequō animō <u>illī</u> pāruērunt. (Cicero – adapted; *describing Romulus' rule*)

7. Bis vincit ille quī <u>sē</u> vincit in **victōriā**. (Publilius Syrus – adapted; *advice on being a humble winner*)

8. … mihi Delphica terra et Claros et Tenedos Patareaque rēgia servit; Iuppiter est pater; per mē, id <u>quod</u> eritque fuitque estque patet. (Ovid – adapted; *Apollo is trying to impress a girl who is fleeing his advances*)

Vocabulary:

cithara, -ae f.	cithara, lyre	Tenedos, -ī f.	Tenedos (an island near Troy)
citharoedus, -ī m.	lyre player		
dēsīderō, -āre	to desire	Patareus, -a, -um	of Pataraea (a city in Lycia)
trepidus, -a, -um	restless, alarmed		
bis (adv.)	twice	rēgia, -ae f.	court, palace
victōria, -ae f.	victory	pateō, -ēre	to lie open, be clear
Delphicus, -a, -um	of Delphi		
Claros, -ī f.	Claros (an island, or a city in Asia Minor)		

Chapter 13 Vocabulary

Nouns

epistula, epistulae f.	letter
*fīnis, fīnis m.	end; border; (pl.) boundary, territory
*mōns, montis m.	mountain
*nāvis, nāvis f.	ship
Rōma, Rōmae f.	Rome
uxor, uxōris f.	wife

Verbs

accipiō, accipere, accēpī, acceptus	to receive
currō, currere, cucurrī, cursūrus	to run
concurrō, concurrere concucurrī, concursūrus	to charge, rush together, clash
discō, discere, didicī	to learn
incolō, incolere, incoluī	to inhabit, to live in
inveniō, invenīre, invēnī, inventus	to find; discover, invent
pōnō, pōnere, posuī, positus	to put, place
spectō, spectāre, spectāvī, spectātus	to watch, look at
vertō, vertere, vertī, versus	to turn, turn around; destroy; change
vincō, vincere, vīcī, victus	to conquer; win

Adjectives

fessus, fessa, fessum	tired
medius, media, medium	middle; middle of (medium mare = "the middle of the sea")
paucī, paucae, pauca (pl.)	few
reliquus, reliqua, reliquum	remaining, rest (of)

Adverbs

hodiē	today
ita	thus, so, in this way

Pronouns

quī, quae, quod

who, which, that – *functions as a subordinating conjunction*

suī, sibi, sē

himself, herself, itself, themselves

Coordinating Conjunction

nam *(sometimes used as a particle)*

for (= because); indeed, truly

(24)

Derivatives: For each English word below, give the Latin word from the Chapter 13 Vocabulary to which it is related and the English word's meaning.

1. vertigo
2. navy
3. inventory
4. piedmont
5. postpone

6. paucity
7. invincible
8. suicide
9. spectator
10. infinity

CHAPTER **14**

Passive Voice (1)
    Present Passive Indicative
    Imperfect Passive Indicative
    Future Passive Indicative
    Present Passive Infinitive
Sentence Pattern: Passive
Ablative of Agent

So far you have learned all the indicative forms in the active voice for all four conjugations. This chapter introduces the passive voice, with passive forms of the present, imperfect and future tenses, and a new sentence pattern in which they appear. It also introduces a new use of the ablative case.

66. **Passive Voice (1)**

A verb in the active voice indicates that the subject is doing the action. A verb in the **passive** voice indicates that the subject is being **acted upon**.

Active	Passive
He is carrying.	He is being carried.
They eat.	They are being eaten.

Exercise 103. In the following passage, copy out all verbs you think are passive and see if you can generate a "rule" for forming the passive in English based on your examples.

As the English language began its formation from the earlier Germanic   1
languages, there were many changes. One was the loss of the passive voice.   2
Although it existed in the Germanic language, as the Indo-European language   3
branched off, the passive voice was not carried over. Thus, the passive voice   4
is nearly nonexistent in Old English. The structure of the language was such   5
that the passive form simply was not used. Slowly, though, the language   6
was changing, and the passive voice was introduced. The first example that   7
is most commonly cited in the history of the English language is that of   8
the verb "building". In the sentence "The house was building," the speaker   9
means "the house was being built", but without the passive form, this was   10
the only structure available. At first only certain verbs could be transformed   11
into the passive, and there was great resistance to its use at all. One scholar   12
has noted that "the usage is fully accepted only in the 16th century, not in   13
literature but in informal and private papers … but [otherwise] it does not   14

come into the open till the end of the 18th century." From that point on,   15
use of the passive continued to develop, and today the passive voice is so   16
accepted and frequently used that many people do not even notice it.   17

In Latin, the passive voice for the present, imperfect and future tenses is signalled by personal endings that are different from those you learned for the active voice (§5). These endings are added to the stem of the verb just as the active endings are. The personal endings for the passive indicative are the same for all conjugations:

	Singular			Plural		
1st person	**-r**	I am _____ed		**-mur**	We are _____ed	
2nd person	**-ris, -re**	You are _____ed		**-minī**	You, you all are _____ed	
3rd person	**-tur**	He, she, it is _____ed	**-ntur**	They are _____ed	

Note: The alternate **-re** ending for the second person singular appears mostly in poetry and will not be stressed in this book.

Sample translations of the present, imperfect, and future passives:

present:	**amātur**	he (she, it) is loved, he is being loved
imperfect:	**amābātur**	he was being loved, he kept being loved, he used to be loved
future:	**amābitur**	he will be loved

67. **Present Passive Indicative**

	1st Conj.	2nd Conj.	3rd Conj.	3rd Conj. –iō	4th Conj.	Endings
1st sg.	amor	moneor	regor	capior	audior	**-r**
2nd sg.	amāris	monēris	regeris	caperis	audīris	**-ris**
3rd sg.	amātur	monētur	regitur	capitur	audītur	**-tur**
1st pl.	amāmur	monēmur	regimur	capimur	audīmur	**-mur**
2nd pl.	amāminī	monēminī	regiminī	capiminī	audīminī	**-minī**
3rd pl.	amantur	monentur	reguntur	capiuntur	audiuntur	**-ntur**

Exercise 104. Following the model verbs above, conjugate **praebeō** and **trahō** in the present passive indicative, singular and plural.

Exercise 105. Identify each of the following verbs by person, number, tense and voice, then give an English translation.

1. iūdicāmur
2. audīris
3. raperis
4. docēminī
5. laudantur
6. cōnstititur
7. fīniuntur
8. dūcor
9. tenētur
10. moventur
11. volvimur
12. relinquuntur
13. iactātur
14. invenior

68. Imperfect Passive Indicative

The **imperfect passive**, like the active (§35, §48), is formed with the tense sign **-bā-** between the verb stem and the personal endings in all four conjugations:

	1st	2nd	3rd	3rd –iō	4th
1st sg.	amābar	monēbar	regēbar	capiēbar	audiēbar
2nd sg.	amābāris	monēbāris	regēbāris	capiēbāris	audiēbāris
3rd sg.	amābātur	monēbātur	regēbātur	capiēbātur	audiēbātur
1st pl.	amābāmur	monēbāmur	regēbāmur	capiēbāmur	audiēbāmur
2nd pl.	amābāminī	monēbāminī	regēbāminī	capiēbāminī	audiēbāminī
3rd pl.	amābantur	monēbantur	regēbantur	capiēbantur	audiēbantur

Exercise 106. Following the model verbs above, conjugate **spectō, teneō** and **pōnō** in the imperfect passive indicative, singular and plural.

69. Future Passive Indicative

The **future passive** of first and second conjugation verbs can be recognized by the tense sign **-bi-** between the verb stem and the personal endings, with **-bo-** and **-bu-** in the first singular and third plural forms respectively, like the future active (§36), and **-be-** in the second person singular. The **future passive** of third and fourth conjugation verbs, like the future active (§49), uses the vowel **-ē-** (**-a-** in the first singular form, **-e-** in the third plural) before the ending:

	1st	2nd	3rd	3rd –iō	4th
1st sg.	amābor	monēbor	regar	capiar	audīar
2nd sg.	amāberis	monēberis	regēris	capiēris	audiēris
3rd sg.	amābitur	monēbitur	regētur	capiētur	audiētur
1st pl.	amābimur	monēbimur	regēmur	capiēmur	audiēmur
2nd pl.	amābiminī	monēbiminī	regēminī	capiēminī	audiēminī
3rd pl.	amābuntur	monēbuntur	regentur	capientur	audientur

Note in the second person singular of the third conjugation, the distinction between present and future is only the length of the stem vowel. This is not an issue for 3rd **-iō** forms:

Present (short -e-)	Future (long -ē-)
regeris	regēris
caperis	capiēris

Exercise 107. Following the model verbs above, conjugate **iūdicō, vincō** and **fīniō** in the future passive indicative, singular and plural.

Exercise 108. Identify each of the following verbs by person, number, tense and voice, then give an English translation.

1.	pōnēbāminī	8.	pōnar
2.	docētur	9.	monēberis
3.	vincentur	10.	spectābitur
4.	traheris	11.	volvuntur
5.	āmittēris	12.	dūcimur
6.	spectābantur	13.	rapiēbar
7.	cōnstituēbātur	14.	iactāris

Exercise 109. Transform each of the following present passive forms into the passive imperfect or future, as indicated, and then translate the new form.

Example: vincitur (future) vincētur – he will be conquered

1.	spectāmur (imperfect)	6.	legor (future)
2.	cōnstituntur (future)	7.	mittor (imperfect)
3.	dēbētur (future)	8.	vocātur (future)
4.	invenīris (imperfect)	9.	sentiuntur (imperfect)
5.	fīnīminī (future)	10.	volvimur (future)

Exercise 110. Translate the underlined words into Latin.

1. He kept being rolled by the waves.
2. You (sg.) will be placed on a throne.
3. Time was lost while we said goodbye.
4. The girls are being disturbed.
5. We will be sent on a quest soon.
6. The cart is being pulled by the horse.
7. Were you (pl.) warned repeatedly?
8. The money will be held by the king.

70. **Present Passive Infinitive**

The **present passive infinitive** of the first, second and fourth conjugations is formed by changing the final -e of the active infinitive to an -ī:

1st Conj.		2nd Conj.		4th Conj.	
amārī	to be loved	monērī	to be advised	audīrī	to be heard
laudārī	to be praised	vidērī	to be seen	fīnīrī	to be finished

The **present passive infinitive** of the third conjugation is formed by replacing the whole -ere of the active infinitive with an -i:

3rd Conj.		3rd Conj. -iō	
regī	to be ruled	capī	to be taken
pōnī	to be put	rapī	to be seized

Exercise 111. Transform each of the following active infinitive forms into the passive, and then translate the new form.

Example: spectāre   spectārī – to be watched

1. invenīre
2. miscēre
3. vincere
4. iactāre
5. habēre
6. pōnere
7. aedificāre
8. sentīre

71. **Sentence Pattern: Passive**

So far you have learned five sentence patterns 1) **Transitive** (§4), 2) **Intransitive** (§4), 3) **Linking** (§33), 4) **Special Intransitive** (§44), and 5) **Factitive** (§47).

The last major sentence pattern is the **passive**. This pattern has two elements:

Passive

• subject
• passive verb

In this pattern, the direct object of the transitive pattern becomes the subject in the passive pattern, and the subject of the transitive pattern may be omitted altogether. This is handy when one doesn't want to name the person doing an action, as in the sentence "Mistakes were made." Compare the following:

transitive pattern: **Fēmina rosam tenet.**   The woman holds a rose.
passive pattern: **Rosa tenētur.**   A rose is (being) held.

Exercise 112. Omit the subject of the original sentence for now and transform each of the following transitive sentences into the passive. Then translate the new sentence.

Example: Dux lēgēs scrībit.   Lēgēs scrībuntur. – The laws are (being) written.

1. Vir amīcōs vocābat.
2. Puellae aquam habent.
3. Ego tē amō.
4. Poēta carmen scrībit.
5. Uxor ignem portat.
6. Homō casam aedificābit.
7. Hostēs pecūniam rapiunt.
8. Nōs vidētis.

72. **Ablative of Agent**

With a passive verb, the person (or animal) by whom something is done is expressed with the preposition **ā/ab** plus an **animate** object. This use is called the **ablative of agent**.

• **Agent** — the person by whom something is done

Puer bonus **ā patre** laudātur.   The good boy is praised **by his father**.
Aqua **ab agricolā** portābātur.   The water was being carried **by the farmer**.

If the action is done by a **thing** rather than a person, Latin uses the same ablative *without a preposition*, which you learned in Chapter 4 (§23):

• **Means (Instrument)** — the thing by or with which something is done

Bellum **armīs** pugnātur.   The war is being fought **with (by means of) weapons**.

Remember that an **ablative of agent** can only occur **when the noun is animate**. Be aware that in a passive sentence it is possible to have a prepositional phrase with **ā/ab** that does not indicate agent:

> Fēminae **ab agrīs** mittuntur.   The women are being sent **away from the fields**.

Exercise 113. Go back to Exercise 112 and add the ablative of agent to the sentences you transformed. Follow the example below.

Example: Lēgēs **ā duce** scrībuntur.   The laws are (being) written **by the leader**.

Exercise 114. Translate each of the following sentences.

1. Illa urbs ā Rōmānīs cōnstituitur.
2. Hic puer ā frātre meō laudātur.
3. Uterque nostrum opēs magnās, sed neuter imperium habet.
4. Poēta quī dīcēbat nec ā puerīs nec puellīs audīrī poterat.
5. Arma in proelium ab mīlitibus portābuntur.
6. Caelum in quō ventīs nūbēs aguntur spectāmus.
7. Ingentēs undae ad lītus volvēbantur, dum nautae nāvēs parant.
8. Per tōtum annum contrā Ītaliam bellum gerēbātur.
9. Sī lēgātō inimīcus es, ā duce īrātō in flūmen trahēris.
10. Ad montem pedibus iter longum ab illīs incipitur.

Exercise 115. Translate into Latin.

1. Love conquers many people, but are all things conquered by love?
2. We are led by such a great love of our state.
3. While he was alive, your friend was always received with great honor in Italy.
4. A letter ought to be sent to my wife.
5. These are the two consuls, who were being elected by the Romans.
6. In a short time, many new families will have come into our city.
7. They are running away from the crowd, which is standing opposite the temple.
8. You (pl.) kept being warned to be good.
9. The race of gods is truly free from fear.
10. The soldier's letter is being read by our brother.

Reading 18 *(adapted)*

Pliny the Younger writes to a friend who has asked about the eruption of Mt. Vesuvius in A.D. 79. See the view of Mt. Vesuvius from Pompeii on p. 290.

> **Praecesserat** per multōs diēs **tremor** terrae; illā vērō nocte invaluit, et nōn sōlum movērī omnia sed etiam vertī crēdēbantur. Irrūpit cubiculum meum māter; iam surrēxī et sēdimus in āreā domūs, quae inter mare et tēctum erat. forsitan propter imprūdentiam (agēbam enim XVIII annum) poscō librum Titī Livī, quod legēbam. Amīcus avunculī quī ad eum ex Hispāniā vēnerat, ubi mē et mātrem sedentēs, mē vērō etiam legentem videt, nōs corripuit. Iam hōra diēī prīma,

et omnia tēcta quassābant; quamquam in apertō locō, angustō tamen erāmus, magnus **ruīnae** timor nōbīs est. Tum dēmum discēdimus ab oppidō multīs cum aliīs.

Multa nova vidēbāmus: mare in sē resorbēbātur et prōcesserat lītus, multaque **animālia** maris siccīs harēnīs **dētinēbat**. Ab alterō latere nūbēs ātra et horrenda longīs **flammīs** rumpēbātur. Tum vērō ille ex Hispāniā amīcus ācrius 'Sī frāter' dīxit 'tuus, tuus avunculus vīvit, optat vestram salūtem; sī periit, superstitēs optat.

Vocabulary:

praecēdō, -ere, -cessī	to precede	angustus, -a, -um	narrow
diēs, -ēī *m.*	day	ruīna, -ae *f.*	falling down (of a building)
tremor, -ōris *m.*	tremor, shaking		
invalescō, -ere, -valuī	to grow strong	dēmum (adv.)	finally, at last
irrumpō, -ere, -rūpī	to rush into	oppidum, -ī *n.*	town
cubiculum, -ī *n.*	bedroom	resorbeō, -ēre	to suck back, swallow again
area, -ae *f.*	courtyard		
domūs (gen. sg.)	house	prōcēdō, -ere, -cessī	to advance
tēctum, -ī *n.*	building, house	animāl, -is *n.*	living; subst. "animal"
forsitan	perhaps	siccīs harēnīs (abl. pl.)	"on the dry sand"
imprudentia, -ae *f.*	ignorance	dētineō, -ēre	to keep back
agēbam annum	"I was in my ____ year"	latus, -eris *n.*	side
		āter, -tra, -trum	black
poscō, -ere	to demand, ask for	horrendus, -a, -um	terrible
Titus Livius *m.*	Livy (the historian)	flamma, -ae *f.*	flame
avunculus, -ī *m.*	uncle	rumpō, -ere, -rūpī	to break
Hispānia, -ae *f.*	Spain	ācrius (adv.)	more urgently
sedentēs (acc. pl.)	"sitting"	salūs, -ūtis *f.*	safety
legentem (acc. sg.)	"reading"	pereō, -ere, -iī	to die, be dead
corripiō, -ere, -uī	to rebuke, chide	superstes, -itis	surviving, outliving; subst. "survivor"
quassō, -āre	to shake violently		
apertus, -a, -um	open		

Practice Sentences

Identify the form and use of the underlined words, then translate.

1. Mittuntur etiam ad eās cīvitātēs lēgātī.   (Caesar)
2. Erunt etiam altera bella atque iterum ad   (Vergil; *giving a prophecy for* Trōiam magnus mittētur Achillēs.   *Rome*)
3. Laudātur ab hīs, culpātur ab illīs.   (Horace; *of a man who goes to one extreme trying to avoid another*)
4. Ā fīliīs in iūdicium vocābātur.   (Cicero)
5. "Ō fortūnātī, quōrum iam moenia surgunt!"   (Vergil; *Aeneas envies Dido's people who are building their city*)
6. Nam sī āmittī vīta beāta potest, beāta esse   (Cicero) nōn potest.
7. Semper pauper eris, sī pauper es, Aemiliāne: (Martial) dantur opēs nūllīs nunc nisi dīvitibus.
8. Flūmen sub undīs scūta virōrum galeāsque   (Vergil – adapted; *of Trojans* et fortia corpora volvit.   *killed in the war with the Greeks*)

Vocabulary:

iterum (adv.)	again, a second time	beātus, -a, -um	happy, blessed
		pauper, -is (adj.)	poor
Achillēs (nom.)	Achilles (a Greek hero who fought at Troy)	Aemiliānus, -ī *m.*	Aemilianus (proper name)
		nisi	if … not, unless
culpō, -āre, -āvī, -ātus	to blame	dīvēs, -itis (adj.)	rich
		scūtum, ī *n.*	shield
fortūnātus, -a, -um	lucky, fortunate	galea, -ae *f.*	helmet

Chapter 14 Vocabulary

Nouns

genus, generis *n.*	birth, origin; kind; race
honor, honōris *m.*	honor, respect; public office
*hostis, hostis *m.* (*usually in* pl.)	enemy
n.b. *hostis is an enemy of the state;* inimīcus (*Ch. 12*) *is a personal enemy*	
iūdicium, iūdiciī *n.*	court; trial; judgment
lēgātus, lēgātī *m.*	delegate, envoy, ambassador; legion commander
lītus, lītoris *n.*	shore, beach, coast
nūbēs, nūbis *f.*	cloud
ops, opis *f.*	power, help; (pl.) wealth, resources
Trōia, Trōiae, *f.*	Troy
unda, undae *f.*	wave, waters; sea

Verbs

āmittō, āmittere, āmīsī, āmissus	to lose
cōnstituō, cōnstituere, cōnstituī, cōnstitūtus	to decide, appoint, establish
rapiō, rapere, rapuī, raptus	to seize, snatch, carry off
stō, stāre, stetī, statūrus	to stand
surgō, surgere, surrēxī, surrēctus	to get up, (a)rise
trahō, trahere, trāxī, tractus	to drag, pull; derive
videor, vidērī, vīsus sum	to seem (*see Ch. 15*); be seen
(*often with dative of the person*)	"it seems best to _____"
vīvō, vīvere, vīxī	to live, be alive
volvō, volvere, volvī, volūtus	to roll, turn/twist around

Adjectives

tantus, tanta, tantum	so much, so great
tantum	only
uterque, utraque, utrumque	both, each (of two)

Adverb

vērō (*postpositive*)	in fact, truly, indeed

Prepositions

ā, ab (+ *animate noun, in a passive sentence*)	by
contrā (+ acc.)	opposite; against; (adv.)
contrā (adv.)	in reply; face to face

(24)

Derivatives: For each English word below, give the Latin word from the Chapter 14 Vocabulary to which it is related and the English word's meaning.

1. vivacious
2. generic
3. inundate
4. judicial
5. constitution
6. revolve
7. insurrection
8. tractor
9. opulent
10. raptor

Caesar's Gaul

CHAPTER 15

Passive Voice (2)
> **Perfect Passive Indicative**
> **Pluperfect Passive Indicative**
> **Future Perfect Passive Indicative**
> **Perfect Passive Infinitive**
Linking Sentence Pattern Revisited
Possessive Adjectives and Possession Using Eius
Ablative of Specification (Respect)

So far you have learned the perfect active forms (Ch. 11), and the present, future and imperfect passive forms of all four conjugations (Ch. 14). This chapter introduces the perfect passive indicative system for all conjugations.

Passive Voice (2)

Latin constructs passive verb forms in the perfect system by combining the fourth principal part with different tenses of **sum**. The fourth principal part is a participle (a verbal adjective), whose ending agrees with the subject in gender and number (see the examples in §73 below).

73. Perfect Passive Indicative

The **perfect passive indicative** is formed by combining the fourth principal part with the present tense forms of **sum**.

1st sg.	amātus (-a, -um)	sum	I was loved/have been loved
2nd sg.	amātus (-a, -um)	es	You were loved/have been loved
3rd sg.	amātus (-a, -um)	est	He, she, it was loved/etc.
1st pl.	amātī (-ae, -a)	sumus	We were loved
2nd pl.	amātī (-ae, -a)	estis	You were loved
3rd pl.	amātī (-ae, -a)	sunt	They were loved

Compare the following participle endings, which agree with the subject of the sentence, in the following examples:

Equus vīs**us** est.	The horse was / has been seen.
Haec cīvitās rēct**a** est.	This state was / has been ruled.
Hoc carmen audīt**um** est.	This song was / has been heard.
Hominēs doct**ī** sunt.	The men were / have been taught.

Remember (§54) that the perfect tense in Latin can either correspond to the simple past tense in English (historical perfect: "I was seen") or stress the present result of a past action (present perfect: "I have been seen").

Exercise 116. Following the model verb above, conjugate **misceō** and **vincō** in the perfect passive indicative, singular and plural.

Exercise 117. Change each of the following perfect active forms into perfect passive, then translate.

Example: rēximus   rēctī sumus; "we have been ruled" or "we were ruled"

1. posuit
2. cēpī
3. āmīsimus
4. trāxērunt
5. sēnsistis
6. petiī
7. cōnstituimus
8. rapuit
9. ēgistī
10. volvistis
11. vertērunt
12. spectāvēre

74. Pluperfect Passive Indicative

The **pluperfect passive indicative** is formed by combining the fourth principal part with the imperfect forms of **sum**.

1st sg.	amātus (-a, -um)	eram	I had been loved
2nd sg.	amātus (-a, -um)	erās	You had been loved
3rd sg.	amātus (-a, -um)	erat	He, she, it had been loved
1st pl.	amātī (-ae, -a)	erāmus	We had been loved
2nd pl.	amātī (-ae, -a)	erātis	You had been loved
3rd pl.	amātī (-ae, -a)	erant	They had been loved

Exercise 118. Following the model verb above, conjugate **habeō** and **vertō** in the pluperfect passive indicative, singular and plural.

Exercise 119. Translate into Latin, using the appropriate principal part from below:

audiō, audīre, audīvī, audītus   to hear
condō, condere, condidī, conditus   to found, build, establish
creō, creāre, creāvī, creātus   to elect
pōnō, pōnere, posuī, positus   to put, place

1. we were establishing
2. they were established
3. he had founded
4. it had been founded
5. she was heard
6. she had been heard
7. she had heard
8. it had been placed
9. they were being placed
10. they have been placed
11. you (sg.) are elected
12. you (sg.) were elected
13. you (pl.) have been elected
14. you (pl.) had been elected

75. Future Perfect Passive Indicative

The **future perfect passive indicative** is formed by combining the fourth principal part with the future forms of **sum**.

1st sg.	amātus (-a, -um)	erō	I shall have been loved
2nd sg.	amātus (-a, -um)	eris	You will have been loved
3rd sg.	amātus (-a, -um)	erit	He, she, it will have been loved
1st pl.	amātī (-ae, -a)	erimus	We shall have been loved
2nd pl.	amātī (-ae, -a)	eritis	You will have been loved
3rd pl.	amātī (-ae, -a)	erunt	They will have been loved

Exercise 120. Following the model verb above, conjugate **relinquō** and **fīniō** in the future perfect passive indicative, singular and plural.

Exercise 121. All the verbs in this exercise are passive. Identify each by person, number and tense, then translate.

Example: caesus erat   third singular pluperfect of caedō: "he had been killed"

1. incēnsum est
2. audītī erimus
3. spectāta erat
4. ācta sunt
5. scrīpta erunt
6. tractī erant
7. raptus es
8. cōnstitūtum erat
9. monitae erunt
10. inventa erant

76. **Perfect Passive Infinitive**

The **perfect passive infinitive** is formed by combining the fourth principal part with the infinitive of **sum**:

Conjugation		
First	amātus (-a, -um) esse	to have been loved
Second	monitus (-a, -um) esse	to have been advised
Third	rēctus (-a, -um) esse	to have been ruled
Fourth	audītus (-a, -um) esse	to have been heard

Exercise 122. Change each of the following present passive infinitives into perfect passive infinitives, then translate.

Example: docērī   doctus esse; "to have been taught"

1. pōnī
2. fīnīrī
3. iactārī
4. prohibērī
5. frangī
6. clāmārī
7. gerī
8. invenīrī

77. **Linking Sentence Pattern Revisited**

In Chapter 5 (§33) you learned about the Linking Sentence Pattern, in which a linking verb connects a subject to a subject complement in the same case: **vir est potēns** (the man is powerful). Chapter 8 (§47) introduced the Factitive Sentence Pattern, in which certain verbs require two accusative objects in a special relationship: **vir ducem bonum habet** (the man considers the leader good).

Passive forms of these verbs frequently occur in linking sentence patterns:

ille Rōmulus **appellātur**	that man **is called** Romulus
duo virī cōnsulēs **creātī erant**	two men **had been elected** consuls
Rōmulus rēx bonus **habitus est**	Romulus **was considered** a good king
vōs amīcī **iūdicāminī**	you (pl.) **are judged** (to be) friends/friendly
vocor fortis.	I **am called** brave

Another common verb in a linking sentence pattern is the passive form of **videō**, which you saw in Chapter 14:

Rōma **vidētur** magna	Rome **seems** big

78. **Possessive Adjectives and Possession Using Eius**

   • **Possessive Adjectives**

   Since Chapter 5 you have been seeing "possessive" adjectives for the first and second persons: **meus, -a, -um** ("my"); **tuus, -a, -um** ("your" sg.); **noster, nostra, nostrum** ("our"); **vester, vestra, vestrum** ("your" pl.). These adjectives may refer back to the subject (reflexive) or not.

Vidēmus casam **nostram**.	We see **our (own)** house. (reflexive)
Videt casam **nostram**.	He sees **our** house. (not reflexive)

   In Latin, the possessive adjective for the third person is always reflexive, refering to the subject as the possessor:

suus, -a, -um	his (her, its, their) own
Puer videt casam **suam**.	The boy sees **his own** house.
Puella videt **suum** equum.	The girl sees **her own** horse.

   Remember that since these words are adjectives, they must agree with the noun they modify in case, number and gender.

   • **Possession using Eius**

   To indicate possession for the third person when it is *not* reflexive, Latin uses the genitive of the pronoun **is, ea, id** (§46).

Vidēmus casam **eius**.	We see **his** house.
	(literally "the house **of him**")
Capiō arma **eōrum**.	I am taking **their** weapons.
	("the weapons **of them**")

   Be careful to distinquish between this and the use of **suus, -a, -um**. Compare the following examples:

Arma **sua** videt.	He sees **his own** weapons.
Arma **eius** videt.	He sees **his** (someone else's) weapons.

Exercise 123. Translate into Latin.

1. They see our friends.
2. They see their own friends.
3. We teach ourselves.
4. He was carrying her books.
5. He carries his own books.
6. He will carry their books.

Exercise 124. Translate each of the following sentences, which have pronouns and/or possessive adjectives.

1.	eam relinquit.	11.	sē docuit.
2.	ea relīquit.	12.	ille suam uxōrem amāvit.
3.	eius frātrem relīquērunt.	13.	ille eius uxōrem amāvit (!)
4.	suum frātrem relīquērunt.	14.	in tuam urbem vēnimus.
5.	suum frātrem relīquit.	15.	in tuam urbem vēnistī.
6.	nostram fīliam laudāvimus.	16.	in vestram urbem vēnit.
7.	eius fīliam laudāvimus.	17.	ex vestrā urbī vēnistis.
8.	meam fīliam laudāvī.	18.	ex suā urbī vēnit.
9.	mē laudāvī.	19.	sibi crēdidit.
10.	eum docuimus.	20.	suae coniugī crēdidit.

79. **Ablative of Specification (Respect)**

The ablative *without a preposition* is used to show **in what respect** something **is** or **is done**:

Vir **corpore** aeger, nōn **animō** est.   The man is weak **in body**, but not **in spirit**.
Dux **nōmine** erat.   He was commander **in name**.

This use of the ablative often occurs with the adjectives **dignus** and **indignus**:

Hī **laude dignī** sunt.   They are **worthy of praise.**
Haec **indigna homine līberō** sunt.   These things are **unworthy of a free man.**

Exercise 125. List all the uses of the ablative case you have had so far and indicate which of these uses require a preposition and which do not.

Exercise 126. Translate each of the following sentences.

1. Urbs ā reliquīs cīvibus magnō cum dolōre relicta erat.
2. Cum surgunt et in iūdiciō stant, nostrī ducēs bonī esse videntur.
3. Ille fuit locus in quō urbs Rōmāna condita erat.
4. Mīlitēs quī in bellō pugnāverant ab omnibus cīvibus vīsī sunt.
5. Rēx Trōiae dignus magnā laude ā suō populō habitus est.
6. Dī vērō etiam fatō rēctī sunt.
7. Virī in perīcula quae nōn vitārī poterant missī sunt.
8. Hostēs longum tempus hāc urbe prohibitī erant.
9. Postquam proelium incēpit, mīlitēs nūmen secundum ōrāvērunt.
10. Nāvēs cēterae ingentibus undīs et ventīs frāctae sunt.

Exercise 127. Translate into Latin.

1. Those dangers had been avoided.
2. The army was led through the countryside of this province by the brave leader.
3. With great labor the truth was discovered by us.
4. Were your letters written during the night?
5. The soldiers were carried around the walls of Troy and into battle by many horses.
6. Romulus seemed to be loved by everyone.
7. Is that delegate considered worthy of our respect?
8. The others will come into their own city, which is on the tall mountain.
9. When the new city was founded, all the Romans were called fortunate.
10. The wealth, which the citizens had received, was suddenly seized by the enemy.

Reading 19 *(adapted)*

Caesar (102 – 44 B.C.) wrote accounts of two of his great military campaigns. This selection comes from the beginning of his Gallic Wars *and describes the various peoples and customs of Gaul. See map of Caesar's Gaul on p. 134.*

Gallia est omnis dīvīsa in partēs trēs, quārum ūnam incolunt Belgae, aliam Aquītānī, tertiam (eī), quī linguā nostrā Gallī appellantur. hī omnēs linguā, īnstitūtīs, lēgibus inter sē **differunt**. Gallōs ab Aquītānīs Garumna flūmen, ā Belgīs Mātrona et Sēquana **dīvidit**. hōrum omnium fortissimī sunt Belgae, quod ā cultū atque hūmānitāte (nostrae) prōvinciae longissimē absunt, proximīque sunt Germānīs, quī trāns Rhēnum incolunt, quibuscum semper bellum gerunt. itaque Helvētiī quoque reliquōs Gallōs virtūte praecēdunt, quod saepe proeliīs cum Germānīs **contendunt**, cum aut suīs fīnibus eōs prohibent, aut in eōrum fīnibus bellum gerunt.

Vocabulary:

dīvidō, -ere, -vīsī, -vīsus	to divide	fortissimī (nom. pl.)	"bravest"
		cultus, -ūs *m.*	civilization
Belgae, -ārum *m.* (pl.)	Belgians	hūmānitās, -tātis *f.*	refinement
Aquītānī, -ōrum *m.* (pl.)	Aquitanians	longissimē (adv.)	furthest
		proximus, -a, -um	nearest
Gallī, -ōrum *m.* (pl.)	Gauls	Rhēnus, -ī *m.*	Rhine (a river)
lingua, -ae *f.*	language	Helvētiī, -ōrum *m.* (pl.)	Helvetians
īnstitūtum, -ī *n.*	way of life		
differō, -ferre	to differ	quoque (adv.)	also
Garumna, -ae *f.*	Garonne (a river)	praecēdō, -ere	to surpass, excel
Mātrona, -ae *f.*	Marne (a river)	contendō, -ere	to contend, fight
Sēquana, -ae *f.*	Seine (a river)		

Practice Sentences

Identify the case and use of the underlined words, then translate.

1. Nēmō enim patriam quia <u>magna</u> est amat, sed quia sua.   (Seneca)

2. Condidit urbem Rōmulus <u>quam</u> ex nōmine suō Rōmam vocāvit.   (Eutropius)

3. Vīta enim mortuōrum in **memoriā** est posita vīvōrum.   (Cicero)

4. Ille mī pār esse <u>deō</u> vidētur, ille, sī fās est, superāre dīvōs.   (Catullus – adapted; *the poet envies the man sitting beside Lesbia, his own beloved*)

5. Prīma dedit lēgēs; Cereris sunt omnia mūnus; ... Certē dea <u>carmine</u> digna est.   (Ovid; *a Muse sings in praise of Ceres*)

6. Ab eō locō in fīnēs Ambianōrum pervĕnit, quī sē suaque omnia sine <u>morā</u> dedidērunt.   (Caesar; *a Gallic tribe reacts to the arrival of Caesar's army*)

7. Aliīs ego tē <u>virtūtibus</u>, ... **gravitātis**, **iūstitiae**, ..., cēterīs omnibus, omnī honōre semper dignum iūdicāvī.   (Cicero – adapted; *speaking to a rival in court*)

8. Fortibus est fortūna <u>virīs</u> data.   (Ennius)

Vocabulary:

mortuus, -a, -um	dead	mūnus, -eris *n.*	gift
vīvus, -a, -um	living, alive	certē (adv.)	surely
memoria, -ae *f.*	memory	Ambianī, -ōrum	Ambiani (a tribe in Gaul)
mī = mihi			
dīvōs = deōs		perveniō, -īre, vēni	to arrive, come through
fās (*n.* indecl.)	right		
Cerēs, -eris *f.*	Ceres, goddess of grain	dēdō, -ere, dedidī	to surrender
		gravitās, -tātis *f.*	gravity, dignity
		iūstitia, -ae *f.*	justice, fairness

Chapter 15 Vocabulary

Nouns

*cīvis, cīvis *m.* or *f.*	citizen
dolor, dolōris *m.*	pain, sorrow
equus, equī *m.*	horse
humus, humī *f.*	ground, earth
Gallia, Galliae *f.*	Gaul
labor, labōris *m.*	work, labor, effort; hardship
laus, laudis *f.*	praise
pectus, pectoris *n.*	breast, chest; heart
perīculum, perīculī *n.*	danger
proelium, proeliī *n.*	battle
prōvincia, prōvinciae *f.*	province
rūs, rūris *n.*	the country(side)

Verbs

condō, condere, condidī, conditus	to found, build, establish
frangō, frangere, frēgī, frāctus	to break, shatter, wreck
incendō, incendere, incendī, incēnsus	to set fire to, burn; inflame
prohibeō, prohibēre, prohibuī, prohibitus	to prohibit, keep from – to keep someone (acc.) from something (abl. – *separation*)
vītō, vītāre, vītāvī, vītātus	to avoid

Adjectives

aequus, aequa, aequum	even, calm, equal
cēterī, cēterae, cētera	the rest, the others
dignus, digna, dignum	worthy; worth, fitting
indignus, indigna, indignum	unworthy; undeserved; shameful
suus, sua, suum	his, her, its, their own

Prepositions

circum/circā (+ acc.)	around
super (+ acc.)	over, above, on (top of)

(24)

Derivatives: For each English word below, give the Latin word from the Chapter 15 Vocabulary to which it is related and the English word's meaning.

1. equanimity
2. rural
3. dolorous
4. abscond
5. circumnavigate
6. humble
7. incendiary
8. civic
9. fractious
10. equestrian

CHAPTER 16

Fourth Declension
Fifth Declension
Locative Case
Other Place Expressions

This chapter introduces the last two declensions and a final case that is only used rarely and indicates place where.

80. **Fourth Declension**

The stem of nouns in the fourth declension ends in **-u**, which usually weakens to **-i** before the plural dative and ablative ending **-bus**. Masculine and feminine nouns share the same endings.

Singular	Masc./Fem.	Neuter	Endings	
Nominative	vult**us**	gen**ū**	**-us**	**-ū**
Genitive	vult**ūs**	gen**ūs**	**-ūs**	**-ūs**
Dative	vult**uī**	gen**ū**	**-uī**	**-ū**
Accusative	vult**um**	gen**ū**	**-um**	**-ū**
Ablative	vult**ū**	gen**ū**	**-ū**	**-ū**
Plural				
Nominative	vult**ūs**	gen**ua**	**-ūs**	**-ua**
Genitive	vult**uum**	gen**uum**	**-uum**	**-uum**
Dative	vult**ibus**	gen**ibus**	**-ibus**	**-ibus**
Accusative	vult**ūs**	gen**ua**	**-ūs**	**-ua**
Ablative	vult**ibus**	gen**ibus**	**-ibus**	**-ibus**

Note the following:

- Most nouns in the fourth declension are masculine. The most common feminine and neuter nouns in this declension are:

Feminine		Neuter	
domus, -ūs	house, home	cornū, -ūs	wing (of an army); horn
manus, -ūs	hand; band (of men)	genū, -ūs	knee

- **Domus** is a fourth declension noun, but also uses some forms from the second declension:

Acc. sg.	**domum**	(to a) home (see §83 below)
Abl. sg.	**domō**	from home
Acc. pl.	**domōs**	to (more than one) homes
Locative sg.	**domī**	at home (see §82 below)

Exercise 128. Identify each of the following nouns by case, number and gender. If the ending is ambiguous, include all possibilities.

1. impetūs
2. flūctibus
3. cornua
4. humum
5. manuī
6. domus
7. genū
8. metū
9. vultuum
10. cāsum

Exercise 129. Following the fourth declension patterns above, decline **cāsus** and **cornū** in all cases, singular and plural. Be sure to check the genitive singular forms in the Chapter Vocabulary to learn what stem to use for each noun.

Exercise 130. Translate the underlined words into Latin using vocabulary in this chapter.

1. Some of the <u>accidents</u> were terrible.
2. They are expecting the army's <u>attack</u>.
3. The <u>destruction</u> of the city was quick.
4. He is building the house <u>by hand</u>.
5. She liked his <u>face</u>. [*use* **vultus**]
6. We are members of the Roman <u>senate</u>.

81. **Fifth Declension**

The stem of nouns in the fifth declension ends in -**ē**.

Singular			**Endings**
Nominative	diēs	rēs	-ēs
Genitive	diēī	reī	-ēī, -eī
Dative	diēī	reī	-ēī, -eī
Accusative	diem	rem	-em
Ablative	diē	rē	-ē
Plural			
Nominative	diēs	rēs	-ēs
Genitive	diērum	rērum	-ērum
Dative	diēbus	rēbus	-ēbus
Accusative	diēs	rēs	-ēs
Ablative	diēbus	rēbus	-ēbus

- The genitive and dative singular endings have -**eī** (instead of -**ēī**) after a consonant.

- Except for **diēs** and **rēs**, most fifth declension nouns don't appear in the plural.

Exercise 131. Identify each of the following nouns by case, number and gender. If the ending is ambiguous, include all possibilities.

1. diērum
2. faciēs
3. speī
4. fidē
5. rēbus
6. spem

Exercise 132. Following the fifth declension patterns above, decline **spēs** and **faciēs** in all cases, singular and plural. Be sure to check the genitive singular forms in the Chapter Vocabulary to learn what stem to use for each noun.

Exercise 133. Translate the underlined words into Latin using vocabulary in this chapter where possible.

1. We will leave on the third <u>day</u>.
2. She thought <u>about his appearance</u>.
3. Did you see the enemy's <u>battle lines</u>?
4. Do you love the <u>state</u>?
5. <u>For seven days</u> they sailed in the ship.
6. You fight us <u>without hope</u> of victory.

82. Locative Case

In Chapter 4 you learned that **place where** is regularly expressed by a preposition + the ablative case (§24). With the names of towns, small islands and a few other words the **locative** case is used instead. The locative endings are the same as the genitive singular in the first and second declension, and elsewhere usually the same as the ablative:

	1st Decl.	2nd Decl.	3rd Decl.	4th Decl.	5th Decl.
Singular	-ae	-ī	-ī *or* –e	[domī]	-ē
Plural	-īs	-īs	-ibus		

Here are some common examples (with the dictionary listings provided for place names you have not learned):

Athēnae, Athēnārum, *f.* Athens
Corinthus, Corinthī, *m.* Corinth
Rhodus, Rhodī, *m.* Rhodes (an island)

Rōmae	at Rome, in Rome	**Rhodī**	at Rhodes, on Rhodes
Corinthī	at Corinth, in Corinth	**Athēnīs**	at Athens, in Athens
domī	at home	**bellī**	in war
humī	on the ground	**rūrī**	in the country

83. Other Place Expressions

With the names of towns and small islands, as well as **domus** and **rūs**, Latin omits the preposition in expressions of **place to which** and **place from which**:

place to which		**place from which**	
Rōmam	to (into) Rome	**Rōmā**	from Rome
Athēnās	to (into) Athens	**Athēnīs**	from Athens
domum	(to) home	**domō**	from home
rūs	to (into) the country	**rūre**	from the country

The preposition is sometimes also omitted with other words in poetry.

In expressions of **place to which** with towns, small islands, **domus** and **rūs**, the presence of a preposition indicates motion towards but not all the way to:

ad Rōmam	to the vicinity of Rome
ad Athēnās	towards Athens
ad domum	homeward

Exercise 134. Translate each of the following sentences.

1. Mīlitēs Rōmae trēs diēs manēbunt.
2. Domūs Corinthī duōs diēs ardēbant, postquam hostēs eās incendērunt.
3. Cīvēs et rūre et ab urbibus vēnerant.
4. Cāsus reī pūblicae hominibus omnibus nocuit.
5. Rhodī multōs diēs manēbimus, inde domum veniēmus.
6. Flūctūs trēs pedēs altī in mediō marī erant.
7. Humī paucās hōrās dormiēbāmus, quia erat nēmō domī.
8. Metūne rūre fugitis?
9. Mīles arma in dextrā manū portāvit tōtum iter.
10. Rōmam aliī festīnāvērunt, sed veniēbam ad templum.

Exercise 135. Translate into Latin.

1. He was resting [*use a form of* **pōnō**] his hands on his knees.
2. Will our leaders abandon the state, if the enemy attacks?
3. You (pl.) will have walked eight miles.
4. That man had been a leader in the
5. senate for many years.
6. In five days he walked to Athens and then sailed home.
6. I stayed in the country for seven days.
7. The citizens had great sorrow [*use dat. of possession*] because the city was burning.
8. They had warned us about him.
9. The soldiers on the right wing were strong, but their fear was great.
10. We will not conquer Gaul with a small band of men.

Reading 20 (*adapted from Livy*)

Livy tells the story of how the Romans and Albans decided to settle their war through a battle fought by two sets of triplets, the Horatii and the Curiatii.

Postquam Rōmānī et Albānī utrimque stābant, cum paucīs mīlitum in medium ducēs prōcēdunt. tum Albānus dux dīcit, "**cupīdō** imperiī duōs populōs ad arma **stimulat**. Sed Etrusca rēs, quae circā nōs tēque est, pollet. iam cum **signum pugnae** dabis, hī mīlitēs pugnābunt et fessī erunt; tum **Etruscī** petent et utrēsque nostrum vincentur! itaque sine multō sanguine utrīusque populī dēcernī potest?" Tullus, quamquam **victōriae** ācer erat, cōnsentit et ratiō invenitur cui fortūna praebuit māteriam.

Vocabulary:

Albānus, -a, um	Alban	pugna, -ae f.	fight
utrimque (adv.)	on both sides	sanguis, -inis m.	blood
prōcēdō, -ere	to proceed, move forward	dēcernō, -ere	to decide the issue
		Tullus, -ī m.	Tullus (king of the Romans)
cupīdō, -inis f.	lust, desire		
stimulō, -āre	to spur on	victōria, -ae f.	victory
Etrusca rēs (nom.)	"Etruscan state"	cōnsentiō, -ere	to agree
polleō, -ēre	to be strong	māteria, -ae f.	means, opportunity
signum, -ī n.	signal, sign		

Reading 21 *(adapted from Livy)*

Livy's story continues.

Forte in duōbus tum exercitibus erant trigeminī frātrēs nec aetāte nec vīribus disparēs, Horātiī et Curiātiī. hī frātrēs cōnstituērunt prō suā quisque patriā pugnāre ferrō. antequam pugnāvērunt, foedus īcēbātur inter Rōmānōs et **Albānōs** hīs lēgibus: imperium erit **victōribus**. tum trigeminī arma capiunt et in medium inter duās aciēs prōcēdunt. cōnsēderant suīs prō castrīs duo exercitūs et **spectāculum** spectāre incēpērunt. datur **signum** īnfestīsque armīs, velut aciēs, trēs iuvenēs magnōrum exercituum animōs gerentēs concurrunt. duo Rōmānī super alium alius exspīrantēs cecidērunt, dum trēs Albānī vulnerantur. **horror** ingēns Rōmānōs perstringit et spēs tōta āmittitur, nam ūnus Rōmānus contrā trēs Curiātiōs stābat. Forte is integer fuit. ... *[continuārī]*

Vocabulary:

trigeminus, -a, -um	triplet	velut	just like
vīrēs, -ium f. (pl.)	strength	iuvenis, -is m.	young man
dispār, disparis	unlike, unequal	gerentēs (nom. pl.)	"displaying"
foedus, -eris n.	treaty	exspīrantēs (nom. pl.)	dying
īcō, -ere, īcī, ictus	to make (a treaty)	vulnerō, -āre	to wound
victor, -ōris m.	victor	horror, -ōris m.	horror, dread
cōnsīdō, -ere, cōnsēdī	to sit down		
īnfestus, -a, -um	hostile, dangerous	perstringō, -ere	to paralyze, chill
		integer, -gra, -grum	unhurt; whole

Practice Sentences

Identify the case and use of the underlined words, then translate.

1. Flēte meōs <u>cāsūs</u>. (Ovid)
2. [Ventī] **vastōs** volvunt ad <u>lītora</u> flūctūs. (Vergil; *describing a storm at sea*)
3. Illō <u>diē</u> dux ad iūdicium omnem suam **familiam** cōgit. (Caesar – adapted)
4. Īrārum tantōs volvis sub pectore <u>flūctūs</u>. (Vergil; *Jupiter, talking to Juno*)
5. <u>Rūrī</u> agere vītam cōnstituit. (Livy – adapted; *of a retired general*)
6. <u>Rēs</u> est magna tacēre. (Martial)
7. Rōmulus excipiet gentem, et Māvortia condet moenia, Rōmānōsque suō dē nomine dīcet. <u>Hīs</u> ego nec mētas rērum nec tempora pōnō; imperium sine fīne dedī. (Vergil; *Jupiter promises a great future for Rome*)
8. **Certum**que eī reī <u>tempus</u> cōnstituitur. (Caesar; *enemies agree to a meeting*)

Vocabulary:

fleō, -ēre	to weep; mourn for	constituō, -ere	to decide
vastus, -a, -um	huge, vast	excipiō, -ere	to renew
familia, -ae *f.*	family	Māvortius, -a,	of Mars =
cōgō, -ere	to gather together, collect	-um	of Rome
		mēta, -ae *f.*	limit
agō, agere	to spend (life)		

Chapter 16 Vocabulary

Nouns

aciēs, aciēī *f.*	battle line
cāsus, cāsūs *m.*	fall; misfortune, destruction; chance, accident
cornū, cornūs *n.*	horn; wing (of an army)
diēs, diēī *m.* or *f.*	day; *fem. used when it is an appointed, or set day*
domus, domūs *f.*	house(hold), home
exercitus, exercitūs *m.*	army
faciēs, faciēī *f.*	face; appearance
fidēs, fideī *f.*	faith, trust; loyalty, trustworthiness
flūctus, flūctūs *m.*	wave; commotion
genū, genūs *n.*	knee
impetus, impetūs *m.*	attack; charge; impulse
manus, manūs *f.*	hand; band (of men)
metus, metūs *m.*	fear, dread; anxiety

passus, passūs *m.*	pace, footstep
mille passūs; mīlia passuum (pl.)	mile (*lit.* "1000 paces"); miles
rēs, reī *f.*	thing, matter, business; court case
rēs pūblica, reī pūblicae *f.*	state, republic
senātus, senātūs *m.*	senate
spēs, speī *f.*	hope
vultus, vultūs *m.*	expression; face

Verbs

ardeō, ardēre, arsī, arsūrus	to burn, be on fire, glow
cadō, cadere, cecidī, cāsūrus	to fall

Adverbs

igitur (*postpositive*)	therefore
inde	from there; then, from that time forth
tam	so, to such a degree

(23)

Derivatives: For each English word below, give the Latin word from the Chapter 16 Vocabulary to which it is related and the English word's meaning.

1. fluctuation
2. meridian
3. domicile
4. decadence
5. meticulous
6. despair
7. impetuous
8. genuflect
9. ardent
10. manicle

READING CHAPTER III

Narrative Reading III: Numa
Dictionary Practice / Form Identification
Review of the Sentence and its Parts
Question Words for Extra Practice
Word Building
 Families of Words
 Consonant Changes
English Abbreviations and Phrases

Narrative Reading III: Numa

(Adapted from Livy)

After the death of Romulus, Numa, a Sabine leader, became king of Rome. He built the famous temple of Janus, established priesthoods and a series of religious rites, and became known for his piety and peaceful policies.

[Numa] **pietāte** omnium pectora **imbuerat**, ita fidēs ac iūs prō lēgum ac poenārum metū cīvitātem regēbant. Lūcus erat, quem medium fons rigābat aquā, ubi saepe Numa sōlus ambulābat, et Camēnīs eum lūcum sacrāvit, quod in hōc locō eārum concilia cum coniuge suā Egeriā erant. Fideī sollemne īnstituit et multa alia **sacrificia** locaque sacrīs quae "Argeōs" pontificēs vocant dēdicāvit.   *continued*

Vocabulary:

pietās, -tātis *f.*	piety (etc.)	Fidēs, -eī *f.*	Faith, personified as a goddess
imbuō, -ere, -uī	to imbue, instill		
ac = et		sollemne, -is *n.*	festival, ceremony
poēna, -ae *f.*	penalty	sacra, -ōrum *n.*	sacrifices
lūcus, -ī *m.*	sacred grove	īnstituō, -ere,	to establish,
fons, fontis *m.*	spring, stream	īnstituī	institute
rigō, -āre	to wet, moisten	sacrificium, -ī *n.*	sacrifice
Camēnae, -ārum *f.*	Muses	Argeī, -ōrum *m.*	shrines (*source*
sacrō, -āre, -āvī	to consecrate		*unknown*)
concilium, -iī *n.*	meeting	pontifex, -icis *m.*	high priest
Egeria, -ae *f.*	Egeria, a nymph and Numa's wife		

151

continued

Omnium tamen maximum eius operum fuit tūtēla per omne rēgnī tempus haud mīnor pācis quam rēgnī. ita duo deinceps rēgēs, alius aliā viā, ille bellō, hic pāce, cīvitātem auxērunt. Rōmulus septem et trīgintā rēgnāvit annōs, Numa trēs et quadrāgintā. nōn sōlum valida sed etiam temperāta et bellī et pācis artibus erat cīvitās.

Vocabulary:

maximus, -a, -um	greatest	augeō, augēre,	to enrich; increase
opus, -eris *n.*	work, act	auxī	
tūtēla, -ae *f.*	protection	validus, -a, -um	strong, powerful
haud mīnor	no less	temperātus,	well-ordered
quam	than	-a, -um	
deinceps (adv.)	in order, successively		
alius aliā viā	"one in one way, the other in another way"		

Dictionary Practice/Form Identification

Identify the words below based on the dictionary entries given. Be sure to indicate the **entry from which each is taken**, and the **part of speech** and to *give all possibilities for ambiguous forms.*

For **nouns** and **adjectives**: give case, number, and gender

For **verbs**: give person, number, tense (present, imperfect, future, perfect, pluperfect, future perfect), voice (active or passive) and mood (indicative or imperative)

A.   dūcō, dūcere, dūxī, ductus: to lead
B.   duo, duae, duo: two
C.   dux, ducis *m.*: leader
D.   ductō, ductāre, ductāvī, ductātus: to cheat
E.   ductus, ductūs *m.*: drawing, form

		Entry	Part of Speech	Form ID
1.	ducibus			
2.	ductus es			
3.	dūc			
4.	duce			
5.	ductāvistī			
6.	duōs			
7.	ductābitur			
8.	ductum			
9.	dūcēmus			
10.	duārum			
11.	dūcunt			
12.	dūcēbam			
13.	ductūs			
14.	dūxērunt			
15.	ductī erāmus			

Review of the Sentence and its Parts

If you are using a "graphic organizer," you can update it to add new material or refocus your review items. Here is the chart from Reading Chapter II, with new items for chapters 11-16:

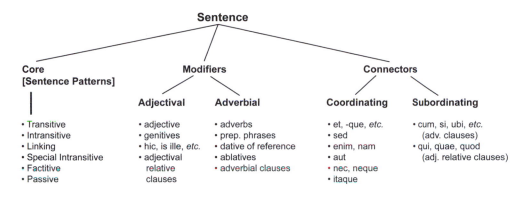

Question Words for Extra Practice

Quis/Quī	who? (animate)
Quem/Quōs	whom? (animate)
Quid/Quae	what? (non-animate)
ā Quō	by whom?
Quō auxiliō	by what means?
Quam diū	how long?
Ubi	where?
Cūr	why?

Based on the narrative reading at the beginning of this chapter, answer the following questions in Latin.

1. Quōrum pectora pietāte imbūta sunt?
2. Quō auxiliō cīvitās regēbātur?
3. Ubi Numa ambulābat?
4. Cūr hunc locum Camēnīs sacrāvit?
5. Quis erat Egeria?
6. Quae erant Argeōs?
7. Quī eīs hoc nōmen dedērunt?
8. Quid fuit maximum opus Numae?
9. Quam diū Rōmulus rēgnāvit?
10. Quis fuit rēx secundus Rōmae?

Word Building

Families of Words

Reading Latin is easier and more fun if you can make good guesses at the meaning of words, rather than always looking everything up. One way to make a good guess is to focus on common roots (see Reading Chapter II), identify the part of speech of the new word, and think of other words you have already learned. This takes practice, but will pay many rewards.

Guess the meaning of each word, and list at least one word you have already learned that is related to it:

Example: iūdex, iūdicis *m.* "judge": iūs, iūris *n.* (justice); iūdicō, iūdicāre (to judge)

1. adventus, adventūs *m.*
2. īnfēlīx, īnfēlīcis
3. servus, servī *m.*
4. spērō, spērāre

Consonant Changes

Certain consonants in combination yield predictable changes. Understanding these patterns can make learning vocabulary (and principal parts) much easier and can help you see connections between words that may not initially seem related (e.g. cadō and cāsus):

- **b** before **s** or **t** becomes **p**
  *scrīb-sī > scrīpsī
  *scrīb-tus > scrīptus
- **g** or **h** before **t** becomes **c**
  *āg-tus > āctus
  *trah-tus > tractus
- **g** or **c** before **s** becomes **x**
  *rēg-s > rēx
  *duc-s > dux

- **d** or **t** before **d, t,** or **s** (**dt, tt, ds, ts**) often becomes **s**
  *cad-tus > cāsus
  *pat-tus > passus
  *ced-sī > cessī
  *mīlet-s > mīles

Explain the consonant changes in the bold form of the following dictionary entries:

Example: **vōx**, vōcis   The nominative form was *vocs, but the **c + s**
turned into **x**

1. **ars**, artis
2. audeō, audēre, **ausus sum**
3. dīcō, dīcere, **dīxī**, dictus
4. lābor, lābī, **lāpsus**
5. videō, vidēre, vīdī, **vīsus**
6. **fēlīx**, fēlīcis
7. ardeō, ardēre, **arsī**, arsus
8. intellegō, intellegere, **intellēxī**, intellēctus

English Abbreviations and Phrases

- A.D.   **annō dominī**   in the year of the Lord
- circa (ca., c.) **circā**   around, approximately *(used with dates)*
- pro tem   **prō tempore**   for the time being, temporarily
- rē   **in rē**   in the matter of, concerning
- vs *or* v.   **versus**   against

- **cum laude**   with honor *(college graduation honorific, based on GPA)*

- **magnā cum laude**   with great honor *(college graduation honorific, based on GPA)*

- **per annum**   through a year, yearly
- **post mortem**   after death

CHAPTER 17

Participles
> **Tenses of the Participle**
> **Participle Uses**
> **Ablative Absolute**

So far you have learned one non-finite verb form, the infinitive ("to _____"). This chapter introduces another non-finite form, the participle. While the infinitive can be used as a noun (§39), the participle is used as an adjective, with or without a noun to modify.

84. Participles

A **participle** is a verbal adjective, so it has attributes of both an adjective and a verb:

The **barking** dog wagged its tail.	The dog **barking** at me wagged its tail.
We visited the **destroyed** city.	We visited the city **destroyed** by the storm.

Like any other adjective in Latin a participle must agree with the word it modifies in case, number and gender. But it also has tense and voice, and may take a direct object:

The dog **eating dinner** wagged its tail.

Latin participles are formed as follows:

present active participle: present stem (**amā**) + **-ns, -ntis: amāns**
  It is declined as a one-ending third declension adjective (§52 and see below).

perfect passive participle: participial stem* (**amāt**) + **-us, -a, -um: amātus**
  *the fourth principal part provides the participial stem
  It is declined as an adjective of the first and second declension like **bonus, bona, bonum** (§27).

future active participle: participial stem (**amāt**) + **-ūr** + **-us, -a, -um: amātūrus**
  It is also declined as an adjective of the first and second declension like **bonus, bona, bonum** (§27).

Here are the participle forms for each conjugation:

		Active	Passive
Present	1	amāns, amantis *(loving)*	
	2	docēns, docentis	- - - - - - - - -
	3	regēns, regentis; capiēns, capientis	
	4	audiēns, audientis	
Perfect	1		amātus, -a, -um *(having been loved)*
	2	- - - - - - - - -	doctus, -a, -um
	3		rēctus, -a, -um
	4		audītus, -a, -um
Future	1	amātūrus, -a, -um *(about to love)*	
	2	doctūrus, -a, -um	[Gerundive]
	3	rēctūrus, -a, -um	
	4	audītūrus, -a, -um	

Note:

- There is no present passive ("being _____ed") form.

- There is no perfect active ("having _____ed") form.

- The future passive ("about to be _____ed") form is called the **gerundive** and will be introduced in Chapter 29.

- **Sum** has only one participle form, the future active: **futūrus, -a, -um.**

Declension of the present active participle:

Singular	**Masc. & Fem.**	**Neuter**
Nominative	regēns	regēns
Genitive	regentis	regentis
Dative	regentī	regentī
Accusative	regentem	regēns
Ablative	regente, regentī*	regente, regentī*
Plural		
Nominative	regentēs	regentia
Genitive	regentium	regentium
Dative	regentibus	regentibus
Accusative	regentēs	regentia
Ablative	regentibus	regentibus

> **Note:**
> - When the present active participle is used as a simple adjective, it uses the **-i stem** ablative ending (**-ī**) common to third declension adjectives: **ab amantī uxōre**, *by the loving wife*
> - When it is used as a noun or is extended by an object or prepositional phrase, it uses the third declension ending common to nouns (**-e**): **ab amante**, *by a lover*; **ā fēminā aquam portante**, *by a woman carrying water*. The **-e** ending will also appear on a participle in an ablative absolute (see §87 below).

Exercise 136. Identify each of the following participles by tense, voice (present active, perfect passive, or future active), case, number and gender. Give all possibilities.

Example: audītārum   perfect passive participle; genitive, pl., *f.*

1.	victae	11.	missus
2.	condentī	12.	currēns
3.	parātā	13.	interfectus
4.	dictum	14.	rapientium
5.	captūra	15.	cantūrō
6.	festīnantem	16.	cadentī
7.	rēctūrīs	17.	patentibus
8.	scrīpta	18.	frāctōs
9.	vulnerantēs	19.	ardentis
10.	monitae	20.	vītāns

85. **Tenses of the Participle**

Sometimes the action of the participle and that of the main verb happen at different times. Participles in Latin show **time relative to the verb** with which they occur. If the action of the participle happens at the same time as that of the main verb, it is expressed in Latin by a present participle. If the action of the participle happened before that of the main verb, Latin uses a perfect participle; if the action is expected but hasn't happened yet, Latin uses a future participle.

This pattern showing the relation between the *time* of the main verb and the *tense* of the participle is very regular and predictable:

Main Verb

Before	*Same Time*	*After*

<--->

Perfect	Present	Future

Tense of the Participle

The present participle is used when the action of the participle occurs at the same time as that of the main verb:

I see him **running**   I saw him **running**   I will see him **running**

The perfect participle is used when the action of the participle has already been completed:

Having been captured, the enemy is dropping their weapons.
Having been captured, the enemy dropped their weapons.

Exercise 137. Using the verbs given below, translate **the participle form only** into Latin. Remember the case, number and gender of the participle must agree with that of the noun it modifies, and the tense of the participle should show time relative to that of the main verb.

inveniō, invenīre, invēnī, inventus	to find
misceō, miscēre, miscuī, mixtus	to disturb
spectō, spectāre, spectāvī, spectātus	to look at
trahō, -ere, trāxī, tractus	to pull

1. Her father called the girl looking at the ships.
2. The ship was overturned by winds disturbing the ocean.
3. Having been pulled out of the ocean and onto the shore, the soldier is happy.
4. Having been pulled out of the ocean and onto the shore, the soldier was tired and weak.
5. About to find his weapon, the soldier was killed.
6. We gave gifts to the citizens looking at the temple.

86. Participle Uses

- You have already seen the perfect passive participle used with different tenses of the verb **sum** to make passive indicative forms in the perfect system (§73-75), You have also seen the perfect passive participle with **esse** to form the perfect passive infinitive (§76). (The most common use of the future active participle will be with **esse** to form the future active infinitive; this use will be introduced in Chapter 19, §92b).

- Often the present active and perfect passive participles (and sometimes the future active, especially in poetry) are used, like any adjective, to modify a noun:

fēmina nōs **audiēns**	The woman **hearing** us
hostēs **captī**	The enemy **having been captured**
puer **discessūrus**	The boy **about to depart**

Latin uses participles all the time instead of the dependent Adverbial (§60) and Relative Adjectival (§64) clauses you learned in Chapters 12 and 13. Latin participles are, therefore, often best translated with a dependent clause in English. Use the context of the sentence to help you decide what kind of clause to use (*if, because, when, who,* etc.). Look at the following examples, which show several ways to translate the same participle clause:

Iuppiter omnia regēns rēx deōrum erat.

Jupiter ruling everything
Jupiter, who ruled everything,
While Jupiter ruled everything, he   } was king of the gods.
Because Jupiter ruled everything, he
As long as Jupiter ruled everything, he

Hostēs captī arma dēmīsērunt.

Having been captured, the enemy
After they were captured, the enemy
When they had been captured, the enemy   } dropped their weapons
Because they had been captured, the enemy
The enemy was captured and

Notice in the last example that the participle has actually been turned into a main verb joined to the original main clause by the conjunction "and." Check with your instructor about translating participles like this.

Exercise 138. In the following sentences, transform each participial clause into two different finite clauses in English. Do not translate into Latin.

Example: The barking dog looks at me.   The dog that is barking looks at me.
                                            The dog looks at me while it is barking.

1. People jumped off the sinking ship.
2. We visited the wounded soldier.
3. Those teaching Latin are happy.
4. The letter never having been read was lost.
5. Do you see the running child?
6. Reading this I learn many things.
7. The men picked up the fallen boxes.
8. The book written by that poet is good.

Exercise 139. Draw an arrow from the participle to the noun it modifies (write in Latin any gapped nouns/pronouns); then translate the whole sentence into English.

1. Cōnsul exercitum timēns discēdere temptat.
2. Mīles ā Gallīs vulnerātus domum vēnit.
3. In casam pecūniam inventam portāvistī.
4. Huic fēminae prō templō stantī dōnum magnum dedī.
5. Audientēs cōnsilium Rōmānī Caesarem laudāvērunt.
6. Dux victus cum mīlitibus fugiet.
7. Dīmīsit illōs virōs in agrīs dormientēs.
8. Puer epistulam legēns domī mānserat.
9. Mīles aquam portāns multa mīlia passuum ambulāvit.
10. Acceptī in urbe ab multīs amīcīs Rōmae manēre cōnstituimus.

87. Ablative Absolute

One of the most common uses of the participle is in a construction called the **ablative absolute**. As the name implies, this construction uses a participle and a noun (or pronoun) in the ablative; the construction is called "absolute" because it is grammatically unattached to the rest of the sentence (**absolūtus** = "free, unconnected"). An ablative absolute is the equivalent of a subordinate (= dependent) clause and usually explains the *time*, *cause* or *condition* of an action that is expressed in the main clause. Consider the following examples:

Subordinate Clause	Ablative Absolute
Cum dux mīlitēs vocat, hostēs fugiunt.	**Duce mīlitēs vocante,** hostēs fugiunt.
When the leader calls the soldiers, the enemy flees.	
Postquam haec verba dicta sunt, cōnsul discessīt.	**Hīs verbīs dictīs,** cōnsul discessīt.
After these words were said, the consul departed.	
Quod bellum fīnītur, omnēs gaudent.	**Bellō fīnītō,** omnēs gaudent.
Everyone rejoices because the war is finished.	
Sī ille regit, bonam fortūnam habēbimus.	**Illō regente,** bonam fortūnam habēbimus.
If that man is ruling, we will have good fortune.	

A literal translation of the ablative absolute can be useful as an intermediate step, but should not, in most cases, be your final translation.

Duce mīlitēs vocante	With the leader calling the soldiers, ...
Hīs verbīs dictīs	With these words having been spoken, ...
Bellō fīnītō	With the war (having been) finished, ...
Illō regente	With that man ruling, ...

Note: Since the verb **sum** has no present participle, an ablative absolute with a linking pattern will consist of only the noun and its subject complement, both in the ablative case:

Caesare duce	With Caesar being leader, When Caesar was leader
secundō diē	Since the day was favorable

Exercise 140. Translate the ablatives absolute below into English, giving the literal and then a more colloquial translation.

Example: puellā missā   with the girl having been sent; after (since, when) the girl was sent

1. omnibus parātīs
2. puerīs canentibus
3. hostibus victīs
4. mātre puerōs vocante
5. cōnsulibus ā populō creātīs
6. Caesare interfectō
7. pāce factā
8. illīs iūssīs
9. annīs volventibus
10. hīs rēbus gestīs

Exercise 141. In the following sentences, transform each dependent clause into an ablative absolute and then translate the sentence.

1. Dum Rōmam exercitus venit, paucī fūgimus.
2. Sī potēns cīvitās est omnēs laetī sunt.
3. Fēminae puellaeque dum hominēs pugnant in urbe manēbant.
4. Cum clāmōrēs turbae audītī sunt, ad montēs cucurristis.
5. Quod Gallia magna erat, mīlitēs multōs diēs ambulābant.
6. Ubi urbs ab hostibus capta erit, omnēs interficiēmur.

Exercise 142. Translate each of the following sentences.

1. Dominō interfectō servus ab urbe cucurrit.
2. Nostrī mīlitēs in hostēs, signō datō, impetum fēcērunt.
3. Crīmine inventō, uterque indignus in iūdicium sextā diē ductus est.
4. Caesar Rōmam virōs captōs dūxit.
5. Moenibus patentibus, equus magnus in urbem Trōiae trahēbātur.
6. Illō duce, nihil timēbimus.
7. Turbā spectante, prīnceps ipse cīvibus persuādēre temptābat.
8. Caesare in Galliā pugnante ducem novum senātus lēgit.
9. Nautae nāvigāre parantēs opēs multās accēpērunt.
10. Propter sua carmina ille poēta Rōmae canēbat.

Exercise 143. Translate into Latin, using participles where possible.

1. When their father walked into the field, the boys began to work.
2. The slave, since he loved his master, came with him to Rome.
3. About to tell a story, the father sat among the boys and girls.
4. Although (their) homes had been burned, the citizens desired to remain in the countryside.
5. The leader, seeing the river, hesitated to pitch camp in that place.
6. After his father was killed, the boy grieved for many days.
7. The doubting man sought the truth from the gods.
8. His name, given to him by the soldiers, was discovered by all.
9. Much money was given to the people of that city when Caesar came home from Gaul.
10. After the letter from her son was received, (his) mother began to sing.

Reading 22 *(adapted)*

Livy continues the story of how the Romans and Albans decided to settle their war through a battle fought by two sets of triplets. Two of the Horatii have been killed, but Horatius remains to fight the three Curiatii.

Ūnus ex Horātiīs integer fuit et contrā trēs Curiātiōs stetit. Quia **sēgregāre pugnam** eōrum optābat, cēpit **fugam**. Iam aliquantum **spatiī** ex eō locō ubi pugnāverant fūgerat, cum respiciēns videt eōs magnīs **intervallīs** currentēs; ūnus haud procul ab sēsē abest. In eum magnō impetū rediit; et dum Albānus exercitus clāmat Curiātiīs, iam Horātius caesō hoste **victor** secundam **pugnam** petēbat. Tunc clāmōre Rōmānī adiuvant mīlitem suum, et ille optāns fīnīre proelium festīnat. Antequam alter, quī nōn procul aberat, venīre poterat, alterum Curiātium cōnficit; iamque duo mīlitēs mānsērunt, sed nec spē nec vīribus parēs. alter intāctum ferrō corpus et duās **victoriās** habēbat, alter, fessum vulnere, fessum cursū trahēns corpus, obicitur hostī. Nec illud proelium fuit. Rōmānus **exsultāns** 'duōs' dīxit, 'frātrum Manibus dedī; tertium causae bellī huius dabō.' Postquam Horātius tertium cecīdit, Rōmānī eum accipiunt magnō cum gaudiō.

Vocabulary:

integer, -gra, -grum	unhurt; whole	victor, -ōris *m.*	victor
sēgregō, -āre	to separate, divide	adiuvō, -āre	to help, encourage
pugna, -ae *f.*	fight, attack		
fuga, -ae *f.*	flight	viribus (abl.)	strength
aliquantus, -a, -um	considerable (amount)	intāctus, -a, -um	unhurt, untouched
spatium, -iī *n.*	space, distance	victōria, -ae, *f.*	victory
respiciō, -ere	to look back	cursus, -ūs, *m.*	running
intervallum, -ī *n*	interval	obiciō, -ere	to expose to (*with* dat.)
haud (adv.)	by no means		
procul (adv.)	far, at a distance	exsultō, -āre	to exult, boast
redeō, -īre, -iī	to go back	Manēs, -ium *m.* (pl.)	Shades, spirits of the dead
caedō, -ere, cecīdī, caesus	to kill		

Practice Sentences

Identify the case and use of the underlined words, then translate.

1. Caesar, acceptīs <u>litterīs</u>, nūntium mittit. (Caesar)
2. Omnibus <u>rēbus</u> comparātīs diem dīcunt. (Caesar)
3. **Invādunt** urbem somnō <u>vīnō</u>que sepultam; caeduntur vigilēs, portīsque patentibus omnīs accipiunt sociōs. (Vergil; *describing the fall of Troy*)
4. …; multōsque per annōs errābant, <u>āctī</u> fātīs, maria omnia circum. (Vergil; *describing the Trojans traveling from Troy to Italy*)
5. <u>Mē</u> duce carpe viam. (Ovid; *Daedalus advises his son to follow him*)
6. Hīs dictīs incēnsō animum inflammāvit amore spemque dedit dubiae <u>mentī</u>. (Vergil; *Queen Dido's sister encourages her amorous feelings for Aeneas*)
7. Ille nūntiō audītō senātum vocāvit. (Cicero – adapted; *Marcus Antonius ("ille") arranges to accuse Caesar of being an enemy to the state*)
8. Germānī post tergum clāmōre audītō, <u>signīs</u> relictīs ex castrīs fūgērunt. (Caesar – adapted; *German soldiers flee when they hear the Romans killing their countrymen*)

Vocabulary:

comparō, -āre, -āvī, -ātus	to prepare	omnīs = omnēs	
invādō, -ere	to invade	carpō, -ere	to pick
sepeliō, -īre, īvī, sepultus	to bury	inflammō, -āre, -āvī	to inflame, set on fire
caedō, -ere	to kill, slaughter	dubius, -a, -um	wavering, uncertain
vigilēs, -um *m.* (pl.)	guards	Germānī, -ōrum *m.* (pl.)	Germans
porta, -ae *f.*	gate, entrance	tergum,-ī *n.*	back

Chapter 17 Vocabulary

Nouns

amor, amōris *m.*	love
Caesar, Caesaris *m.*	Julius Caesar (a Roman general)
castra, castrōrum *n.* (pl.)	camp
castra ponere	to pitch camp
clāmor, clāmōris *m.*	shout; cheer
crīmen, crīminis *n.*	crime; accusation, charge
fātum, fātī *n.*	fate, destiny
ferrum, ferrī *n.*	iron; sword
gaudium, gaudiī *n.*	joy, delight
nūntius, nūntiī, *m.*	messenger; message
prīnceps, prīncipis *m.*	leader, chief; first citizen, emperor
servus, servī *m.*	slave, servant
signum, signī *n.*	sign, token, signal; (military) standard
vīnum, vīnī *n.*	wine
vulnus, vulneris *n.*	wound

Verbs

interficiō, interficere, interfēcī, interfectus	to kill, destroy
canō, canere, cecinī, cantus	to sing
pateō, patēre, patuī	to be open, stand open
persuādeō, persuādēre, persuāsī, persuāsus (+ dat.)	to persuade
vulnerō, vulnerāre, vulnerāvī, vulnerātus	to wound
temptō, temptāre, temptāvī, temptātus	to try, attempt; test, prove

Subordinating Conjunction

quamquam	although

(21)

Derivatives: For each English word below, give the Latin word from the Chapter 17 Vocabulary to which it is related and the English word's meaning.

1. announce
2. invulnerable
3. servile
4. paramour
5. attempt
6. gaudy
7. patent
8. vintage
9. exclaim
10. signet

CHAPTER 18

Dependent Clauses (3)
     Noun Use: Relative Clause
Interrogative Pronoun: quis, quid
Interrogative Adjective: quī, quae, quod
Intensive Pronouns: īdem; ipse

So far you have learned about relative adjectival clauses, which modify an antecedent in the main clause (§64). This chapter introduces relative noun clauses, sometimes called "indefinite" clauses because they have no antecedent. It also introduces two new pronouns and an adjective, which follow declension patterns you have already learned.

88. **Dependent Clauses: Noun Use—Relative Clause**

Just as a regular adjective can be used as a substantive, without an accompanying noun, (§29), so too the antecedent of a relative clause may not always be expressed. In this situation, the relative clause itself functions as a noun in the main clause. Compare the examples below.

As a Subject
Vir est fortis.   The **man** is strong.
Quī in agrō labōrat fortis est.   **Whoever/He who works in the field** is strong.

As a Direct Object
Fortēs laudāmus.   We praise the **brave (men)**.
Quōs Caesar amāvit laudāmus.   We praise **those whom Caesar loved**.

When the relative clause has no expressed antecedent, it is often called an **indefinite relative clause**. When you translate the clause into English, you will need to supply an antecedent (he who ... / those who ...) or use the English indefinite form (whoever ...).

Exercise 144. Bracket the relative clauses in the following sentences and identify each as adjectival or noun. Then translate.

1. Cōnsul cui erant ingentēs oculī nōn pulcher erat.
2. Quī semper vēritātem dīxit laudāvimus.
3. Capiēturne quī hoc scelus fēcit ab mīlitibus?
4. Caelum in quō ventī nūbēs agunt spectāmus.
5. Nautae quōrum nāvis frangitur sunt fortēs.
6. Quī hās nāvēs aedificāvit artem magnam habet, sed pecūniā caret.

89a. **The Interrogative Pronoun: quis, quid**

The **interrogative pronoun** asks the question "who?" or "what?". It occurs more commonly in the singular, where the masculine and feminine forms are the same. The plural forms are identical to those of the relative pronoun, with the masculine and feminine endings distinct from each other.

Singular	Masc. & Fem.		Neuter	
Nominative	quis	who?	quid	what?
Genitive	cuius	of whom?, whose?	cuius	of what?
Dative	cui	to/for whom?	cui	to/for what?
Accusative	quem	whom?	quid	what?
Ablative	quō	(by/with…) whom?	quō	(by/with…) what?

Plural	Masculine	Feminine	Neuter
Nominative	quī	quae	quae
Genitive	quōrum	quārum	quōrum
Dative	quibus	quibus	quibus
Accusative	quōs	quās	quae
Ablative	quibus	quibus	quibus

Exercise 145. Translate the underlined word(s) in each sentence with the correct Latin form. Use the singular form unless plural is indicated.

1. <u>Whose</u> wine is this?
2. <u>What</u> are you doing?
3. <u>To whom</u> (pl.) are you talking?
4. <u>With what</u> will you write?
5. <u>Who</u> let the dogs out?
6. <u>Whom</u> (pl.) of the men do you choose?

Exercise 146. Identify the case, number and use of each interrogative pronoun below. Then translate the questions and their answers.

1. Quid nautīs nocet?   Ventus.
2. Quid aedificābit?   Casam.
3. Ad quem veniēmus?   Ad tē.
4. Cuius carmina audīs?   Huius poētae.
5. Quōs vincēbātis?   Mīlitēs.
6. Quae tibi dedī?   Pulchra dōna.

89b. **The Interrogative Adjective: quī, quae, quod**

The interrogative adjective looks exactly like the relative pronoun (§63). It modifies a noun and asks the question "which _____?" "what _____?". See the following examples.

Quī vir est fortis?	**Which man** is brave?
Quem virum vulnerāvistī?	**Which man** did you wound?
Quae nāvis frācta est?	**Which ship** was wrecked?
Cui puellae carmen illud dedit?	**To which girl** did he give that poem?
Quibus armīs mīlitēs interfectī sunt?	**With which weapons** were the soldiers killed?

Exercise 147. Identify each interrogative as a pronoun or adjective; if it is an adjective, draw an arrow to the noun it modifies. Then translate the whole sentence.

1. Quī erant ducēs?
2. Quī vir illōs mīlitēs ducit?
3. Quās spēs Rōmānī ducibus habuērunt?
4. Cuius ferrum in agrīs āmittēbātur?
5. Quod scelus Rōmae factum est?
6. Quibuscum multōs annōs bellum Caesar gerēbat?

90. Intensive Pronouns: ipse; īdem

Intensive pronouns, like the other demonstrative pronouns **hic, ille** (§50) and **is** (§46), can be used either in place of nouns or as adjectival modifiers, which agree in case, number and gender with a noun. They are used to emphasize a noun (or pronoun).

Ipse (except for the nom. sg. masc. form) is declined exactly like the irregular adjectives you learned in Chapter 11. The "odd" genitive and dative singular forms are in bold below.

ipse, ipsa, ipsum _____self, himself, herself, itself, themselves; very

Singular	Masculine	Feminine	Neuter
Nominative	ipse	ipsa	ipsum
Genitive	**ipsīus**	**ipsīus**	**ipsīus**
Dative	**ipsī**	**ipsī**	**ipsī**
Accusative	ipsum	ipsam	ipsum
Ablative	ipsō	ipsā	ipsō
Plural			
Nominative	ipsī	ipsae	ipsa
Genitive	ipsōrum	ipsārum	ipsōrum
Dative	ipsīs	ipsīs	ipsīs
Accusative	ipsōs	ipsās	ipsa
Ablative	ipsīs	ipsīs	ipsīs

Because **ipse, ipsa, ipsum** may refer to a man, woman, thing, or even a pronoun, its English definition will vary according to the context. Compare the following examples:

Caesar ipse mīlitēs dūcet.	**Caesar himself** will lead the soldiers.
Ipse mīlitēs dūxī.	**I myself** led the soldiers.
Tē ipsum laudāmus.	We praise **you yourself**.
Mīlitēs ipsōs laudāvimus.	We praised **the soldiers themselves**.

It is especially important not to confuse **ipse** with the reflexive pronoun (§65). Compare the following examples:

Servus **sē** videt.	The slave sees **himself**.
Servus **ipse** signum videt.	The slave **himself** sees the signal.
Servus **ipsum** signum videt.	The slave sees the signal **itself**.

īdem is a compound of **is, ea, id** (§46). The bold forms below show where letter changes have occurred, probably for ease of pronunciation: **eum + dem = eundem**, **is + dem = īdem**.

īdem, eadem, idem   **the same**

Singular	Masculine	Feminine	Neuter
Nominative	**īdem**	eadem	idem
Genitive	eiusdem	eiusdem	eiusdem
Dative	eīdem	eīdem	eīdem
Accusative	**eundem**	**eandem**	idem
Ablative	eōdem	eādem	eōdem
Plural			
Nominative	eīdem	eaedem	eadem
Genitive	**eōrundem**	**eārundem**	**eōrundem**
Dative	eīsdem	eīsdem	eīsdem
Accusative	eōsdem	eāsdem	eadem
Ablative	eīsdem	eīsdem	eīsdem

Exercise 148. Translate the following.

1. We teach ourselves.
2. We ourselves are women.
3. They themselves obey the same laws.
4. I will come to the citadel itself today.
5. You (sg.) should fear nothing but fear itself.
6. Exercitus Caesaris ipsīus fūgit.
7. Urbī ipsī magna moenia erant.
8. Vōs ipsōs pugnāre dubitāvērunt.
9. Dūxistīne ipse illōs?
10. Mōs īdem nobīs ipsīs est.

Exercise 149. Translate each of the following sentences.

1. Paucī Trōiānōrum suās nāvēs incendērunt.
2. Quid cognōvistī postquam epistulam prīncipis ipsīus accēpistī?
3. Quī dolōre caret fēlīx est, nam nātūra mortālibus mala saepe facit.
4. Lēgātus cuius equus ab amīcō tenēbātur Rōmam ambulāvit.
5. Quī tibi persuadēbunt? Cui credēs?
6. In quā arce illud aurum inventum est?
7. Quibus librōs dedistī quōs scrīpseram?
8. Prīmā lūce mīlitēs ad eundem locum ubi aciēs prīma cecīderat cucurrērunt.
9. Eadem vōx quae inter hominēs saepe audīta erat nunc tacuit.
10. Ō cīvēs, quae fāta effēcērunt, cum gaudiō accipere temptāte.

Exercise 150. Translate into Latin.

1. The world itself is large and full of many customs.
2. We praise the same girls who found the gold.
3. Human beings can not avoid what the gods bring about.
4. The farmers by whom the house was being built were Greek.
5. Because of the heat, the same army, which walked many miles during the night, will remain at home today.
6. Who is worthy of his own father?
7. After a difficult journey on foot, the army pitched camp between those very mountains.
8. The old man with whom we used to sail did not like [*use* **āmō**] the heat.
9. Her brother, whom we left in the country, had always been faithful to the state.
10. We were pleased by the arrival of both delegates to whom we had given the same message.

Reading 23 *(adapted)*

Caesar describes a disaster at sea with his transport ships.

Hīs rēbus pāce **cōnfirmātā**, diē quartō postquam in **Britanniam** vēnimus, nāvēs XVIII, quae equitēs sustulerant, ex **portū** levī ventō navigāvērunt. cum adpropinquābant Britanniae et ex castrīs vidērentur, magna tempestās subitō coorta est et nūlla eārum cursum tenēre potuit.

continued

Vocabulary:

cōnfirmō, -āre, -āvī -ātus	to confirm, ratify	portus, -ūs *m.*	port, harbor
		adpropinquō, -āre	to approach
Britannia, -ae *f.*	Britain	coorta est	"arose, appeared"
eques, equitis *m.*	horseman	cursus, -ūs *m.*	course, direction
tollō, -ere, sustulī	to carry, transport		

continued

Eādem nocte cum erat lūna plēna, is diēs, quī **maritimōs** aestūs maximōs in **ōceanō** efficere cōnsuēvit, vēnit nostrīsque id erat **incognitum**. ita ūnō tempore et longās nāvēs, quibus Caesar exercitum trānsportāverat quāsque in **āridum** subdūxerat, aestus complēbat, et eās <nāvēs>, quae ad **ancorās** erant dēligātae, tempestās adflictābat, neque ūllum nostrīs auxilium dabātur. multīs nāvibus frāctīs, reliquae, fūnibus, **ancorīs**, reliquīsque armāmentīs āmīssīs, nāvigāre nōn poterant. magna, id quod **necesse** erat, tōtīus exercitūs perturbātiō facta est. neque enim nāvēs erant aliae, quibus portārī poterant.

Vocabulary:

maritimus, -a, -um	of the sea, marine	dēligō, -āre, -āvī, -ātus	to fasten
maximus, -a, -um	greatest, very big		
ōceanus, -ī *m.*	ocean	adflictō, -āre, -āvī	to knock about
cōnsuēscō, -ere, -ēvī (+ inf.)	to be accustomed (to), usually ___	fūnis, -is *m.*	rope
incognitus, -a, -um	unknown	armāmenta, -ōrum *n.* (pl.)	equipment
āridum, -ī *n.*	dry land		
subdūcō, -ere, -dūxī	to pull up, haul	necesse (adv.)	necessary, inevitable
compleō, -ēre, -ēvī	to fill	perturbātiō, -iōnis *f.*	disturbance, commotion
ancora, -ae *f.*	anchor		

Reading 24 (adapted)

In this selection Ovid adopts the voice of a lover chiding his girlfriend, Corinna. She has bleached her hair and it is now falling out.

Dīcēbam, "Medicāre tuōs **dēsiste** capillōs!"
    tingere quam potes, iam tibi nūlla coma est.
Cui est coma tam longa, tam pulchra?
nec tamen āter erat neque erat tamen aureus ille
    sed, quamvīs neuter, mixtus uterque **color**.
Adde quod et docilēs et centum flexibus aptī
    et tibi nūllīus causa dolōris erant.
quam sē praebuērunt ferrō **patienter** et ignī,
    clāmābam: "scelus est illōs, scelus ūrere crīnēs!"
Nunc tibi **captīvōs** mittet Germānia crīnēs.
    tūta triumphatae munere gentis eris.
Saepe comās aliquō laudante, rubēbis
    et dīcēs, "ēmptā nunc ego merce laudar!"

Vocabulary:

tingō, -ere	to dye	quam (adv.)	how
medicō, -āre	to treat	patienter (adv.)	patiently
(complementary inf.)		ūrō, -ere	to burn, scorch
dēsistō, -ere	to stop	crīnis, -is *m.*	hair
capillus, -ī *m.*	(a single) hair	captīvus, -a, -um	captive, of
coma, -ae *f.*	hair		captives
tam (adv.)	so	Germānia, -ae *f.*	Germany
āter, ātra, ātrum	black, dark	tūtus, -a, -um	safe
quamvīs	although	triumphatae	"conquered"
mixtus	= mixtus est	munus, -eris *n.*	gift
color, -ōris *m.*	color	aliquis, aliquid	someone,
adde quod	"and besides"		something
docilis, -e	manageable	rubeō, -ēre	to blush
flexus, -ūs *m.*	"style"	ēmptus, -a, -um	bought
		merx, mercis *f.*	merchandise – *i.e.* a wig – (§53 abl. of cause)

Practice Sentences

Identify the case and use of the underlined words, then translate.

1. Nam quis <u>hoc</u> nōn intellegit? Quis hoc nōn perspicit? — (Cicero; *prosecuting a former proconsul for flagrant abuses*)
2. Frangitur ipsa suīs Rōma superba <u>bonīs</u>. — (Propertius)
3. <u>Quis</u> est quī mē vocat? — (Plautus)
4. Quid ab hīs tot maleficiīs <u>sceleris</u> abesse vidētur? — (Cicero; *defending a man charged with parricide, Cicero talks about the many crimes of the accusers*)
5. Stultum est timēre <u>quod</u> vītārī nōn potest. — (Publilius Syrus)
6. <u>Quī</u> hoc dicunt videntur mihi errāre. — (Seneca)
7. Ante mare et terrās et quod tegit omnia caelum ūnus erat tōtō nātūrae vultus in orbe, <u>quem</u> dīxēre "chaos". — (Ovid; *describing the very beginning of the universe*)
8. Sed Caesar <u>lēgī</u> pāruit ipse suae; — lex erat. — (Martial; *two evenly-matched gladiators fight, and the crowd wants both to be released, but that would be against the rules*)

Vocabulary:

intellegō, -ere	to understand	maleficium, -iī *n.*	wrong,
perspiciō, -ere	to see through, observe		misdeed
superbus, -a, -um	proud	stultus, -a, -um	stupid
		tegō, -ere	to cover

Chapter 18 Vocabulary

Nouns

adventus, adventūs *m.*	arrival
aestus, aestūs *m.*	heat; tide
*arx, arcis *f.*	citadel, summit
aurum, aurī *n.*	gold
auxilium, auxiliī *n.*	aid, help; *in pl. often* auxiliary troops
mōs, mōris *m.*	custom, tradition
*orbis, orbis *m.*	circle; universe
orbis terrārum	the world
scelus, sceleris *n.*	crime, wicked deed, wickedness
senex, senis *m.*	old man
vōx, vōcis *f.*	voice

Verbs

cognōscō, cognōscere, cognōvī cognitus	to learn, recognize, understand
efficiō, efficere, effēcī, effectus	to bring about, produce

Adjectives

aureus, aurea, aureum	golden, of gold
Graecus, Graeca, Graecum	Greek
levis, leve	light, easy; swift
quī, quae, quod	which _____?, what _____?
tot	so many, as many

Pronouns

īdem, eadem, idem	the same
ipse, ipsa, ipsum	_____self; himself, herself, itself, themselves; very
quis, quid	who?, what?

(20)

Derivatives: For each English word below, give the Latin word from the Chapter 18 Vocabulary to which it is related and the English word's meaning.

1.	auxiliary		6.	orbit
2.	mores		7.	effect
3.	cognitive		8.	adventure
4.	aleve		9.	vociferous
5.	senile		10.	auriferous

CHAPTER 19

Infinitive Forms
    Perfect Active Infinitive
    Future Active Infinitive
    Review of All Infinitive Forms
Noun Clause: Indirect Statement
    Tenses of the Infinitive in Indirect Statement

This chapter provides a review of the infinitive forms you have already learned and introduces the perfect and future active infinitives. It also introduces an infinitive noun clause called the indirect statement.

91. **Infinitive Forms**

In previous chapters you have learned the regular Present Active (§5, 45), Passive (§70) and Perfect Passive (§76) infinitive forms. The two new forms of the infinitive follow the patterns you have already seen.

91a. **Perfect Active Infinitive**

The **perfect active infinitive** is formed by adding **-isse** to the perfect stem in each conjugation:

Conjugation		
First	amā**visse**	to have loved
Second	monu**isse**	to have advised
Third	rēx**isse**	to have ruled
Fourth	audī**visse**	to have heard

91b. **Future Active Infinitive**

The **future active infinitive** is formed by combining the future active participle with the infinitive of **sum**:

Conjugation		
First	amātūrus (-a, -um) esse	to be about to love
Second	monitūrus (-a, -um) esse	to be about to advise
Third	rēctūrus (-a, -um) esse	to be about to rule
Fourth	audītūrus (-a, -um) esse	to be about to hear

91c. Review of all Infinitive Forms

The formation of infinitives is very regular and therefore predictable:

present active infinitive	= present stem + **-re:**	**amāre**
present passive infinitive	= present stem + **-rī:**	**amārī**
(except third conj.)	> present stem + **-ī:**	**capī**
perfect active infinitive	= perfect stem + **-isse:**	**amāvisse**
perfect passive infinitive	= participial stem* + **-us, -a, -um** + **esse: amātus esse**	

* the fourth principal part provides the participial stem

future active infinitive =   participial stem + **-ūr** + **-us, -a, -um** + **esse: amātūrus esse**

The future passive infinitive is very rare and its form is given in the chart of endings below only for reference.

Summary of infinitive endings:

	Active		Passive	
Present	-re	to _____	-rī (-ī)	to be _____ed
Perfect	-isse	to have _____ed	-us esse*	to have been _____ed
Future	-ūrus esse*	to be about to _____	[-um īrī]	[to be about to be _____ed]

> **Note: esse** is sometimes omitted from the infinitive in these forms. When this happens, the infinitive looks like a participle and it is necessary to depend on the context to decide whether the form is a participle or infinitive.

Here is a review of the infinitive forms for each conjugation:

		Active			Passive
Present	1	amāre	1	amārī	
	2	monēre	2	monērī	
	3	regere	3	regī	
	4	audīre	4	audīrī	
Perfect	1	amāvisse	1	amātus (-a, -um) esse	
	2	monuisse	2	monitus (-a, -um) esse	
	3	rēxisse	3	rēctus (-a, -um) esse	
	4	audīvisse	4	audītus (-a, -um) esse	
Future	1	amātūrus (-a, -um) esse			
	2	doctūrus (-a, -um) esse			‒ ‒ ‒ ‒ ‒ ‒ ‒ ‒
	3	rēctūrus (-a, -um) esse			
	4	audītūrus (-a, -um) esse			

The infinitives of **sum** and **possum** are:

Present	esse	posse
Perfect	fuisse	potuisse
Future	futūrus esse *or* fore	-------

Exercise 151. Write the principal parts and give all the infinitive forms (except the future passive) for the following verbs:

1. vītō
2. pōnō
3. iubeō
4. capiō

5. caedō
6. inveniō
7. dīcō
8. spērō

92. **Noun Clause: Indirect Statement**

A dependent noun clause with an infinitive verb and accusative subject can be expected with verbs of saying, thinking, and perceiving. This clause is called an **indirect statement** (sometimes also indirect discourse, or *ōrātiō oblīqua*). Unlike the other dependent clauses you have learned, an indirect statement has no clause marker in Latin. To recognize this construction, therefore, you need to recognize the presence of these three elements:

- infinitive
- accusative subject of the infinitive
- main verb of saying, thinking, perceiving (some people call these verbs of mental action "head" verbs)

Although Latin indirect statements use a non-finite verb (the infinitive), they are often best translated by a finite clause in English, with or without the clause marker "that":

Videt **tē manēre**.	He sees **(that) you are staying**.
Gaudent **nōs venīre**.	They are glad **(that) we are coming**.
Crēdimus **eōs pugnāre**.	We believe **(that) they are fighting**.
Caesar respondit **sē ventūrum esse**.	Caesar replied **that he (Caesar) would come.**

> **Note:**
> - If the perfect passive or future active infinitive is used in an indirect statement, the participle ending must agree with the subject of the infinitive in case (accusative), number, and gender.
> - The reflexive pronoun (**sē**) in indirect statement typically refers to the subject of the main (governing) verb.

Here are some verbs that may be followed by an indirect statement:

Verbs of saying, speaking, telling:

ait, aiunt; āiō	he says, they say; I say
dīcō, dīcere, dīxī, dictus	to say
moneō, monēre, monuī, monitus	to warn, advise
nārrō, nārrāre, nārrāvī, nārrātus	to tell
negō, negāre, negāvī, negātus	to deny, say that … not
nūntiō, nūntiāre, nūntiāvī, nūntiātus	to announce, report
respondeō, respondēre, respondī, respōnsus	to answer, reply
trādō, trādere, trādidī, trāditus	to report

Verbs of thinking:

cōgitō, cōgitāre, cōgitāvī, cōgitātus	to think
iūdicō, iūdicāre, iūdicāvī, iūdicātus	to judge, decide
putō, putāre, putāvī, putātus	to think, consider
spērō, spērāre, spērāvī, spērātus	to hope

Verbs of knowing, believing:

cognōscō, cognōscere, cognōvī, cognitus	to know, recognize, understand
crēdō, crēdere, crēdidī, crēditus	to believe
nesciō, nescīre, nescīvī, nescītus	not to know
sciō, scīre, scīvī, scītus	to know

Verbs of perceiving:

audiō, audīre, audīvī *or* audiī, audītus	to hear
cernō, cernere, crēvī, crētus	to see, discern, perceive, decide
intellegō, intellegere, intellēxī, intellēctus	to understand, perceive, realize
sentiō, sentīre, sēnsī, sēnsus	to feel, perceive
videō, vidēre, vīdī, vīsus	to see

Others:

gaudeō, gaudēre, gāvīsus sum	to rejoice, be glad
ostendō, ostendere, ostendī, ostentus/ostēnsus	to show, reveal
scrībō, scrībere, scrīpsī, scrīptus	to write

Exercise 152. Translate each of the following into Latin.

1. I say that all men love the gods.
2. He writes that we are coming.
3. The leaders know the men are brave.
4. We see that those boys are running.
5. Do you think the ship is being wrecked?
6. The messenger announces that the king is preparing to rule.

93. **Tenses of the Infinitive in Indirect Statement**

Sometimes the action of the infinitive and that of the main verb happen at different times. Latin uses the same pattern of tenses for the infinitive that you learned with participles (§85). In all the sentences from Exercise 152, the action of the infinitive happens at the same time as that of the main verb and is expressed in Latin by a present infinitive. If the action of the infinitive happened before that of the main verb, Latin uses a perfect infinitive; if the action is expected, but hasn't happened yet, Latin uses a future infinitive.

This pattern showing the relation between the *time* of the main verb and the *tense* of the infinitive is very regular and predictable:

Main Verb

Before	*Same Time*	*After*
<- ->		
Perfect	Present	Future

Tense of the Participle

Study the following examples:

Time of Main Verb			Action of Infinitive
Present	Dīcō eum **vēnisse**.	I say that he came.	*already happened*
	Dīcō eum **venīre**.	I say that he is coming.	*same time*
	Dīcō eum **ventūrum esse**.	I say that he will come.	*hasn't happened yet*
Past	Dīxī eum **vēnisse**.	I said that he had come.	*already happened*
	Dīxī eum **venīre**.	I said that he was coming.	*same time*
	Dīxī eum **ventūrum esse**.	I said that he would come.	*hasn't happened yet*

Exercise 153. Translate each of the following into Latin

1. We say that all men used to love the gods.
2. He says that all men will love the gods.
3. They said that all men used to love (= had loved) the gods.
4. She said that all men would love the gods.
5. You (sg.) deny that the war was fought there.
6. I denied that the war had been fought there.
7. He answered that the women would take the water.
8. He answered that the women were being taken.
9. He answered that the men had been taken.
10. They thought the citizens were appointing a new leader.
11. Do you think the leaders are ruling well?
12. He thinks that he will rule well.
13. The envoy believes that we are burning the city.
14. The envoy believed that you (pl.) were burning the city.
15. The enemy will report that they burned the city.

Exercise 154. Translate each of the following sentences.

1. Nūntius ipse nōs timēre cernit?
2. Lēgātī dīxērunt hostēs urbem trādidisse.
3. Servus negāvit sē dominum suum interfēcisse.
4. Epistula senātuī nūntiāvit Galliam ā Caesare superātam esse.
5. Senēs spērant līberōs mātrēs patrēsque audītūrōs esse.
6. Caesar ante dīxit sē ducem cōpiīs fore.*
7. Putant id esse dolum, sed nōn est.
8. Poēta dīcēbat montēs verbīs suīs mōtōs esse.
9. Intellegō ratiōnem mentem sed gaudium timōremque pectus regere.
10. Scīvistīne caedem aciēī illīus factūram esse?

* see §91c

Exercise 155. Translate into Latin.

1. The boy's father said he was brave, but had a loud voice.
2. The god of the sea says he will help the Roman sailors.
3. After he read our letter, (our) son wrote that he would come home in three days.
4. The emperor revealed that he had great wealth and much gold.
5. The farmer, whose house had been burned by the soldiers, desires to build a new house.
6. Children should be seen and not heard.
7. Before the enemy attacked, the people believed the gods would help them.
8. I know that you (sg.) listened to the plan of the consuls before.
9. Did the messenger report that the consuls had been called to Rome?
10. The poet wrote that the winds were swift but the ocean itself calm.

Reading 25 *(adapted)*

Cornelius Nepos (c. 99-24 B.C.) writes about Themistocles' trip to Asia, preferring the Greek historian Thucydides as a source about whether Themistocles made the trip during the reign of the Persian ruler Xerxes or Artaxerxes.

Sciō multōs scrīpsisse Themistoclēn Xerxē **rēgnante** in **Asiam** trānsisse. Sed egō potissimum Thūcydidī crēdō, quod aetāte proximus dē iīs, quī illōrum tempōrum **historiam** relīquērunt, et eiusdem cīvitātis fuit. Is ait ad Artaxerxēn eum vēnisse atque hīs verbīs epistulam mīsisse: Themistoclēs vēnī ad tē, quī plūrima mala omnium Graecōrum in domum tuam intulī quam diū mihi necesse fuit adversum patrem tuum **bellāre** patriamque meam **dēfendere**.

Vocabulary:

Themistoclēs, -is *m.* Themistoclēs		iīs = eīs	
Themistoclēn (*Greek acc. form*)		historia, -ae *f.*	history
Xerxēs, -is *m.*	Xerxes	Artaxerxēn	Artaxerxes
rēgnō, -āre	to reign, to rule	*Greek acc. form*	
Asia, -ae *f.*	Asia	plūrimus, -a, -um	most
trānseō, trānsīre, trānsiī	to cross, go across	īnferō, īnferre, intulī	to bring
potissimum (adv.)	above all, chiefly	quam diū	as long as
Thūcydidēs, -is *m.*	Thucydides	adversum (+ acc.)	against
proximus, -a, -um	closest, nearest	bellō, -āre	to fight a war
dē (+ abl.)	among	dēfendō, -ere	to defend

Reading 26 *(adapted)*

Livy tells how the Romans, under the leadership of Scipio, capture the city of New Carthage, a settlement established by the Carthaginians in Spain. Mago is the Carthaginian commander (and the brother of Hannibal).

inde [Scipiō], cum fugientēs vīdit hostēs, aliōs ad tumulum, quī tenēbātur D mīlitum praesidiō, aliōs in arcem, in quam et ipse Māgo cum omnibus ferē **armātīs** quī mūrīs pulsī fuerant, refūgerat, partem cōpiārum ad tumulum mittit, partem ipse ad arcem dūcit. et tumulus prīmō impetū est captus, et Māgo arcem temptāvit **dēfendere**, sed cum omnia hostium plēna vīdit neque spem ūllam esse, sē arcemque et praesidium dēdidit. quia dēdita arx est, caedēs tōtā urbe passim factae sunt et omnis pūbēs quī obvius fuit interficiēbātur; tum signō datō caedibus fīnis factus est et ad praedam **victōrēs** versī sunt, quae ingēns fuit. inde quī cīvēs Novae Carthāginis erant dīmīsit urbemque et sua omnia restituit.

Vocabulary:

tumulus, -ī *m.*	hill	dēfendō, -ere	to defend
Māgo, -ōnis *m.*	Mago	dēdō, -ere, -idī, -itus	to surrender
praesidium, -ī *n.*	garrison	passim	here and there
armō, -āre, -āvī, -ātus	to arm, equip	pūbēs, puberis	adult
ferē (adv.)	almost	obvius, -a, -um	at hand, in the way
mūrus, -ī *m.*	wall	victor, -ōris *m.*	victor
pellō, -ere, -pulsus	to drive back	Carthāgō, -inis *f.*	Carthage
refugiō, -ere, rēfūgī	to take refuge	dīmittō, -ere, -mīsī	to let go, send away
		restituō, -ere	to restore, give back

Practice Sentences

Identify the form and use of the underlined words, then translate.

1. Tamen putābat ... causam calumniae <u>sē</u> repertūrum [esse]. — (Cicero; *explaining one of Verres' schemes*)

2. "Omnēs" inquit "iūrant esse mē Iovis <u>filium</u>, sed vulnus hoc hominem esse mē clāmat" — (Seneca; *quoting Alexander*)

3. Lāocoōn ardēns summā **dēcurrit** ab arce, et procul: "ō miserī, quae tanta **insānia**, cīvēs? Crēditis āvectōs [esse] <u>hostēs</u>? Aut ūlla putātis dōna carēre dolīs Danaum?" — (Vergil; *Laocoon was the only Trojan to warn against accepting the Trojan Horse*)

4. "Āiō tē, Aiacida, Rōmānōs <u>vincere</u> posse." — (Ennius; *quoting a famously ambiguous oracle*)

5. Nōn amō tē, Sabidī, nec possum dīcere quārē: <u>hoc</u> tantum possum dīcere, nōn amō tē. — (Martial)

6. Crēdō equidem, ..., <u>genus</u> esse deōrum. — (Vergil; *Dido describing Aeneas to her sister*)

7. Multīque cogitant <u>bellum</u> eō diē potuisse finīrī. — (Caesar – adapted)

8. Fuit ōlim, quasi ego sum, senex; <u>eī</u> filiae duae erant, quasi nunc meae sunt; eae erant duōbus nuptae frātribus, quasi nunc meae sunt vōbīs. — (Plautus; *a father begins telling a story to two brothers*)

Vocabulary:

calumnia, -ae *f.*	false charge
reperiō, -īre, repperī, repertus	to discover, find
iūrō, -āre	to swear
Iuppiter, Iovis *m.*	Jupiter, Jove (king of the Roman gods)
summus, -a, -um	the top of
dēcurrō, -ere = dē + currō	to run down (from)
insānia, -ae *f.*	madness, folly
āvehō, -ere, -vēxī, -vectus	to carry away; (*passive*) sail away, be carried
Danaum = Graecōrum	
Aiacida (= *Greek acc. form*)	descendant of Aeacus (i.e. Achilles' son, Pyrrhus) *Pyrrhus asked the Delphic oracle if he should fight the Romans
Sabidius, -ī *m.*	Sabidius (proper name)
quārē (adv.)	why
equidem	truly, indeed
quasi	just as
nūbō, -ere, -psī, -ptus	to marry

Chapter 19 Vocabulary

Nouns

*caedēs, caedis *f.*	slaughter, murder
cōpia, cōpiae *f.*	abundance, plenty, resources, wealth; (pl.) troops
dolus, dolī *m.*	trick, deceit
līberī, līberōrum *m.* (pl.)	children

Verbs

ait, aiunt; āiō	he says, they say; I say
caedō, caedere, cecīdī, caesus	to kill, cut; sacrifice (of animals)
cernō, cernere, crēvī, crētus	to see, discern, perceive, decide
cōgitō, cōgitāre, cōgitāvī, cōgitātus	to think, consider
gaudeō, gaudēre, gāvīsus sum	to rejoice, be glad; delight in (+ abl.)
inquit	he said *(introduces a direct quotation)*
negō, negāre, negāvī, negātus	to deny, say that ... not
nesciō, nescīre, nescīvī, nescītus	not to know
ostendō, ostendere, ostendī, ostentus/ostēnsus	to show, reveal
putō, putāre, putāvī, putātus	to think, consider; suppose
respondeō, respondēre, respondī, respōnsus	to answer, reply; correspond to
sciō, scīre, scīvī, scītus	to know; know how to (+ inf.)
spērō, spērāre, spērāvī, spērātus	to hope, hope for *(+ acc. and future inf.)*
trādō, trādere, trādidī, trāditus	to hand over, surrender; hand down, report

Adverbs

ante	before *(of space or time)*, in front; previously
bene	well
ibi	there

(21)

Derivatives: For each English word below, give the Latin word from the Chapter 19 Vocabulary to which it is related and the English word's meaning.

1. despair
2. homicide
3. benefactor
4. gaudy
5. tradition
6. responsive
7. compute
8. ostensibly
9. science
10. negate

Mosaics outside Merchant's Office Complex, Ostia, end 2nd c. A.D.

CHAPTER 20

Irregular Verbs: volō, nōlō, mālō
Negative Commands with nōlō
Noun Clause: Objective Infinitive

So far you have learned the irregular verbs **sum** and **possum**. This chapter introduces three more common irregular verbs. In the previous chapter, you learned that the infinitive could be used as the verb of a noun clause following verbs of speaking, thinking (etc.). This chapter introduces another infinitive noun clause, this time dependent on verbs of commanding, preventing, wishing and the like.

94. Irregular Verbs: volō, nōlō, mālō

The verbs **volō, nōlō, mālō** have irregular forms in the present tense. They have no passive forms, and their perfect forms are completely regular.

Here is the present active indicative of these irregular verbs, followed by the present infinitive, imperative and participle forms where they exist:

	To Want	Not To Want	To Prefer
1st sg.	volō	nōlō	mālō
2nd sg.	vīs	nōn vīs	māvīs
3rd sg.	vult	nōn vult	māvult
1st pl.	volumus	nōlumus	mālumus
2nd pl.	vultis	nōn vultis	māvultis
3rd pl.	volunt	nōlunt	mālunt
Infinitive	velle	nōlle	mālle
Imperative	(none)	nōlī nōlīte	(none)
Participle	volēns, -entis	nōlēns, -ntis	(none)

95. Negative Commands with nōlō

The imperative forms of **nōlō** are often used with a complementary infinitive (§7b) to express a negative command:

| **Nōlī** hoc **facere**. | **Do not do** this! |
| **Nōlīte rapere** illa. | **Do not take** those things! |

Exercise 156. Translate each of the following into Latin.

1. He wants.
2. They prefer.
3. Do not speak! (sg.)
4. We are unwilling.
5. Are you (sg.) willing?

6. Do not kill (pl.) us!
7. I do not want to flee.
8. You (sg.) prefer to do that.
9. They dare to want these things.
10. You (pl.) are unwilling to wage war.

96. **Noun Clause: Objective Infinitive**

Verbs with the meaning "to order" or "to wish" (and the like) often appear with an infinitive clause as their object. This use is therefore called the **objective infinitive**. It is similar to the complementary infinitive (§7b), except that the objective infinitive has its own subject:

I want **to stay**.	complementary	They dare **to fight**.	complementary
I want **you to stay**.	objective	We advise **them to fight**.	objective

In Latin, the **subject of the infinitive** is in the **accusative** case:

Volō **tē manēre**.	I want **you to stay**.
Vetāmus **eōs pugnāre**.	We forbid **them to fight**.
Nōlunt **nōs venīre**.	They do not want **us to come**.
Prohibet **mīlitēs pugnāre**.	He prevents **the soldiers from fighting.**

Here are some of the common verbs that may be followed by this construction:

cōgō, cōgere, coēgī, coāctus	to force, compel
cupiō, cupere, cupīvī *or* cupiī, cupītus	to want, desire
iubeō, iubēre, iūssī, iūssus	to order, command
mālō, mālle, māluī	to prefer, want (something) more
nōlō, nōlle, nōluī	to be unwilling, not want
postulō, postulāre, postulāvī, postulātus	to demand
prohibeō, prohibēre, prohibuī, prohibitus	to prevent
sinō, sinere, sīvī, sītus	to allow, permit; let alone
vetō, vetāre, vetuī, vetitus	to forbid; order ... not
volō, velle, voluī	to wish, want, be willing

You have now had four uses of the infinitive:

complementary	§7b	Chapter 1
as a noun ("subjective")	§39	Chapter 8
verb in indirect statement	§92	Chapter 19
objective	§96	Chapter 20

Review these uses before you do the next exercise.

Exercise 157. In each of the following sentences, identify the form and use of each infinitive.

Example: Ille prohibet mīlitēs pugnāre.   pugnāre: present active inf.; objective

1. Cōnsul haec audīre solēbat.
2. Semper multa cupere bonum nōn est.
3. Nōluit fugere.
4. Nōluērunt vōs fugere.
5. Senex multōs annōs vīvere potuerat.
6. Rōmānīs dulce erat prō patriā pugnāvisse.
7. Caesar iūssit arma rapī.
8. Virī dīxērunt hostēs arma trādidisse.
9. Virī hostēs arma trādere postulābant.
10. Vidēre est crēdere.
11. Dolōs illīus fugere volumus.
12. Hostēs ab nostrīs mīlitibus vincī posse putās?

Exercise 158. Translate the sentences from Ex. 157.

Exercise 159. List all the uses of the accusative case you have had so far and indicate which of these uses require a preposition and which do not.

Exercise 160. Translate each of the following sentences.

1. Ab hostibus capī nōlumus.
2. Uxor tristis Rōmam cum coniuge venīre vult.
3. Patriam tuam amāre dēbēs et quī eī nocent fortiter pugnāre.
4. Nōlīte vestram urbem in tālī locō condere!
5. Caesar mīlitēs celeriter moenia decem pedēs alta condere iūssit.
6. Graecīs multae nāvēs erant.
7. Cōgitāsne Caesarem ipsum cēterōs victūrum esse?
8. Superī vetant illōs sacra ē templō capere.
9. Post vīnum multum postulāvērunt poētam carmina tristia clārā cum vōce canere.
10. Multī senēs in Graeciā sapientēs sunt, sed nōn omnēs.

Exercise 161. Translate into Latin.

1. Do you (pl.) prefer to be mortal?
2. I want this money to be given to him within six days.
3. Many of the Greeks who sailed to Troy did not want to fight.
4. It is the custom to praise one wise man, but not the multitude.
5. It was necessary to move the sacred gifts quickly when the temple began to burn.
6. He forbids those soldiers to flee and sends a messenger to Caesar.
7. Caesar was not willing to send troops into this province.
8. Our father allowed us to sing songs at night.
9. The destruction of the citadel had been desired by many.
10. Free men prefer to live with war (rather) than without freedom.

Reading 27 *(adapted)*

Caesar describes how Cicero's brother, Quintus Cicero, managed to get important letters through to Caesar and his legion commanders when he was besieged during the Roman campaign in Gaul.

Multae litterae nuntiīque ad Caesarem mittēbantur, quōrum pars dēprehensa in conspectū nostrōrum mīlitum necābatur. erat ūnus intus Nervius, nōmine Verticō, quī ā prīmā obsidiōne ad Cicerōnem perfūgerat suamque eī fidem praestiterat. hic servō spē lībertātis magnīsque persuadet praemiīs, ita servus litterās ad Caesarem portat. hās ille iaculō inligātās effert et Gallus inter Gallōs sine ūllā **suspiciōne** versātus ad Caesarem pervenit. ab eō dē perīculīs Cicerōnis **legiōnis**que cognōscit. Caesar acceptīs litterīs hōrā circiter ūndecimā diēī statim nūntium ad Marcum Crassum **quaestōrem** mittit, cuius hīberna aberant ab eō mīlia passuum xxv; iubet mediā nocte **legiōnem** castra relinquere celeriterque ad sē venīre. exit cum nūntiō Crassus. alterum ad Gāium Fabium lēgātum mittit, et iubet eum in Atrebatium fīnēs **legiōnem** addūcere.

Vocabulary:

dēprehendō, -ere, -dī, -sus	to seize, catch	suspiciō, -ōnis *f.*	suspicion
conspectus, -ūs *m.*	sight	versātus, -a, -um	coming and going
necō, -āre	to kill	perveniō, -īre	to reach
intus (adv.)	within, "in the army"	legiō, -iōnis *f.*	Roman legion
Nervius, -a, -um	a Nervian (Nervians were a tribe in Gaul)	circiter (adv.)	around, about
		statim (adv.)	immediately
obsidiō, -iōnis *f.*	siege	quaestor, -ōris *m.*	quaestor
perfugio, -ere, perfūgī	to desert, flee for refuge	hīberna, -ōrum *n.* (pl.)	winter quarters
praestō, -āre, -stitī	to show, prove	exeō, -īre	to leave, go out
praemium, -iī *n.*	reward	Atrebatēs, -ium *m.* (pl.)	Atrebates (Gallic tribe)
iaculum, -ī *n.*	javelin		
inligātus, -a, -um	attached		
efferō, efferre, extulī, ēlātus	to carry out		

Reading 28

Terence was born in North Africa and came to Rome as a slave, but was later freed because of his education and abilities. He wrote six comedies that have survived, including the Heauton Timoroumenos *("Self-Tormenter"), which was produced in 163 B.C. and was modeled on an earlier Greek play. This reading comes from the prologue, in which the speaker does not summarize the plot of the play, as most prologue-speakers did. Instead he explains that the poet wants him to be an "advocate," to convince the spectators they should judge the play themselves, rather than relying on critics who complain that the author was just copying earlier Greek plays.*

Ōrātōrem voluit esse mē, nōn **prologum**.

Vestrum iūdicium fēcit; mē āctōrem dedit.

Sed hic āctor tantum poterit ā fācundiā,

Quantum ille potuit cōgitāre commodē

Quī **ōrātiōnem** hanc scrīpsit, quam dictūrus sum.   5

Nam quod rūmōrēs distulērunt malevolī,

Multās contāminasse Graecās, dum facit

Paucās **Latīnās**, id esse factum hic nōn negat,

... et deinde factūrum (esse) autumat.

Vocabulary:

ōrātō, -iōnis *m.*	advocate	rūmor, -ōris *m.*	rumor
voluit (*subject is the poet, Terence*)		differō, -ferre, distulī	to spread abroad
		malevolus, -a, -um	spiteful (people)
prologus, -ī *m.*	prologue speaker	multās	many (plays)
āctor, -ōris *m.*	advocate	contāminasse, -āre	to blend, unite
tantum poterit	"will have as much power"	(*infinitive in indirect statement with Terence as the understood subject*)	
fācundia, -ae, *f.*	eloquence	paucās	few (plays)
quantum	"as"	Latīnus, -a, -um	Latin
commodē (adv.)	skilfully, well	hic	= Terence
ōrātiō, -iōnis *f.*	speech	deinde (adv.)	"again"
nam quod	"as for the fact that"	autumō, -āre	to say

Practice Sentences

Identify the form and use of the underlined words, then translate.

1. [Catō] esse quam vidērī <u>bonus</u> mālēbat. (Sallust)
2. Magna sunt ea <u>quae</u> dīcō, mihi crēde; nōlī haec contemnere. (Cicero)
3. <u>Nōlīte</u> perturbārī. (Petronius)
4. Hominēs <u>id</u> quod volunt crēdunt. (Caesar)
5. Omnēs <u>diēs</u> iubēmus esse iūridicōs. (C.Th. 2.8.18)
6. Multa ēveniunt <u>hominī</u> quae vult, quae nōn vult. (Plautus – adapted)
7. Ō <u>superī</u>, mortālia facta vidētis? (Ovid; *a spurned lover complains to the gods*)
8. Simul cēnāre et in eōdem locō somnum <u>capere</u> voluērunt. (Cicero)

Vocabulary:

contemnō, -ere	to disparage, think light of	ēveniō, -īre	to happen, turn out
perturbō, -āre	to confuse, disturb	simul	at the same time
iūridicus, -a, -um	open for court proceedings	cēnō, -āre	to dine, eat
		somnus, -ī *m.*	sleep

Chapter 20 Vocabulary

Nouns

multitūdō, multitūdinis *f.*	multitude, great number, crowd
Graecia, Graeciae *f.*	Greece

Verbs

cōgō, cōgere, coēgī, coāctus	to force, compel; collect
cupiō, cupere, cupīvī *or* cupiī, cupītus	to want, desire
iubeō, iubēre, iūssī, iūssus	to order, command
mālō, mālle, māluī	to prefer, want (something) more
necesse est	it is necessary
nōlō, nōlle, nōluī	to be unwilling, not want
postulō, postulāre, postulāvī, postulātus	to demand, claim; prosecute
sinō, sinere, sīvī, sītus	to allow, permit
vetō, vetāre, vetuī, vetitus	to forbid; order ... not
volō, velle, voluī	to wish, want, be willing

Adjectives

mortālis, mortāle	mortal, transient; human
sacer, sacra, sacrum	sacred
sapiēns, sapientis	wise, sensible
superus, supera, superum	upper, higher, above
superī, superōrum *m.* (pl.)	gods
tālis, tāle	such, of such a kind
tristis, triste	sad; gloomy

Adverbs

celeriter	quickly
fortiter	bravely, forcefully
numquam	never

(21)

Derivatives: For each English word below, give the Latin word from the Chapter 20 Vocabulary to which it is related and the English word's meaning.

1. superior
2. postulate
3. benevolent
4. multitude
5. cogitate
6. sapient
7. veto
8. fortitude
9. jussive
10. cupidity

CHAPTER 21

Comparison of Adjectives
    Declension of Comparatives
    Irregular Comparison
Comparison with quam & Ablative of Comparison
Indefinite Pronoun: quīdam, quaedam, quoddam

So far most of the adjectives you have learned have been in the positive degree ("big"). This chapter introduces forms of the comparative ("bigger") and superlative ("biggest") degrees. It also introduces a new use of the ablative case, and another pronoun.

97. **Comparison of Adjectives**

Positive:

> This is the form you learned in Chapters 5 (first and second declension adjectives) and 10 (third declension adjectives). The stem of a Latin adjective can be found by dropping the genitive singular ending.

Comparative:

> In English, we usually form the comparative of an adjective by adding *-er* to its positive stem, or by using *more* (*rather,* or *quite*) with the positive form: *dearer, more dear, rather dear, quite dear*

> In Latin, most adjectives form the comparative by adding **-ior, -ius** to their stem. The comparative *always* uses third declension endings (see §98 below).

Superlative:

> In English, we usually form the superlative of an adjective by adding *-est* to its stem, or by using *most* or *very* with the positive form: *dearest, most dear, very dear*

> In Latin, most adjectives form the superlative by adding **-issim-** to the stem, followed by first and second declension endings. Superlatives decline like **bonus, bona, bonum** (§27).

Positive	Comparative	Superlative
longus, longa, longum (long)	longior, longius (longer)	longissimus, longissima, longissimum (longest)
dignus, digna, dignum (worthy)	dignior, dignius (more worthy)	dignissimus, dignissima, dignissimum (most worthy)
laetus, laeta, laetum (happy)	laetior, laetius (happier)	laetissimus, -a,-um (happiest)
tristis, triste (sad)	tristior, tristius (sadder)	tristissimus, -a, -um (saddest)
sapiēns, sapientis (wise)	sapientior, sapientius (wiser)	sapientissimus, -a, -um (wisest)

Exercise 162. Using the models above, form the comparative and superlative of the following adjectives.

1. iūstus, iūsta, iūstum
2. fortis, forte
3. plēnus, plēna, plēnum
4. brevis, breve
5. potēns, potentis
6. novus, nova, novum
7. turpis, turpe
8. ingēns, ingentis

Regular Exceptions:

1) Adjectives in **-er** form the **superlative** by adding **-rimus (-a, -um)** to the nominative singular masculine of the positive.

2) Four common adjectives in **-lis** form the **superlative** by adding **-limus (-a, -um)** to the stem of the positive.

Positive	Comparative	Superlative
miser, misera, miserum	miserior, miserius	miserrimus, -a, -um
pulcher, pulchra, pulchrum	pulchrior, pulchrius	pulcherrimus, -a, -um
ācer, ācris, ācre	ācrior, ācrius	ācerrimus, -a, -um
facilis, facile	facilior, facilius	facillimus, -a, -um
difficilis, difficile	difficilior, difficilius	difficillimus, -a, -um
similis, simile	similior, similius	simillimus, -a, -um
dissimilis, dissimile	dissimilior, -ius	dissimillimus, -a, -um

98. **Declension of Comparatives**

Comparatives follow the declension of consonant stem nouns, which you learned in Chapter 7 (§41). This means that, unlike third declension adjectives in the positive, they have **-e** (not -ī) in the ablative singular, and they lack the -ī in genitive plural and nom./acc. pl. neuter.

	Singular		Plural	
	Masc./Fem.	Neuter	Masc./Fem.	Neuter
Nominative	longior	longius	longiōrēs	longiōra
Genitive	longiōris	longiōris	longiōrum	longiōrum
Dative	longiōrī	longiōrī	longiōribus	longiōribus
Accusative	longiōrem	longius	longiōrēs	longiōra
Ablative	longiōre	longiōre	longiōribus	longiōribus

99. Irregular Comparison

As in English, some Latin adjectives have irregular comparative and superlative forms. Because these forms are not predictable, they must be memorized carefully.

Positive	Comparative	Superlative
bonus, -a, -um (good)	melior, melius (better)	optimus, -a, -um (best)
magnus, -a, -um (big)	maior, maius (bigger)	maximus, -a, -um (biggest)
malus, -a, -um (bad)	pēior, pēius (worse)	pessimus, -a, -um (worst)
multus, -a, -um (much; many)	plūs, plūris* (more)	plūrimus, -a, -um (most)
parvus, -a, -um (small)	minor, minus (smaller, less)	minimus, -a, -um (smallest, least)
superus, -a, -um (upper)	superior, superius (higher)	summus, -a, -um (highest, furthest; top of) suprēmus, -a, -um (highest, last)

*Note: plūs, plūris in the singular is a neuter noun and is often followed by a partitive genitive:

plūs pecūniae   more money (*literally*: "more of money")

In the plural plūrēs, plūra is an adjective:

plūrēs mīlitēs   more soldiers

For the declension of plūs, see the Morphology Reference Section at the back of the book.

Exercise 163. Identify the following adjectives by degree, case, number and gender. Include all possibilities for ambiguous forms. Then translate each form.

Example: **sapientissimum** superlative, acc. sg. m. or nom./acc. sg. n., "wisest, very wise"

1. dulcissimā
2. maius
3. clārissimōs
4. longior
5. summī
6. celerrimus
7. fidēliōrem
8. plūrimīs
9. meliōre
10. sacerrima
11. fortēs
12. potentiōra
13. pēiōrum
14. facillimō

100. Comparison with quam & Ablative of Comparison

When you see a comparative form, you should be ready to expect a comparison between two items. Latin can express this comparison in two different ways:

- **quam** — **quam** (*than*) can be used as a coordinating conjunction linking the two items being compared. The connected items are in the same case.

  Pater sapientior est **quam filius**.   The father is wiser **than** (his) **son**.
  Is laude dignior **quam culpā** est.   He is more worthy of praise **than blame**.

- **ablative of comparison** — the ablative (*than*) can be used instead of **quam** when the first item is in the nominative or accusative case.

  Pater sapientior est **filiō**.   The father is wiser **than** (his) **son**.
  Crēdunt hanc viam breviōrem esse **illā**. They believe that this path is shorter than **that (one)**.

Exercise 164. Translate each of the following sentences using both comparative constructions where applicable.

1. We think that he is stronger than she.
2. These things were more difficult than those.
3. Are bigger cities better than smaller ones?
4. He denied that the mind of men was swifter than the body.
5. Some kings are stronger than others.
6. They held the most beautiful gifts.

101. Indefinite Pronoun: quīdam, quaedam, quoddam

The pronoun **quīdam, quaedam, quoddam** ("a certain, a sort of") is declined like the relative pronoun **quī, quae, quod** (§63) with **-dam** appended to the end of the word. Note that -**m** becomes -**n** before -**d**: eu**nd**am, eōru**nd**am; que**nd**am, qua**nd**am, etc.

Like the other demonstratives you have learned, these pronouns can be used in place of nouns or as adjectival modifiers:

Quīdam in urbem vēnit.	A certain (man) came into the city.
Quīdam dux bene pugnat.	A certain leader fights well.
Quaedam ab agrīs currit.	A certain (woman) is running away from the fields.
Quaedam dōna accēpimus.	We received certain gifts.

Exercise 165. Translate each of the following sentences.

1. Erantne lēgēs Rōmānae iūstiōrēs lēgibus Graecīs?
2. Sapientēs intellēxērunt nihil esse vēritātis lūce dulcius.
3. Numquam rēs pūblica nec melior nec iūstior fuit.
4. Quīdam ad urbem adveniēbant, quamquam aliī nōlēbant.
5. Contrā commūne perīculum dux noster fortissimus omnium erat.
6. Quis omnium dignissimus fuit?
7. Putant eam aptiōrem rūrī quam urbī esse.
8. Rēgīna amōris causā infēlicissima sē cōnfēcit.
9. Rōmānī numquam maius aut pulchrius templum vīderant.
10. Plūs aurī quam sapientiae mālunt.

Exercise 166. Translate into Latin.

1. The longest journey begins with one step.
2. My love is deeper than the deepest sea.
3. Are two heads in fact better than one in a trial?
4. A certain poet was the ugliest of all men, but he used to sing with the sweetest words.
5. He answered that this was easier to say than to do.
6. The emperor commanded the troops to wage war bravely.
7. When the battle was made, the enemy were fighting more with deceit than force.
8. Some men prefer good wine, others water.
9. Since the dangers were quite serious, the crowd (multitude) sought help.
10. That man was full of loyalty and accomplished very many things for the public good.

Reading 29 *(adapted)*

Cicero writes a remorseful letter from exile to his beloved wife, Terentia, who had to bring up their son, look after their 20-year-old daughter, and manage Cicero's estate and affairs in his absence, as well as work for his return. He blames himself for putting his wife and children in this situation and says he wishes he had followed another course.

Accēpī ab Aristocritō trēs epistulās, quās ego lacrimīs prope dēlēvī. cōnficior enim maerōre, mea Terentia, nec meae mē miseriae magis excruciant quam tuae vestraeque. Ego autem hōc miserior sum quam tū, quae es miserrima, quod ipsa **calamitās** commūnis est utrīusque nostrum, sed culpa mea propria est. Meum fuit officium vel lēgātiōne vītāre perīculum vel **dīligentiā** et cōpiīs resistere vel cadere fortiter. Hōc miserius, turpius, indignius nōbīs nihil fuit. quārē cum dolōre cōnficior tum etiam pudōre; pudet enim mē uxōrī meae optimae, suāvissimīs līberīs virtūtem et diligentiam nōn praestitisse .... Tū modo ad mē omnia dīligentissimē scrībe; etsī magis iam rem quam litterās dēbeō spectāre. Curā et tibi persuādē, mihi tē cārius nihil esse nec umquam fuisse. Valē, mea Terentia, quam ego vidēre videor itaque dēbilitor lacrimīs. Valē.

Vocabulary:

Aristocritus, -ī *m.*	Aristocritus, a friend of Cicero	pudor, -ōris *m.*	shame
		pudeō, -ēre	to cause shame
prope (adv.)	nearly	*(with acc. + subjective infinitive)*	
maeror, -ōris *m.*	grief, sorrow	suāvis, -e	sweet, delightful
miseria, -ae *f.*	misery, distress	praestō, -āre, -stitī	to distinguish oneself
excruciō, -āre	to torture	*(to someone* – dat., *in some way* – abl.)	
calamitās, -tātis *f.*	disaster, damage	exspectō, -āre	to hope for
proprius, -a, -um	one's own	dīligentissimē (adv.)	very carefully,
officium, -iī *n.*	duty		in greatest detail
vel ... vel ... vel	either ... or ... or	etsī (conj.)	although
lēgātiō, -iōnis *f.*	post of ambassador	umquam (adv.)	ever
dīligentia, -ae *f.*	careful management	dēbilitō, -āre	to disable,
quārē (conj.)	therefore		weaken

Practice Sentences

Identify the case and use of the underlined words, then translate.

1. Patria mihi <u>vītā</u> meā est cārior. (Cicero – adapted)
   Ipsā rē publicā nihil mihi est <u>cārius</u>. (Cicero)
   Potius vītā quam <u>patriā</u> carēbō. (Cicero)

2. Nec enim bonitās est pessimīs esse (Seneca)
   <u>meliōrem</u>.

3. Quaedam **remedia** graviōra ipsīs (Seneca)
   <u>perīculīs</u> sunt.

4. Cato enim <u>ipse</u> iam servīre quam (Caesar)
   pugnāre māvult.

5. Quid enim <u>nōbīs</u> duōbus, iūdicēs, (Cicero; *talking about himself*
   labōriōsius? *and his client*)

6. Rēx erat Aenēās <u>nōbīs</u>, quō iūstior alter (Vergil; *a Trojan speaks about his*
   nec pietāte fuit, nec bellō maior et armīs. *leader, whom he fears is dead*)

7. "Quae mea culpa tuam," dīxit (Ovid; *a wife is upset when her*
   "<u>cārissime</u>, mentem vertit?" *husband plans a long journey*)

8. Post **pugnam** ad Regillum lacum nōn (Livy; *Rome conquered the Latins*
   alia illīs <u>annīs</u> **pugna** clārior fuit. *here in c. 496 B.C.*)

Vocabulary:

potius (adv.)	rather	pietās, -tātis *f.*	piety — *abl. of*
bonitās, -tātis *f.*	goodness, excellence		*specification/*
remedium, -iī *n.*	remedy, cure		*respect (§79)*
iūdex, -icis *m.*	judge	pugna, -ae *f.*	fight
labōriōsus, -a, -um	troubled,	ad Regillum	"at Lake Regillus"
	full of labor	lacum	

Chapter 21 Vocabulary

Noun

plūs, plūris *n.* (*often* + gen.)	more

Verbs

adveniō, advenīre, advēnī, adventūrus	to arrive, come to; happen
cōnficiō, cōnficere, cōnfēcī, cōnfectus	to finish, accomplish; weaken, kill
cūrō, cūrāre, cūrāvī, cūrātus	to care for/about, pay attention to; cure
dēleō, dēlēre, dēlēvī, dēlētus	to destroy; blot out
intellegō, intellegere, intellēxī, intellēctus	to understand
quaerō, quaerere, quaesīvī (-iī), quaesītus	to look for, seek; ask
resistō, resistere, restitī (*often* + dat.*)	to resist, oppose, make a stand

Adjectives

commūnis, commūne	shared, common; public
gravis, grave	heavy; serious, important; difficult
iūstus, iūsta, iūstum	just, fair
quīdam, quaedam, quoddam	a certain _____, a sort of _____
turpis, turpe	shameful, base; ugly, foul

** *irregular comparatives and superlatives in §99*

Pronoun

quīdam, quaedam, quoddam	a certain _____, a sort of _____

can also be used as an adjectival modifier

Coordinating Conjunction

quam	(rather) than, as (*in comparison*)

Subordinating Conjunction

quoniam	since, seeing that

(15 + chart in §99)

Derivatives: For each English word below, give the Latin word from the Chapter 21 Vocabulary to which it is related and the English word's meaning.

1. turpitude
2. intelligence
3. confection
4. advent
5. ameliorate
6. gravity
7. delete
8. resistant
9. pejorative
10. curator

READING CHAPTER IV

Narrative Reading IV: Tullus and the Treachery of Mettius
Dictionary Practice / Form Identification
Review of the Sentence and its Parts
Question Words for Extra Practice
Word Building: Compounds
English Abbreviations and Phrases

Narrative Reading IV: Tullus and the Treachery of Mettius
(Adapted from Livy)

The Albans, after the battle of the Horatii and Curiatii, swear allegiance to the Romans. But their leader, Mettius, induces two Roman allies, the Fidenates and the Veientes, to revolt, promising that he will help them. When the battle is engaged, however, Mettius helps neither the Romans nor the allies, but withdraws to see which side will be victorious. When Tullus and the Romans win, they invite the Albans to a thanksgiving ceremony. Tullus offers quite different rewards to the Albans and their leader.

Nec diū pāx **Albāna** mānsit. invidia vulgī, quod tribus mīlitibus fortūna pūblica commissa erat, vānum ingenium **dictātōris** corrupit, et quoniam rēcta cōnsilia nōn bene **ēvēnerant**, prāvīs reconciliāre populī animōs coepit. igitur ut prius

(continued)

Vocabulary:

Albānus, -a, -um	Alban, of the Albans	dictātor, -ōris *m.*	dictator
invidia, -ae *f.*	discontent	corrumpō, -ere, -rūpī	to corrupt
vulgus, -ī *n.*	people, the masses	rēctus, -a, -um	honest
committo, -ere, -mīsī, -missus	to entrust	ēveniō, -īre, -vēnī	to turn out
		prāvus, -a, -um	evil, improper
vānus, -a, -um	weak, idle	reconciliō, -āre	to win back
ingenium, -iī *n.*	nature, character	coepit	"he began"
		ut prius	"just as before"

Narrative Reading IV *(continued)*

in bellō pācem, sīc in pāce bellum quaerēns, quia suae cīvitātī animōrum plūs quam vīrium cernēbat esse, bellum gerere aliōs concitat populōs. Fīdēnātēs, **colōnia** Rōmāna, et Vēientēs **pactō** trānsitiōnis Albānōrum ad bellum atque arma **incitantur**. Cum Fīdēnae apertē dēsciērunt, Tullus Mettiō exercitūque eius ab Albā accītō contrā hostēs dūcit*. Tullus adversus Vēientem hostem dērigit suōs, Albānōs contrā legiōnem Fīdēnātium conlocat. Albānō nōn plūs animī erat quam fideī. nec manēre ergō nec trānsīre apertē ausus est, sed sēnsim ad montēs succēdit; inde ubi satis discessisse sēsē putāvit, dērigit tōtam aciem et mānsit. Nōn alia ante Rōmāna **pugna** ācrior fuit.

Postquam Rōmānī vīcērunt, Albānus exercitus, **spectātor pugnae**, vēnit in campōs. Proximō diē, parātīs omnibus, Tullus vocārī ad contiōnem utrumque exercitum iubet. Tum ita Tullus inquit: "Rōmānī, sī umquam ante ūllō in bellō necesse fuit prīmum dīs immortālibus grātiās agere, tum vestrae virtūtī, hesternum id proelium fuit. Pugnāvistis enim nōn magis cum hostibus quam, quae **pugna** maior atque **perīculōsior** est, cum perfidiā sociōrum. Mettius ille est foederis Rōmānī Albānīque ruptor. Centuriōnēs armātī Mettium circumsistunt et Tullus inquit: "Albānī, populum omnem Albānum Rōmam trādūcere in animō est, cīvitātem dare plēbī, prīmōrēs in patrēs legere, ūnam urbem, ūnam rem pūblicam facere. Mettī, ut ante animum inter Fīdēnātem Rōmānamque rem **dīvīsistī**, ita iam corpus **dīvidētur**." itaque Mettius duōs in currūs distentus inligātus est. tum in partēs dīversās equī concitātī sunt et lacerum in utrōque currū corpus portāvērunt. avertēre omnēs ab tantā foeditāte spectāculī oculōs. prīmum ultimumque illud supplicium apud Rōmānōs exemplī parum memoris lēgum hūmānārum fuit.

Vocabulary:

vīrēs, -ium *f. (pl.)*	strength	pactum, -ī *n.*	promise, pact
concitō, -āre	to stir up, rouse	trānsitiō, -iōnis *f.*	desertion
colōnia, -ae *f.*	colony	incitō, -āre	to incite, stir up
Fīdēnātēs, -um *m.*	citizens of Fidenae, a town near Rome	Fīdēnae, -ārum *f.*	Fidenae (a town in Latium)
Vēientēs, -um *m.*	citizens of Veii, an Etruscan town near Rome	apertē (adv.)	openly
		dēscīscō, -ere, -iī	to revolt

Tullus, -ī *m.* — Tullus, 3rd king of Rome

Mettius, -ī, *m.* — Mettius, leader of the Albans

Alba, -ae *f.* — Alba Longa, town near Rome

acciō, -ere, accīvī, -ītus — to summon

*dūcō, -ere — to march, move
   used without an object

adversus, -a, -um — facing, opposing

dērigō, -ere — to direct, turn

legiō, -iōnis *f.* — legion

conlocō, -āre — to place, station

ergō (adv.) — therefore

trānseō, -īre — to desert

sēnsim (adv.) — gradually

succēdō, -ere, -dī — to retreat

satis (adv.) — enough

pugna, -ae *f.* — fight, battle

spectātor, -ōris *m.* — spectator

campus, -ī *m.* — plain

contiō, -iōnis *f.* — meeting

umquam (adv.) — ever

hesternus, -a, -um — of yesterday

perīculōsus, -a, -um — dangerous

perfidia, -ae *f.* — treachery

foedus, -eris *n.* — treaty

ruptor, -ōris *m.* — breaker

circumsistō, -ere — to surround

centuriōnēs (pl.) — (Roman) captains

trādūcō, -ere — to transfer

plēbs, -is *f.* — common people

prīmōrēs, -um *m.* — first rank

dīvidō, -ere, -īsī — to divide, split

currus, -ūs *m.* — chariot, team of horses

distentus, -a, -um — stretched out

inligō, -āre, -āvī, -ātus — to attach

dīversus, -a, -um — opposite

lacer, -era, -erum — torn

āvertō, -ere, -tī — to avert, turn away

foeditās, -tātis *f.* — horror, hideousness

spectāculum, -ī *n.* — sight

ultimus, -a, -um — last

supplicium, -iī *n.* — punishment

apud (+ acc.) — among

exemplī parum memoris — "of a type too little mindful of"

Dictionary Practice/Form Identification

Identify the words below based on the dictionary entries given. Be sure to indicate the **entry from which each is taken**, and the **part of speech** and to *give all possibilities for ambiguous forms.*

For **nouns** and **adjectives**: give case, number, and gender

For **verbs**: give person, number, tense, voice (active *or* passive) and mood (indicative or imperative); if infinitive, give tense and voice

    A.   servīlis, servīle: slavish, servile
    B.   serviō, servīre, servīvī : to be a slave
    C.   servitūs, servitūtis *f.*: slavery
    D.   servō, servāre, servāvī, servātus: to watch over

		Entry	Part of Speech	Form ID
1.	servātī erunt			
2.	servitūtī			
3.	servīvērunt			
4.	servābar			
5.	servīle			
6.	serviam			
7.	servīlēs			
8.	servāvistī			
9.	servīvisse			
10.	servitūs			
11.	servātus sum			
12.	servī			
13.	servābunt			
14.	servīlibus			
15.	servātum esse			

Review of the Sentence and its Parts

Chapters 17-21 have added new dependent clauses, several with non-finite verbs. Finite clauses are often easier to recognize because they have clause markers, while non-finite clauses typically do not. Notice that sometimes the function of a non-finite and a finite clause is the same: participles and adjectival relative clauses both modify nouns; ablatives absolute and the clauses introduced in Chapter 12 both function as adverbial modifiers providing information about (e.g.) when, why, and under what conditions the action of the main verb happens. It may be useful at this stage to review the old and new dependent clauses by their function in the sentence.

	Adjectival Modifier	Adverbial Modifier	Noun
Finite	Relative Clause (Ch. 13) marked by **quī, quae, quod**	Clause (Ch. 12) marked by **cum, dum, sī, ubi,** etc.	Relative Clause (Ch. 18) marked by **quī, quae, quod**
Non-Finite	Participle (Ch. 17)	Ablative Absolute (Ch. 17)	Indirect Statement (Ch. 19)
			Objective Infinitive (Ch. 20)

Question Words for Extra Practice

Quis/Quī	who? (animate)
Quem/Quōs	whom? (animate)
Quid/Quae	what? (non-animate)
ā Quō	by whom?
Quō auxiliō	by what means?
Quam diū	how long?
Ubi	where?
Cūr	why?

Based on the narrative reading at the beginning of this chapter, answer the following questions in Latin.

1. Quam diū pāx Albāna mānsit?
2. Quis erat dux Albānōrum?
3. Quid ingenium dictātōris corrupit?
4. Quō auxiliō reconciliābat populī animōs?
5. Quī ad bellum atque arma incitantur?
6. Pugnā inceptā, quid Mettius agit?
7. Ubi Albānus exercitus stetit post pugnam?
8. Cui Tullus cīvitātem dedit?
9. Quid rēx Rōmānus fēcit?
10. Cur Mettius interfectus est?

Word Building: Compounds

A good way to help build your Latin vocabulary is to watch for compound words made up of simple stems you already know. Words in Latin are compounded in predictable ways, so you can learn to pull them apart and make educated guesses even about words you've never seen before. (Review Reading Chapter II for spelling changes!) Here are some examples:

- **Verbs with prefixes that come from prepositions**

Preposition	Verb	Compound Word	Meaning
ā/ab	mittere	āmittere	to send away, lose
ad	venīre	advenīre	to come to, arrive
ante	pōnere	antepōnere	to place before, prefer
circum	dare	circumdare	to put around, surround
cum (com-, con-)	currere	concurrere	to run together, charge
in	capere	incipere	to take in (hand), begin
sub (sup-)	iacēre	subiacēre	to lie under, be close to
super	sedēre	supersedēre	to sit over, preside

- **Other compounds**

Type of Formation	Parts of the Compound	Compound Word	Meaning
two adjectives	omnis + potēns	omnipotēns	all-powerful
adjective + noun	māgnus + animus	magnanimus	great-spirited
noun + verb	ager + colō (to till, cultivate)	agricola	farmer

Guess the meaning of each compound below and identify the two parts in each compound:

1. subscrībō
2. addūcunt
3. excidimus
4. manūmittit
5. armiger
6. dēpōnō
7. mātricīda
8. āmēns

English Abbreviations and Phrases

- c.v. *or* vita	**curriculum vitae**	course of life
- ibid.	**ibidem**	in the same place
- id.	**idem**	the same (man/author)
- M.A.	**Magister artium**	Master of Arts (*graduate degree*)
- op. cit.	**opus citatum** *or* **opere citato**	the work cited
- p.s.	**post scriptum**	after what has been written
- q.v.	**quod videre**	which to see (*i.e. Go look at*)
- **deo volente**		God willing
- **quid pro quo**		this for that

CHAPTER 22

Comparison of Adverbs
More on quam
Deponent Verbs
   Special Intransitive: Deponent Verbs used with an Ablative Object

In Chapter 21 you learned about the comparison of adjectives. This chapter introduces the comparison of adverbs, as well as a group of verbs that lacks active forms.

102. Comparison of Adverbs

The comparative and superlative of adverbs follows the same pattern as that of the adjectives to which they are related.

Positive:

Many adverbs are formed from adjectives as follows:

1st and 2nd declension adjectives add **-ē** to their stem

cārus, -a, -um	**cārē**
miserus, -a, -um	**miserē**
pulcher, -chra, -chrum	**pulchrē**

3rd declension adjectives add **-(i)ter** to their stem (stems in **-nt** and **-tt > t**)

celer, -is, -e	**celeriter**
sapiēns, -ntis	**sapienter**

The positive form of other adverbs must simply be memorized.

Comparative adverbs end in **-ius**. They are the same as the accusative singular neuter form of the comparative adjective.

Superlative adverbs are formed by replacing the superlative adjective endings with **-ē**.

The following chart illustrates sample adverb forms, including five common irregular ones.

Positive	Comparative	Superlative
celeriter (quickly)	celerius (more quickly)	celerrimē (most quickly)
fortiter (bravely)	fortius (more bravely)	fortissimē (most bravely)
longē (far)	longius (farther)	longissimē (farthest)
bene (well)	melius (better)	optimē (best)
male (badly)	pēius (worse)	pessimē (worst)
multum (much)	plūs (more – quantity)	plūrimum (most, very much)
magnopere (greatly)	magis (more – quality)	maximē (most, especially)
parum (little)	minus (less)	minimē (least)

103. More on quam

Quam is used as a connector with **comparative** adverbs, just as it is with comparative adjectives (§100). It appears instead of the Ablative of Comparison, except in poetry:

hic mīles **fortius** pugnāvit **quam** ille   this soldier fought **more bravely than** that one

Quam can also be used as an adverb to modify the **superlative** of either an adjective or an adverb, indicating the greatest possible degree. A common way to translate **quam** + superlative is "as _____ as possible":

quam laetissimus   as happy as possible
quam celerrimē   as quickly as possible

104. Deponent Verbs

Deponent verbs have *passive forms* but *active meanings*. (They are called "deponent" because they literally "put down" [dē + **pōnere**] their passive meanings.) They are conjugated like the passive of regular verbs.

	Present	Imperfect	Future	Perfect
1st sg.	cōnor	cōnābar	cōnābor	cōnātus, -a, -um sum
2nd sg.	cōnāris	cōnābāris	cōnāberis	cōnātus, -a, -um es
3rd sg.	cōnātur	cōnābātur	cōnābitur	cōnātus, -a, -um est
1st pl.	cōnāmur	cōnābāmur	cōnābimur	cōnātī, -ae, -a sumus
2nd pl.	cōnāminī	cōnābāminī	cōnābiminī	cōnātī, -ae, -a estis
3rd pl.	cōnantur	cōnābantur	cōnābuntur	cōnātī, -ae, -a sunt

You will be able to identify a deponent verb from its dictionary listing, because the first form will end in **-or** instead of **-ō**, the second form will be a passive infinitive and the listing will have only three forms:

Present Indicative		Present Infinitive	Perfect Indicative
moror	"I delay"	morārī	morātus sum
loquor	"I talk"	loquī	locūtus sum

Note: More than half of all deponent verbs are regular, first conjugation verbs.

Imperatives of deponent verbs are formed as follows:

2nd sg.: Add **-re** to the verb stem (morāre, loquere) – these forms look like a present active infinitive for each conjugation

2nd pl.: Add **-minī** to the verb stem (morāminī, loquiminī) – these forms look like the 2nd pl. indicative, but the context of the sentence should make the mood clear

Deponents retain the following Active forms:

Future Infinitive (morātūrus esse, locūtūrus esse)
Present and Future Participles, Gerund and Supine (to be learned later)

See the Morphology Reference Section (pp. 320-331) for imperative, infinitive and participle forms for all four conjugations.

A few verbs have regular active forms, except in the perfect system where they have only passive forms. These are called **semi-deponent** verbs, and you have already learned three of the most common ones:

audeō, audēre, ausus sum	to dare
fidō, fidere, fisus sum	to trust
gaudeō, gaudēre, gavīsus sum	to rejoice
soleō, solēre, solitus sum	to be accustomed

Remember that when you are identifying most *forms* of deponent verbs, they are *passive*, even though their meanings are *active*.

Exercise 167. From the dictionary entries below, identify which verbs are deponent.

1. cōnfiteor, cōnfitērī, cōnfessus sum
2. rōdō, rōdere, rōsī, rōsus
3. hortor, hortārī, hortātus sum
4. fateor, fatērī, fassus sum
5. carpō, carpere, carpsī, carptus
6. moror, morārī, morātus sum
7. reor, rērī, ratus sum
8. impleō, implēre, implēvī, implētus

Exercise 168. Identify each of the following verbs by person, number, tense, voice, and mood, and then translate into English.

Example: cōnātus eris   second sg., future perfect, deponent, indic.:   "you will have tried"

1.	frūctus esse	7.	cōnātī erātis
2.	ingredimur	8.	ūtor
3.	potītus eram	9.	fūnctus est
4.	ūsī eritis	10.	vesceris
5.	sequitur	11.	ingressus es
6.	patimur	12.	ausae sumus

105. **Special Intransitive: Deponent Verbs used with an Ablative Object**

In Chapter 7 (§44) you learned that some verbs take their object in the dative or ablative case instead of the accusative. The deponent verbs **ūtor, fruor, fungor, potior, vescor** (and some of their compounds) typically take their object in the ablative case, in the same "special intransitive" sentence pattern.

Exercise 169. Translate each of the following sentences.

1. Dux ipse mīlitēs ingredī Rōmam sinit.
2. Nōlīte sequī illōs!
3. Vir multa vulnera patī solitus est.
4. Creditisne hīs magis quam illīs?
5. Quōdam tempore lēgātī maius bellum quam pācem cūrābant.
6. Vescī quibusdam cibīs tē aegrum faciet.
7. Prīnceps ipse cibō pōtūque frūctus est dum Rōma ardet.
8. Morārī quam hostem petere māvis?
9. Cōgitāsne Caesarem ipsum Gallōs victūrum esse?
10. Bellō inceptō, Caesar cōpiās ex Ītaliā in Galliam quam celerrimē dūxit.

Exercise 170. Translate into Latin.

1. Certain women will acquire fame.
2. I judged that the fault was mine alone and I am very sad.
3. Tradition forbids women to enter the temple.
4. The senate did not want to make the crowd angry.
5. Those who follow that leader into the hostile province will not live many days.
6. To use deceit was not their custom.
7. We ourselves will depart rather quickly on the seventh day.
8. The children enjoyed the same books.
9. The soldiers were following the leader himself.
10. The part of the city that is near the river was being attacked as fiercely as possible by the army.

Reading 30 *(slightly edited)*

Caesar tells how the Germans were defeated and his summer campaign in Gaul ended. Labienus was a prominent legion commander in Caesar's Gallic campaign.

Ita proelium restitūtum est, atque omnēs hostēs terga vertērunt neque prius fugere **dēstitērunt**, quam ad flūmen Rhēnum, mīlia passuum ex eō locō circiter quīndecim, pervēnērunt. ... hōc proeliō trāns Rhēnum nūntiātō Suēbī, quī ad rīpās Rhēnī vēnerant, domum **revertī** coepērunt. quōs ubi, quī proximī Rhēnum incolunt, perterritōs sēnsērunt, īnsecutī magnum ex hīs numerum occīdērunt. Caesar ūnā aestāte duōbus maximīs bellīs cōnfectīs, in hīberna in Sequanōs exercitum **dēdūxit**. hībernīs Labiēnum praeposuit, ipse in citeriōrem Galliam profectus est.

Vocabulary:

restituō, -ere, -uī, -ūtus	to restore, renew	perterreō, -ēre, -uī, -itus	per = very
tergum, -ī *n.*	back	īnsequor, -ī, īnsecūtus sum	to pursue
prius ... quam	before		
dēsistō, -ere, -stitī	to stop (+ inf.)	aestās, -tātis *f.*	summer
circiter (adv.)	around, about	cōnficiō, -ere	to bring to an end
perveniō, -īre, -vēnī	to arrive	hīberna, -ōrum *n.* (pl.)	winter quarters
Rhēnus, -ī *m.*	the Rhine river	Sequanī, -ōrum *m.* (pl.)	the Sequani (a German tribe)
Suēbī, -ōrum *m.* (pl.)	the Suebi (a German tribe)	praepōnō, -ere (+ acc. & dat.)	to set ____ as a commander (over)
rīpa, -ae *f.*	bank (of a river)	dēdūcō, -ere, -xī	to lead down
revertor, -ī	to turn back	citerior, -ius	on this side, nearer
coepērunt	(they) began		
quōs = hōs			

Practice Sentences

Identify the case and use of the underlined words, then translate.

1. Ille, ubi mātrem cognōvit, tālī fugientem <u>vōce</u> secūtus est. (Vergil – adapted; *Venus departs revealing herself to her son, Aeneas [ille], who calls after her*)

2. Ipsī ex silvīs rārī **prōpugnābant** nostrōsque intrā **mūnītiōnēs** ingredī prohibēbant. (Caesar – adapted; *describing an enemy's battle strategy*)

3. Dum loquor, <u>hōra</u> fugit. (Ovid)

4. Nōn omnēs <u>eadem</u> mīrantur amantque. (Horace)

5. Maximum **remedium** īrae <u>mora</u> est. (Seneca)

6. Somnus in ignōtōs oculōs <u>sibi</u> vēnit, et aurō **hērōs** Aesonius potitur. (Ovid; *describing how Jason overcame the dragon [sibi], which guarded the golden fleece*)

7. [Eum] populus Rōmānus meliōrem <u>virum</u> quam histriōnem esse arbitrātur. (Cicero; *speaking of the famous actor, Quintus Roscius*)

8. [Hannibal,] hāc **pugnā** pugnātā, Rōmam profectus est nūllō **resistente**. In propinquīs <u>urbī</u> montibus morātus est. (Cornelius Nepos; *describing Hannibal's march to Rome*)

Vocabulary:

rārus, -a, -um	scattered, here and there	sibi	*refers to the dragon*
prōpugnō, -āre	to rush out to fight		
intrā (+ acc.)	inside, within	hērōs *(nom. sg.)*	hero
mūnītiō, -iōnis *f.*	fortification	Aesonius, -a, -um	descended from Aeson, Jason
remedium, -iī *n.*	remedy, cure		
somnus, -ī *m.*	sleep		
ignōtus, -a, -um	not knowing	histriō, -iōnis *m.*	actor

Chapter 22 Vocabulary

Nouns

cibus, cibī *m.*	food
culpa, culpae *f.*	fault, blame
mora, morae *f.*	delay
pōtus, pōtūs *m.*	drink

Verbs

arbitror, arbitrārī, arbitrātus sum	to think, judge
cōnor, cōnārī, cōnātus sum	to try
fīdō, fīdere, fīsus sum (+ dat.)	to trust, confide in
fruor, fruī, frūctus sum (+ abl.)	to enjoy
fungor, fungī, fūnctus sum (+ abl.)	to perform, do
ingredior, ingredī, ingressus sum	to enter; march, walk
loquor, loquī, locūtus sum	to speak, talk, say
mīror, mīrārī, mīrātus sum	to wonder (at), be surprised at; admire
moror, morārī, morātus sum	to delay
patior, patī, passus sum	to suffer, allow
potior, potīrī, potītus sum (+ abl.)	to get hold of, acquire
proficīscor, proficīscī, profectus sum	to set out, depart
sequor, sequī, secūtus sum	to follow, accompany; pursue
ūtor, ūtī, ūsus sum (+ abl.)	to use
vescor, vescī (+ abl.)	to eat, feed on

Adjective

propinquus, propinqua, propinquum	near (to), neighboring; near, not far off *(of time)*
propinquus, propinquī *m.*	relative, kinsman

Adverb

quam	how, how much; as _____ as possible *(with superlatives)*

(21)

Derivatives: For each English word below, give the Latin word from the Chapter 22 Vocabulary to which it is related and the English word's meaning.

1. loquacious
2. function
3. arbitrate
4. potable
5. ingress

6. culpable
7. moratorium
8. consequence
9. abuse
10. passion

CHAPTER 23

Irregular Verbs
    eō, īre, iī (īvī), itūrus (to go)
        Compounds of eō
    ferō, ferre, tulī, lātus (to carry, bear)
        Compounds of ferō
Paradigm of vīs, vīs, f.

Irregular Verbs

So far you have learned the irregular verbs **sum, possum, volō, nōlō** and **mālō**. This chapter introduces two more common irregular verbs. It also introduces an irregular noun.

106. eō, īre, iī (īvī), itūrus (to go)

The verb **eō** (to go) is irregular in the present tense and must be memorized. Its other forms are regular, but are given here for convenience:

Indicative

	Present	Imperfect	Future	Perfect	Pluperfect	Future Perfect
1st sg.	eō	ībam	ībō	iī, (īvī)	ieram	ierō
2nd sg.	īs	ībās	ībis	iistī > īstī	ierās	ieris
3rd sg.	it	ībat	ībit	iit	ierat	ierit
1st pl.	īmus	ībāmus	ībimus	iimus	ierāmus	ierimus
2nd pl.	ītis	ībātis	ībitis	iistis > īstis	ierātis	ieritis
3rd pl.	eunt	ībant	ībunt	iērunt	ierant	ierint

Imperatives

2nd sg.	ī
2nd pl.	īte

Infinitives

Present	īre
Perfect	īsse
Future	itūrus esse

Participles

Present	iēns, euntis
Future	itūrus, -a, -um

Compounds of eō

There are many common compounds of **eō**. These follow the pattern of forms given above.

Exercise 171. See if you can guess the principal parts and meanings of the following:

Example: abeō   abīre, abiī, abitūrus: to go away, depart

1. adeō	4. redeō
2. exeō	5. subeō
3. ineō	6. trānseō

Exercise 172. Translate the following into Latin using **eō** or its compounds, and identify the tense of each form:

Example: I depart   abeō; present tense

1. They entered	6. He wants (*use* **volō**) to go
2. We will go	7. They will cross
3. He was returning	8. We had undergone
4. You (sg.) approached	9. Are you (pl.) going out?
5. Go away! (pl.)	10. They will have gone away

107. ferō, ferre, tulī, lātus (to carry, bear)

The verb **ferō** is also irregular in the present tense and must be memorized. The imperfect and future active and the future passive are given here for convenient reference, but the perfect (**tulī, tulistī, tulit,** etc.) can be found in the Morphology Reference Section at back of the book:

Indicative

	Active			Passive	
	Present	**Imperfect**	**Future**	**Present**	**Future**
1st sg.	ferō	ferēbam	feram	feror	ferar
2nd sg.	fers	ferēbās	ferēs	ferris	ferēris
3rd sg.	fert	ferēbat	feret	fertur	ferētur
1st pl.	ferimus	ferēbāmus	ferēmus	ferimur	ferēmur
2nd pl.	fertis	ferēbātis	ferētis	feriminī	ferēminī
3rd pl.	ferunt	ferēbant	ferent	feruntur	ferentur

Imperatives

2nd sg.	fer (n.b. §45)
2nd pl.	ferte

Infinitives

	Active	Passive
Present	ferre	ferrī
Perfect	tulisse	lātus esse
Future	lātūrus esse	

Participles

	Active	**Passive**
Present	ferēns, ferentis	
Perfect		lātus, -a, -um
Future	lātūrus, -a, -um	

Compounds of ferō

There are many common compounds of **ferō**. These follow the pattern of forms given above. Note especially the following and their principal parts:

auferō, auferre, abstulī, ablātus	to carry away
cōnferō, cōnferre, contulī, collātus	to bring together, compare; contribute
īnferō, īnferre, intulī, illātus	to bring to, introduce
offerō, offerre, obtulī, oblātus	to offer
referō, referre, rettulī, relātus	to carry back, bring back, report

Exercise 173. Translate the following into Latin using **ferō** or its compounds, and identify the tense of each form:

1. They will offer
2. It is reported
3. She was carried
4. You (pl.) had been carried away
5. I will bear
6. To be introduced
7. They will contribute
8. Having been offered (neuter sg.)
9. They will have been compared
10. He was reporting

Exercise 174. Translate each verb form and be ready to identify it by person, number, tense and voice.

1. adeunt
2. lātae erātis
3. inībit
4. fers
5. tuleris
6. auferēs
7. abībāmus
8. sustulērunt
9. fertur
10. collāta sunt

108. ## Paradigm of vīs, vīs, *f.*

The third declension word **vīs** (stem: **vī-**) has some unusual forms in the singular, and in the plural it is easily confused with the second declension noun **vir**. It is worth memorizing these forms now so they won't cause trouble later:

	vīs, vīs *f.* power; pl. strength		**vir, virī** *m.* man	
	Singular	**Plural**	**Singular**	**Plural**
Nominative	vīs	vīrēs	vir	virī
Genitive	[vīs – *rarely seen*]	vīrium	virī	virōrum
Dative	[vī – *rarely seen*]	vīribus	virō	virīs
Accusative	vim	vīrēs	virum	virōs
Ablative	vī	vīribus	virō	virīs

Exercise 175. Translate each of the following sentences.

1. Clāmōre sublātō hostēs petīvimus prīmā lūce.
2. Eōdemque tempore fortēs virī proelium ineunt et multī perīre incipiunt.
3. Infēlīcēs mīlitēs domum trāns Graeciam sē cōnferunt.
4. Scītisne Caesarem Galliae cunctae bellum intulisse?
5. Quibus vīrēs magnae erant labōrem nōn vītāvērunt.
6. Ā nūntiō territō malum commūne relātum erat.
7. Lēge carēns cīvitās celerius perībit, nam bonī cīvēs abībunt.
8. Auxiliō lātō, fēminae līberīque gaudēbant.
9. Fīlius frātrēsque parēs patrī erant et virtūte et vīribus.
10. Omnēs abiimus, turbā clāmōrem tollente.

Exercise 176. Translate into Latin.

1. Scared by the shouts, the boys ran into the forest.
2. The soldiers collected all their own weapons after the battle.
3. The unlucky band (of men) was killed when the hostile army arrived.
4. In a few days I think I will go to Rome.
5. The sailor's wife will return home when the ship departs.
6. Because of the heat, we threw ourselves into that river.
7. The king's servants are carrying fire for their master.
8. About to cross the road, she fell (down).
9. I see many men bearing arms.
10. Although they kept trying to cross the river, they could not bring aid to their friends.

Reading 31 *(adapted)*

Tacitus tells a story of intrigue and murder in the Roman Empire. Agrippina, the second wife of Emperor Claudius, persuaded him to adopt her son by a previous marriage, Nero. Four years later, Claudius died — probably poisoned by Agrippina — and Nero, three or four years older than Claudius' son, Britannicus, became emperor. But Agrippina subsequently lost influence over Nero and began to support her stepson Britannicus as the rightful heir. This prompted Nero to plot the poisoning death of Britannicus at a banquet in A.D. 55, as Tacitus describes.

Turbātus est Agrippīnae minīs Nerō et, propinquō diē, quō quartum decimum aetātis annum Britannicus fīniēbat, eum ōdisse incēpit. quia nūllum crīmen neque iubēre caedem frātris palam audēbat, occulta mōlītur parārīque venēnum iubet.

Mōs habēbātur prīncipum līberōs cum cēterīs idem aetātis **nōbilibus** vescī in **aspectū** propinquōrum propriā et parciōre mēnsā. illīc epulānte Britannicō, quia cibōs pōtūsque eius ūnus ex ministrīs gustū explōrābat, hic dolus inventus est. innoxius ac praecalidus et lībātus pōtus datur Britannicō; tum,

postquam fervōre aspernābātur, frīgidā in aquā adfunditur
venēnum, quod celeriter cunctōs eius artūs **pervāsit.** celerrimē
et vōx et spīritus raptī sunt. trepidant quī **circumsedent,**
diffugiunt nesciī; sed, quibus altior intellectus, manent dēfixī
et Nerōnem spectantēs. ille, ut erat **reclīnis** et nesciō similis,
solitum esse ita ait per comitiālem morbum quō prīmā ab
infantiā adflictārētur Britannicus, et reditūrōs esse paulātim
vīsus sēnsūsque. at Agrippīnae pavor, ea **cōnsternātiō** mentis,
quamvīs vultū premerētur, ēmicuit. sibi suprēmum auxilium
ēreptum esse intellegēbat. Ita post breve **silentium** repetīta
convīviī laetitia est.

Vocabulary:

turbō, -āre	to disturb	circumsedeō, -ēre	to sit around
propinquō diē	abl. absolute	diffugiō, -ere	to scatter
mina, -ae f.	threat	nescius, -a, -um	unaware, not
ōdisse (pf. inf.)	to dislike, hate		knowing
palam (adv.)	openly	quibus (+ est)	(dative of
occultum, -ī n.	secret plan		possession)
mōlior, -īrī, -ītus sum	to devise; undertake	altior (adj.)	better
venēnum, -ī n.	poison	intellēctus, -ūs m.	understanding
idem aetātis	"of the same age"	dēfixus, -a, -um	rooted
nōbilis, -e	noble		(in their seats)
aspectus, -ūs m.	sight	ut	as
propriā et parciōre	"at their own, less	reclīnis, -e	reclining
mēnsā	luxurious table"	solitus, -a, -um	normal,
illīc (adv.)	there		customary
epulor, -ārī, -ātus sum	to feast	comitiālis, -is m.	epilepsy
minister, -trī m.	servant	morbus, -ī m.	illness,
gustus, -ūs m.	tasting		ailment
explōrō, -are	to investigate, test	īnfantia, -ae f.	infancy
innoxius, -a, -um	harmless	adflictārētur	"(he) had been
praecalidus, -a, -um	very hot		afflicted"
		paulātim (adv.)	gradually
lībō, -āre, -āvī -ātus	to taste	vīsus, -ūs m.	sight
		sēnsus, -ūs m.	sense;
fervor, -ōris m.	boiling heat		consciousness
aspernor, -ārī	to reject	pavor, -ōris, m.	trembling
adfundō, -ere	to pour in		(from fear)
pervādō, -ere, -vāsī, -vāsus	to spread, pervade	cōnsternātiō, -iōnis f.	alarm, distress
spīritus, -ūs m.	breath	quamvīs	although
trepidō, -āre	to be afraid, anxious	premerētur	"she tried to conceal"

ēmicō, -ere, -uī	to be conspicuous	repetō, -ere, -īvī,	to renew,
sibi	(*dative of*	-ītus	begin again
	reference)	silentium, -ī *n.*	silence
ēripiō, -ere, -rēpī	to take away	convīviī laetitia	joy of the
			banquet

Reading 32 *(adapted)*

Ovid, in his Fasti, *tells the story of how Persephone, daughter of Ceres and Jupiter, is abducted by her uncle, Pluto (Jupiter's brother), to become his wife and queen of the underworld.*

Terram pulchra Cerēs et multās **possidet** urbēs,	1
in quibus est cultō **fertilis** Henna solō.	2
Fīlia Persephonē Cereris, comitāta puellīs,	3
errābat **nūdō** per sua prāta pede.	4
Valle sub umbrōsā locus est plēnus melilōtō	5
et aliīs flōribus quībus nitēbat humus.	6
Quam simul aspexit, "comitēs, accēdite" dīxit	7
"et mēcum plēnōs flōre referte sinūs."	8
Hanc videt et vīsam patruus **vēlōciter** aufert,	9
rēgnaque caeruleīs in sua portat equīs.	10
Illa quidem clāmābat, "iō, cārissima māter,	11
auferor!" ipsa suōs abscideratque sinūs.	12
Panditur intereā Dītī via, dum deus ībat	13
in celerī cūrrū virgine perterritā.	14
Attonita est plangōre Cerēs quae vēnerat Hennam.	15
nec mora, "Mē miseram! Fīlia, " dīxit, "ubi es?"	16

Vocabulary:

Cerēs, Cereris *f.*	Ceres, goddess of agriculture	umbrōsus, -a, -um	shaded
		melilōtos, -ī *m.*	clover
possideō, -ēre	to hold, possess	flōs, flōris *m.*	flower
colō, -ere, coluī, cultus	to till, cultivate	niteō, -ēre	to be bright
		quam simul	as soon as
fertilis, -e	fertile, productive	aspiciō, -ere, -spexī	to see
Henna, -ae *f.*	Henna, a town in Sicily	comes, -itis *m.* or *f.*	companion
		accēdō, -ere	to come near
solum, -ī *n.*	ground, soil	sinus, -ūs *m.*	fold (of clothing), lap
comitātus, -a, -um	accompanied (by)		
nūdus, -a, -um	bare	patruus, -ī *m.*	uncle
prātum, -ī *n.*	meadow	vēlōciter (adv.)	quickly
vallis, -is *f.*	valley	caeruleus, -a, -um	dark blue, dark

quidem (adv.)	indeed	perterreō, -ēre,	to terrify
abscindō, -ere,	to tear	-uī, -itus	thoroughly
abscidī, -scīssus		attonitus, -a, -um	stunned
pandō, -ere	to open	plangor, -ōris *m.*	wailing
Dīs, Dītis *m.*	Pluto, god of the	nec mora	*supply* erat
	underworld	mē miseram	*accusative is used*
currus, -ūs *m.*	chariot		*for an exclamation*

Practice Sentences

Identify the case and use of the underlined words, then translate.

1. Ūnum hoc sciō, <u>quod</u> fors feret ferēmus aequō animō. — (Terence)

2. Ō nāvis, rēferent in <u>mare</u> tē novī flūctūs. Ō quid agis? — (Horace; *the poet uses a ship metaphor to refer to the troubles besetting the state.*)

3. Quidquid id est, timeō Danaōs et <u>dōna</u> ferentēs. — (Vergil; *the priest, Laocoon, tries to warn the Trojans not to accept the Greek horse.*)

4. Ūnus erit quem tū tollēs in caerula caelī <u>templa</u>. — (Ennius; *Jupiter foretells to Mars that only one of his sons will be deified*)

5. Hennā tū simulācrum Cereris tollere audēbās, Hennā tū dē <u>manū</u> Cereris Victoriam ēripere et deam deae dētrahere cōnātus es? — (Cicero; *this is part of a speech against Verres, who is accused of stealing sacred statues from the shrine at Henna*)

6. <u>Nāvem</u>, scīs, putō, nōn morātur ūnus. — (Martial; *the same can be said of airplanes in the modern world*)

7. In longum sermōnem mē vocās, Attice, <u>quem</u> tamen, nisi Quīntus aliud quid nōs agere māvult, suscipiam. — (Cicero; *the author talks with two friends about civil law*)

8. Gratiās agimus et ducibus vestrīs et exercitibus, quod <u>oculīs</u> magis quam auribus crēdidērunt. — (Livy; *the dictator of Tusculum speaks to the Roman senate*)

Vocabulary:

fors, fortis *f.*	chance, fortune	sermō, -ōnis *m.*	conversation
quisquis, quidquid	whoever, whatever	Atticus, -ī m.	Atticus, a friend of Cicero
Danaī, -ōrum *m.*	the Greeks		
caerulus, -a, -um	dark blue, dark	nisi	unless
simulācrum, -ī *n.*	image, statue	Quīntus, -ī m.	Quīntus, a friend of Cicero
Victoria, -ae *f.*	the goddess, Victory		
ēripiō, -ere	to snatch	aliud quid	some other (activity), something else
dētrahō, -ere, -xī, -ctus	to take away		
		suscipiō, -ere	to undertake
		auris, -is *f.*	ear

Chapter 23 Vocabulary

Noun

vīs, vīs *f.*	power, force, violence;
vīrēs, vīrium (pl.)	strength

Verbs

eō, īre, iī *or* īvī, itūrus	to go
abeō, abīre, abiī, *or* -īvī, abitūrus	to go away, depart
adeō, adīre, adiī, *or* -īvī, aditūrus	to go towards, approach
exeō, exīre, exiī, *or* -īvī, exitūrus	to go out, exit
ineō, inīre, iniī, *or* -īvī, initūrus	to enter; begin
pereō, perīre, periī, *or* -īvī, peritūrus	to perish, die
redeō, redīre, rediī *or* -īvī, reditūrus	to go back, return
subeō, subīre, subiī *or* -īvī, subitūrus	to go up; to undergo; to approach
trānseō, trānsīre, trānsiī, *or* -īvī, trānsitūrus	to go across, cross
ferō, ferre, tulī, lātus	to carry, bear, endure; report, say
adferō, adferre, attulī, adlātus	to bring to; cause
auferō, auferre, abstulī, ablātus	to carry away, take away
cōnferō, cōnferre, contulī, collātus	to bring together, collect; compare; contribute
sē cōnferre	to proceed, go
īnferō, īnferre, intulī, illātus	to bring in, introduce; inflict
offerō, offerre, obtulī, oblātus	to offer, bring forward
referō, referre, rettulī, relātus	to carry back, bring back, report
tollō, tollere, sustulī, sublātus	to lift up, raise; remove, carry off, steal

Adjectives

īnfēlix, īnfēlīcis	unhappy, unlucky
cunctus, cuncta, cunctum	the whole, all (collectively)

(20)

Derivatives: For each English word below, give the Latin word from the Chapter 23 Vocabulary to which it is related and the English word's meaning.

1.	perish	6.	adit
2.	ablative	7.	infelicitous
3.	infer	8.	collate
4.	relative	9.	transitory
5.	exit	10.	violent

CHAPTER 24

Present Active Subjunctive
Present Passive Subjunctive
Present Subjunctive of sum, possum and volō
Independent Uses of the Subjunctive
    Exhortation / Command
    Wish
    Doubt
    Possibility

So far all the finite verbs you have learned have been in the indicative or imperative mood. This chapter introduces the present tense of the third mood, the **subjunctive**, in the active and passive voice of all conjugations, including the irregular verb **sum**. It also introduces some common uses of the subjunctive as a main verb. Unlike the indicative, which indicates real or factual information, the subjunctive often suggests doubt, possibility or anticipated action.

A note on the subjunctive in English: Use of the subjunctive in English has gradually decreased over the years so that it now appears only in a few expressions. Among these are:

• impossible wishes	I wish he **were** here (but he is not).
	I wish I **were** in Italy.
• contrary to fact statements	If I **were** rich, I would feed the hungry.
	She acts as if she **were** my mother!
• clauses after certain verbs	I suggest that **he come** back soon.
of asking, recommending	He demanded that she **leave**.

Even in some of the above examples the indicative replaces the subjunctive in common speech. Latin uses the subjunctive in several different kinds of expressions, but note that the English translation of these does not necessarily use an English subjunctive.

109. Present Active Subjunctive

The **present active subjunctive** uses the same personal endings as the indicative (**-m** for **-ō** in first sg.), but can be recognized by a change in the stem vowel: the signal for the subjunctive is **-ā-** in all conjugations except the first, where (because the indicative already has an **-a-**) it is an **-ē-** instead. Note that the long vowel is shortened (as always) before the first singular and both third person endings.

	1st Conj. (e)	2nd Conj. (ea)	3rd Conj. (a)	3rd Conj. –iō (ia)	4th Conj. (ia)
1st sg.	amem	moneam	regam	capiam	audiam
2nd sg.	amēs	moneās	regās	capiās	audiās
3rd sg.	amet	moneat	regat	capiat	audiat
1st pl.	amēmus	moneāmus	regāmus	capiāmus	audiāmus
2nd pl.	amētis	moneātis	regātis	capiātis	audiātis
3rd pl.	ament	moneant	regant	capiant	audiant

There are many mnemonic devices for remembering the vowels for each conjugation. Two common ones are the following sentences:

First	**Second**	**Third**	**Third –iō & Fourth**
Cl**e**m	St**ea**ms	Cl**a**ms in	S**ia**m
Sh**e**	R**ea**ds	**A**	D**ia**ry

110. Present Passive Subjunctive

The present passive subjunctive uses the same stem vowels as the active with the passive personal endings you already know. Deponent verbs follow the same pattern.

	1st Conj. (e)	2nd Conj. (ea)	3rd Conj. (a)	3rd Conj. –iō (ia)	4th Conj. (ia)	Passive Endings
1st sg.	amer	monear	regar	capiar	audīar	**-r**
2nd sg.	amēris (-re)	moneāris (-re)	regāris (-re)	capiāris (-re)	audiāris (-re)	**-ris** (-re)
3rd sg.	amētur	moneātur	regātur	capiātur	audiātur	**-tur**
1st pl.	amēmur	moneāmur	regāmur	capiāmur	audiāmur	**-mur**
2nd pl.	amēminī	moneāminī	regāminī	capiāminī	audiāminī	**-minī**
3rd pl.	amentur	moneantur	regantur	capiantur	audiantur	**-ntur**

Exercise 177. Following the model verbs just given, conjugate **laudō**, **dēleō** and **cernō** in the present active and passive subjunctive, singular and plural.

Exercise 178. Identify the conjugation and then transform each of the following verbs from indicative to subjunctive.

1. rogant
2. patēs
3. resistunt
4. vulnerāmus
5. auditur
6. ardētis
7. rapiō
8. spectāris
9. dormīmus
10. tacent
11. cadit
12. vetor
13. trahitis
14. cernis

111. Present Subjunctive of sum, possum and volō

The subjunctive of **sum, possum** and **volō** is signalled by **-ī-** in the present:

	sum	**possum**	**volō**
1st sg.	sim	possim	velim
2nd sg.	sīs	possīs	velīs
3rd sg.	sit	possit	velit
1st pl.	sīmus	possīmus	velīmus
2nd pl.	sītis	possītis	velītis
3rd pl.	sint	possint	velint

The verbs **nōlō** and **mālō** follow the pattern of **sum** (**nōlim, nōlīs, nōlit,** etc.; **mālim, mālīs, mālit,** etc.). The verbs **eō** and **ferō** have regular subjunctive forms (**eam, eās, eat,** etc.; **feram, ferās, ferat,** etc.). See the Morphology Reference Section for the subjunctive paradigms of these verbs (pp. 320-331).

Exercise 179. Identify each of the following verb forms by person, number, tense and mood and translate the indicative forms.

1. adest
2. adeunt
3. redīverim
4. eātis
5. absint
6. adfuērunt
7. pereās
8. velit

112. Independent Uses of the Subjunctive

While the indicative mood is used to give or get factual information, the subjunctive is used to convey the opinion or feeling of the speaker (writer). It has a variety of different uses as an independent (main) verb in Latin, but three common uses are:

1)	to urge or demand an action	Let's get pizza! Let them eat cake!
2)	to wish for something	I wish he would come! (or) Would that he might come!
3)	to indicate doubt, often by asking for advice or expressing surprise	What should I do? Who would have thought it?!
4)	to indicate a possibility	That may happen. He might come.

These uses of the subjunctive are referred to by different terms in different grammars:

1) Exhortation/Command

> **hortatory** – always 1st person (usually pl.); negative is **nē**
>
> > In urbem **eāmus.** **Let us (Let's) go** into the city.
> > Nē dēspērēmus. **Let us not despair.**
>
> **jussive** – usually 3rd person (sg. or pl.)
>
> > Fābulam illam **dīcat.** **Let him/her tell** that story.
> > Omnēs cīvēs **veniant.** **Let** all the citizens **come.**

prohibition = negative command – 2nd or 3rd person, usually perfect subjunctive (§117) + **nē**

| Hoc **nē fēcerīs** | **Do not do** this! |
| **Nē dēspērāverītis** | **Do not despair!** |

* compare this with the more common negative imperative construction, which you have already learned (§95)

| **Nōlī** hoc **facere!** | **Do not do** this! |
| **Nōlīte dēspērāre** | **Do not despair!** |

2) Wish

optative – often accompanied by **utinam**; negative is **nē**

Utinam **fugiat** hostēs!	**I hope he will escape** the enemy!
Nē ille **pereat!**	**May** he **not die!**
Omnēs laetī **sint!**	**If only** all people **would be** happy!

A present tense signals that the wish is possible; an imperfect (§113-114) or pluperfect (§118, 123) that it is/was not accomplished. The perfect occurs for wishes only in archaic texts.

3) Doubt

deliberative – expressed as a question; negative is **nōn**

| Quid **scrībam?** | What **should I write?** |
| Quid **facerem?** | What **should I have done?** (imperfect §113-114) |

Often a so-called "deliberative question" isn't so much a question which expects an answer as it is a rhetorical expression or an exclamation expressing doubt, disbelief, surprise or indignation. A deliberative question about the present uses the present subjunctive; one about the past uses the imperfect subjunctive.

4) Possibility

potential – sometimes accompanied by **forsitan**; negative is **nōn**

The potential subjunctive is likely to appear in forms such as **velim** (*I would like*), **mālim** (*I would prefer*), **possim** (*I could*) and in the second person singular of verbs of perception:

Forsitan **dīcat** hoc.	Perhaps he **may say** this.
Nōlim pūtēs illud.	**I wouldn't want** you to think that.
Vidērēs pontum.	**You could have seen** the ocean. (imperfect §113-114)

Exercise 180. Identify the following English examples as expressing exhortation/command, wish, doubt or possibility. (Do *not* translate these into Latin.)

1. Let's meet at noon.
2. They might come tomorrow.
3. May they return soon!
4. What am I to do?
5. Let him try to deny his guilt.
6. Would that he is innocent.
7. Who would believe it?
8. Perhaps I am making a mistake.

Exercise 181. Translate each of the following and identify the use of the subjunctive. Be ready to say how you decided on the use you identify.

1. Hīs celerius serviāmus.
2. Utinam exercitus veniat.
3. Quid nunc agam?
4. Sit.
5. Forsitan glōria magna tibi sit.
6. Nē morī timeant.
7. Dīcāmus an taceāmus?
8. Nocte eōs audiās.
9. Omnēs gaudeāmus.
10. Diū vīvās flōreāsque.

Exercise 182. Translate each of the following sentences.

1. Virōs haec dōna ad templa deōrum portāre hortēmur.
2. Ille rēx suōs populōs iūstissimē semper regat.
3. Utinam quī bonus rēctusque est flōreat.
4. Nē putent tē reliquīs aegriōrem esse.
5. Quis eum cognōscat post decem annōs?
6. Rōmam nostrīs cum amīcīs eāmus.
7. Utinam beātam vītam agās et nūlla mala accidant.
8. Nōn illa faciant; nam plūrimī cīvium nōn volunt.

Exercise 183. Translate into Latin.

1. Let us always fight very fiercely on behalf of our country.
2. I wish the citizens would hear many good things about the new consuls.
3. Let him depart; for he was captured trying to save the children.
4. Should I send them away?
5. He might finally enjoy great profits.
6. After the war is finished, let us thank Caesar.
7. Should we sail in a few days or begin to march today?
8. May fortune help the brave and let us keep them in our memory for many years!

Reading 33

Cicero exhorts his fellow citizens to live a noble life and defend the state against evil. He uses the leader of Carthage (Rome's enemy in the Punic Wars), Hannibal, and the Bruti and Camilli, famous Roman families, as examples.

Quis Carthāginiēnsium plūris fuit Hannibale cōnsiliō, virtūte, rēbus gestīs, quī ūnus cum tot imperātoribus nostrīs per tot annōs dē imperiō et dē glōriā dēcertāvit? hunc suī cīvēs ē cīvitāte **ēiēcērunt**: nōs etiam hostem litterīs nostrīs et memoriā vidēmus **esse celēbrātum**. quā rē **imitēmur** nostrōs Brūtōs, Camillōs, … **innumerābilīs** aliōs quī hanc rem pūblicam **stabilivērunt**; quōs equidem in deōrum **immortalium** coetū ac **numerō** repōnō. amēmus patriam, pāreāmus senātuī, cōnsulāmus bonīs; **praesentīs** frūctūs neglegāmus, **posteritātis** glōriae serviāmus; id esse optimum putēmus quod erit rēctissimum; spērēmus quae volumus, sed quod acciderit ferāmus; cōgitēmus dēnique corpus virōrum fortium, magnōrum hominum esse mortāle, animī vērō mōtūs et virtūtis glōriam sempiternam.

Vocabulary:

Carthāgiēnsis, -e	Carthaginian	immortālis, -e	immortal, undying
plūris	"of more value"	coetus, -ūs *m.*	company; assembly
Hannibal, -alis *m.*	Hannibal	numerus, -ī *m.*	number
rēs gestae	"military achievements"	repōnō, -ere	place, put; reckon
imperātor, -tōris *m.*	general		among
dēcertō, -āre, -āvī	to fight, contend	cōnsulō,	to look after, consult
ēiciō, -ere, -iēcī	to throw out, expel	-ere (+ dat.)	the interests of
celēbrō, -āre, -āvī, -ātus	to celebrate	praesentīs	present, immediate
quā rē	therefore	= praesentēs *(acc. pl.)*	
imitor, -ārī	to imitate	posteritās, -tātis *f.*	posterity
innumerābilīs	countless, innumerable	sempiternus, -a, -um	everlasting
= innumerābilēs *(acc. pl.)*			
stabiliō, -īre, -īvī	to make stable		

Practice Sentences

Identify the form and use of each subjective verb and translate.

1. Vivāmus, mea Lesbia, atque amēmus, (Catullus; *these lines*
   rūmōrēsque senum **sevēriōrum** *are addressed to his*
   omnēs ūnius aestimēmus assis. *adulterous lover*)

2. Quid ego faciam? Maneam an abeam? (Plautus)

3. Valeant cīvēs meī! sint incolumēs, sint flōrentes, (Cicero; *quoting Milo*
   sint beātī! stet haec urbs praeclāra! *while defending him*)

4. Commūnis libertātis causā arma capiant. (Caesar – adapted)

5. Quis genus Aeneadum, quis Trōiae nesciat urbem? (Vergil; *Dido is*
   speaking)

6. Quī beneficium dedit, taceat; narret quī accēpit. (Seneca)

7. Commūnem hunc **ergō** populum paribusque regāmus (Vergil; *Juno proposes*
   auspiciīs. *to Venus that they unite*
   the Carthaginians and
   Trojans)

8. Dīxit vērō Deus, "**congregentur** aquae quae sub (Vulgate; *describing the*
   caelō sunt in locum unum et **appāreat** ārida," *origin of the world*)
   factumque est ita et vocāvit Deus āridam 'terram'
   congregātiōnēsque aquārum appellāvit 'maria'.

Vocabulary:

rūmor, -ōris *m.*	rumor, public opinion	Aeneadae, -(ār)um *m.* (pl.)	"followers of Aeneas"
sevērus, -a, -um	severe, stern	beneficium, -iī *n.*	favor, kindness
aestimō, -āre, -āvī	to value, count as worth (+ gen. §44)	ergō	therefore
as, assis *m.*	as; a copper coin *roughly* = "penny"	auspicium, -iī *n.*	auspices, power
		congregō, -āre	to gather
		appāreō, -ēre	to appear
incolumis, -e	safe, unharmed	āridus, -a, -um	dry
praeclārus, -a, -um	glorious, distinguished	congregātiō, -iōnis *f.*	collection

Chapter 24 Vocabulary

Nouns

frūctus, frūctūs *m.*	fruit, enjoyment; profit
glōria, glōriae *f.*	glory, fame; ambition, boasting
memoria, memoriae *f.*	memory, recollection; history
mōtus, mōtūs *m.*	emotion, impulse; movement

Verbs

accidō, accidere, accidī	to fall at *or* near; happen
adsum, adesse, adfuī, adfutūrus	to be present, be near
appellō, appellāre, appellāvī, appellātus	to name, call upon, address
bibō, bibere, bibī, bibitūrus	to drink
dēspērō, dēspērāre, dēspērāvī, dēspērātus	to despair
dīmittō, dīmittere, dīmīsī, dīmissus	to send away, send forth; dismiss; abandon
flōreō, flōrēre, flōruī	to bloom; prosper, flourish
hortor, hortārī, hortātus sum	to urge, encourage
neglegō, neglegere, neglēxī, neglēctus	to ignore, neglect

Adjectives

beātus, beāta, beātum	happy, blessed; prosperous
rēctus, rēcta, rēctum	straight, upright; right; virtuous, honest

Adverbs

dēnique	finally, at last; in short; in fact
equidem	truly, indeed
forsitan	perhaps
utinam	*signals a wish;* if only, would that

Coordinating Conjunction

an	or

(20)

Derivatives: For each English word below, give the Latin word from the Chapter 24 Vocabulary to which it is related and the English word's meaning.

1. accident
2. rectangle
3. fructose
4. negligent
5. florid
6. appellation
7. dismiss
8. glorious
9. motor
10. exhortation

CHAPTER 25

Imperfect Active Subjunctive
Imperfect Passive Subjunctive
Imperfect Subjunctive of sum, possum and volō
Dependent Uses of the Subjunctive: Adverbial Clauses
    Purpose
    Result

This chapter introduces the imperfect subjunctive, active and passive, of all conjugations, including deponent and irregular verbs. It also introduces two common uses of the subjunctive in dependent clauses.

113. Imperfect Active Subjunctive

The **imperfect active subjunctive** looks like the present active infinitive (second principal part, **-re**) with the regular personal endings added. Note that the **-e-** is short (as always) before the first singular and both third person endings, but otherwise long.

	1st Conj.	2nd Conj.	3rd Conj.	3rd Conj. –iō	4th Conj.
1st sg.	amārem	monērem	regerem	caperem	audīrem
2nd sg.	amārēs	monērēs	regerēs	caperēs	audīrēs
3rd sg.	amāret	monēret	regeret	caperet	audīret
1st pl.	amārēmus	monērēmus	regerēmus	caperēmus	audīrēmus
2nd pl.	amārētis	monērētis	regerētis	caperētis	audīrētis
3rd pl.	amārent	monērent	regerent	caperent	audīrent

114. Imperfect Passive Subjunctive

The imperfect passive subjunctive looks like the present active infinitive with passive personal endings added.

	1st Conj.	2nd Conj.	3rd Conj.	3rd Conj. –iō	4th Conj.
1st sg.	amārer	monērer	regerer	caperer	audīrer
2nd sg.	amārēris	monērēris	regerēris	caperēris	audīrēris
3rd sg.	amārētur	monērētur	regerētur	caperētur	audīrētur
1st pl.	amārēmur	monērēmur	regerēmur	caperēmur	audīrēmur
2nd pl.	amārēminī	monērēminī	regerēminī	caperēminī	audīrēminī
3rd pl.	amārentur	monērentur	regerentur	caperentur	audīrentur

Deponent verbs form the imperfect subjunctive in the same way, as if they had a present active infinitive.

	1st Conj.	2nd Conj.	3rd Conj.	4th Conj.
1st sg.	morārer	verērer	loquerer	potīrer
2nd sg.	morārēris	verērēris	loquerēris	potīrēris
3rd sg.	morārētur	verērētur	loquerētur	potīrētur
1st pl.	morārēmur	verērēmur	loquerēmur	potīrēmur
2nd pl.	morārēminī	verērēminī	loquerēminī	potīrēminī
3rd pl.	morārentur	verērentur	loquerentur	potīrentur

Exercise 184. Following the model verbs above, conjugate **vetō**, **taceō** and **neglegō** in the imperfect active and passive subjunctive, singular and plural.

115. **Imperfect Subjunctive of sum, possum and volō**

The subjunctive of **sum, possum** and **volō** is regular:

	Sum	Possum	Volō
1st sg.	essem	possem	vellem
2nd sg.	essēs	possēs	vellēs
3rd sg.	esset	posset	vellet
1st pl.	essēmus	possēmus	vellēmus
2nd pl.	essētis	possētis	vellētis
3rd pl.	essent	possent	vellent

The verbs **nōlō, mālō, eō** and **ferō** also have regular imperfect subjunctive forms. See the Morphology Reference Section for the full paradigms of these verbs (pp. 326-331).

116. **Dependent Uses of the Subjunctive: Adverbial Clauses**

The subjunctive is used in a variety of dependent clauses. Two common uses are to indicate:

1) **Purpose** – introduced by **ut** (**utī**); negative is **nē** (never **ut** + **nōn**)

While English often expresses purpose with an infinitive, Latin uses a dependent clause with a subjunctive verb to indicate intention or will (rather than fact). In the examples below, the first translation is the most idiomatic in English. Because a purpose clause always refers to an incomplete action, (happening either at the same time or after the main verb), only present and imperfect tenses of the subjunctive are commonly used; the present after a present tense main verb, the imperfect after a past tense. More details about tenses of the subjunctive in dependent clauses will be discussed in the next chapter (§121).

Ut tē videāmus venimus.   We come { **to see you.** / (**in order that we may see you.**) }

Ut tē vidērēmus vēnimus.   We came { **to see you.** / (**in order that we might see you.**) }

Currunt **nē hostēs sē capiant.**	They run	so the enemy will not capture them (in order that the enemy not capture them.)
Cucurrit **nē hostēs sē caperent.**	He ran	so the enemy would not capture him (in order that the enemy not capture him.)

A purpose clause (sometimes called a final clause) functions as an adverbial modifier by giving the purpose of the main verb; it answers the question *"why?" / "for what purpose?"*

2) **Result** – introduced by **ut** (**utī**); negative is **ut nōn** (or another negative word)

Latin uses an adverbial dependent clause with a subjunctive verb to express the result of an action or condition in the main clause. When there is a result clause (sometimes called a consecutive clause) in a sentence, the main clause often has a "signpost word" (an adjective or adverb) such as:

ita	thus, so	**tam**	so, to such a degree
sīc	thus, so	**tot**	so many
tālis, tāle	such, of such a kind	**totiēns**	so often
tantus, -a, -um	so much, so great		

Even in the absence of a signpost word in the main clause, a result clause can be identified by asking the question *"so that what?" / "with what result?"* Sometimes this is the only way to decide if a clause in Latin (or English!) is expressing purpose or result. As with purpose clauses, result clauses most commonly use the present and imperfect subjunctive; the present after a present tense main verb, the imperfect after a past tense main verb.

Ita facimus **ut omnēs nōbīs pāreant.**	We act in such a way **that everyone will obey us.**
Totiēns dīcit **ut nōn audīre cupiāmus.**	He speaks so often **that we do not want to listen.**
Tam sapienter rēxit **ut nēmō rēgnum relinquere cuperet.**	He ruled so wisely **that no one wanted to leave the kingdom.**

Exercise 185. Bracket and identify each of the dependent clauses as **purpose** or **result**, and then translate the underlined verb into Latin.

Daedalus was such a clever architect that King Minos <u>brought</u> (**ferō**) him to Crete <u>to build</u> (**aedificō**) the labyrinth. The king kept him imprisoned on the island for so many years that Daedalus <u>wanted</u> (**volō**) to leave very badly. He invented wings <u>to escape</u> (**fugiō**), and he arranged the feathers in such a way that they <u>were</u> (**sum**) similar to birds' wings. Icarus was so bold that he <u>did</u> not <u>listen</u> (**audiō**) to his father. To <u>look for</u> (**petō**) his son, Daedalus flew near the sea. He is so sad that he <u>doesn't</u> <u>know</u> (**sciō**) what to do, so he journeys to Sicily <u>to find</u> (**inveniō**) peace. There the king's admiration was so great that he <u>received</u> (**accipiō**) him kindly and <u>gave</u> (**dō**) Daedalus refuge.

Exercise 186.

Translate each of the following sentences.

1. Vēnērunt ut nōs vidērent, sed nēmō domī erat.
2. Reī pūblicae vīrēs ingentēs fuērunt ut hostēs petere nōllent.
3. Tantum vīnī biberam ut ē casā amīcī discēderem et domum īrem.
4. Circum pontem mūrumque pugnāvērunt nē urbs verterētur.
5. Utinam ā nōbīs iūs cīvīle dīscerent.
6. Glōriae cupīdō tē ita aget ut multa perīcula subeās.
7. Tot cīvēs illum cōnsulem creāvērunt ut aliī eī resistere nōn audērent.
8. Pācem dēnique petunt ut bellum quam celerrimē fīniant.
9. Quī scelus facit poenam dare dēbet nē plūrēs scelera faciant.
10. Tollāmusne illud aurum ut opem magnam habeāmus?

Exercise 187.

Translate into Latin.

1. Rome was so great that other nations were afraid to attack.
2. Those soldiers are fleeing in order not to be wounded.
3. His talent was such that everyone admired him.
4. Let them have fair laws in order that they may live more freely.
5. He may perhaps be lying because of his eagerness.
6. The boys ran so quickly that no one saw them.
7. Let us set out at dawn in order to arrive at the specified time.
8. Should I encourage these unhappy men?
9. They had fought fiercely with their weapons in order to defeat the enemy.
10. The messenger will come today to announce delay of the army.

Reading 34 *(slightly edited)*

The historian Florus reviews the qualities of Rome's first seven kings: Romulus, Numa, Tullus Hostilius, Ancus, [Tarquin, Servius,] and Tarquinius Superbus.

Haec est prīma aetās populī Rōmānī et quasi **infantia**, quam habuit sub rēgibus septem, quādam fātōrum industriā tam variīs ingeniō, ut reī pūblicae ratiō et ūtilitās postulābat. nam quis Rōmulō ardentior? tālī opus fuit, ut invāderet rēgnum. quis Numā religiōsior? ita rēs poposcit, ut ferōx populus deōrum metū **mītigārētur**. quid ille **mīlitiae** artifex Tullus? bellātōribus virīs quam **necessārius** [fuit], ut acueret ratiōne virtūtem! quid **aedificātor** Ancus, ut urbem **colōniā extenderet**, ponte iungeret, mūrō tuērētur? ... Postrēmō Superbī illīus inportūna **dominātiō** nōn nihil, plūrimum vērō prōfuit. Sic enim **agitātus** iniūriīs populus cupiditāte lībertātis incendēbātur.

Vocabulary:

quasi (adv.)	as it were	bellātor, -ōris	warlike
infantia, -ae *f.*	infancy	quam necessārius	"how necessary"
industria, -ae *f.*	diligence, activity	acuō, -ere	to sharpen
tam variīs … ut	"so different … as"	aedificātor, -ōris *m.*	architect, builder
variīs *modifies* rēgibus		colōnia, -ae *f.*	colony (Ostia)
ūtilitās, -tātis *f.*	advantage, usefulness	extendō, -ere	to extend, expand
ardēns, -ntis	eager, passionate, bold	tueor, -ērī	to guard, protect
invādō, -ere	to seize, take hold of	postrēmō (adv.)	finally
religiōsus, -a, -um	pious, religious	inportūnus, -a, -um	savage, uncivil
poscō, -ere, poposcī	to demand, require	dominātiō, -iōnis *f.*	dominion, rule
ferōx, -ōcis	fierce, insolent, wild	prōsum, -desse,	to be useful,
mītigō, -āre	to tame, soften	prōfuī	benefit
quid	"what about?"	agitō, -āre, -āvī,	to agitate, disturb
mīlitia, -ae *f.*	army	-ātus	
artifex, -ficis *m.*	creator, originator		

Reading 35 A-C

Martial wrote several epigrams about not wanting to share his own poems lest his listeners ask him to hear their own work. The first two selections here are on this theme, with the first addressed to Theodorus and the second to Pontilianus, probably a fictitious friend, who is the subject of the third selection too.

A. Nōn dōnem tibi cūr meōs libellōs
　　　Ōrantī totiēns et exigentī,
　　Mīrāris, Theodōre? Magna causa est:
　　　Dōnēs tū mihi nē tuōs libellōs.

B. Cūr nōn mittō meōs tibi, Pontīliane, libellōs?
　　nē mihi tū mittās, Pontīliane, tuōs.

C. Mentīris, crēdō: recitās mala carmina, laudō:
　　Cantās, cantō: bibis, Pontīliane, bibō:
　　Pēdis, dissimulō: gemmā vīs lūdere, vincor:
　　Rēs ūna est, sine mē quam facis, et taceō.
　　Nīl tamen omnīnō praestās mihi. "Mortuus," inquis,
　　"Accipiam bene tē." Nīl volō: sed morere.

Vocabulary:

dōnō, -āre	to give	gemma, -ae, *f.*	gem, precious stone
libellus, -ī *m.*	little book		used as a piece in a
exigō, -ere	to demand		game like chess
recitō, -āre	to recite, read aloud	ludō, -ere	to play
cantō, -āre	to sing	nīl omnīnō	nothing at all
pēdō, -ere	to fart	praestō, -āre	to provide, show
dissimulō, -āre	to pretend not to notice; conceal, hide	accipiō bene	to treat well

Practice Sentences

Identify the form and use of each subjunctive verb and translate.

1. Ea tanta est urbs ut ex quattuor urbibus maximīs cōnstāre dicātur. (Cicero; *describing the Sicilian city, Syracuse*)

2. Quis in hanc rem fuit **arbiter**? Utinam is quidem Rōmae esset! Rōmae est. Utinam adesset in iūdiciō! Adest. Utinam sedēret in cōnsiliō C. Pisōnis! Ipse C. Pīsō est. Eundemne tū arbitrum et iūdicem sūmēbās? (Cicero; *the amount of a legal claim has already been set by an* arbiter *and now comes before a* iūdex *who will decide if the claim should be paid, but the plaintiff wants to argue again about the amount of the claim*)

3. Ita ferī ut sē morī sentiat. (Suetonius; *with these words Caligula ordered men put to death by multiple small wounds*)

4. Quis **temperet** ā lacrimīs? (Vergil; *Aeneas explains that his story is very sad*)

5. Tantus in cūriā clāmor factus est ut populus concurreret. (Cicero)

6. Utinam populus Rōmānus ūnam **cervīcem** habēret! (Suetonius; *Caligula lashed out in anger at a crowd which opposed him*)

7. Quis tam **dēmēns** [est], ut suā **voluntāte** maereat? (Cicero)

8. Lēgum omnēs servī sumus ut līberī esse possīmus. (Cicero)

Vocabulary:

cōnstō, -āre	to consist (of)	cūria, -ae *f.*	Curia, senate building
arbiter, -trī *m.*	arbitrator		
sedēre in cōnsiliō	to sit in judgment	cervīx, -īcis *f.*	neck
C. Pīsō, -ōnis *m.*	Gaius Piso	dēmēns, -ntis	crazy
sūmō, -ere	to take, accept	voluntās, -tātis *f.*	will, choice
feriō, -īre	to strike, kill	maereō, -ēre	to be sad, mourn
temperō, -āre	to refrain, keep from		

Chapter 25 Vocabulary

Nouns

cupiditās, cupiditātis *f.*	desire, wish, longing, eagerness
cupīdō, cupidinis *f.*	desire, wish, longing, eagerness
ingenium, ingeniī, *n.*	talent, (innate) nature, character
iniūria, iniūriae *f.*	injury, harm; insult; wrong
opus, operis *n.*	work, labor, task
opus est (+ dat.)	there is a need/use (for)
mūrus, mūrī *m.*	wall; fortification wall for a city
*pons, pontis *m.*	bridge

Verbs

iungō, iungere, iūnxī, iūnctus	to join, unite, connect; yoke
mentior, mentīrī, mentītus sum	to lie, speak *or* say falsely
morior, morī, mortuus sum	to die

Adjectives

certus, certa, certum	fixed, established, certain; specified; reliable, sure
certē (adv.)	certainly, surely, of course; at least
quantus, quanta, quantum	how much

Adverbs

autem *(postpositive)*	however; on the contrary
cūr	why?
nē	not *(used with imperative & perfect subjunctive)*
quidem *(postpositive)*	indeed, certainly, in fact
nē ... quidem	not ... even
totiēns	so often

Coordinating Conjunction

at	but; at least; then

Subordinating Conjunctions

nē	in order that ... not *(used with subjunctive)*
ut	in order that; so that

(20)

Derivatives: For each English word below, give the Latin word from the Chapter 25 Vocabulary to which it is related and the English word's meaning.

1. mortality
2. pontiff
3. ingenuity
4. quantify
5. opera
6. conjunction
7. certify
8. mural

Street. Pompeii, 1st c. A.D.

CHAPTER 26

Perfect Active Subjunctive
Pluperfect Active Subjunctive
Perfect and Pluperfect Subjunctive of sum and possum
Tenses in Independent Uses of the Subjunctive
Tenses in Dependent Uses of the Subjunctive: Sequence of Tenses
Dependent Uses of the Subjunctive: Adverbial Clauses
      Circumstance, Cause, Concession
      Time, with anticipation

This chapter introduces the active voice of the last two subjunctive tenses: the perfect and pluperfect; there is no future or future perfect subjunctive. It provides information about how the four tenses of the subjunctive (present, imperfect, perfect, pluperfect) are used, both in the main and in dependent clauses. It also introduces more uses of the subjunctive in adverbial dependent clauses.

117. Perfect Active Subjunctive

The **perfect active subjunctive** adds **-erī-** to the perfect stem of the third principal part and uses the same personal endings as the present subjunctive. The long **-ī** shortens to **-i** before **-m**, **-t**, and **-nt** and, over time, shortened in the other endings too, so the perfect subjunctive and future perfect indicative looked the same, except in the first person singular. Many texts now print a short **-i** in all the perfect subjunctive forms, but this book will retain the original long **-ī** to help distinguish them from the future perfect indicative.

	1st Conj.	2nd Conj.	3rd Conj.	4th Conj.
1st sg.	amāverim	monuerim	rēxerim	audīverim
2nd sg.	amāverīs	monuerīs	rēxerīs	audīverīs
3rd sg.	amāverit	monuerit	rēxerit	audīverit
1st pl.	amāverīmus	monuerīmus	rēxerīmus	audīverīmus
2nd pl.	amāverītis	monuerītis	rēxerītis	audīverītis
3rd pl.	amāverint	monuerint	rēxerint	audīverint

Exercise 188. Following the model verbs above, conjugate **exspectō, flōreō** and **dormiō** in the perfect active subjunctive, singular and plural.

Exercise 189. Transform each of the following verbs from indicative to subjunctive.

1. vulnerāvistis
2. scīvērunt
3. rēxistī
4. advēnit
5. sēnsimus
6. nocuistī
7. ōrāvit
8. mānsī

235

Exercise 190. Identify each of the following verbs by person, number, tense and mood. Include all possibilities for any ambiguous forms.

1.	errat	10.	clāment
2.	iactēs	11.	laudāveris
3.	audeāmur	12.	laudāverīs
4.	bibam	13.	resistant
5.	mentīrer	14.	flōrētis
6.	docuerō	15.	peream
7.	sciat	16.	advēnērunt
8.	ēgeram	17.	imperētis
9.	dēlēvistī	18.	dīmīserint

118. Pluperfect Active Subjunctive

The **pluperfect active subjunctive** adds **-isse-** to the perfect stem of the third principal part and uses the same endings as the present subjunctive. Note that the **-e-** is short (as always) before the first singular and both third person endings, but otherwise long. The pluperfect active subjunctive looks like the perfect active infinitive with personal endings added.

	1st Conj.	2nd Conj.	3rd Conj.	4th Conj.
1st sg.	amāvissem	monuissem	rēxissem	audīvissem
2nd sg.	amāvissēs	monuissēs	rēxissēs	audīvissēs
3rd sg.	amāvisset	monuisset	rēxisset	audīvisset
1st pl.	amāvissēmus	monuissēmus	rēxissēmus	audīvissēmus
2nd pl.	amāvissētis	monuissētis	rēxissētis	audīvissētis
3rd pl.	amāvissent	monuissent	rēxissent	audīvissent

Exercise 191. Following the model verbs above, conjugate **nuntiō, iubeō** and **aperiō** in the pluperfect active subjunctive, singular and plural.

119. Perfect and Pluperfect Subjunctive of sum and possum

The subjunctives of **sum** and **possum** are regular in the perfect and the pluperfect:

	Sum		Possum	
	Perfect	**Pluperfect**	**Perfect**	**Pluperfect**
1st sg.	fuerim	fuissem	potuerim	potuissem
2nd sg.	fuerīs	fuissēs	potuerīs	potuissēs
3rd sg.	fuerit	fuisset	potuerit	potuisset
1st pl.	fuerīmus	fuissēmus	potuerīmus	potuissēmus
2nd pl.	fuerītis	fuissētis	potuerītis	potuissētis
3rd pl.	fuerint	fuissent	potuerint	potuissent

Exercise 192. Identify each of the following verbs by person, number, tense and mood. Include all possibilities for any ambiguous forms.

1.	vēnissēs	6.	sītis	11.	ferrēmus
2.	dent	7.	portārēmus	12.	ēgit
3.	steterat	8.	posuerō	13.	neglegant
4.	mīserint	9.	trādideris	14.	adfuistis
5.	moneātis	10.	trāderis	15.	adesset

120. Tenses in Independent Uses of the Subjunctive

The present tense is much more common than the perfect in the independent uses of the subjunctive. Similarly, the imperfect is more common than the pluperfect in these uses. The following chart is provided as a summary of the most common tense uses; if no example is given, the tense is not commonly used for that independent use. *This chart is for reference only and need not be memorized!*

Sample verb: **eō, īre, iī, itūrus**   to go

	Present	Imperfect	Perfect	Pluperfect
Hortatory	**eāmus.** let's go.			
Jussive	**eat.** let him go.	**īret.** he should have gone.		
negative ("*Prohibition*")			**nē ierīs.** don't go.	
Optative	**(utinam) eant.** I wish they would go (in the future).	**(utinam) īrent.** I wish they were going (now).		**(utinam) īssent.** I wish they had gone (in the past).
Deliberative	**eam?** should I go?	**īrem?** should I have gone?		
Potential	**eant.** they may go.	**īrent.** they might have gone.	**ierint.** they may/ might go.	

Exercise 193. Translate each of the following and identify the subjunctive use.

1. Utinam plūs aquae portāvissēmus.
2. Rogāret nōs.
3. Domum quam celerrimē currāmus.
4. Forsitan ille scelus fēcerit.
5. Bona sit fortūna cīvibus.
6. Should I try (**temptō**) to speak?
7. I wish our leaders had listened!
8. You could have seen the strangest things.
9. Now let us drink wine!
10. He should have come.

121. **Tenses in Dependent Uses of the Subjunctive: Sequence of Tenses**

The tense of the subjunctive in a dependent clause shows action relative to that of the main clause: incomplete (happening at the same time as that of the main clause, or at some time in the future), or completed (before the action of the main verb). Happily, there is a clear pattern of usage for what tense to expect in each clause.

Tenses of a Latin verb are grouped in two categories, primary and secondary (or "historical").

> A **primary** tense is anything that is not a past tense:
> present, future, present perfect (§54; *he has come*) or future perfect.

> A **secondary** tense is a past tense:
> imperfect, historical perfect (§54; *he came*) or pluperfect.

A primary tense in the main clause is accompanied by a primary tense (either present or perfect subjunctive) in the dependent clause. If the main clause has a secondary tense, the verb of the dependent clause will be secondary (either imperfect or pluperfect subjunctive). This pattern is often called the "sequence of tenses." The following chart shows how the typical pattern works:

	Main Verb	Subjunctive Verb (dependent clause)	
Primary Sequence	Present Future Present Perfect Future Perfect *(rare)*	Present	(incomplete action *or* same time as main verb)
		Perfect	(completed action)
Secondary Sequence	Any Past Tense	Imperfect	(incomplete action *or* same time as main verb)
		Pluperfect	(completed action)

Result clauses (§116) do not always follow this sequence of tenses, e.g., the perfect subjunctive can be used after a secondary tense to emphasize the result:

> Vulnus tantum erat **ut perierit.**   The wound was so great **that he died.**

Exercise 194. Which tense of the subjunctive would you use for each of the underlined dependent verbs, and why? (Do *not* translate into Latin.)

1. We are going in order <u>to buy</u> food.
2. We were going in order <u>to buy</u> food.
3. We will go in order <u>to buy</u> food.
4. He was so strong that <u>he was able</u> to win.
5. He is so strong that <u>he is able</u> to win.
6. He is so strong that <u>he will be able</u> to win.

Exercise 195. Translate each of the underlined verbs into Latin.

1. If only <u>I were able</u> to leave now.
2. He <u>may be</u> the next consul.
3. They work hard so <u>they can</u> live well.
4. We lied so <u>you would be</u> safe.
5. I wish <u>they had been able</u> to come.
6. They arrived so late that <u>you could</u> not see them.

122. Dependent Uses of the Subjunctive: Adverbial Clauses

1) **Circumstance, Cause, Concession** – introduced by **cum**; negative is **nōn**

As you learned in Chapter 12 (§60), a **cum** clause with an indicative verb indicates a specific time. When the dependent verb is subjunctive, the clause indicates the situation or circumstances under which an action occurred. The context of the sentence may suggest the best way to understand or translate the clause, but it is not always possible to distinguish among these three uses. **Cum** circumstantial typically uses only the imperfect and pluperfect subjunctive.

Cum hoc scīret, bellum gessit.	He waged war	**when he knew this.**
		because he knew this.
		although he knew this.

Circumstance (When):

> **Cum litterās mīsisset,** discessit. **When he had sent the letter,** he departed.

Cause (Because, Since):

> **Cum nāvigāre timeat,** in lītore manet. He stays on the shore, **because he is afraid to sail.**

Concession (Although):

> Cēnam parat **cum aegra sit.** She prepares dinner, **although she is sick.**

Tamen is commonly found with cum clauses indicating concession.

2) **Time, with anticipation** – introduced by **dum**

As you learned in Chapter 12 (§60), **dum** with a present indicative means "while, as long as." With a present or imperfect subjunctive, it means "until," in a dependent clause indicating time with the idea of anticipation or expectation.

> Exspectāmus **dum ille haec dīcat.** We are waiting **until he says these things.**

The following rhyme has helped many students remember this use:

> These words in feeble minds instill:
> **dum** with subjunctive means "until"

Antequam ("before") is similarly used with the imperfect subjunctive to indicate expectation, or even purpose.

Exercise 196. Translate each of the following sentences.

1. Scrībēsne ad nōs cum Rōmam vēneris?
2. Bellum gerere Rōmānīs difficile nōn est cum Rōmae multī et fortēs cīvēs sint.
3. Iūdicium ita factum est ut malus poenam dederit.
4. Mīlitēs cum multī dēspērāvissent tamen pugnābant.
5. Vōs exspectāvistis dum nāvis advenīret.

6. Cum mīles ab hostibus captus ducem appropinquantem vidēret, timōre tremēbat.
7. Oppidum pulchrum vīdī tum cum trānsiī lātum pontem.
8. Oppidum pulchrum vīdī cum trānsīrem lātum pontem.
9. Haec cum ita sint, nē appropinquāverīs.
10. Cum sōlem in caelō videāmus, omnēs noctem appropinquāre scīmus.

Exercise 197. Translate into Latin.

1. The war was so long that the citizens began to despair.
2. Since night is approaching, let them go home with their friends.
3. Although she was very tired, nevertheless she kept on walking in order to find water.
4. The brave soldier was killed when he was fighting.
5. They went into the city since there was no food at home.
6. They went into the city in order to find food.
7. At the time when my mother and father were in Rome, I was away.
8. Let us rejoice because we will be free in a few days.
9. Wait until he comes.
10. When he had heard your (sg.) message, he was silent.

Reading 36 *(slightly edited)*

Hyginus (c. 64 B.C. – A.D. 17) wrote many works which are lost, but his collection of 300 mythological stories has survived. This selection summarizes part of the myth of Hercules and will seem very disjointed to those who know the full myth; for those who don't, a list of the proper names follows the Vocabulary section below.

Īnfāns cum esset, **dracōnēs** duōs duābus manibus necāvit, quōs Iūnō mīserat. Leōnem Nemaeum, quem Lūna nūtrīerat in antrō, necāvit, cuius pellem prō tegumentō habuit. Hydram Lernaeam, Typhōnis filiam, cum capitibus novem ad fontem Lernaeum interfēcit. Haec tantam vim venēnī habuit, ut afflātū hominēs necāret, et sī quis eam dormientem trānsīerat, vestīgia eius afflābat et maiōrī **cruciātū** moriēbātur. Hanc Minervā mōnstrānte interfēcit et exinterāvit et eius venēnō sagittās suās tinxit; itaque quicquid posteā sagittīs fīxerat, mortem nōn effugiēbat, unde posteā et ipse periit in Phrygiā.

Hērculēs cum ad Cerberum esset missus ab Eurystheō rēge et [cum] Lycus, Neptūnī filius, putāvisset eum periisse, Megaram, uxōrem eius, et filiōs interficere voluit et rēgnum occupāre. Hercules eō intervēnit et Lycum interfēcit; posteā, ab Iūnōne **īnsāniā** obiēctā, Megaram et filiōs suōs interfēcit. Postquam suam mentem recēpit, ab Apolline petiit darī sibi responsum, quōmodo scelus pūrgāret. quod eī Apollō sortem reddere nōluit, Herculēs irātus dē templō eius **tripodem** sustulit, quem posteā Iōvis iussū reddidit et nōlentem sortem dare iussit. Herculēs ob id ā Mercuriō Omphalae rēgīnae in **servitūtem** datus est.

Vocabulary:

īnfāns, -ntis *m.*	infant	tingō, -ere, tinxī	to stain, wet
dracō, -ōnis *m.*	snake	figō, -ere, -xī	to pierce
necō, -āre, -āvī	to kill	effugiō, -ere	to escape
nūtriō, -īre, -iī	to nourish, raise, nurture	occupō, -āre	to take possession of
		eō (adv.)	there
pellis, -is *f.*	hide	interveniō, -īre	to come on the scene
tegumentum, -ī *n.*	armor, protective covering	recipiō, -ere, -cēpī	to regain
fōns, fontis *m.*	spring (of water)	quōmodo …	"how he could
venēnum, -ī *n.*	venom, poison	pūrgāret	clear"
afflātus, -ūs *m.*	breath	sors, sortis *f.*	oracular response
quis = aliquis		reddō, -ere, -didī	to utter in reply; return
vestīgium, -iī *n.*	track, footprint	tripūs, -odis *m.*	tripod, 3-legged stand at the Delphic oracle
afflō, -are	to breathe on (*subject is Hydra*)	iussū	"by order of"
cruciātus, -ūs *m.*	severe pain, torture		
exinterō, -āre, -āvī	to gut, disembowel		
sagitta, -ae *f.*	arrow		
servitūs, -tūtis *f.*	bondage, servitude		

Proper Names:

Iūnō, -ōnis *f.*	Juno, queen of the gods	Eurystheus, -ī *m.*	Eurystheus, king who sends Hercules on his labors
Leō, -ōnis *m.*	lion		
Nemaeus, -a, -um	of Nemea (a city), Nemean	Lycus, -ī *m.*	Lycus, a king of Thebes
Lūna, -ae *f.*	Luna, goddess of the Moon	Neptūnus, -ī *m.*	Neptune, sea god
Hydra, -ae, *f.*	Hydra, monstrous snake	Megara, -ae *f.*	Megara, daughter of king Creon
Lernaeus, -a, -um	of Lerna (a city), Lernaean	Apollo, -inis *m.*	Apollo, god of prophecy
Typhō, -ōnis *m.*	Typhon, a monster	Iuppiter, Iovis *m.*	Jupiter, king of the gods
Minerva, -ae *f.*	Minerva, goddess who helps Hercules	Mercurius, -iī *m.*	Mercury, messenger god and son of Jupiter
Phrygia, -ae *f.*	Phrygia, an area in modern Turkey	Omphala, -ae *f.*	Omphale, queen of Lydia
Cerberus, -ī *m.*	Cerberus, 3-headed guard-dog of Hades		

Reading 37 *(slightly edited)*

From 55 to 44 B.C. Cicero wrote various philosophical works, among them De Senectute (On Old Age). *In this excerpt he writes about the immortal nature of the soul and concludes with some comforting words that the Persian leader Cyrus, on his deathbed, said to his sons. Cicero typically uses long sentences, but to make this selection more intelligible, it has been broken into shorter sentences joined by "et."*

Sic persuāsī mihi, sic sentiō, cum tanta **celeritās** animōrum sit, tanta memoria praeteritōrum futūrōrumque prūdentia, tot artēs, tantae **scientiae**, tot **inventa**, nōn posse eam nātūram, quae rēs eās **contineat**, esse mortālem. et cumque semper **agitētur** animus nec principium **mōtūs** habeat, quia sē ipse moveat, [sentiō] nē fīnem mōtūs quidem habitūrum esse, quia numquam sē ipse sit relictūrus. et, cum **simplex** animī esset nātūra, neque habēret in sē quicquam **admixtum dispār** suī atque **dissimile**, [sentiō] nōn posse eum dīvidī; et, sī nōn posset [dīvidī], nōn posse interīre; ....

moriēns Cyrus maior haec dīcit: 'Nōlīte arbitrārī, Ō mihi cārissimī fīliī, mē, cum ā vōbīs discesserō, nūsquam aut nūllum fore. Nec enim, dum eram vōbīscum, animum meum vidēbātis, sed eum esse in hōc corpore ex eīs rēbus quās gerēbam intellegēbātis. Eundem igitur esse crēdite, etiamsī nūllum vidēbitis.'

Vocabulary:

celeritās, -tātis *f.*	speed	admisceō, -ēre, -uī, -mixtus	to mix, combine
praeteritus, -a, -um	past events, the past		
futūrus, -a, -um	future events, the future	dispār, -aris	different in kind
		dissimilis, -e	dissimilar
prūdentia, -ae *f.*	foreknowledge	dīvidō, -ere	to divide, separate
scientia, -ae *f.*	knowledge, erudition	intereō, -īre	to perish, die
inventum, -ī *n.*	discovery	Cyrus maior	Cyrus the elder, "Cyrus the Great," ruler of the Persian empire
contineō, -ēre	to contain (§132)		
agitō, -āre	to move; *pass.* move oneself		
principium, -iī *n.*	primary cause, origin		
mōtus, -ūs *m.*	motion, movement	nūsquam (adv.)	nowhere
simplex, -icis	single, consisting of one element	fore = futūrum esse	
		etiamsī (*sub. conj.*)	although

Practice Sentences

Identify the form and the use of each subjunctive verb.

1. Is pāgus appellābātur Tigurīnus; nam omnis cīvitās Helvētia in quattuor pāgōs dīvīsa est. Hic pāgus ūnus cum domō exīsset (patrum nostrōrum memoriā) cōnsulem interfēcerat et eius exercitum sub iugum mīserat.

    (Caesar; *telling how a group of the Helvetians had killed one of his ancestors*)

2. Dīxerat "Ō mōrēs! Ō tempora!" Tullius ōlim,
    Sacrilegum strueret cum Catilīna nefās,
    Cum gener atque socer dīrīs concurreret armīs
    Maestaque cīvīlī caede madēret humus.

    (Martial)

3. Multa quoque et bellō passus [est], dum conderet urbem
        īnferretque deōs Latiō.

    (Vergil; *describing Aeneas' fate*)

4. Cum sōlitūdō et vīta sine amīcīs insidiārum et metūs plēna sit, ratiō ipsa monet amīcitiās comparāre.

    (Cicero)

5. Nōn ut edam vīvō, sed ut vīvam edō.

    (Quintilian; *illustrating antithesis*)

6. Numquam mē rēvocās, veniās cum saepe vocātus.

    (Martial; *complaining to a friend who never reciprocates his invitations*)

7. Populus autem eōdem annō mē cōnsulem [creāvit], cum cōnsul uterque bellō cecidisset.

    (Augustus; *explaining in his* Res Gestae *how he became consul at only 19 years of age*)

8. Rōmānī signa intulērunt: prīma et secunda aciēs, ut victīs ac summōtīs resisteret, tertia, ut venientēs sustinēret.

    (Caesar – adapted; *describing how he fought the phalanx of the Gauls*)

Vocabulary:

pāgus, -ī *m.*	district, community	socer, -erī *m.*	father-in-law
Tigurīnus, -a, -um	of Tigurinus, Tigurine	madeō, -ēre, -uī	to be wet
Helvētia, -ae, *f.*	Helvetia, Switzerland	Latium, -iī *n.*	Latium, a city
iugum, -ī *n.*	yoke	Latiō = ad Latium	
cūria, -ae *f.*	Curia, senate building	sōlitūdō, -inis *f.*	solitude, loneliness
		insidiae, -ārum, *f.*	ambush, plot, trap
sacrilegus, -a, -um	profane, impious	amīcitia, -ae *f.*	friendship
Tullius, -iī *m.*	Cicero	comparō, -āre	to establish, make
struō, -ere, struxī	to devise, arrange	edō, -ere, ēdī	to eat
		rēvocō, -āre	to invite back
Catilīna, -ae *m.*	Catiline, a political enemy of Cicero	summoveō, -ēre, -mōvī, -mōtus	to repulse, push back
gener, -erī *m.*	son-in-law	sustineō, -ēre	to stop, withstand

Chapter 26 Vocabulary

Nouns

nefās *n. (indeclinable)*	sin, crime (against divine law), wrong
poena, poenae *f.*	penalty
poenam dare	to pay the penalty
sōl, sōlis *m.*	sun

Verbs

appropinquō, appropinquāre, appropinquāvī, appropinquātūrus	to approach, draw near
exspectō, exspectāre, exspectāvī, exspectātus	to wait for, expect; hope for
tremō, tremere, tremuī	to tremble, shake

Adjectives

dīrus, dīra, dīrum	awful, horrible
lātus, lāta, lātum	wide, broad
maestus, maesta, maestum	sad, mournful

Adverbs

posteā	afterwards
quoque	also
unde	from where, whence

Pronouns

aliquis, aliquid	someone, something, anyone, anything
quisquis, quicquid (quidquid)	whoever, whatever; everyone who

Subordinating Conjunctions

cum	when; because, since; although
dum	until *(with the subjunctive)*

(16)

Derivatives: For each English word below, give the Latin word from the Chapter 26 Vocabulary to which it is related and the English word's meaning.

1. dire
2. nefarious
3. expectation
4. subpoena
5. latitude
6. solar

CHAPTER 27

Perfect and Pluperfect Passive Subjunctive
Adverbial Clauses: Conditions
    Simple conditions
    Subjunctive conditions

This chapter introduces the perfect and pluperfect subjunctive passive forms. It also expands on what you have already learned about conditions, adverbial dependent clauses, and uses of the subjunctive.

123. Perfect and Pluperfect Passive Subjunctive

These tenses are formed like the perfect (**amātus sum**) and pluperfect (**amātus eram**) passive indicative, except that the form of the verb **sum** is in the subjunctive instead of the indicative. Deponent verbs follow the same pattern.

Perfect

	1st Conj.	2nd Conj.	3rd Conj.	4th Conj.
1st sg.	amātus **sim**	monitus **sim**	rēctus **sim**	audītus **sim**
2nd sg.	amātus **sīs**	monitus **sīs**	rēctus **sīs**	audītus **sīs**
3rd sg.	amātus **sit**	monitus **sit**	rēctus **sit**	audītus **sit**
1st pl.	amātī **sīmus**	monitī **sīmus**	rēctī **sīmus**	audītī **sīmus**
2nd pl.	amātī **sītis**	monitī **sītis**	rēctī **sītis**	audītī **sītis**
3rd pl.	amātī **sint**	monitī **sint**	rēctī **sint**	audītī **sint**

Pluperfect

	1st Conj.	2nd Conj.	3rd Conj.	4th Conj.
1st sg.	amātus **essem**	monitus **essem**	rēctus **essem**	audītus **essem**
2nd sg.	amātus **essēs**	monitus **essēs**	rēctus **essēs**	audītus **essēs**
3rd sg.	amātus **esset**	monitus **esset**	rēctus **esset**	audītus **esset**
1st pl.	amātī **essēmus**	monitī **essēmus**	rēctī **essēmus**	audītī **essēmus**
2nd pl.	amātī **essētis**	monitī **essētis**	rēctī **essētis**	audītī **essētis**
3rd pl.	amātī **essent**	monitī **essent**	rēctī **essent**	audītī **essent**

Exercise 198. Following the model verbs above, conjugate **dēleō, legō** and **inveniō** in the perfect and pluperfect passive subjunctive, singular and plural.

Exercise 199. Identify each of the following verbs by person, number, tense, voice and mood.

1.	dūcerer	11.	trādar
2.	cōnātī sumus	12.	dīxissent
3.	habitae essētis	13.	exspectāta sint
4.	eāmus	14.	scīrētur
5.	dēleātur	15.	ēripiāmus
6.	laudēminī	16.	coācta sim
7.	vēneris	17.	iungerentur
8.	missus sit	18.	lātus esset
9.	invenīrentur	19.	pōnam
10.	vocātī erāmus	20.	agāre

Exercise 200. Transform each of the following from indicative to subjunctive.

1.	ductus est	6.	inventa es
2.	accipiēbāmur	7.	clāmātur
3.	iūnxeris	8.	cōnābantur
4.	appellātī erātis	9.	interfectī sunt
5.	proficīscuntur	10.	movēmur

124. Adverbial Clauses: Conditions

A conditional sentence has a main clause and a dependent adverbial clause usually introduced by **sī** *(if)*. You have already seen some conditions in this book, all of which so far have used the indicative. Conditions in Latin may be divided into two types according to whether they use the indicative or subjunctive:

1) **simple conditions** – introduced by **sī, nisi**, etc.; verbs in the **indicative**

   This type of condition implies nothing about whether or not the situation is real. The same tense of the indicative is generally used in both the dependent and main clauses.

Time	Tense of Indicative	If clause (= protasis)	Main clause (= apodosis)
past	any past tense	**Sī ēgistī id,** If you did that,	**sapiēns fuistī.** you were wise.
present	present	**Sī agis id,** If you do that,	**sapiēns es.** you are wise.
future	future	**Sī agēs id,** If you (will) do that,	**sapiēns eris.** you will be wise.

2) **subjunctive conditions** – introduced by **sī, nisi**, etc.; verbs in the **subjunctive**

   These conditions *do* imply something about the situation, either that it is not true, or that there is some doubt about the condition. The same tense of the subjunctive is generally used in both the main and dependent clause. The following chart shows the usual pattern, along with the names commonly given to each of these conditions:

Name of Condition	Time	Subj. Tense	Example
contrary-to-fact (*not true*)	past	pluperfect	**Sī id ēgissēs, sapiēns fuissēs.** If you had done that, you would have been wise.
contrary-to-fact (*not true*)	present	imperfect	**Sī id agerēs, sapiēns essēs.** If you were doing that, you would be wise.
less vivid (*doubtful*)	future	present (*or* perfect in the **sī** clause)	**Sī id agās/ēgerīs, sapiēns sīs.** If you should do (were to do) that, you would be wise.

Special Note: The pronoun **aliquis, aliquid** (someone, something) which you learned in the last chapter can sometimes be hard to recognize. After certain words, the prefix **ali-** drops off, making this pronoun look like **quis, quid** (who?, what?). Use the context to help you decide which word is intended and use the following jingle to help remember when the prefix typically drops off:

After **sī**, **nisi**, **num** and **nē**, all the **ali-**'s fade away.

This book has encouraged you to read the Latin text as it appears (left to right) and to let each word lead you to expect what is likely to come next. The following chart summarizes conditions from the perspective of a careful reader.

		Dependent clause		Main clause	Type of condition
Indicative					
	sī, nisi	past	→	past	= Past Simple
		present	→	present	= Present Simple
		future *or* future perfect	→	future *or* future perfect	= Future Simple
Subjunctive					
	sī, nisi	present *or* perfect	→	present	= Future Less Vivid ("should - would")
	sī, nisi	pluperfect	→	pluperfect	= Past Contrary to Fact
		imperfect	→	imperfect	= Present Contrary to Fact

Exercise 201. Identify the type of condition and say what person, number, tense, voice, and mood would be needed in Latin for each verb. Do not translate.

1. They would have been lost at sea, if the storm had come then.
2. If it should rain today, we would not go on a picnic.
3. If you were all rich, you would not be stealing money from others.
4. If we go to the store later today, we will buy you some wine.
5. Would she stay with us if her parents allowed it?

Exercise 202. Identify the tense and mood of each underlined verb and name the condition represented in each sentence. Then translate.

1. Sī iūdex tibi <u>crēdet</u>, nūllam poenam dare cōgēris.
2. Magnam opem cōpiamque habērēs, sī <u>essēs</u> rēx.
3. Sī rēx fuissem, magnā cum sapientiā populum <u>rēxissem</u>.
4. Sī quis nōs <u>videat</u>, ab hostibus celeriter capiāmur.
5. Cīvēs <u>gaudērent</u>, sī imperātor venīret.

Exercise 203. Translate each of the following sentences.

1. Hodiē cōnsul in senātum vēnit ut audīrētur.
2. Sī sociī Rōmānī auxilia mittant, nōs omnēs cōnservēmur.
3. Currāmus celerrimē nē videāmur.
4. Cucurrimus tam celeriter ut nōn vidērēmur.
5. Sī sapientēs essētis, fīliōs philosophiam docērētis.
6. Venī mēcum ut mare et multās celerēs nāvēs videās.
7. Sī lūna plēna fuisset, Caesar lītus Galliae cōnspicere potuisset.
8. Ā nostrō duce petimus nē dīmittāmur.
9. Sī amīcitiam sacram habēmus, multī amīcī nōbīs erunt.
10. Sī amīcitiam sacram habeāmus, multī amīcī nōbīs sint.

Exercise 204. Translate into Latin.

1. The city would have fallen if the enemy had burned all the houses and temples.
2. Although a new judge had been chosen, nevertheless the trial did not begin for ten days.
3. If someone had brought food, we could have eaten dinner quickly.
4. The wise men will be happy if there is any perception after death.
5. If I were your ally, then I would be able to help you.
6. Few men returned although many had set out.
7. The trees were so tall that the boys could not see their highest parts.
8. If the consuls had announced the victory, the people would have shouted with joy.
9. We would be able to overcome all hardships if we were strong in courage.
10. Our companions laughed when the very serious delegate fell.

Reading 38

In 63 B.C. Catiline attempted to overthrow the Roman government, a plot which included the assassination of the consul, Cicero. Catiline's plans were discovered, and Cicero hastily summoned the senators to a meeting at which Catiline himself was present. In the following excerpt Cicero expresses surprise that Catiline would choose to remain in Rome where he is hated and feared by so many.

Servī mehercule meī sī mē metuerent, ut tē metuunt omnēs cīvēs tuī, domum meam relinquere dēbēre mē putārem; tū urbem [relinquere dēbēre tē] nōn arbitrāris? et, sī mē meīs cīvibus indignē suspectum tam graviter atque offēnsum [esse] vidērem, carēre mē aspectū cīvium quam īnfestīs omnium oculīs cōnspicī māllem; tū, cum conscientiā scelerum tuōrum agnōscās odium omnium [esse] iūstum et iam diū tibi dēbitum, dubitās, quōrum mentēs sēnsūsque vulnerās, eōrum aspectum praesentiamque vītāre? Sī tē parentēs timērent atque ōdissent tuī neque eōs ūllā ratiōne plācāre possēs, ut opinor, ab eōrum oculīs aliquō [locō] concēderes. Nunc tē patria, quae communis est parens omnium nostrum, ōdit ac metuit et iam diū nihil tē iūdicat nisi dē parricīdiō suō cōgitāre; huius tū neque auctoritātem verebere nec iūdicium sequere nec vim pertimēscēs?

Vocabulary:

mehercule	"by Hercules!"	praesentia, -ae *f.*	presence
ut (+ indic.)	as	parēns, -ntis *m.* or *f.*	parent
indignē (adv.)	undeservedly	plācō, -āre	to appease, reconcile (with)
suspectus, -a, -um	suspected, mistrusted		
offensus, -a, -um	offensive, odious	opīnor, -ārī	to think, believe
aspectus, -ūs *m.*	sight	parricīdium, -iī *n.*	murder of a parent
īnfestus, -a, -um	hostile		
conscientia, -ae *f.*	knowledge, consciousness	auctoritās, -tātis *f.*	authority
		pertimēscō, -ere	to fear greatly
agnōscō, -ere	to recognize		

Reading 39

In Ovid's account of the great flood sent by Jupiter (cf. Ch. 7, Reading 5), he describes what the husband (Deucalion) says to his wife (Pyrrha) about their situation as the flood's only survivors.

"namque ego (crēde mihi), sī tē quoque pontus habēret,
tē sequerer, coniunx, et mē quoque pontus habēret.
ō utinam possim populōs reparāre **paternīs**
artibus atque animās **fōrmātae** īnfundere terrae!
nunc genus in nōbīs restat mortāle duōbus.
sic vīsum superīs: hominumque exempla manēmus."

Vocabulary:

namque	certainly; for; now	īnfundō, -ere (+ dat.)	to pour into
reparō, -āre	to restore, recover		
paternus, -a, -um	father's, paternal	restō, -āre	to remain, be left
anima, -ae *f.*	breath (of life)	vīsum (est)	to seem best
fōrmō, -āre, -āvī, -ātus	to form, fashion, mold		

Practice Sentences

Identify the form and use of each subjunctive verb then translate the full sentence.

1. Sī vīveret, verba eius audīrētis. (Cicero; *explaining why he can't call a witness*)

2. Ego sī Scipiōnis dēsīderiō mē movērī negem certē mentiar. ... Vīta tālis quidem fuit vel fortūnā vel glōriā, ut nihil posset accēdere. (Cicero; *Laelius here talks about the life and death of his friend Scipio*)

3. Caesarī cum id nūntiātum esset eōs per prōvinciam nostram iter facere cōnārī, mātūrat ab urbe proficīscī. (Caesar; *Caesar hears that the Helvetians are preparing to march*)

4. Nisi tū āmīsissēs, numquam recēpissem. (Cicero; *quoting Fabius, who won back the town of Tarentum after the addressee had lost that town to the enemy*)

5. Nōlīte existumāre maiōrēs nostrōs armīs rem pūblicam ex parvā magnam fēcisse! Sī ita esset, multō pulcherrimam eam nōs habērēmus; quippe sociōrum atque cīvium, praetereā armōrum atque equōrum maiōr cōpia nōbīs quam illīs est. Sed alia fuēre, quae illōs magnōs fēcēre, quae nōbīs nūlla sunt. (Sallust)

6. Sī tacuissēs, **philosophus** mānsissēs. (attributed to Boethius)

7. Sit tibi terra levis. (Traditional epitaph)

8. Caveat emptor. (Justinian)

Vocabulary:

Scipiō, -iōnis *m.*	Scipio (a Roman leader)	existumō, -āre	to judge, think
multō	"much"	maiōrēs (nom. pl.)	"ancestors"
dēsīderium, -iī *n.*	sense of loss	quippe	for, inasmuch as
vel ... vel	either ... or	praetereā (adv.)	besides, moreover
accēdō, -ere	to be added	philosophus, -ī *m.*	philosopher
mātūrō, -āre	to hasten	caveō, -ēre	to beware
recipiō, -ere, -cēpī	to get back, regain	emptor, -ōris *m.*	buyer

Chapter 27 Vocabulary

Nouns

amīcitia, amīcitiae *f.*	friendship
imperātor, imperātōris *m.*	general; emperor
iūdex, iūdicis *m.*	judge
odium, odiī *n.*	hatred, unpopularity
philosophia, philosophiae *f.*	philosophy
sēnsus, sēnsūs *m.*	sense, perception; emotion; idea
socius, sociī *m.*	companion, comrade, ally
victōria, victōriae *f.*	victory

Verbs

concēdō, concēdere, concessī, concessūrus	to go away, withdraw; yield to, submit; allow; forgive
cōnservō, cōnservāre, cōnservāvī, cōnservātus	to save, preserve, keep
cōnspiciō, cōnspicere, cōnspexī, cōnspectus	to observe, catch sight of, look at
metuō, metuere, metuī, metūtus	to fear, dread
ōdī, ōdisse	to hate; dislike
vereor, verērī, veritus sum	to fear, be afraid; respect

Adverb

num	*signals a question which expects the answer "no"*; whether *(in indirect question §126)*

Subordinating Conjunctions

nisi = nī	unless, if … not
sīn	but if, if however

(17)

Derivatives: For each English word below, give the Latin word from the Chapter 27 Vocabulary to which it is related and the English word's meaning.

1. conservation
2. odium
3. odious
4. society
5. judge
6. conspicuous
7. sensory
8. concession

CHAPTER 28

Irregular Verb: fīō, fierī, factus sum
Dependent Uses of the Subjunctive: Noun Clauses
    Noun Result
    Indirect Question
    Indirect Command
    Clauses of Fearing

The dependent clauses you learned in the last two chapters function as adverbs, answering questions like "why?", "when?", "with what result?" and "under what condition?". This chapter introduces dependent noun clauses that use the subjunctive. It also gives the irregular forms of **fīō**, a verb often accompanied by a noun result clause.

125. Irregular Verb: fīō, fierī, factus sum

The verb **fīō** has forms of the fourth conjugation except for the infinitive (**fierī**) and the imperfect subjunctive (**fierem**, etc.) which look like third conjugation forms. It is used as the passive of **faciō** and has the same passive forms as **faciō** in the perfect system.

	Indicative			Subjunctive	
	Present	**Imperfect**	**Future**	**Present**	**Imperfect**
1st sg.	fīō	fīēbam	fīam	fīam	fierem
2nd sg.	fīs	fīēbās	fīēs	fīās	fierēs
3rd sg.	fit	fīēbat	fīet	fīat	fieret
1st pl.	fīmus	fīēbāmus	fīēmus	fīāmus	fierēmus
2nd pl.	fītis	fīēbātis	fīētis	fīātis	fierētis
3rd pl.	fīunt	fīēbant	fīent	fīant	fierent

126. Dependent Uses of the Subjunctive: Noun Clauses

Remember that the direct object, or sometimes the subject, of a main verb may be a dependent clause (§88, 92, 96). The dependent clauses in this chapter all have a clause marker and a verb in the subjunctive, and generally follow the regular sequence of tenses (§121). The key to identifying how each clause is used is to know the meaning of the main verb.

1) Noun Result – introduced by **ut** (**utī**); negative is **ut … nōn**

The result clauses you have seen before function adverbially and are (usually) signaled by a signpost word in the main clause (§116, 2). A *noun* result clause functions as the direct object or subject (or subject complement) of certain governing verbs and impersonal expressions with the meaning "bring about" or "happen."

Here are some of the common verbs which should lead you to expect a noun result clause:

Main Verb	Meaning	Noun Clause functions as
faciō (*and its compounds*)	to make	direct object
efficiō	to bring about	direct object
cōnficiō	to accomplish	direct object
efficitur (*passive of above verbs*)	be brought about	subject
accidit	happen	subject
fit (§125)	come about	subject
mōs est	it is the custom	subject/subject complement
necesse est*	it is necessary	subject/subject complement

*often without **ut**; *also used with an infinitive construction* (§39)

<u>Efficiam</u> **ut omnēs intellegant.**	I will make **them all understand.**
Saepe enim <u>accidit</u> **ut nēmō longum iter sōlus facere velit.**	For it often happens **that no one wants to make a long journey alone.**
Sīc <u>fit</u> **ut rēs pūblica valeat.**	So it happens **that the state is strong.**
<u>Erat mōs</u> Rōmānōrum **ut deōs colerent.**	It was the custom of the Romans **to worship the gods.**

Exercise 205. Translate into Latin.

1. It is the custom of men to be unwilling to seek peace.
2. The king brought it about that he had all the towns in his power.
3. Did he cause you to understand these things?
4. It is often necessary to fight for our fatherland.

2) Indirect Question – introduced by a question word (e.g., **quis?, ubi?, cūr?**)

Verbs of *asking, telling, seeing, hearing, knowing* and the like (§92) are often accompanied by an indirect question. This construction follows the regular sequence of tenses (§121), except that it *indicates a future action by using the future participle + either the present or imperfect subjunctive of* **sum**. Study the following examples:

Time of Main Verb			Action of Subjunctive Verb
Primary *Present/* *(Future)*	Rogō quid **fēcerit.** Rogō quid **faciat.** Rogō quid **factūrus sit.**	I ask what he did. I ask what he is doing. I ask what he will do.	*already happened (completed)* *same time* *hasn't happened yet*
Secondary *Past*	Rogāvī quid **fēcisset.** Rogāvī quid **faceret.** Rogāvī quid **factūrus esset.**	I asked what he had done. I asked what he was doing. I asked what he would do.	*already happened (completed)* *same time* *hasn't happened yet*

Exercise 206. Translate each of the underlined dependent clauses into Latin.

1. I know <u>who you (sg.) are</u>.
2. I wonder <u>how often they will come</u>?
3. Will you know <u>how to find us</u>?
4. We didn't know <u>where they were staying</u>.
5. She wondered <u>what he would say</u>?
6. He doesn't know <u>where they live</u>.
7. She asked us <u>what we had done</u>.
8. We know <u>who is coming</u>.
9. We knew <u>why he had come</u>.
10. They asked <u>how many people were giving gifts</u>.

3) **Indirect Command** – introduced by **ut** (**utī**); negative is **nē**

Verbs of *asking, telling, advising, persuading, commanding* and the like are often accompanied by an indirect command, which some grammar books call a **substantive clause of purpose.** Some common verbs which should lead you to expect an indirect command are:

hortor	to urge	**petō**	to ask
imperō	to command	**postulō**	to demand
moneō	to advise, warn	**precor**	to pray
ōrō	to beg, pray	**quaerō**	to ask
persuadeō	to persuade	**rogō**	to ask

<u>Moneō</u> vōs **ut illī ducī crēdātis.** — I advise you to trust that leader.

<u>Rogābant</u> nōs **ut abīrēmus statim.** — They were asking us to depart immediately.

Cīvibus <u>persuāsit</u> **ut in urbe manērent.** — He persuaded the citizens to stay in the city.

<u>Petō</u> ā tē **ut scrībās ad tuōs.** — I beg (from) you to write to your (people).

<u>Ōrābat</u> **nē sē relinquerēs.** — He kept begging you not to leave him.

Note: there are *three verbs* which do *not* use this construction. They are followed instead by an objective infinitive (§96):

iubeō   I order
vetō   I forbid
cupiō   I want

Exercise 207. Translate each of the underlined dependent verbs into Latin.

1. They were begging us <u>to rescue</u> them.
2. She asks that <u>we help</u> her.
3. Did the enemy demand that <u>he give</u> gifts?
4. He forbade them <u>to burn</u> the temple.
5. He will try to persuade us <u>to fight</u>.
6. I urge you (pl.) not <u>to drink</u> that.
7. They wanted us <u>to elect</u> him leader.
8. We prayed to the gods <u>to save</u> us.

   4) Clauses of Fearing – introduced by **nē**; negative is **ut**

Verbs of fearing (e.g. **timeō**, **metuō**, **vereor**) often govern clauses introduced by **nē** and **ut**. However, special care needs to be given to the meanings of the clause markers here, since their meanings are the reverse of what they mean elsewhere, perhaps because this use of the subjunctive is optative in origin (§112). The fear is that the wish will not come true: **optō ut scrībat** (I wish that he would write) – [but] I fear that he won't (**timeō ut scrībat**); **optō nē discēdat** (I wish he would not go away) – [but] I fear that he will (**timeō nē discēdat**).

	Indicates a Fear that	Translate as
nē	something will happen	that, lest
ut	something will *not* happen	that … not

Note: **nē nōn** sometimes replaces **ut**, and always does when the main clause has a negative.

Metuō **nē** veniant.	I fear **that** they will come. *or* I fear **lest** they (may) come.
Metuō **ut** veniant.	I fear **that** they will **not** come.
Timuit **nē** abīssēmus.	He feared **that** we had gone away.
Timuit **ut** venīrēmus.	He feared **that** we would **not** come.
<u>Nōn</u> timuit **nē nōn** venīrēmus	He did *not* fear **that** we would **not** come.

Exercise 208. Translate.

1. Prīncipēs verentur nē interficiantur.
2. Metuit ut nūntius audītus esset.
3. Omnēs timēmus nē hostēs adsint.
4. Timeō ut tantum iter ingredī possim.
5. Caesar fears that the army will be attacked.
6. Were you (sg.) afraid that he wouldn't stay?
7. I kept fearing that the dog would eat my food.
8. They are afraid that you (pl.) won't believe them.

Exercise 209. Translate each of the following sentences and be ready to identify the type of each dependent clause.

1. Rogāvit vōs ad quem gladiōs missōs essent.
2. Lēgātus metuēbat ut mīlitēs flūmen altum trānsīre possent.
3. Uxōrēs semper timēbunt nē coniugēs aliās fēminās ament.
4. Pater meus mihi persuāsit nē sōla Rōmae manērem.
5. Nōlī mē rogāre cūr illae arborēs caesae sint.
6. Fit ut rēs pūblica valeat illīs bonīs regentibus.
7. Rēx nōbīs imperāvit ut prō patriā pugnārēmus.
8. Cognōscimus quōmodō tēlīs nostrīs ūtāmur.
9. Vereor nē labōrēs aetātis gaudia vītae vincant.
10. Nauta nōs monuit ut quam celerrimē ante tempestātem nāvigārēmus.

Exercise 210. Translate into Latin.

1. They kept asking who the new king was and whether he was wise.
2. Did you fear that the senate would not make peace with the enemy?
3. The captives *(use a participle)* begged to be allowed to live.
4. We were surprised how many men were being forced to destroy their homes.
5. They feared that the enemy would burn their camp and carry off their weapons.
6. He had warned the citizens not to try to free your (pl.) slaves.
7. Do you know why the boy was left with his father?
8. The general commanded the Greek towns to surrender immediately.
9. It happened that no one was killed when the enemy attacked the city.
10. The general asked that his soldiers be given more money.

Reading 40

Caesar tells about the Helvetians (one of the tribes in Gaul) and their leader, Orgetorix, who urges his people to push beyond the natural boundaries of their territory.

Apud Helvētiōs longē nōbilissimus fuit et dītissimus Orgetorīx. Is, M. Messālā, M. Pīsōne cōnsulibus, rēgnī cupiditāte **inductus** coniūrātiōnem **nōbilitātis** fēcit, et cīvitātī persuāsit, ut dē fīnibus suīs cum omnibus cōpiīs exīrent, [dīcēns] facile esse, cum virtūte omnibus praestārent, tōtius Galliae imperiō potīrī. Id facilius eīs persuāsit, quod undique locī nātūrā Helvētiī

continued

Vocabulary:

dīs, dītis	rich	coniūrātiō, -iōnis *f.*	conspiracy
M. Messāla, -ae *m.*	Marcus Messala	nōbilitās, -tātis *f.*	nobility
M. Pīsō, -onis *m.*	Marcus Piso	praestō, -āre (+ dat.)	to be superior to
indūcō, -ere, -dūxī, -ductus	to lead on, induce		

continued

continentur: ūnā ex parte flūmine Rhēnō, lātissimō et altissimō, quī agrum Helvētium ā Germānīs **dīvidit**; alterā ex parte monte Iūrā altissimō, quī est inter Sēquanōs et Helvētiōs; tertiā, lacū Lemannō et flūmine Rhodanō, quī prōvinciam nostram ab Helvētiīs **dīvidit**. Hīs rēbus fīēbat ut et minus lātē vagārentur et minus facile fīnitimīs bellum īnferre possent.

Vocabulary:

contineō, -ēre	to contain, hem in	lacus, -ūs *m.*	lake
		Lemannus, -ī *m.*	(lake) Geneva
Rhēnus, -ī *m.*	Rhine (river)	Rhodanus, -ī *m.*	Rhone (river)
Iūra, -ae *f.*	Jura (a mountain)	vagor, -ārī	to wander
dīvidō, -ere	to divide, separate	fīnitimus, -a, -um	neighboring
Sēquanī, -ōrum *m.* (pl.)	Sequani (a tribe)		

Practice Sentences

Identify the form and use of each subjunctive verb and translate.

1. Eādem nocte accidit ut esset lūna plēna. (Caesar)
2. Timeō nē male facta **antīqua** mea sint inventa omnia. (Plautus; *a young man who has fathered a child worries the truth will come out*)
3. Quanta multitūdō hominum **convēnerit** ad hoc iūdicium, vidēs. (Cicero; *addressing the court at the beginning of a speech*)
4. Potest fierī ut fallar. (Cicero; *admitting that he is not always right*)
5. Albānus exercitus **inclāmāvit** Curiātiīs utī opem ferant frātrī. (Livy)
6. Forsitan et Priamī fuerint quae Fāta requīrās. (Vergil; *Aeneas tells of the fall of Troy and its king*)
7. Metuōque et timeō, nē hoc tandem prōpalam fiat nimis. (Plautus; *a man watches two lovers*)
8. Cīvitās quae sit cōgitā, quid petās, quī sis. (attributed to Cicero; *advice to a budding politician*)

Vocabulary:

male (adv.)	unfortunately	inclāmō, -āre, -āvī	to cry out (to), call upon
antīquus, -a, -um	old		
conveniō, -īre, -vēnī	to come together, assemble	Curiātiī, -ōrum *m.*	the Curiatii (family)
		Priamus, -ī *m.*	Priam, king of Troy
fallō, -ere	to deceive; (*pass.*) be mistaken	prōpalam (adv.)	openly
		nimis (adv.)	too (much)
Albānus, -a, -um	Alban		

Chapter 28 Vocabulary

Nouns

canis, canis *m.* or *f.*	dog
gladius, gladiī *m.*	sword
oppidum, oppidī *n.*	town
tēlum, tēlī *n.*	weapon; spear
tempestās, tempestātis *f.*	storm; weather

Verbs

ēripiō, ēripere, ēripuī ēreptus	to snatch away; rescue, free
fiō, fierī, factus sum	to happen, occur; be done, be made
imperō, imperāre, imperāvī, imperātus (+ dat)	to command, order; rule (over)
mōs est	it is the custom, habit, way
requīrō, requīrere, requīsīvī (-iī), requīsītus	to search for; ask, inquire after; demand
rogō, rogāre, rogāvī, rogātus	to ask, ask for

Adjective

quot (*indeclinable*)	how many?

Adverbs

quōmodo	how
quotiēns	how often?
statim	immediately, at once
undique	on all sides

Preposition

apud (+ acc.)	among, with, near, at (the house of)

(17)

Derivatives: For each English word below, give the Latin word from the Chapter 28 Vocabulary to which it is related and the English word's meaning.

1. interrogate
2. stat! (hospital slang)
3. imperative
4. tempestuous
5. requirement
6. canine
7. fiat
8. quota

Neptune on his Chariot and Sea Creatures. Mosaic from Ostia, 2nd c. A.D.

CHAPTER 29

The Gerund
The Gerundive
    Passive Periphrastic
    Dative of Agent

You have already learned that certain verb forms can be used as nouns (infinitives §39) and others as adjectives (participles §84). This chapter introduces a second type of verbal noun called the gerund, and a new verbal adjective form called the gerundive, along with several common uses of these forms.

127. **The Gerund**

A **gerund** is a verbal noun, like the infinitive. In English, it can be hard to distinguish between a gerund (noun) and some participles (adjective) because both end with **-ing**. In examples such as the third one below, this can lead to real ambiguity and, sometimes, humor:

Gerund (= Noun)	Participle (= Adjective)

I like **hunting** rabbits.
    hunting is the direct object of "like"
	The **hunting** dogs are very quick.
	    hunting describes the dogs

They succeeded by **working** hard.
    working is the object of the
    preposition "by"
	The man **working** in the field ate lunch.
	    working describes the man

Visiting relatives can be difficult.
    It can be difficult **to visit** relatives.
	Visiting relatives can be difficult.
	    Relatives **who visit** can be difficult.

Exercise 211. Identify each **-ing** word below as either a gerund or a participle. If it is a participle, draw an arrow to the noun it modifies.

1. She learned to speak Italian by practicing all the time.
2. Did you see him leaving early?
3. Being young, we enjoyed sneaking out at night.
4. While swimming in the lake, the boys saw a huge fish eating insects.
5. He was afraid of answering the questions incorrectly.
6. My dog loves the woman training her.
7. Already running late, he took a cab for the sake of arriving on time.
8. The Romans appointed many days for worshipping the gods.

Unlike in English, a Latin gerund does *not* look like a present active participle. The gerund is formed by adding -nd- to the present stem of the verb, followed by the neuter singular endings of the second declension. Notice that the vowel before the -nd- is short, and that there is no nominative form.

	1st Conj.	2nd Conj.	3rd Conj.	3rd Conj. -Iō	4th Conj.
Nominative	-----	-----	-----	-----	-----
Genitive	amandī	docendī	regendī	capiendī	audiendī
Dative	amandō	docendō	regendō	capiendō	audiendō
Accusative	amandum	docendum	regendum	capiendum	audiendum
Ablative	amandō	docendō	regendō	capiendō	audiendō

Deponent verbs follow the same pattern, but the irregular verb **eō** does not:

	morior	eō
Nominative	-----	-----
Genitive	morandī	eundī
Dative	morandō	eundō
Accusative	morandum	eundum
Ablative	morandō	eundō

Like the infinitive when used as a noun, the gerund is always neuter and singular, and can be modified by an adverb (as in the first example below). Unlike in English, a Latin gerund is never used as the subject or direct object of a verb; instead, the infinitive plays those roles (§39, 96). The dative case is relatively rare, and the accusative is used only as the object of a few prepositions.

Here are the most common uses for each case of the gerund:

Genitive

1) with nouns and adjectives as an objective or explanatory genitive (§30)

   ars bene vīvendī   the art of living well
   cupidus discendī   desirous of learning; eager to learn

2) with **causā** or **grātiā** to show cause/purpose (§53)

   pugnandī causā   for the sake of fighting; in order to fight

Dative

1) with adjectives denoting fitness or suitability

   nāvis apta nāvigandō   a ship fit for sailing

Accusative

1) with **ad** (and sometimes **in**) to show purpose

   ad pugnandum   for fighting; in order to fight
   ad audiendum convēnērunt they gathered to listen

   *in this use, the gerund never takes a direct object in Latin

Ablative

1) without a preposition, to indicate means (and, less often, manner or cause)

dīcendō dīcere discimus   we learn to speak by speaking

2) with certain prepositions (**ā/ab, dē, ex** or **in**)

dē bene vīvendō dīxērunt   they spoke about living well

Exercise 212. Translate the underlined phrases into Latin using a gerund.

1. They came <u>in order to listen</u>.
2. <u>By fighting well</u> they won the war.
3. He talks <u>for the sake of delaying</u>.
4. Do you get pleasure <u>from learning</u>?
5. She has a great love <u>of reading</u>.
6. Good shoes are useful <u>for walking</u>.
7. He was experienced <u>at speaking</u>.
8. They went inside <u>to sleep</u>.

128. **The Gerundive**

The **gerundive**, or future passive participle (§84, Chapter 17), is a verbal adjective. It looks like the gerund but, like other adjectives, it can occur in the singular or plural of any case (including the Nominative) or gender. The gerundive uses first and second declension endings like **bonus, bona, bonum**:

Singular	Masculine	Feminine	Neuter
Nominative	amandus	amanda	amandum
Genitive	amandī	amandae	amandī
Dative	amandō	amandae	amandō
Accusative	amandum	amandam	amandum
Ablative	amandō	amandā	amandō
Plural			
Nominative	amandī	amandae	amanda
Genitive	amandōrum	amandārum	amandōrum
Dative	amandīs	amandīs	amandīs
Accusative	amandōs	amandās	amanda
Ablative	amandīs	amandīs	amandīs

Remember, the gerund is a noun; the gerundive is an adjective.

Exercise 213. Identify each of the following as a gerund, gerundive or present active participle, and give its case, number and gender. If a form is ambiguous, identify all possibilities.

1. līberandās
2. metuentium
3. metuendum
4. incendentī
5. conveniendīs
6. flōrentis
7. ostendendus
8. cōnspiciendō
9. iungentem
10. eundī

The gerundive has only two common uses in Latin:

1) **To show obligation, necessity or propriety** (see especially §129 below)

crīmina nōn **ferenda**	crimes not **to be tolerated**
vir **laudandus**	a man **to be praised**
librōs **legendōs**	books **worth reading**

2) **To replace the gerund with a direct object**

A gerund in the genitive or ablative (without a preposition) can have a direct object, but most Latin authors prefer to use a gerundive construction instead. This gerundive construction always replaces a gerund in the dative or a gerund dependent on a preposition if the gerund would have had a direct object. In this construction, the noun takes the case the gerund would have been in and, like any adjective, the gerundive agrees with the noun in case, number and gender:

	Gerundive	**Gerund + Direct Object**
	cōnsilium bellī **gerendī**	cōnsilium **gerendī** bellum
literal translation	"a plan for the war **to be waged**"	"a plan **for waging** war"

In the gerundive construction, the deponent verbs that take their object in the ablative (§105) behave as transitive verbs do:

ad **fruendās** voluptātēs   for enjoying pleasures

Verbs that take a dative object can use the gerund construction:

ad vōbīs **pārendum**   to obey you

The gerundive construction is best understood (and translated) in the same way as the gerund construction. Here are some additional examples for each case:

	Gerundive (preferred)	Gerund + Direct Object
Genitive	**urbis capiendae** causā for the sake of capturing the city	**urbem capiendī** causā for the sake of capturing the city
Ablative	**pāce petendā** by seeking peace	**pācem petendō** by seeking peace
Dative	ūtilis **temperandīs animīs** useful for governing passions	(not possible)
Accusative	**ad pācem petendam** (in order) to seek peace	(not possible)

Exercise 214. Translate each of the following phrases and say whether a gerund or gerundive is used.

1.	scrībendō	6.	studium pugnandī
2.	ad virtūtem laudandam	7.	studium bellī gerendī
3.	victōriae nūntiandae causā	8.	ad voluptātem petendam
4.	aptus legendō	9.	spēs vincendī
5.	metus pereundī	10.	eīs persuādendī causā

Exercise 215. Translate the underlined phrases into Latin and say whether a gerund or gerundive is used.

1. you won <u>by running</u> quickly
2. you won <u>by wounding the soldier</u>
3. I came <u>to listen</u>
4. I came <u>to see the dog</u>
5. he is writing a book <u>about sailing</u>
6. he wrote a book <u>about navigating the sea</u>

129. Passive Periphrastic and Dative of Agent

The most common use of the gerundive is in a construction called the **passive periphrastic**, in which the gerundive is used with a form of **sum, esse, fuī** to indicate obligation or necessity. If expressed, the person to whom the obligation attaches (the person who will do the action) is indicated by a **dative of agent** instead of the ablative, unless the dative would cause ambiguity (see Ex. 217.6, below). Notice that even though the Latin expression is passive, colloquial English usually prefers an active translation:

Carthāgō dēlenda est.	Carthage must be destroyed.
	We must destroy Carthage.
Hoc mihi faciendum erat.	This had to be done by me.
	I had to do this.
Dī omnibus colendī sunt.	The gods must be worshipped by everyone.
	Everyone must worship the gods.
Putō proelium committendum esse.	I think the battle must be joined (begun).
	I think we must begin the battle.

Exercise 216. Translate each of the following. Use the passive periphrastic where possible.

1. Equus mittendus est.
2. Omnia fīnienda erant.
3. Dīxit Caesarem laudandum esse.
4. Fēminae eī cōnservandae fuērunt.
5. Senātuī pārendum est.
6. Caesar must do these things.
7. We must harm the shameful men.
8. The army had to destroy the bridge.
9. You (sg.) ought to drink the wine.
10. The city must be founded.

Exercise 217. Translate each of the following sentences.

1. Ex discendō capiunt voluptātem.
2. Multī Athēnās ad vīvendum ierant.
3. Exībant ad condendam urbem.
4. Lēgātī dīxērunt sē Rōmam cōnsulis inveniendī causā vēnisse.
5. Vēnērunt oppidī capiendī causā.
6. Grātiae deīs vōbīs agendae sunt.
7. Arbitrātī sunt cibum pōtumque statim mittendum esse.
8. Spectandō sē in aquā, Narcissus sē amāre incēpit. (Narcissus, -ī *m.* a boy's name)
9. Signum datum est ut mīlitēs proelium committerent.
10. Nesciō quid mihi agendum sit.

Exercise 218. Translate into Latin, using a gerund or gerundive where possible.

1. This water is not useful for drinking.
2. Caesar had to fight many battles in Gaul.
3. Working at night is difficult.
4. They accomplished many things by working with great care.
5. Did he say we must carry all those weapons?
6. The leader called the soldiers to prepare the great ships.
7. He thought by killing the king he would free the state.
8. Iron is useful for making swords.
9. Do you know why the women had to sing those songs?
10. I will use the whole time for speaking.

Reading 41

Cicero writes for his Roman countrymen about the different Greek schools of philosophy. Here he is talking about the philosopher Epicurus' belief that the Greatest (highest) Good in life is living pleasantly. Epicurus defined pleasure (voluptās) as the avoidance of pain (dolor).

Fatendum est summum esse bonum iūcundē vīvere. Id, quī in ūnā virtūte pōnunt et **splendōre** nōminis captī, quid nātūra postulet nōn intellegunt, **errōre** maximō, sī Epicūrum audīre voluerint, līberābuntur. istae enim vestrae eximiae pulchraeque virtūtēs nisi voluptātem efficerent, quis eās aut **laudābilēs** aut expetendās [esse] arbitrārētur? Ut[1] enim medicōrum **scientiam** nōn ipsīus artis, sed bonae valetūdinis causā probāmus, et gubernātōris ars, quia bene nāvigāndī ratiōnem habet, **ūtilitāte**, nōn arte laudātur, sīc sapientia, quae ars vīvendī putanda est, nōn expeterētur, sī nihil efficeret; nunc expetitur, quod est tamquam artifex conquīrendae et comparandae voluptātis. nam cum **ignōrātiōne** rērum bonārum et malārum māximē hominum vīta **vexētur**, ob eumque errōrem et voluptātibus māximīs saepe prīventur et dūrissimīs animī dolōribus torqueantur, sapientia est adhibenda, quae et **terrōribus** cupiditātibusque dētractīs et omnium **falsārum opīniōnum** temeritāte dērepta certissimam sē nōbīs ducem praebeat ad voluptātem.

Note:
1. **Ut** *here* = "as," "just as"

Vocabulary:

fateor, -ērī	to admit, accept as true	artifex, -icis *m.*	maker, author
iūcundē (adv.)	agreeably, pleasantly	conquīrō, -ere	to search for
Id	*refers to* iūcundē vīvere	comparō, -āre	to acquire
splendor, -ōris *m.*	splendor	ignōrātiō, -iōnis *f.*	ignorance
error, -ōris *m.*	error (abl. separation)	vexō, -āre	to trouble, upset
Epicūrus, -ī *m.*	Epicurus	prīvō, -āre	to deprive (of)
iste, ista, istud	that		(+ abl. separation)
eximius, -a, -um	fine, excellent	torqueō, -ēre	to twist; torment
laudābilis, -e	worthy of praise	adhibeō, -ēre	to use
expetō, -ere	to seek out, desire	terror, -ōris *m.*	fear
medicus, -ī *m.*	doctor	dētrahō, -ere	to remove
scientia, -ae *f.*	knowledge, skill	falsus, -a, -um	false
valetūdō, -inis *f.*	health	opiniō, -iōnis *f.*	opinion, belief
gubernātor, -ōris *m.*	pilot, navigator	temeritās, -tātis *f.*	recklessness
ūtilitās, -tātis *f.*	utility, usefulness	dēripiō, -ere, -uī,	to remove
	(abl. cause)		-reptus

Practice Sentences

1. Magna sunt ea quae dīcō, mihi crēde; nōlī haec **contemnere**. Dīcenda, **dēmōnstranda**, **explicanda** sunt omnia, causa nōn sōlum expōnenda, sed etiam **graviter cōpiōsē**que agenda est; perficiendum est, sī quid agere aut prōficere vīs, ut hominēs tē nōn sōlum audiant, vērum etiam **libenter studiōsē**que audiant.

   (Cicero; *arguing that he, not a rival, should take charge of a case*)

   n.b. the first sentence here is Practice Sentence 20.2

2. Nihil hōrum sine timōre mīrāmur. Et cum timendī sit causa nescīre, nōn est tantī scīre, nē timeās?

   (Seneca; *explaining that earthquakes are not caused by the gods*)

3. Ūnus homō nōbīs cūnctandō restituit rem. Nōn enim rūmōrēs pōnēbat ante salūtem.

   (Ennius; *speaking of Quintus Fabius Maximus, who saved Rome in the second Punic War by refusing to engage in a full battle with Hannibal*)

4. Sed legendī semper occāsiō est, audiendī nōn semper.

   (Pliny; *urging a friend to come hear an old and masterful speaker rather than to stay home and read*)

5. Nihil agendō hominēs male agere discunt.

   (Cato)

6. Natūrā inest in mentibus nostrīs **insatiābilis** quaedam cupiditās vērī videndī.

   (Cicero)

7. Ācerrimus ex omnibus nostrīs sēnsibus est sēnsus videndī.

   (Cicero)

8. Sī quis in hōc artem populō nōn nōvit amandī, hoc legat et lēctō carmine doctus amet. Arte citae vēlōque ratēs rēmōque reguntur, arte levēs currūs: arte regendus Amor.

   (Ovid; *offering his services as an instructor in the ways of love*)

9. Semper metuendō sapiēns ēvītat malum.

   (Publilius Syrus)

10. Hominis autem mēns discendō alitur et cōgitandō, semper aliquid aut anquīrit aut agit videndīque et audiendī dēlectātiōne ducitur.

    (Cicero)

Vocabulary:

contemnō, -ere	to disparage, condemn	salūs, -ūtis *f.*	safety
		rēs = rēs pūblica	
dēmōnstrō, -āre	to explain; prove	insum, -esse	to be in, be present in
explicō, -āre	to explain, set forth	insatiābilis, -e	insatiable
expōnō, -ere	to explain, set forth	nōscō, -ere, nōvī	to know
graviter (adv.)	seriously	citus, -a, -um	swift, quick
cōpiōsē (adv.)	fully, in detail	vēlum, -ī *n.*	sail

perficiō, -ere	to accomplish	ratis, -is *f.*	boat, ship; raft
prōficiō, -ere	to be successful	rēmus, -ī *m.*	oar
lībenter (adv.)	freely, with pleasure	currus, -ūs *m.*	chariot
studiōsē (adv.)	eagerly, enthusiastically	ēvītō, -āre	to avoid
		alō, -ere	to nourish
tantī esse	to be important	anquīrō, -ere	to investigate, inquire into
cūnctor, -ārī	to delay		
restituō, -ere, -stituī	to restore	dēlectātiō, -iōnis *f.*	pleasure, delight
rūmor, -ōris *m.*	reputation, popular opinion		

Chapter 29 Vocabulary

Nouns

occāsiō, occāsiōnis *f.*	occasion, opportunity
studium, studiī *n.*	eagerness, zeal; study
voluptās, voluptātis *f.*	pleasure, delight

Verbs

committō, committere, commīsī, commissus	to join, unite, engage in
conveniō, convenīre, convēnī conventūrus	to assemble, gather; meet; agree
probō, probāre, probāvī, probātus	to approve (of); prove, show

Adjectives

cīvīlis, cīvīle	civil, public, political
perītus, perīta, perītum	experienced, skilful
ūtilis, ūtile	useful, profitable
vērus, vēra, vērum	true
vērum, vērī *n.*	truth, what is true

Adverbs

male	badly
tamquam	as, just as, just like

(12)

Derivatives: For each English word below, give the Latin word from the Chapter 29 Vocabulary to which it is related and the English word's meaning.

1. civilization
2. veritable
3. probation
4. voluptuous
5. utility
6. malefactor
7. convention
8. occasional

CHAPTER **30**

More on Relative Pronouns
>**Connecting Relative**
>**Clauses of Characteristic**
>**Clauses of Purpose**

Review of Cases
>**Nominative**
>**Vocative**
>**Accusative**

Dictionary Practice / Form Identification

This is the first of three chapters that will introduce constructions you are likely to meet as you move to the next level of Latin, and that will provide a general review of the case uses you have learned so far. This chapter expands on the uses of the relative pronoun you have seen and introduces two additional dependent clauses whose verb is in the subjunctive.

130. **More on Relative Pronouns**

So far you have learned that relative pronouns are used to introduce dependent clauses with an indicative verb (§64, 88). These pronouns have additional uses, among which the most common are the following:

1) **Connecting Relative** – a relative pronoun can function as a coordinating conjunction. At the beginning of a sentence (or after a colon or semi-colon) a relative pronoun is often used to connect that sentence with the preceding one. In this use, the relative pronoun refers either to the whole preceding sentence or to one item in that sentence. A connecting relative can be translated as a demonstrative or personal pronoun, often preceded by "and":

Quī = et is / hic	"(And) he"
Quae = et ea /haec	"(And) she"
Quod = et id / hoc	"(And) this"

Caesar exercitum suum in urbem dūxit. **Quod** cum vīdissent hostēs, fūgērunt.

>Caesar led his army into the city. **And** when the enemy saw/had seen **this**, they fled.

Eōrum fīnēs Nerviī attingēbant. **Quōrum** dē nātūrā mōribusque Caesar, cum quaereret, sīc reperiēbat.

The Nervii bordered on their territory. **And** when Caesar asked about **their** nature and customs, he found the following.

Exercise 219. Translate each of the following, using the vocabulary help given.

1. Videāmus nunc id quod caput est. id vērō, iūdicēs, etiam dubitandum et diūtius cōgitandum est? rēs loquitur ipsa, iūdicēs. quae semper valet plūrimum.　(Cicero; *arguing in court that the facts of his case are obvious*)

2. Tertiae cohortis centuriōnēs ex eō, quō stābant, locō recessērunt suōsque omnēs remōvērunt, et vōcibus hostēs vocāre coepērunt; quōrum prōgredī ausus est nēmō.　(Caesar)

3. Caesar statuit exspectandam [esse] classem. quae ubi convēnit ac prīmum ab hostibus vīsa est, circiter CCXX nāvēs eōrum profectae ex portū nostrīs adversae constitērunt.　(Caesar)

Vocabulary:

caput	"the main point"	statuō, -ere	to decide
diūtius	*comparative of* diū	portus, -ūs *m.*	harbor
cohors, -tis *f.*	cohort, division	adversus, -a, -um	opposite, facing
centuriō, -iōnis, *m.*	centurion, captain		(+ dat.)
rēcēdō, -ere, -cessī	to withdraw	constō, -āre, -stitī	to take up a position
removeō, -ēre, -mōvī	to move back		
prōgredior, -ī	to come forward		

2) **Clauses of Characteristic** – a relative clause with a subjunctive verb often describes a characteristic quality or behavior of an antecedent that is not otherwise defined. While a relative clause + indicative specifies "a specific person who does/is something", a clause of characteristic + subjunctive indicates "a person/thing *of the sort that* does/is something".

Sunt **quī dīcant**	There are those **who say** ....
Is **quī multa sciat.**	He is **the sort of man who knows many things**.
Multa sunt **quae mentem moveant.**	There are many things **which influence the mind.**

Exercise 220. Translate each of the following.

1. Is erat vir quī Graeciam rēxit.
2. Is erat vir quī Graeciam regeret.
3. Nihil videō quod timeam.
4. Aliquid vīdī quod timuī.
5. That was the man everyone praised.
6. He was the sort of man whom everyone praised.
7. They are the men who did this.
8. They are the men to do this.

3) **Clauses of Purpose** – a relative pronoun often replaces **ut** to introduce a purpose clause.

Mīlitēs mīsit **quī urbem caperent**.	He sent soldiers **to capture the city**.
Scrībēbat ōrātiōnēs **quās aliī dīcerent**.	He used to write speeches **for others to deliver**.

Exercise 221. Translate each of the following.

1. Hostēs lēgātum lēgērunt quī pācem peteret.
2. Servōs mittit quī equum domum ducant.
3. Fēminae veniunt quae coniugēs Rōmānōrum sint.
4. Ille dux quī novam gentem conderet ad Ītaliam missus est.

131. **Review of Cases**

This book has presented the basic uses of each case to help you learn to read and understand Latin texts. As you begin to read more unadapted texts, you will find that there are more uses for each case than would be appropriate to include in a beginning textbook. Reference grammar books are available which give many details about uses of each case, for those who are interested. This section, and the similar sections in the next two chapters, will summarize what you should know so far about the general meaning, form, and specific uses of individual cases.

1) **Nominative** – is the "naming" case (from **nōmen**)

Form: for neuters, the nominative and accusative endings are always the same; neuter plurals end in **-a** in all declensions

Use:

- **subject of a finite verb** (§8b)
- **subject complement** = predicate nominative (§33)

2) **Vocative** – is the case of direct address (from **vocō**)

Form: the vocative endings are the same as the nominative, except for 2nd declension words whose nominative singular ends **-us**; these have **-e** in the vocative singular Proper names and a few nouns in **-ius** use **-ī**.

Use:

- **identifies the person (thing) being spoken to** (§17)

3) **Accusative** – is the case of the direction or goal

   Form: the accusative ending for all masculine and feminine words is **-m**; the plural is **-s.** For neuters, the accusative and nominative endings are always the same; neuter plurals end in **-a** in all declensions

   Use:

- **direct object** (§8b)
- **second accusative**
    object complement with factitive verbs (§47)
    with verbs of teaching (**doceō**) & asking (**ōrō**) (§47)
- **subject of an infinitive**
    indirect statement (§92)
    objective infinitive clause (§96)
- **adverbial modifer**
    place to which (§24, §83)
    length of time (§59)
    extent of space (§61)
    degree (§61)
    object of a preposition (with a variety of meanings)

Dictionary Practice/Form Identification

Identify the words below based on the dictionary entries given. Be sure to indicate the **entry from which each is taken** and the **part of speech,** and to *give all possibilities for ambiguous forms.*

   For **nouns** and **adjectives**: give case, number, and gender
   For **verbs**: give person, number, tense, voice and mood

    if infinitive, give tense and voice
    if participle, give case, number, gender, tense and voice

     A.   volātus, volātūs, *m*: flight
     B.   volō, volāre, volāvī: to fly
     C.   volō, velle, voluī: to wish
     D.   volo, volōnis, *m*.: volunteer

	Entry	Part of Speech	Form ID
1. volantī			
2. voluerās			
3. volātis			
4. volātibus			
5. volēns			
6. velītis			
7. volat			
8. volārent			
9. volātūs			
10. volēbam			
11. volōnēs			
12. volem			
13. volāverant			
14. volōnum			
15. voluisse			

Reading 42

Cicero here talks about the nature of the soul (animus), which the Stoics believed was made of fire (sometimes a kind of fiery breath), and about why it rises quickly into the heavens above the denser and more compact air near the earth.

Accēdit ut facilius animus **ēvādat** ex hōc āere ... eumque perrumpat, quod nihil est animō **vēlōcius**, nūlla est **celeritās** quae possit cum animī celeritāte contendere. quī sī **permanet incorruptus** suīque similis, necesse est ita ferātur, ut **penetret** et **dīvidat** omne caelum hoc, in quō nūbēs imbrēs ventīque cōguntur, quod et ūmidum et cālīginōsum est propter exhālātiōnēs terrae.

Vocabulary:

accēdit ut	"it is also true that"	penetrō, -āre	to penetrate, pierce
ēvādō, -ere	to escape	dīvidō, -ere	to break open, divide
āēr, āeris *m.*	air		
perrumpō, -ere	to break through	imber, -bris *m.*	rain
vēlōx, vēlōcis	swift	ūmidus, -a, -um	moist, damp
celeritās, -tātis *f.*	speed	cālīginōsus, -a, -um	misty, foggy
contendō, -ere	to compare		
permaneō, -ēre	to last, remain	exhālātiō, -iōnis *f.*	evaporation
incorruptus, -a, -um	uncorrupted, genuine		

Reading 43

Ovid tells the story of Daedalus and Icarus (cf. Ch. 17, Practice Sentence 5). Daedalus, a famous inventor, is imprisoned on the island of Crete by King Minos. He finally figures out a way to escape, and invents wings, constructed with wax and feathers, so that he and his young son, Icarus, can escape the island of Crete by flying away. Despite his father's warnings, Icarus flies too close to the sun, whose heat has a predictable effect on the wax holding the wings together....

"terrās licet" inquit "et undās	1
obstruat: at caelum certē patet; ībimus illāc:	
omnia **possideat**, nōn **possidet** āera Mīnōs."	
dīxit et ignōtās animum dīmittit in artēs	
nātūramque novat. nam pōnit in **ōrdine** pennās	5
ut vērās imitētur avēs. puer Īcarus ūnā	
stābat .... [Daedalus]	
instruit et nātum, "mediō"que "ut līmite currās,	
Īcare," ait "moneō, nē, sī dēmissior ībis,	10
unda gravet pennās, sī celsior, ignis adūrat:	
inter utrumque volā. …	
mē duce carpe viam!" pariter **praecepta** volāndī	
trādit et ignōtās umerīs accommodat ālās. …	
et patriae **tremuēre** manūs; dedit ōscula nātō	15
nōn iterum **repetenda** suō, …	
hortāturque sequī damnōsāsque ērudit artēs	
et movet ipse suās et nātī rēspicit ālās. …	
cum puer audācī coepit gaudēre volātū	
dēseruitque ducem caelīque cupīdine tractus	20
altius ēgit iter. …	
tābuerant cērae: **nūdōs** quatit ille lacertōs,	
rēmigiōque carēns nōn ūllās percipit aurās,	
ōraque caeruleā patrium clāmantia nōmen	
excipiuntur aquā, quae nōmen trāxit ab illō.	25
at pater īnfēlīx, nec iam pater, "Īcare," dīxit,	
"Īcare," dīxit,"ubi es? quā tē **regiōne** requīram?"	
"Īcare," dīcēbat: pennās aspēxit in undīs	
dēvōvitque suās artēs corpusque sepulcrō	
condidit, et tellūs ā nōmine dicta sepultī.	30

Vocabulary:

(note the Latin uses plural for singular – and vice versa – in several places here)

licet	"although"	āla, -ae, *f.*	wing
obstruō, -ere	to barricade	patrius, -a, -um	of a father, father's
illāc (adv.)	that way, there	osculum, -ī, *n.*	kiss
possideō, -ēre	to possess, be master of	repetō, -ere	to repeat
		damnōsus, -a, -um	destructive
āera (acc.)	air	ērudiō, -īre	to instruct, teach
Mīnōs (nom.)	Minos, king of Crete	rēspiciō, -ere	to look back, look at
		volātus, -ūs *m.*	flight, flying
ignōtus, -a, -um	unknown, strange, unfamiliar	dēserō, -ere, -uī	to desert, leave
		tābēscō, -ere, -uī	to melt
novō, -āre	to change, make anew	cēra, -ae *f.*	wax
		nūdus, -a, -um	bare
ōrdō, -inis, *m.*	order, row(s)	quatiō, -ere	to shake; "flap" (as with wings)
penna, -ae *f.*	feather		
imitor, -ārī	to imitate, act like	lacertus, -ī *m.*	arm
avis, -is *f.*	bird	rēmigium, -ī *n.*	"wings"
ūnā (adv.)	in the same place; together with him	percipiō, -ere, -cēpī	to get hold of
		caeruleus, -a, -um	dark blue
instruō, -ere	to instruct, teach	excipiō, -ere, -cēpī	to catch, receive
līmes, -itis *m.*	way, path	regiō, -iōnis *f.*	direction, region
dēmissus, -a, -um	low	requīrō, -ere	to look for, search for
gravō, -āre	to weigh down		
adūrō, -ere	to set fire to, scorch	aspiciō, -ere, -pēxī	to catch sight of
		dēvoveō, -ēre, -vōvī	to curse
volō, -āre	to fly	sepulcrum, -ī *n.*	grave, tomb
pāriter (adv.)	equally, as well	condō, -ere, -didī	to bury
praeceptum, -ī, *n.*	rule, precept	dicta (est)	*third sg. perfect pass.*
umerus, - ī, *m.*	shoulder	sepeliō, -īre, -iī, -ultus	to bury
accommodō, -āre	to fit, put on		

Practice Sentences

Translate and identify the use of each subjunctive verb.

1. Haec habuī, dē **senectūte** quae dīcerem.

   (Cicero; *Cato, at 84 years, sums up his discourse on old age at the end of Cicero's* Dē Senectūte)

2. Quis homō est quī dīcat mē dīxisse illud?

   (Plautus – slightly edited; *denying an accusation*)

3. "Neque is sum," inquit, "quī gravissimē ex vōbīs mortis perīculō terrear."

   (Caesar; *Sabinus, a Roman general, boasts to his men of his courage, which ensuing events prove an idle boast*)

4. Sed est mōs hominum ut nōlint eundem plūribus rēbus **excellere**.

   (Cicero)

5. Dēnique nūllum est iam dictum quod nōn dictum sit prius.

   (Terence – slightly edited)

6. Urbem Rōmam ... condidēre atque habuēre initiō Trōiānī, quī Aeneā duce profugī ... vagābantur.

   (Sallust; *on the founding of Rome*)

7. Virtūs facit ut eōs dīligāmus in quibus ipsa inesse videātur.

   (Cicero)

8. Quis tālia fandō
   Myrmidonum Dolopumve aut dūrī mīles Ulixī temperet ā lacrimīs?

   (Vergil; *Aeneas agrees to describe the fall of Troy, but warns the story is painful*)

Vocabulary:

senectūs, -tūtis *f.*	old age	Myrmidonēs, -um *m.* (pl.)	Myrmidons (Greeks from Thessaly)
excellō, -ere	to excel		
for, fārī	to speak, tell		
initium, -iī *n.*	beginning	Dolopēs, -um *m.* (pl.)	Dolopes (more Greeks from Thessaly)
profugus, -a, -um	exiled, fugitive		
vagor, -ārī	to wander, roam		
dīligō, -ere	to value, love	Ulixēs, -is *m.*	Ulysses (= Odysseus)
insum, -esse	to be in, belong to		

Chapter 30 Vocabulary

Nouns

Aenēās, Aenēae *m.*	Aeneas, leader of the Trojans
Aenēan (acc.)	
aura, aurae *f.*	breeze; air

Verbs

coepī, coepisse, coeptus	began (*a "defective" verb with no present system*)
nāscor, nāscī, nātus sum	to be born
nātus, -ī *m.*	son

Adjectives

celsus, celsa, celsum	high
Trōiānus, Trōiāna, Trōiānum	Trojan

Adverbs

circiter	about, near
deinde	then, next
iterum	again, a second time
prīmum	first, in the first place, for the first time
prius	before, sooner

Coordinating Conjunction

-ve	or

(12)

CHAPTER 31

Subordinate Clauses in Indirect Speech
Impersonal Constructions
More on the Dative
> **Dative with Compound Verbs**
> **Dative of Purpose**
Review of Cases
> **Genitive**
> **Dative**
Dictionary Practice/Form Identification

This chapter introduces one more use of the subjunctive in a dependent clause, a very common verbal construction, and two new uses of the dative case.

132. Subordinate Clauses in Indirect Speech

Dependent clauses that occur within an indirect statement, indirect command, or indirect question have their verb in the subjunctive:

Putāmus virōs **quī pugnent** fortēs esse.	We think the men **who are fighting** are brave.
Rogāvit sī lēgēs scrīptās essent **quod multa crīmina essent.**	He asked if laws had been written **because there were many crimes.**
Imperat mīlitibus ut urbem **quam hostēs incendant** relinquant.	He orders the soldiers to leave the city **which the enemy is burning.**

This is the twelfth use of the subjunctive in a dependent clause that you have learned:

	Name of Clause		Introduced by	Type of Clause
1.	Circumstantial	§122	cum	Adverbial
2.	Causal	§122	cum	Adverbial
3.	Concessive	§122	cum	Adverbial
4.	Expectation	§122	dum, antequam	Adverbial
5.	Conditions	§124	sī, nisi	Adverbial
6.	Purpose	§116	ut, nē, quī, quae, quod	Adverbial
7.	Result	§116 §126	ut, ut … nōn	Adverbial Noun
8.	Indirect Question	§126	quis, quid, ubi, cūr, other question words	Noun
9.	Indirect Command	§126	ut, nē	Noun
10.	Fearing	§126	nē, ut	Noun
11.	Characteristic	§130	quī, quae, quod	Adv., Adj., Noun
12.	Subordinate Clauses in Indirect Speech	§132	any	Adverbial, Noun

133. Impersonal Constructions

There are many impersonal expressions in Latin, some of which can seem very awkward to English speakers. It is common to translate these expressions with "it" as a "dummy subject" in English.

- 3rd singular verbs such as the following should lead you to expect an infinitive subject (§39):

decet	it is fitting	oportet	it is right, necessary
iuvat	it is pleasing	vidētur	it seems good (Ch. 14)
licet	it is permitted		

- Some phrases are also regularly used in this way (or with a noun result clause – §126):

fās est	it is right	mōs est	it is the custom (Ch. 28)
nefās est	it is wrong	necesse est	it is necessary

- You have already seen several verbs which lead you to expect a noun result clause as subject (§126)

accidit	it happens
efficitur	it is brought about
fit	it comes about

- In addition, a few intransitive verbs can also be used impersonally, in what looks like a 3rd singular passive form and is, therefore, often called an "impersonal passive." A literal English equivalent for these does not exist, so it is usually best either to translate the verb as active, with "one" as the subject, or to use "there" with a gerund. In a passage, the full context will make other translations possible too:

| bibitur | one drinks | pugnātur | there (is) fighting |
| itur | one enters | venītur | one comes |

The following are typical examples of impersonal constructions:

Licet mihi īre. **It is permitted** for me to go.
   (*or* **I am allowed** to go.)

Oportet mē īre. **It is right** for me to go. (*or* **I should** go.)

Multās diēs **pugnātum est.** **They fought (there was fighting)** for many days.

Ventum est. **They came.**

Illud **videndum est.** We (one) **must see** that.

Exercise 222. Bracket and identify the type of each dependent clause, then translate using the vocabulary help given.

Context: In 58 B.C. when the Helvetians (inhabitants of ancient Switzerland) decide to migrate from their own lands to an area near southwest Gaul (France), their route leads through a province under Roman control (near Geneva). Caesar learns of this and hurries to stop them. The Helvetians, in turn, try to reassure him of their peaceful intentions.

Ubi dē eius adventū Helvētiī certiōrēs factī sunt, lēgātōs ad eum mittunt nōbilissimōs cīvitātis, ... quī dīcerent sibi esse in animō sine ūllō maleficiō iter per prōvinciam facere, quod aliud iter habērent nūllum: rogāre ut eius voluntāte id sibi facere liceat.

Vocabulary:

Helvētiī, -ōrum *m.*	Helvetians	maleficium, -iī *n.*	offence, harm,
nōbilis, -e	renowned, well-known		wrong
voluntās, -tātis *f.*	will, consent		

134. More on the Dative

The following two uses of the dative should be added to those you have already had. The first is an extension of the indirect object, and the second often pairs with a dative of reference or the like.

1) Dative with Compound Verbs

Many compound verbs with the prefixes **ad-**, **ante-**, **circum-**, **cum- (con-)**, **in-**, **inter-**, **ob-**, **post-**, **prae-**, **sub-** and **super-** take a dative indirect object (with or without a direct object). This is also true of compounds of **sum**, except **absum** which takes an ablative.

Caesar **Galliae cunctae** bellum **intulit**	Caesar imposed war on all Gaul
eī pater **subrīdet**	Her father smiles at her
amīcīs adsum	I am with (near) friends
illīs mīlitibus ducem **praefēcit**	He put the leader in charge of those soldiers

284 INTRODUCTION TO LATIN

2) Dative of Purpose

The dative can be used to indicate the purpose or end of an action and, in this use, often occurs with a second dative of the person (or thing) affected, which is sometimes characterized as a Dative of Reference. When these two appear together, the construction is frequently called a "double dative." The dative of purpose appears in two different contexts.

- as the complement in a linking sentence

ille dux Rōmānīs **auxiliō** erat	that leader was (**of**) **help** to the Romans
hic mihi **cūrae** est	this is a **care** to/for me
fīlius patrī **impedimentō** fuit	the son was **a hindrance** to his father

- as an adverbial modifier

optāvit locum **rēgnō**	he chose a place **for a kingdom**
eum ducem **bellō** creant	they make him leader **for the war**
exercitus urbī **auxiliō** vēnit	the army came **as an aid** to the city

Exercise 223. Translate each of the following, using the vocabulary help given.

1. impōnit fīnem sapiēns et rēbus honestīs. (Juvenal)
2. sed tacitī respectābant somnōque sepultī, dum roseā face sōl īnferret lūmina caelō. (Lucretius; *on the "savage" period mankind*)
3. ... [gentem] enim Trōiānō ā sanguine dūcī audīverat Tyriās ōlim quae verteret arcēs; hinc populum lātē rēgem bellōque superbum ventūrum [esse] excidiō Libyae: (Vergil; *Juno hates the Trojans partly because she knows they will destroy her favorite city, Carthage*)
4. ego vōs hortārī tantum possum ut amīcitiam omnibus rēbus hūmānīs antepōnātis; nihil est enim tam nātūrae aptum. (Cicero)
5. locum insidiīs circumspectāre Poenus coepit. (Livy; *Hannibal plans his military strategy*)
6. pontō nox incubat ātra (Vergil; *describing a storm*)

Vocabulary:

impōnō, -ere	to put on, impose	lātē (adv.)	widely
tacitus, -a, -um	silent	superbus, -a, -um	proud, arrogant
respectō, -āre	to wait	excidium, -iī *n.*	destruction
somnus, -ī *m.*	sleep	Libya, -ae *f.*	Libya
sepultus, -a, -um	buried	antepōnō, -ere	to put before, prefer
roseus, -a, -um	rose-colored	circumspectō, -āre	to look around
fax, facis *f.*	torch, fire	Poenus, -a, -um	the Phoenician = Hannibal
sanguis, -inis *m.*	blood; race	āter, -tra, -trum	black, dark
Tyrius, -a, -um	Tyrian, of Carthage	incubō, -āre	to lie on, sit upon

135. Review of Cases

1) **Genitive** – expresses the relation of one noun to another and identifies the attributes of a noun

Form: the genitive singular is given as the 2nd form in dictionary listings for all nouns and for one-ending adjectives; all genitive plurals end **-um**

Use:

- **With Nouns – adjectival modifier**

  possession (§18)
  of the whole / partitive (§18)
  explanatory (§30)
  objective (§30)
  subjective (§30)
  with **causā** & **grātiā** to show cause/purpose (§53)

- **With Adjectives – limits the meaning of the adjective**

  with adjectives such as **plēnus** (Ch. 8), **perītus** (Ch. 29), **cupidus** (eager for), **ignārus** (unaware of), **memor** (mindful of) and the like

2) **Dative** – usually identifies the person (sometimes the thing) involved as recipient, beneficiary, interested party, etc., but it can also express a purpose, limit or direction

Form: the dative and ablative plural endings are always the same

Use:

- **Adverbial modifier**

  indirect object (§19)
  reference (§19)
  possession (§40)
  with adjectives meaning *friendly, unfriendly, similar, dissimilar, faithful, suitable, fit, equal, near,* etc. (§62)
  agent (§129)
  (indirect) object of compound verbs (§134)
  purpose (§134)

- **Part of Sentence Core**

  dative object of special intransitive verbs (§44)
  purpose (§134)

Dictionary Practice/Form Identification

Identify the words below based on the dictionary entries given. Be sure to indicate the **entry from which each is taken** and the **part of speech**, and to *give all possibilities for ambiguous forms.*

For **nouns** and **adjectives**: give case, number, and gender
For **verbs**: give person, number, tense, voice and mood

> if infinitive, give tense and voice
> if participle, give case, number, gender, tense and voice

> A.   dicāx, dicācis: witty, sarcastic
> B.   diciō, diciōnis *f.*: power
> C.   dicō, dicāre, dicāvī, dicātus: to dedicate, devote
> D.   dīcō, dīcere, dīxī, dictus: to say, speak

		Entry	Part of Speech	Form ID
1.	dicārentur			
2.	diciōnum			
3.	dicācēs			
4.	dicta sint			
5.	dicāvissem			
6.	dicācissimae			
7.	diciōnī			
8.	dīxērunt			
9.	dicāta eram			
10.	dicantis			
11.	dīcerēs			
12.	dicācius			
13.	dīcī			
14.	dicās			
15.	dīcās			

Reading 44

Cicero explains why self-control is so important.

> temperantia est enim, quae in rēbus aut expetendīs aut fugiendīs
> ut ratiōnem sequāmur monet. nec enim satis est iūdicāre quid
> faciendum nōn faciendumve sit, sed stāre etiam oportet in eō,
> quod sit iūdicātum.

Vocabulary:

temperantia, -ae *f.*   restraint, self-control,   expetō, -ere   to desire, ask for
                        moderation   satis (adv.)   enough

Reading 45

Cicero has been discussing dreams and has gotten off the subject. He returns to the subject here to tell how Hannibal avoided the anger of Juno by heeding the warning she gave him in a dream.

Redeāmus ad **somnia**. Hannibalem Coelius[1] scrībit,* cum **columnam** auream, quae esset in fānō Iunōnis Lacīniae, auferre vellet dubitāretque utrum ea **solida** esset an extrīnsecus inaurata, perterebrāvisse, cumque **solidam** invēnisset, statuisse tollere; eī secundum quiētem vīsam esse Iunōnem praedīcere nē id faceret, minārīque, sī fēcisset, sē cūrātūram [esse], ut eum quoque oculum[2], quō bene vidēret, āmitteret, idque ab homine acūtō nōn esse neglēctum; itaque ex eō aurō, quod exterebrātum esset, būculam cūrāsse faciendam et eam in summā **columnā** conlocāvisse.

Notes:

* Notice that *scrībit* in the first line introduces an indirect statement that lasts for the rest of the passage.
[1] Coelius wrote a history of Rome, c. 120 B.C.
[2] Hannibal had previously lost the sight in one eye to disease.

Vocabulary:

somnium, -ī *n.*	dream	statuō, -ere, -uī	to decide
Hannibal, -is *m.*	Hannibal	secundum quiētem	"after sleep (came)"
columna, -ae *f.*	column	praedīcō, -ere	to warn
fānum, -ī *n.*	= templum	(+ dat.)	
Lacīnius, -a, -um	Lacinian, of Lacinium	minor, -ārī	to threaten
		acūtus, -a, -um	intelligent, sharp
utrum (adv.)	whether	exterebrō, -āre, -āvī	to bore out
solidus, -a, -um	solid	-ātus	
extrīnsecus (adv.)	on the outside	būcula, -ae *f.*	heifer
inaurō, -āre, -āvī,	to gild	cūrāsse	= cūrāvisse
-ātus		conlocō, -āre, -āvī	to place
perterebrō, -āre	to bore through		

Practice Sentences

1. Itur in **antīquam** silvam.

   (Vergil; *Aeneas and a comrade gather wood for a funeral pyre*)

2. Gallīs magnō ad **pugnam** erat impedīmentō.

   (Caesar; *describing the effect of a Roman javelin pinning several Gallic shields together*)

3. Nihil enim sine ratiōne faciendum est; nōn est autem beneficium, nisi quod ratiōne datur, quoniam ratiō omnis honestī comes est.

   (Seneca)

4. Pugnātum est ab utrīsque ācriter.

   (Caesar, slightly edited; *explaining a battle technique*)

5. Dē gustibus nōn disputandum est.

   (traditional)

6. Nōn ignāra malī, miserīs succurrere discō.

   (Vergil; *Dido reassures Aeneas that she will help him*)

7. Nunc est bibendum, nunc pede līberō pulsanda tellūs.

   (Horace; *the beginning of a famous drinking song, perhaps in celebration of the defeat of Cleopatra*)

8. Rē nūntiātā, Caesar omnem ex castrīs equitātum suīs auxiliō mīsit.

   (Caesar)

Vocabulary:

antīquus, -a, -um	ancient	gustus, -ūs *m.*	taste
Gallī, -ōrum, *m.*	the Gauls	disputō, -āre	to argue
pugna, -ae, *f.*	fight	succurrō, -ere	to help
beneficium, -iī *n.*	kindness, favor	pulsō, -āre	to strike, tap
comes, -itis *m.*	companion	equitātus, -ūs *m.*	cavalry
ācriter (adv.)	fiercely		

Chapter 31 Vocabulary

Nouns

fās *n. (indeclinable)*	right; divine law
fās est	it is right
nefās est	it is wrong
impedimentum, impedimentī *n.*	hindrance, obstacle
īnsidiae, īnsidiārum *f.* (pl.)	ambush, plot; treachery
lūmen, lūminis *n.*	light, lamp, torch; eye
tellūs, tellūris *f.*	the earth; land, ground

Verbs

licet, licēre, licuit (*impersonal* + dat.)	it is allowed, it is lawful
oportet, oportēre, oportuit (*impersonal* + acc.)	it is right, one should; it is necessary

Adjectives

dūrus, dūra, dūrum	hard, harsh, rough
honestus, honesta, honestum	honest, worthy, honorable
ignārus, ignāra, ignārum	ignorant (of), unaware (of)

Adverbs

hīc	here
hinc	from this place; hence

(12)

Forum with Mt. Vesuvius in the distance. Pompeii, 1st c. A.D.

CHAPTER 32

The Supine
Ut + Indicative
More on the Ablative
> **Description (Quality)**
> **Degree of Difference**
Review of Cases
> **Ablative**
> **Locative**
Dictionary Practice/Form Identification

This chapter introduces a new verbal noun and expands on the use of **ut** and on the ablative case.

136. **The Supine**

The **supine** is a verbal noun which adds endings of the fourth declension to the participial stem (§84) and is found only in the accusative and the ablative singular.

	1st Conj.	2nd Conj.	3rd Conj.	3rd Conj. -iō	4th Conj.
Accusative	amā**tum**	doc**tum**	rēc**tum**	cap**tum**	audī**tum**
Ablative	amā**tū**	doc**tū**	rēc**tū**	cap**tū**	audī**tū**

The accusative is used after verbs of motion to indicate purpose, and may take its own object:

| vēnit **iuvātum** | he came **to help** |
| lēgātōs mīsit **rogātum pācem** | he sent envoys **to ask for peace** |

The ablative is used as an ablative of specification (§79) after adjectives and a few nouns (**fās, nefās, opus**), and never has an object. There are only a handful of common supines in -**ū**:

nefās **audītū**	a crime **to hear**
difficile **cognitū**	hard **to understand**
mīrābile **dictū**	strange **to say**
optimum **factū**	best **to do**
minimus **nātū**	youngest **by birth**
facile **vīsū**	easy **to see**

Exercise 224. Translate each of the following.

1. Illud facile factū est.
2. Urbem captum gladiīs ībant.
3. Hoc fās est vīsū.
4. Carmina illīus poētae dulcia audītū sunt.
5. Nihil dignum dictū actum erat.
6. Dictum ad senātum vēnit.

Exercise 225. Translate each of the following, using the vocabulary help given.

1. Vēnātum Aenēās ūnāque miserrima Dīdō in nemus īre parant.   (Vergil)
2. Tītan quī maior nātū erat postulat ut ipse regnāret.   (Ennius)
3. In ea castra lēgātī ab Rōmā vēnērunt questum iniūriās et ex eō foedere rēs repetītum.   (Livy; *an Italian tribe violates their treaty with Rome and pays*)

Vocabulary:

vēnor, -ārī	to hunt	Tītan, -ānis *m.*	Titan, brother of Saturn
ūnā (adv.)	together	queror, -ī, questus	to complain, protest at
Dīdō, -ōnis *f.*	Dido, queen of Carthage	foedus, -eris *n.*	treaty, agreement
nemus, -oris *n.*	forest, wood	repetō, -ere, -īvī -ītus	to demand, claim (what is due)

137. Ut + the Indicative

In Chapter 25 (§116) you learned that **ut** could be used to introduce dependent clauses with a subjunctive verb. **Ut** has a number of other uses (and meanings), among the most common of which is to introduce dependent clauses with an indicative verb. The following can be added to the clause-markers you learned in Chapter 12 (§60):

Adverbial Clause Marker	English Meaning	Category
ut	when	time
ut	as	comparison

Exercise 226. Translate each of the following and identify the type of **ut** clause (with subjunctive or indicative verb).

1. Ut summō cōnspexit ab monte terrās īnfēlix, timōre tremuit.
2. Ille tantum pecūniae habuerat, ut beātus semper vidērētur.
3. Puellae tacent nec, ut ante solēbant, clāmantēs ambulant.
4. Haec omnia fēcērunt ut pācem celeriter habērent.
5. Ut Rōma ardēbat imperātor cecinisse dīcitur.
6. Oportet hominēs ut vīvant pugnāre.
7. Ut diū pugnātum est, fortiōrēs vīcērunt.
8. Ut cōnsul in senātū loquēbātur, alter clāmābat.

138. **More on the Ablative**

Two additional uses of the ablative are not as common as others you have learned, but are useful to know for specific contexts.

1) **Description (Quality)**

A noun in the ablative, always accompanied by an adjectival modifier, is used to describe physical characteristics and other qualities of another noun. Because this ablative describes qualities, it is sometimes called the Ablative of Quality.

vir **parvīs pedibus**	a man **with small feet**
vir **magnā virtūte**	a man **of great courage**
coma **colōre aurī**	hair **the color of gold**

2) **Degree of Difference**

The ablative is used with comparatives, and words which indicate a comparison (especially **ante** and **post**) to specify the degree of difference. You saw this construction (with **multō**) in Practice Sentence 27.5 (first example below):

multō pulcherrimam	much more beautiful (*more beautiful by much*)
arbor altior **duōbus pedibus**	a tree two feet higher (*higher by two feet*)
paucīs diēbus ante	a few days before (*before by a few days*)

Exercise 227. Translate each of the following, using the vocabulary help given.

1. Patria mihi vītā meā multō est cārior. (Cicero)
2. Catilīna, nōbilī genere nātus, fuit magnā vī et animī (Sallust)
   et corporis sed ingeniō malō.
3. Bonus dēfensor nēmō nisi quī ēloquentissimus fuit; (Quintilian; *talking*
   tantō est accūsāre quam dēfendere facilius. *about law courts*)
4. Neque hominēs inimīcō animō temperātūrōs [esse] (Caesar; *not trusting the*
   ab iniūriā et maleficiō exīstimābat. *Helvetians*)
5. At paulō post audita vōx est monentis, ut prōvidērent, (Cicero; *talking about*
   nē ā Gallīs Rōma caperētur. *oracles*)

Vocabulary:

Catilīna, -ae *m.*	Catiline	temperō, -āre	to refrain (from)
nōbilis, -e	noble	maleficium, -iī *n.*	crime, misdeed
dēfensor, -ōris *m.*	defender	exīstimō, -āre	to think
ēloquēns, -entis	eloquent, articulate	prōvideō, -ēre	to be cautious,
accūsō, -āre	to prosecute, accuse		make preparations
dēfendō, -ere	to defend	Gallī, -ōrum, *m.*	the Gauls

139. Review of Cases

1) **Ablative** – originally indicated **separation / source** (**ab-latus**, from **abferō**) but, over time, absorbed the functions of two other cases, the **instrumental** and the **locative**. Thus the uses of the ablative can, for the most part, be derived from these three categories, although there is some overlap and scholars disagree on the derivation of some uses. The ablative can be the object of a few verbs, but otherwise it functions as an adverbial modifier.

Form: the ablative singular ends in a long vowel, except in the 3rd declension consonant stem, where it ends in **-e**; the ablative and dative plural endings are always the same.

Use:

- **separation / source**

place from which (§24)	
[separation] (§44)	*object of **careō***
cause (§53)	*without prep.*
agent (§72)	
comparison (§102)	*without prep.*

- **instrumental**

means (instrument) (§23)	*without prep.*
manner (§34)	
accompaniment (§34)	
specification (respect) (§79)	*without prep.*
ablative absolute (§87)	
object of **ūtor** etc. (§105)	*part of sentence core*
degree of difference (§138)	
description (quality) (§138)	

- **locative**

place where (§24)	
time when (§59)	*without prep.*
time within which (§59)	*without prep.*

2) **Locative** – was originally a separate case in Proto-Indo-European indicating place where (in, at) as an adverbial modifier. Over time it was largely absorbed into the ablative case in Latin, but it survives in the names of towns, small islands and a few other words.

Form: the locative singular ending was **–i** which, in the first and second declensions, came to look like the genitive singular ending (Roma**i** > Rom**ae**, bell**i**). The other endings have merged with those of the ablative.

Use:

- **place where** (§82)

Dictionary Practice/Form Identification

Identify the words below based on the dictionary entries given. Be sure to indicate the **entry from which each is taken** and the **part of speech**, and to *give all possibilities for ambiguous forms.*

For **nouns** and **adjectives**: give case, number, and gender
For **verbs**: give person, number, tense, voice and mood

if infinitive, give tense and voice
if participle, give case, number, gender, tense and voice

A.   rēgius, rēgia, rēgium: royal
B.   regnō, regnāre, regnāvī, regnātus: to be a king; reign
C.   rēgnum, rēgnī *n.*: kingdom
D.   regō, regere, rēxī, rēctus: to rule; guide
E.   rēx, rēgis, *m.*: king

		Entry	Part of Speech	Form ID
1.	rēgna			
2.	regnā			
3.	rēxisse			
4.	rēgiō			
5.	regēmur			
6.	rēgum			
7.	regar			
8.	regnātū			
9.	rēgnō			
10.	regnātūrōs			
11.	rēgēs			
12.	regerēs			
13.	regnandae			
14.	rēgiā			
15.	rēxerint			

Reading 46

Cicero, in his treatise on Old Age, relates a story credited to Lysander, a Spartan general who defeated the Athenians. Lysander spoke about a time when the Spartans showed proper respect for an elderly Athenian man, when the Athenians themselves did not.

Lysander Lacedaemonius dīcere solitus est Lacedaemonem esse honestissimum **domicilium** senectūtis: nusquam enim tantum tribuitur aetātī, nusquam est senectūs honōrātior. equidem trāditum est, cum Athēnīs lūdīs quīdam in **theātrum** grandis nātū vēnisset, magnō consessū locum nusquam eī datum [esse] ā suīs cīvibus. cum autem ad Lacedaemoniōs accessisset, quī, lēgātī cum essent, certō in locō consēderant, consurrexisse omnēs illī dīcuntur et senem sessum recēpisse. quibus cum ā cunctō consessū plausus multus datus esset, ex eīs quīdam dīxit Athēniēnsēs scīre, quae rēcta essent, sed facere nōlle.

Vocabulary:

Lysander, -drī, *m.*	Lysander	grandis, -e	old
Lacedaemonius, -a, -um	Spartan	consessus, -ūs, *m.*	crowd
Lacedaemōn, -onis *f.*	Sparta	magnō consessū	"although the
domicilium, -iī, *n.*	home, dwelling place	(*abl. absolute*)	crowd was big"
senectūs, -tūtis, *f.*	old age	accēdō, -ere, -essī	to approach,
nusquam (adv.)	nowhere		come near
tribuō, -ere	to give, show	consīdō, -ere, -sēdī	to be seated, settle
honōrātus, -a, -um	honored, respected	consurgō, -ere,	to stand up together,
Athēnae, -ārum, *f.*	Athens	-surrexī	rise (up) together
lūdus, -ī, *m.*	game (Panathenaic	sessum	*supine from* sedeō
	festival in honor	plausus, -ūs, *m.*	applause, clapping
	of Athena)	Athēniēnses, -ium, *m.*	the Athenians
theātrum, -ī, *n.*	theater		

Reading 47

Sallust describes how and why Rome began to decline.

Ubi labōre atque **iūstitiā** rēs pūblica crēvit, rēgēs magnī bellō domitī [sunt], **natiōnēs** ferae et populī ingentēs vī subāctī [sunt], ..., cuncta maria terraeque patēbant, **saevīre** fortūna ac miscēre omnia coepit. Quī labōrēs, perīcula, dubiās atque asperās rēs facile **tolerāverant**, eīs ōtium dīvitiaeque, [ea] optanda aliās, onerī **miseriae**que fuēre. Igitur prīmō pecūniae, deinde imperī cupīdō crēvit: eae causae omnium malōrum fuēre. Namque **avāritia** fidem probitātem cēterāsque artēs bonās vertit; prō hīs, superbiam, **crūdēlitātem**, deōs neglegere, ēdocuit.

Vocabulary:

iūstitia, -ae *f.*	justice	dīvitiae, -ārum *f.*	riches, wealth
crēscō, -ere, crēvī	to grow	aliās (adv.)	in other circumstances
domō, -āre, -uī, -itus	to tame, conquer	onus, -eris *n.*	burden
natiō, -iōnis *f.*	nation	miseria, -ae *f.*	misery
subigō, -ere, -ēgī, -āctus	to subdue	avāritia, -ae *f.*	greed
		probitās, -tātis *f.*	honesty
saeviō, -īre	to be cruel; rage	superbia, -ae *f.*	insolence
dubius, -a, -um	uncertain, dangerous	crūdēlitās, -tātis *f.*	cruelty, inhumanity
tolerō, -āre, -āvī	to tolerate	ēdoceō, -ēre, -uī	to teach
ōtium, -iī *n.*	leisure		

Reading 48

*Vergil incorporates Roman legend and history in a speech by Jupiter in the first
book of the* Aeneid. *Here Jupiter promises Venus that her son, Aeneas, will reach
Italy and that the race he founds will go on to great success.*

[Aenēās] bellum ingēns geret Ītaliā populōsque ferōcīs	1
contundet mōrēsque virīs et moenia pōnet,	2
...	
Rōmulus excipiet gentem et Māvortia condet	3
moenia Rōmānōsque suō dē nōmine dīcet.	4
Hīs ego nec mētās rērum nec tempora pōnō:	5
imperium sine fīne dedī. Quīn aspera Iūnō,	6
quae mare nunc terrāsque metū caelumque fatīgat,	7
cōnsilia in melius referet, mēcumque fovēbit	8
Rōmānōs, rērum dominōs gentemque togātam.	9
Sīc placitum. . . .	10
Nāscētur pulchrā Troiānus orīgine Caesar,	11
imperium Ōceanō, fāmam quī terminet astrīs.	12

Vocabulary

contundō, -ere	to crush	in melius	"for the better"
excipiō, -ere	to inherit, take up	foveō, -ēre	to cherish
Māvortius, -a, -um	of Mars (patron god of Rome)	togātus, -a, -um	toga-clad
		orīgō, -inis *f.*	origin, source
dīcet = vocābit [gentem]	*(factitive pattern)*	Ōceanus, -ī *m.*	Oceanus, *the ocean was thought of as a great river which encircled the earth*
mēta, -ae *f.*	limit, boundary		
quīn	but indeed		
Iūnō, -ōnis *f.*	Juno, queen of the gods	terminō, -āre	to limit
fatīgō, -āre	to tire (out), harass	astrum, -i *n.*	star

Practice Sentences

1. **Horrendum** et dictū videō mīrābile mōnstrum. (Vergil; *Aeneas tells of his travels*)

2. Bellō **Helvetiōrum** cōnfectō ... Galliae lēgātī ad Caesarem **grātulātum** convēnērunt. (Caesar)

3. Id dictū quam rē, ut plēraque, facilius erat. (Livy; *commenting on those who second-guessed a military strategy*)

4. Cētera, quamquam ferenda nōn sunt, ferāmus. (Cicero; *in a letter to his wife from exile*)

5. Pompēius ut equitātum suum pulsum vīdit, aciē excessit. (Caesar; *Caesar defeats Pompey in 48 B.C.*)

6. Haec rēs magnō ūsuī nostrīs fuit. (Caesar – slightly edited; *Caesar repositions war ships to startle the enemy fighting at the edge of the water*)

7. Forsitan hoc quod dictūrus sum mīrābile audītū esse videātur, sed certē id dīcam quod sentiō. (Cicero; *addressing the senate after his return from exile*)

8. Quod erat **dēmōnstrandum**. (Euclid; *this is the meaning of the standard abbreviation, Q.E.D., at the end of a proof*)

Vocabulary:

horrendus, -a, -um	horrible, terrible	equitātus, -ūs *m.* (pl.)	cavalry
monstrum, -ī *n.*	portent, omen		
Helvetiī, -ōrum *m.*	the Helvetians	pellō, -ere, pepulī, pulsus	to beat
grātulō, -āre, -āvī, -ātus	to congratulate	excēdō, -ere, -cessī	to leave, withdraw
plēraque (adv.)	"in most cases"	ūsus, -ūs *m.*	use, value
Pompēius, -ī *m.*	Pompey	dēmōnstrō, -āre	to explain; prove

Chapter 32 Vocabulary

Verb

recipiō, recipere, recēpī
  receptus

to receive, accept; take back
  regain

Adjectives

asper, aspera, asperum
ferōx, ferōcis
ferus, fera, ferum
mīrābilis, mīrābile
paulus, paula, paulum

rough, harsh; cruel
fierce, bold; wild, savage
wild, fierce; cruel; uncivilized
wonderful, extraordinary
little, small

Adverb

prīmō

at first

Coordinating Conjunction

ut

as, when

(8)

LIST OF LATIN SOURCES

Readings

Reading #	Author	Source	Chapter #
1	Ennius	*Varia* 107-108	4
2	Ennius	*Varia* 9-10	5
3	Florus	*Epitome* 1.1	5
4	Florus	*Epitome* 1.1	6
5	Ovid	*Metamorphoses* 1.366ff.	7
6	Ennius	*Varia* 113-115	7
7	Pliny	*Epistulae* 9.32	8
8	Ovid	*Metamorphoses* 1.1-7	8
9	Pliny	*Epistulae* 1.11	9
10	Plautus	*Pseudolus* 2.2	9
11	Tacitus	*Germania* 7	10
12	Cicero	*Pro Cluentio* 146.5ff.	10
13	Cicero	*De Natura Deorum* 1.34	11
14	Cicero	*Epistulae ad Familiares* 14.5	11
15	Livy	*Ab Urbe Condita* 1.16	12
16	Varro	*Res Rustica* 3.1.4-5	12
17	Eutropius	*Breviarum Historiae Romanae* 1.8-9	13
18	Pliny	*Epistulae* 6.20.3-10	14
19	Caesar	*Bellum Gallicum* 1.1	15
20	Livy	*Ab Urbe Condita* 1.23	16
21	Livy	*Ab Urbe Condita* 1.24-25	16
22	Livy	*Ab Urbe Condita* 1.25ff.	17
23	Caesar	*Bellum Gallicum* 4.28-29	18
24	Ovid	*Amores* 1.14	18
25	Cornelius Nepos	*Themistocles* 9	19
26	Livy	*Ab Urbe Condita* 26.46-47	19
27	Caesar	*Bellum Gallicum* 5.45-46	20
28	Terence	*Heauton Timoroumenos, Prologus* 10-21	20
29	Cicero	*Epistulae ad Familiares* 14.3	21
30	Caesar	*Bellum Gallicum* 1.53	22
31	Tacitus	*Annales* 13.15-16	23
32	Ovid	*Fasti* 4.426-450	23
33	Cicero	*Pro Sestio* 142-143	24
34	Florus	*Epitome* 1.2.8.1	25
35	Martial	*Epigrammata* 5.73; 7.3; 12.40	25
36	Hyginus	*Fabulae* 5.30, 32	26
37	Cicero	*Cato Maiore De Senectute* 21-22	26
38	Cicero	*In Catilinam* 1.17	27
39	Ovid	*Metamorphoses* 1.361-366	27
40	Caesar	*Bellum Gallicum* 1.2	28
41	Cicero	*De Finibus* 1.42.11-43.9	29
42	Cicero	*Tusculanae Disputationes* 1.43	30
43	Ovid	*Metamorphoses* 8.185-235	30

44	Cicero	*De Finibus* 1.14.47	31
45	Cicero	*De Divinatione* 1.48.2-11	31
46	Cicero	*Cato Maiore De Senectute* 63-64	32
47	Sallust	*Bellum Catilinae* 10	32
48	Vergil	*Aeneid* 1.263-287	32

Narrative Readings

Reading Chapter #	Author	Source
2	Livy	*Ab Urbe Condita* 1.1
3	Livy	*Ab Urbe Condita* 1.21.5-6
4	Livy	*Ab Urbe Condita* 1.27-28

Practice Sentences

Ch. Sentence #	Author	Source
3.1	Vergil	*Aeneid* 1.8
3.2	Ovid	*Metamorphoses* 7.456
3.3	Sallust	*Bellum Catilinae* 12.3
4.1	Pliny	*Naturalis Historia* 11.145.7
4.2	Ennius	*Varia* 60
4.3	Vergil	*Aeneid* 7.23
5.1	Publilius Syrus	*Sententiae* N 51
5.2	Publilius Syrus	*Sententiae* M 30
5.3	Publilius Syrus	*Sententiae* N 36
5.4	Cicero	*Laelius de Amicitia* 54.6
5.5	Plautus	*Mostellaria* 702
5.6	Ovid	*Metamorphoses* 3.163
6.1	St. Jerome	*Epistulae* 57.12.3
6.2	Vergil	*Aeneid* 1.378-79
6.3	Seneca	*Epistulae Morales ad Lucilium* 115, 16.1
6.4	Vergil	*Aeneid* 1.11
6.5	Sallust	*Bellum Catilinae* 49.3
6.6	Cicero	*De Finibus* 5.84
7.1	Traditional Hymn	
7.2	Publilius Syrus	*Sententiae* B 28
7.3	Vergil	*Aeneid* 1.507
7.4	Cicero	*Epistulae ad Atticum* 6.4
7.5	Vulgate	*John* 8.12
7.6	Vulgate	*Romans* 8.8
7.7	Cicero	*De Re Publica* 6.26
7.8	Vergil	*Aeneid* 1.364
8.1	Cicero	*De Natura Deorum* 2.167.7
8.2	Cicero	*Tusculanae Disputationes* 5.25.9
8.3	Publilius Syrus	*Sententiae* V 14
8.4	Publilius Syrus	*Sententiae* L 13
8.5	Cicero	*Epistulae ad Atticum* 2.1
8.6	Cicero	*Pro Caecina* 35.8
8.7	Cicero	*Pro Rege Deiotaro* 26.13
8.8	Cicero	*De Finibus* 3.4.12
9.1	Ovid	*Metamorphoses* 11.297-298
9.2	Cicero	*Pro Milone* 4.11
9.3	Livy	*Ab Urbe Condita* 7.32.12
9.4	Ovid	*Metamorphoses* 10.147-149
9.5	Vergil	*Aeneid* 1.203

9.6	Cicero	*Philippicae* 14.32.1-2
9.7	Terence	*Andria* 4.1.51
9.8	Cicero	*In Verrem* 2.3.102
10.1	Ennius	*Varia* 51
10.2	Vergil	*Aeneid* 4.314
10.3	Seneca	*De Ira* 1.9
10.4	Cicero	*De Re Publica* 2.67.13
10.5	Modern	MGM motto
10.6	Anonymous	
10.7	Pliny	*Epistulae* 9.24
10.8	Pliny	*Epistulae* 8.10.2
11.1	Ovid	*Metamorphoses* 7.452
11.2	Livy	*Ab Urbe Condita* 1.31.8
11.3	Vergil	*Aeneid* 1.133-134
11.4	Vergil	*Aeneid* 5.790-791
11.5	Caesar	*Bellum Gallicum* 7.77.14.4
11.6	Cicero	*Ad Familiares* 16.14
11.7	Vergil	*Aeneid* 1.251
11.8	Cicero	*Ad Atticum* 6.3.9
12.1	Cicero	*Pro Rabirio Perduellionis* 11
12.2	Livy	*Ab Urbe Condita* 3.69.2
12.3	Terence	*Heauton Timorumenos* 272
12.4	Cicero	*Pro Caelio* 6
12.5	Seneca	*Epistulae Morales ad Lucilium* 66.12.4
12.6	Seneca	*De Beneficiis* 7.7.3.4
12.7	Vergil	*Aeneid* 1.47-48
12.8	Cicero	*Philippicae* 11.13.34
13.1	Varro	*Res Rusticae* 2.1.3.3-4
13.2	Seneca	*Epistulae Morales ad Lucilium* 1.7.8
13.3	Cicero	*Cato Maiore De Senectute* 14.47
13.4	Livy	*Ab Urbe Condita* 2.12.8
13.5	Plautus	*Stichus* 243
13.6	Cicero	*De Re Publica* 2.4
13.7	Publilius Syrus	*Sententiae* B 21
13.8	Ovid	*Metamorphoses* 1.515-518
14.1	Caesar	*Bellum Gallicum* 3.23.3
14.2	Vergil	*Eclogues* 4.35-36
14.3	Horace	*Sermones* 1.2.11
14.4	Cicero	*Cato Maiore De Senectute* 22.8
14.5	Vergil	*Aeneid* 1.437
14.6	Cicero	*De Finibus* 2.86.9
14.7	Martial	*Epigrammata* 5.81
14.8	Vergil	*Aeneid* 1.100-101
15.1	Seneca	*Epistulae Morales ad Lucilium* 66.26.7
15.2	Eutropius	*Breviarium Ab Urbe Condita* 1.2
15.3	Cicero	*Philippicae* 9.5.10
15.4	Catullus	*Carmina* 51.1
15.5	Ovid	*Metamorphoses* 5.343, 345
15.6	Caesar	*Bellum Gallicum* 2.15.2
15.7	Cicero	*Pro Murena* 23.5
15.8	Ennius	*Annales* 7.233
16.1	Ovid	*Amores* 1.12.1
16.2	Vergil	*Aeneid* 1.86
16.3	Caesar	*Bellum Gallicum* 1.4
16.4	Vergil	*Aeneid* 12.831

16.5	Livy	*Ab Urbe Condita* 7.39.12
16.6	Martial	*Epigrammata* 4.80.6
16.7	Vergil	*Aeneid* 1.276-279
16.8	Caesar	*Bellum Civile* 3.19.5.1
17.1	Caesar	*Bellum Gallicum* 5.46
17.2	Caesar	*Bellum Gallicum* 1.6.4
17.3	Vergil	*Aeneid* 2.265-267
17.4	Vergil	*Aeneid* 1.31-32
17.5	Ovid	*Metamorphoses* 8.208
17.6	Vergil	*Aeneid* 4.54-55
17.7	Cicero	*Philippicae* 5.9.24
17.8	Caesar	*Bellum Gallicum* 4.15
18.1	Cicero	*In Verrem* 2.1.9.8
18.2	Propertius	*Elegiae* 3.13.60
18.3	Plautus	*Mercator* 808
18.4	Cicero	*Pro Roscio Amerino* 30.4
18.5	Publilius Syrus	*Sententiae* S 7
18.6	Seneca	*Epistulae Morales ad Lucilium* 57.8.1
18.7	Ovid	*Metamorphoses* 1.5-8
18.8	Martial	*Liber de Spectaculis* 29.4-5
19.1	Cicero	*In Verrem* 2.2.21.11
19.2	Seneca	*Epistulae Morales ad Lucilium* 59.12.7
19.3	Vergil	*Aeneid* 2.41-44
19.4	Ennius	*Annales* 6.167
19.5	Martial	*Epigrammata* 1.32
19.6	Vergil	*Aeneid* 4.12
19.7	Caesar	*Bellum Civile* 3.51
19.8	Plautus	*Stichus* 539-541
20.1	Sallust	*Bellum Catilinae* 54.6.3
20.2	Cicero	*In Q. Caecilium* 39.2
20.3	Petronius	*Satiricon* 16.4.3
20.4	Caesar	*Bellum Gallicum* 3.18.7
20.5	Theodosian Law Code	C.Th. 2.8.18
20.6	Plautus	*Trinummus* 361
20.7	Ovid	*Metamorphoses* 14.729
20.8	Cicero	*De Inventione* 2.14.7-8
21.1	Cicero	*In Catilinam* 1.27; *Epistulae ad Fam.* 2.15; *Epistulae ad Att.* 3.26
21.2	Seneca	*Epistulae Morales ad Lucilium* 79.11.2
21.3	Seneca	*Controversiae* 6.7.1.16
21.4	Caesar	*Epistulae ad Atticum* 7.15.2
21.5	Cicero	*Pro Milone* 5
21.6	Vergil	*Aeneid* 1.544-545
21.7	Ovid	*Metamorphoses* 11.421-22
21.8	Livy	*Ab Urbe Condita* 2.31.3
22.1	Vergil	*Aeneid* 1.405-406
22.2	Caesar	*Bellum Gallicum* 5.9.6
22.3	Ovid	*Amores* 1.11.15
22.4	Horace	*Epodi* 2.2.58
22.5	Seneca	*De Ira* 2.29
22.6	Ovid	*Metamorphoses* 7.155-56
22.7	Cicero	*Pro Roscio Comodeo* 17.10
22.8	Cornelius Nepos	*Liber De Excellentibus Ducibus (Hannibal)* 23.5
23.1	Terence	*Phormio* 137-138
23.2	Horace	*Carmina* 1.14.1-2
23.3	Vergil	*Aeneid* 2.49

23.4	Ennius	*Annales* 1.54
23.5	Cicero	*In Verrem* 2.4.112
23.6	Martial	*Epigrammata* 10.104.19
23.7	Cicero	*De Legibus* 1.13.9
23.8	Livy	*Ab Urbe Condita* 6.26.5
24.1	Catullus	*Carmina* 5.1-3
24.2	Plautus	*Curculio* 589
24.3	Cicero	*Pro Milone* 93
24.4	Caesar	*Bellum Gallicum* 7.4.4
24.5	Vergil	*Aeneid* 1.565
24.6	Seneca	*De Beneficiis* 2.11.2
24.7	Vergil	*Aeneid* 4.102-103
24.8	Vulgate	*Genesis* 1.9-10
25.1	Cicero	*In Verrem* 2.4.118
25.2	Cicero	*Pro Roscio Comodeo* 12
25.3	Suetonius	*De Vitis Caesarum (Caligula)* 30.1.4
25.4	Vergil	*Aeneid* 2.6, 8
25.5	Cicero	*In Verrem* 2.2.47
25.6	Suetonius	*Life of Caligula* 30.2.7
25.7	Cicero	*Tusculanae Disputationes* 3.71
25.8	Cicero	*Pro Cluentio* 147
26.1	Caesar	*Bellum Gallicum* 7.12
26.2	Martial	*Epigrammata* 9.70.1
26.3	Vergil	*Aeneid* 1.5-6
26.4	Cicero	*De Finibus* 1.66
26.5	Quintilian	*Institutio Oratoria* 9.3.85
26.6	Martial	*Epigrammata* 3.27.1
26.7	Augustus	*Res Gestae* 1
26.8	Caesar	*Bellum Gallicum* 1.25
27.1	Cicero	*Pro Roscio Comodeo* 42
27.2	Cicero	*Laelius de Amicitia* 10-12
27.3	Caesar	*Bellum Gallicum* 1.7
27.4	Cicero	*Cato Maiore De Senectute* 11
27.5	Sallust	*Bellum Catilinae* 52.19
27.6	Boethius *(attributed)*	perhaps inspired by *Consolatio Philosophiae* 2.P7
27.7	Traditional	epitaph
28.1	Caesar	*Bellum Gallicum* 4.29
28.2	Plautus	*Truculentus* 774
28.3	Cicero	*Pro Roscio Amerino* 5.11
28.4	Cicero	*Ad Familiares* 13.73
28.5	Livy	*Ab Urbe Condita* 1.25.9
28.6	Vergil	*Aeneid* 2.506
28.7	Plautus	*Miles Gloriosus* 1348
28.8	Cicero *(attributed)*	*De Petitione Consulatus*
29.1	Cicero	*In Q. Caecilium* 39.2-7
29.2	Seneca	*Quaestiones Naturales* 6.3.4
29.3	Ennius	*Annales* 12.363-365
29.4	Pliny	*Epistulae* 2.3
29.5	Cato	*De Agri Cultura* fr. 7.2
29.6	Cicero	*Tusculanae Disputationes* 1.19
29.7	Cicero	*De Oratore* 2.357
29.8	Ovid	*Ars Amatoria* 1.1-4
29.9	Publilius Syrus	*Sententiae* S 24
29.10	Cicero	*De Officiis* 1.105
30.1	Cicero	*Cato Maiore De Senectute* 85

30.2	Plautus	*Bacchides* 4.7
30.3	Caesar	*Bellum Gallicum* 5.30.2
30.4	Cicero	*Brutus* 84
30.5	Terence	*Eunuchus, Prologus* 40-41
30.6	Sallust	*Bellum Catilinae* 6.1
30.7	Cicero	*De Officiis* 1.17.56
31.1	Vergil	*Aeneid* 6.179
31.2	Caesar	*Bellum Gallicum* 1.25.3
31.3	Seneca	*De Beneficiis* 4.10.2
31.4	Caesar	*Bellum Gallicum* 4.26.1
31.5	Traditional	proverb
31.6	Vergil	*Aeneid* 1.630
31.7	Horace	*Carmina* 1.37.1-2
31.8	Caesar	*Bellum Gallicum* 4.37.2
32.1	Vergil	*Aeneid* 3.26
32.2	Caesar	*Bellum Gallicum* 1.30
32.3	Livy	*Ab Urbe Condita* 31.38.4
32.4	Cicero	*Epistulae ad Familiares* 14.4
32.5	Caesar	*Bellum Civile* 3.94
32.6	Caesar	*Bellum Gallicum* 4.25.1
32.7	Cicero	*In Pisonem* 32.10
32.8	Euclid	Medieval translation from the original Greek

Exercises

219.1	Cicero	*Pro Milone* 53
219.2	Caesar	*Bellum Gallicum* 5.43
219.3	Caesar	*Bellum Gallicum* 3.14
222	Caesar	*Bellum Gallicum* 1.7
223.1	Juvenal	*Saturae* 6.444
223.2	Lucretius	*De Rerum Natura* 5.609-610
223.3	Vergil	*Aeneid* 1.19-22
223.4	Cicero	*Laelius de Amicitia* 17
223.5	Livy	*Ab Urbe Condita* 21.53
223.6	Vergil	*Aeneid* 1.89
225.1	Vergil	*Aeneid* 4.117-119
225.2	Ennius	*Euhemerus*, fr. 3.64
225.3	Livy	*Ab Urbe Condita* 3.25
227.1	Cicero	*In Catilinam* 1.11
227.2	Sallust	*Bellum Catilinae* 5.1
227.3	Quintilian	*Institutio Oratoria* 5.13.3
227.4	Caesar	*Bellum Gallicum* 1.7
227.5	Cicero	*De Divinatione* 2.69.4

MORPHOLOGY REFERENCE SECTION

Nouns
first declension
second declension
third declension
fourth declension
fifth declension
vīs (irregular)

Adjectives
first & second declension
third declension
    three endings
    two endings
    one ending
comparative
plūs
irregular comparison

Adverbs

Numerals

Pronouns
personal
demonstrative
reflexive
intensive
relative
interrogative

Verbs
indicative active
    present, imperfect, future
    perfect, pluperfect, future perfect
subjunctive active
imperative active
infinitive active
participle active

indicative passive
    present, imperfect, future
    perfect, pluperfect, future perfect
subjunctive passive
imperative passive
infinitive passive
participle passive
deponent verbs
    imperative
    infinitive

    participle

irregular verbs
    sum
    possum
    volō, nōlō, mālō
    eō
    ferō
    fīō

Nouns

	First Declension	Second Declension		
Singular	**Feminine**	**Masculine**	**Masculine**	**Neuter**
Nominative	fēmina	animus	puer	rēgnum
Genitive	fēminae	animī	puerī	rēgnī
Dative	fēminae	animō	puerō	rēgnō
Accusative	fēminam	animum	puerum	rēgnum
Ablative	fēminā	animō	puerō	rēgnō
Vocative	fēmina	anime	puer	rēgnum
Plural				
Nominative	fēminae	animī	puerī	rēgna
Genitive	fēminārum	animōrum	puerōrum	rēgnōrum
Dative	fēminīs	animīs	puerīs	rēgnīs
Accusative	fēminās	animōs	puerōs	rēgna
Ablative	fēminīs	animīs	puerīs	rēgnīs
Vocative	fēminae	animī	puerī	rēgna

Third Declension: Masculine and Feminine

Singular	[—]	[-s]	[i-stem]
Nominative	cōnsul	rēx	ars
Genitive	cōnsulis	rēgis	artis
Dative	cōnsulī	rēgī	artī
Accusative	cōnsulem	rēgem	artem
Ablative	cōnsule	rēge	arte
Vocative	cōnsul	rēx	ars

Plural			
Nominative	cōnsulēs	rēgēs	artēs
Genitive	cōnsulum	rēgum	artium
Dative	cōnsulibus	rēgibus	artibus
Accusative	cōnsulēs	rēgēs	artēs
Ablative	cōnsulibus	rēgibus	artibus
Vocative	cōnsulēs	rēgēs	artēs

Third Declension: Neuter

Singular	[Consonant stem]	[i-stem]
Nominative	caput	mare
Genitive	capitis	maris
Dative	capitī	marī
Accusative	caput	mare
Ablative	capite	marī
Vocative	caput	mare

Plural	[Consonant stem]	[i-stem]
Nominative	capita	maria
Genitive	capitum	marium
Dative	capitibus	maribus
Accusative	capita	maria
Ablative	capitibus	maribus
Vocative	capita	maria

Fourth Declension

Singular	M (& F)	Neuter
Nominative	vultus	genū
Genitive	vultūs	genūs
Dative	vultuī	genū
Accusative	vultum	genū
Ablative	vultū	genū
Vocative	vultus	genū

Plural		
Nominative	vultūs	genua
Genitive	vultuum	genuum
Dative	vultibus	genibus
Accusative	vultūs	genua
Ablative	vultibus	genibus
Vocative	vultūs	genua

Fifth Declension

Singular	Masculine	Feminine
Nominative	diēs	rēs
Genitive	diēī	reī
Dative	diēī	reī
Accusative	diem	rem
Ablative	diē	rē
Vocative	diēs	rēs

Plural

Nominative	diēs	rēs
Genitive	diērum	rērum
Dative	diēbus	rēbus
Accusative	diēs	rēs
Ablative	diēbus	rēbus
Vocative	diēs	rēs

vīs, vīs, *f.*

	Singular	**Plural**
Nominative	vīs	vīrēs
Genitive	[vīs – *rarely seen*]	vīrium
Dative	[vī – *rarely seen*]	vīribus
Accusative	vim	vīrēs
Ablative	vī	vīribus

Adjectives

First and Second Declension

Singular	**Masculine**	**Feminine**	**Neuter**
Nominative	bonus	bona	bonum
Genitive	bonī	bonae	bonī
Dative	bonō	bonae	bonō
Accusative	bonum	bonam	bonum
Ablative	bonō	bonā	bonō
Plural			
Nominative	bonī	bonae	bona
Genitive	bonōrum	bonārum	bonōrum
Dative	bonīs	bonīs	bonīs
Accusative	bonōs	bonās	bona
Ablative	bonīs	bonīs	bonīs

Third Declension
Three-Ending Adjectives

Singular	**Masculine**	**Feminine**	**Neuter**
Nominative	ācer	ācris	ācre
Genitive	ācris	ācris	ācris
Dative	ācrī	ācrī	ācrī
Accusative	ācrem	ācrem	ācre
Ablative	ācrī	ācrī	ācrī
Plural			
Nominative	ācrēs	ācrēs	ācria
Genitive	ācrium	ācrium	ācrium
Dative	ācribus	ācribus	ācribus
Accusative	ācrēs	ācrēs	ācria
Ablative	ācribus	ācribus	ācribus

Two-Ending Adjectives

Singular	**M & F**	**Neuter**
Nominative	omnis	omne
Genitive	omnis	omnis
Dative	omnī	omnī
Accusative	omnem	omne
Ablative	omnī	omnī
Plural		
Nominative	omnēs	omnia
Genitive	omnium	omnium
Dative	omnibus	omnibus
Accusative	omnēs	omnia
Ablative	omnibus	omnibus

One-Ending Adjectives

Singular	M & F	Neuter
Nominative	ingēns	ingēns
Genitive	ingentis	ingentis
Dative	ingentī	ingentī
Accusative	ingentem	ingēns
Ablative	ingentī	ingentī

Plural	M & F	Neuter
Nominative	ingentēs	ingentia
Genitive	ingentium	ingentium
Dative	ingentibus	ingentibus
Accusative	ingentēs	ingentia
Ablative	ingentibus	ingentibus

Comparative Adjectives

Singular	M & F	Neuter
Nominative	longior	longius
Genitive	longiōris	longiōris
Dative	longiōrī	longiōrī
Accusative	longiōrem	longius
Ablative	longiōre	longiōre

Plural	M & F	Neuter
Nominative	longiōrēs	longiōra
Genitive	longiōrum	longiōrum
Dative	longiōribus	longiōribus
Accusative	longiōrēs	longiōra
Ablative	longiōribus	longiōribus

plūs, plūris

Singular	M & F	Neuter
Nominative	_____	plūs
Genitive	_____	plūris
Dative	_____	_____
Accusative	_____	plūs
Ablative	_____	plūre

Plural	M & F	Neuter
Nominative	plūrēs	plūra
Genitive	plūrium	plūrium
Dative	plūribus	plūribus
Accusative	plūrēs	plūra
Ablative	plūribus	plūribus

Irregular Comparison

Positive	Comparative	Superlative
bonus, -a, -um (good)	melior, melius (better)	optimus, -a, -um (best)
magnus, -a, -um (big)	maior, maius (bigger)	maximus, -a, -um (biggest)
malus, -a, -um (bad)	pēior, pēius (worse)	pessimus, -a, -um (worst)
multus, -a, -um (much; many)	plūs, plūris (more)	plūrimus, -a, -um (most)
parvus, -a, -um (small)	minor, minus (smaller, less)	minimus, -a, -um (smallest, least)
superus, -a, -um (upper)	superior, superius (higher)	summus, -a, -um (highest, furthest; top of)
		suprēmus, -a, -um (highest, last)

Adverbs

Positive	Comparative	Superlative
celeriter (quickly)	celerius (more quickly)	celerrimē (most quickly)
fortiter (bravely)	fortius (more bravely)	fortissimē (most bravely)
longē (far)	longius (farther)	longissimē (farthest)
bene (well)	melius (better)	optimē (best)
male (badly)	pēius (worse)	pessimē (worst)
multum (much)	plūs (more – *quantity*)	plūrimum (most, very much)
magnopere (greatly)	magis (more – *quality*)	maximē (most, especially)
parum (little)	minus (less)	minimē (least)

Numerals

	Cardinal		Ordinal	
1	ūnus, -a, -um	I	prīmus, -a, -um	first
2	duo, duae, duo	II	secundus, -a, -um	second
3	trēs, tria	III	tertius, -a, -um	third
4	quattuor	IV	quārtus, -a, -um	fourth
5	quīnque	V	quīntus, -a, -um	fifth
6	sex	VI	sextus, -a, -um	sixth
7	septem	VII	septimus, -a, -um	seventh
8	octō	VIII	octāvus, -a, -um	eighth
9	novem	IX	nōnus, -a, -um	ninth
10	decem	X	decimus, -a, -um	tenth
11	ūndecim	XI	ūndecimus, -a, -um	eleventh
12	duodecim	XII	duodecimus, -a, -um	twelfth
20	vīgintī	XX		
30	trīgintā	XXX		
40	quādrāgintā	XL		
50	quīnquāgintā	L		
60	sexāgintā	LX		
70	septuāgintā	LXX		
80	octōgintā	LXXX		
90	nōnāgintā	XC		
100	centum	C		
500	quīngentī, -ae,-a	D		
1,000	mīlle	M		
2,000	duo mīlia	MM		

ūnus, -a, -um

Singular	Masculine	Feminine	Neuter
Nominative	ūnus	ūna	ūnum
Genitive	ūnīus	ūnīus	ūnīus
Dative	ūnī	ūnī	ūnī
Accusative	ūnum	ūnam	ūnum
Ablative	ūnō	ūnā	ūnō

duo, duae, duo   **trēs, tria**

Plural	Masculine	Feminine	Neuter	M & F	Neuter
Nominative	duo	duae	duo	trēs	tria
Genitive	duōrum	duārum	duōrum	trium	trium
Dative	duōbus	duābus	duōbus	tribus	tribus
Accusative	duōs	duās	duo	trēs	tria
Ablative	duōbus	duābus	duōbus	tribus	tribus

Pronouns

Personal Pronouns

ego, tū   **I, you**

Singular	1st Person	2nd Person
Nominative	ego	tū
Genitive	meī	tuī
Dative	mihi	tibi
Accusative	mē	tē
Ablative	mē	tē

Plural		
Nominative	nōs	vōs
Genitive	nostrum, nostrī	vestrum, vestrī
Dative	nōbīs	vōbīs
Accusative	nōs	vōs
Ablative	nōbīs	vōbīs

Third Person Pronoun uses the Demonstrative is, ea, id (see below)

Demonstrative Pronouns

is, ea, id   **he, she, it; this; that**

Singular	Masculine	Feminine	Neuter
Nominative	is	ea	id
Genitive	eius	eius	eius
Dative	eī	eī	eī
Accusative	eum	eam	id
Ablative	eō	eā	eō

Plural			
Nominative	eī	eae	ea
Genitive	eōrum	eārum	eōrum
Dative	eīs	eīs	eīs
Accusative	eōs	eās	ea
Ablative	eīs	eīs	eīs

hic, haec, hoc   **this, these; the latter**

Singular	Masculine	Feminine	Neuter
Nominative	hic	haec	hoc
Genitive	huius	huius	huius
Dative	huic	huic	huic
Accusative	hunc	hanc	hoc
Ablative	hōc	hāc	hōc

Plural			
Nominative	hī	hae	haec
Genitive	hōrum	hārum	hōrum
Dative	hīs	hīs	hīs
Accusative	hōs	hās	haec
Ablative	hīs	hīs	hīs

ille, illa, illud   **that, those; the famous; the former**

Singular	Masculine	Feminine	Neuter
Nominative	ille	illa	illud
Genitive	illīus	illīus	illīus
Dative	illī	illī	illī
Accusative	illum	illam	illud
Ablative	illō	illā	illō

Plural			
Nominative	illī	illae	illa
Genitive	illōrum	illārum	illōrum
Dative	illīs	illīs	illīs
Accusative	illōs	illās	illa
Ablative	illīs	illīs	illīs

Reflexive Pronouns   **myself, yourself, him/herself**

Singular	1st Person	2nd Person	3rd Person
Genitive	meī	tuī	suī
Dative	mihi	tibi	sibi
Accusative	mē	tē	sē, sēsē
Ablative	mē	tē	sē, sēsē

Plural			
Genitive	nostrum, nostrī	vestrum, vestrī	suī
Dative	nōbīs	vōbīs	sibi
Accusative	nōs	vōs	sē, sēsē
Ablative	nōbīs	vōbīs	sē, sēsē

Intensive Pronouns

ipse, ipsa, ipsum   _____self, himself, herself, itself, themselves

Singular	Masculine	Feminine	Neuter
Nominative	ipse	ipsa	ipsum
Genitive	ipsīus	ipsīus	ipsīus
Dative	ipsī	ipsī	ipsī
Accusative	ipsum	ipsam	ipsum
Ablative	ipsō	ipsā	ipsō

Plural			
Nominative	ipsī	ipsae	ipsa
Genitive	ipsōrum	ipsārum	ipsōrum
Dative	ipsīs	ipsīs	ipsīs
Accusative	ipsōs	ipsās	ipsa
Ablative	ipsīs	ipsīs	ipsīs

īdem, eadem, idem   **the same**

Singular	Masculine	Feminine	Neuter
Nominative	īdem	eadem	idem
Genitive	eiusdem	eiusdem	eiusdem
Dative	eīdem	eīdem	eīdem
Accusative	eundem	eandem	idem
Ablative	eōdem	eādem	eōdem

Plural			
Nominative	eīdem	eaedem	eadem
Genitive	eōrundem	eārundem	eōrundem
Dative	eīsdem	eīsdem	eīsdem
Accusative	eōsdem	eāsdem	eadem
Ablative	eīsdem	eīsdem	eīsdem

Relative Pronoun

qui, quae, quod   who, which, that

Singular	Masculine	Feminine	Neuter
Nominative	quī	quae	quod
Genitive	cuius	cuius	cuius
Dative	cui	cui	cui
Accusative	quem	quam	quod
Ablative	quō	quā	quō

Plural			
Nominative	quī	quae	quae
Genitive	quōrum	quārum	quōrum
Dative	quibus	quibus	quibus
Accusative	quōs	quās	quae
Ablative	quibus	quibus	quibus

Interrogative Pronoun*

quis, quid   who?, what?

Singular	Masculine & Feminine	Neuter
Nominative	quis	quid
Genitive	cuius	cuius
Dative	cui	cui
Accusative	quem	quid
Ablative	quō	quō

plural forms look like the Relative Pronoun above

Verbs

Indicative Active

Present

	1st Conj.	2nd Conj.	3rd Conj.	3rd Conj. -iō	4th Conj.
1st sg.	amō	moneō	regō	capiō	audiō
2nd sg.	amās	monēs	regis	capis	audīs
3rd sg.	amat	monet	regit	capit	audit
1st pl.	amāmus	monēmus	regimus	capimus	audīmus
2nd pl.	amātis	monētis	regitis	capitis	audītis
3rd pl.	amant	monent	regunt	capiunt	audiunt

Imperfect

	1st Conj.	2nd Conj.	3rd Conj.	3rd Conj. -iō	4th Conj.
1st sg.	amābam	monēbam	regēbam	capiēbam	audiēbam
2nd sg.	amābās	monēbās	regēbās	capiēbās	audiēbās
3rd sg.	amābat	monēbat	regēbat	capiēbat	audiēbat
1st pl.	amābāmus	monēbāmus	regēbāmus	capiēbāmus	audiēbāmus
2nd pl.	amābātis	monēbātis	regēbātis	capiēbātis	audiēbātis
3rd pl.	amābant	monēbant	regēbant	capiēbant	audiēbant

Future

	1st Conj.	2nd Conj.	3rd Conj.	3rd Conj. -iō	4th Conj.
1st sg.	amābō	monēbō	regam	capiam	audiam
2nd sg.	amābis	monēbis	regēs	capiēs	audiēs
3rd sg.	amabit	monēbit	reget	capiet	audiet
1st pl.	amābimus	monēbimus	regēmus	capiēmus	audiēmus
2nd pl.	amābitis	monēbitis	regētis	capiētis	audiētis
3rd pl.	amābunt	monēbunt	regent	capient	audient

Perfect

	1st Conj.	2nd Conj.	3rd Conj.	4th Conj.
1st sg.	amāvī	monuī	rēxī	audīvī
2nd sg.	amāvistī	monuistī	rēxistī	audīvistī
3rd sg.	amāvit	monuit	rēxit	audīvit
1st pl.	amāvimus	monuimus	rēximus	audīvimus
2nd pl.	amāvistis	monuistis	rēxistis	audīvistis
3rd pl.	amāvērunt/	monuērunt/	rēxērunt/	audīvērunt/
	amāvēre	monuēre	rēxēre	audīvēre

Pluperfect

	1st Conj.	2nd Conj.	3rd Conj.	4th Conj.
1st sg.	amāveram	monueram	rēxeram	audīveram
2nd sg.	amāverās	monuerās	rēxerās	audīverās
3rd sg.	amāverat	monuerat	rēxerat	audīverat
1st pl.	amāverāmus	monuerāmus	rēxerāmus	audīverāmus
2nd pl.	amāverātis	monuerātis	rēxerātis	audīverātis
3rd pl.	amāverant	monuerant	rēxerant	audīverant

Future Perfect

	1st Conj.	2nd Conj.	3rd Conj.	4th Conj.
1st sg.	amāverō	monuerō	rēxerō	audīverō
2nd sg.	amāveris	monueris	rēxeris	audīveris
3rd sg.	amāverit	monuerit	rēxerit	audīverit
1st pl.	amāverimus	monuerimus	rēxerimus	audīverimus
2nd pl.	amāveritis	monueritis	rēxeritis	audīveritis
3rd pl.	amāverint	monuerint	rēxerint	audīverint

Subjunctive Active
Present

	1st Conj.	2nd Conj.	3rd Conj.	3rd Conj. -iō	4th Conj.
1st sg.	amem	moneam	regam	capiam	audiam
2nd sg.	amēs	moneās	regās	capiās	audiās
3rd sg.	amet	moneat	regat	capiat	audiat
1st pl.	amēmus	moneāmus	regāmus	capiāmus	audiāmus
2nd pl.	amētis	moneātis	regātis	capiātis	audiātis
3rd pl.	ament	moneant	regant	capiant	audiant

Imperfect

	1st Conj.	2nd Conj.	3rd Conj.	3rd Conj. -iō	4th Conj.
1st sg.	amārem	monērem	regerem	caperem	audīrem
2nd sg.	amārēs	monērēs	regerēs	caperēs	audīrēs
3rd sg.	amāret	monēret	regeret	caperet	audīret
1st pl.	amārēmus	monērēmus	regerēmus	caperēmus	audīrēmus
2nd pl.	amārētis	monērētis	regerētis	caperētis	audīrētis
3rd pl.	amārent	monērent	regerent	caperent	audīrent

Perfect

	1st Conj.	2nd Conj.	3rd Conj.	4th Conj.
1st sg.	amāverim	monuerim	rēxerim	audīverim
2nd sg.	amāverīs	monuerīs	rēxerīs	audīverīs
3rd sg.	amāverit	monuerit	rēxerit	audīverit
1st pl.	amāverīmus	monuerīmus	rēxerīmus	audīverīmus
2nd pl.	amāverītis	monuerītis	rēxerītis	audīverītis
3rd pl.	amāverint	monuerint	rēxerint	audīverint

Pluperfect

	1st Conj.	2nd Conj.	3rd Conj.	4th Conj.
1st sg.	amāvissem	monuissem	rēxissem	audīvissem
2nd sg.	amāvissēs	monuissēs	rēxissēs	audīvissēs
3rd sg.	amāvisset	monuisset	rēxisset	audīvisset
1st pl.	amāvissēmus	monuissēmus	rēxissēmus	audīvissēmus
2nd pl.	amāvissētis	monuissētis	rēxissētis	audīvissētis
3rd pl.	amāvissent	monuissent	rēxissent	audīvissent

Imperative Active
Present

	1st Conj.	2nd Conj.	3rd Conj.	3rd Conj. -iō	4th Conj.
2nd sg.	amā	monē	rege	cape	audī
2nd pl.	amāte	monēte	regite	capite	audīte

Infinitive Active

	1st Conj.	2nd Conj.	3rd Conj.	4th Conj.
Present	amāre	monēre	regere	audīre
Perfect	amāvisse	monuisse	rēxisse	audīvisse
Future	amātūrus,	monitūrus,	rēctūrus,	audītūrus,
	-a, -um esse	-a, -um esse	-a, -um esse	-a, -um esse

Participle Active

	1st Conj.	2nd Conj.	3rd Conj.	4th Conj.
Present	amāns, -ntis	monēns, -ntis	regēns, -ntis	audiēns, -ntis
Future	amātūrus,	monitūrus,	rēctūrus,	audītūrus,
	-a, -um	-a, -um	-a, -um	-a, -um

Indicative Passive
Present

	1st Conj.	2nd Conj.	3rd Conj.	3rd Conj. -iō	4th Conj.
1st sg.	amor	moneor	regor	capior	audīor
*2nd sg.**	amāris	monēris	regeris	caperis	audīris
3rd sg.	amātur	monētur	regitur	capitur	audītur
1st pl.	amāmur	monēmur	regimur	capimur	audīmur
2nd pl.	amāminī	monēminī	regiminī	capiminī	audīminī
3rd pl.	amantur	monentur	reguntur	capiuntur	audiuntur

Imperfect

	1st Conj.	2nd Conj.	3rd Conj.	3rd Conj. -iō	4th Conj.
1st sg.	amābar	monēbar	regēbar	capiēbar	audiēbar
*2nd sg.**	amābāris	monēbāris	regēbāris	capiēbāris	audiēbāris
3rd sg.	amābātur	monēbātur	regēbātur	capiēbātur	audiēbātur
1st pl.	amābāmur	monēbāmur	regēbāmur	capiēbāmur	audiēbāmur
2nd pl.	amābāminī	monēbāminī	regēbāminī	capiēbāminī	audiēbāminī
3rd pl.	amābantur	monēbantur	regēbantur	capiēbantur	audiēbantur

Future

	1st Conj.	2nd Conj.	3rd Conj.	3rd Conj. -iō	4th Conj.
1st sg.	amābor	monēbor	regar	capiar	audīar
*2nd sg.**	amāberis	monēberis	regēris	capiēris	audiēris
3rd sg.	amābitur	monēbitur	regētur	capiētur	audiētur
1st pl.	amābimur	monēbimur	regēmur	capiēmur	audiēmur
2nd pl.	amābiminī	monēbiminī	regēminī	capiēminī	audiēminī
3rd pl.	amābuntur	monēbuntur	regentur	capientur	audientur

*2nd sg. alternate ending for **-ris** is **-re** (*mostly in poetry*)

Perfect**

	1st Conj.	2nd Conj.	3rd Conj.	4th Conj.
1st sg.	amātus sum	monitus sum	rēctus sum	audītus sum
2nd sg.	amātus es	monitus es	rēctus es	audītus es
3rd sg.	amātus est	monitus est	rēctus est	audītus est
1st pl.	amātī sumus	monitī sumus	rēctī sumus	audītī sumus
2nd pl.	amātī estis	monitī estis	rēctī estis	audītī estis
3rd pl.	amātī sunt	monitī sunt	rēctī sunt	audītī sunt

***Note: Only the masculine form is listed here for the perfect system. See §73.*

Pluperfect

	1st Conj.	2nd Conj.	3rd Conj.	4th Conj.
1st sg.	amātus eram	monitus eram	rēctus eram	audītus eram
2nd sg.	amātus erās	monitus erās	rēctus erās	audītus erās
3rd sg.	amātus erat	monitus erat	rēctus erat	audītus erat
1st pl.	amātī erāmus	monitī erāmus	rēctī erāmus	audītī erāmus
2nd pl.	amātī erātis	monitī erātis	rēctī erātis	audītī erātis
3rd pl.	amātī erant	monitī erant	rēctī erant	audītī erant

Future Perfect

	1st Conj.	2nd Conj.	3rd Conj.	4th Conj.
1st sg.	amātus erō	monitus erō	rēctus erō	audītus erō
2nd sg.	amātus eris	monitus eris	rēctus eris	audītus eris
3rd sg.	amātus erit	monitus erit	rēctus erit	audītus erit
1st pl.	amātī erimus	monitī erimus	rēctī erimus	audītī erimus
2nd pl.	amātī eritis	monitī eritis	rēctī eritis	audītī eritis
3rd pl.	amātī erunt	monitī erunt	rēctī erunt	audītī erunt

Subjunctive Passive

Present

	1st Conj.	2nd Conj.	3rd Conj.	3rd Conj. -iō	4th Conj.
1st sg.	amer	monear	regar	capiar	audiar
*2nd sg.**	amēris	moneāris	regāris	capiāris	audiāris
3rd sg.	amētur	moneātur	regātur	capiātur	audiātur
1st pl.	amēmur	moneāmur	regāmur	capiāmur	audiāmur
2nd pl.	amēminī	moneāminī	regāminī	capiāminī	audiāminī
3rd pl.	amentur	moneantur	regantur	capiāntur	audiantur

Imperfect

	1st Conj.	2nd Conj.	3rd Conj.	3rd Conj. -iō	4th Conj.
1st sg.	amārer	monērer	regerer	caperer	audīrer
*2nd sg.**	amārēris	monērēris	regerēris	caperēris	audīrēris
3rd sg.	amārētur	monērētur	regerētur	caperētur	audīrētur
1st pl.	amārēmur	monērēmur	regerēmur	caperēmur	audīrēmur
2nd pl.	amārēminī	monērēminī	regerēminī	caperēminī	audīrēminī
3rd pl.	amārentur	monērentur	regerentur	caperentur	audīrentur

**2nd sg. alternate ending for* -ris *is* -re (*mostly in poetry*)

Perfect

	1st Conj.	2nd Conj.	3rd Conj.	4th Conj.
1st sg.	amātus sim	monitus sim	rēctus sim	audītus sim
2nd sg.	amātus sīs	monitus sīs	rēctus sīs	audītus sīs
3rd sg.	amātus sit	monitus sit	rēctus sit	audītus sit
1st pl.	amātī sīmus	monitī sīmus	rēctī sīmus	audītī sīmus
2nd pl.	amātī sītis	monitī sītis	rēctī sītis	audītī sītis
3rd pl.	amātī sint	monitī sint	rēctī sint	audītī sint

Pluperfect

	1st Conj.	2nd Conj.	3rd Conj.	4th Conj.
1st sg.	amātus essem	monitus essem	rēctus essem	audītus essem
2nd sg.	amātus essēs	monitus essēs	rēctus essēs	audītus essēs
3rd sg.	amātus esset	monitus esset	rēctus esset	audītus esset
1st pl.	amātī essēmus	monitī essēmus	rēctī essēmus	audītī essēmus
2nd pl.	amātī essētis	monitī essētis	rēctī essētis	audītī essētis
3rd pl.	amātī essent	monitī essent	rēctī essent	audītī essent

Imperative Passive
Present

	1st Conj.	2nd Conj.	3rd Conj.	4th Conj.
2nd sg.	amāre	monēre	regere	audīre
2nd pl.	amāminī	monēminī	regiminī	audīminī

Infinitive Passive

	1st Conj.	2nd Conj.	3rd Conj.	4th Conj.
Present	amārī	monērī	regī	audīrī
Perfect	amātus esse	monitus esse	rēctus esse	audītus esse
Future	amātum īrī	monitum īrī	rēctum īrī	audītum īrī

Participle Passive

	1st Conj.	2nd Conj.	3rd Conj.	4th Conj.
Perfect	amātus, -a, -um	doctus, -a, -um	rēctus, -a, -um	audītus, -a, -um
Future /	amandus,	docendus,	regendus,	audiendus,
Gerundive	-a, -um	-a, -um	-a, -um	-a, -um

Deponent Verbs
Indicative   — *see Passive forms of regular verbs above*
Subjunctive   — *see Passive forms of regular verbs above*

Imperative (Present)

	1st Conj.	2nd Conj.	3rd Conj.	4th Conj.
2nd sg.	morāre	verēre	loquere	potīre
2nd pl.	morāminī	verēminī	loquiminī	potīminī

Infinitive

	1st Conj.	2nd Conj.	3rd Conj.	4th Conj.
Present	morārī	verērī	loquī	potīrī
Perfect	morātus esse	veritus esse	locūtus esse	potītus esse
Future	morātūrus esse	veritūrus esse	locūtūrus esse	potītūrus esse

Participles

	1st Conj.	2nd Conj.	3rd Conj.	4th Conj.
Present	morāns	verēns	loquēns	potiēns
Future	morātūrus	veritūrus	locūtūrus	potītūrus
	-a, -um	-a, -um	-a, -um	-a, -um
Perfect	morātus	veritus	locūtus	potītus
	-a, -um	-a, -um	-a, -um	-a, -um
Gerundive	morandus	verendus	loquendus	potiendus
	-a, -um	-a, -um	-a, -um	-a, -um

Irregular Verbs

sum, esse, fuī	to be
possum, posse, potuī	to be able
volō, velle, voluī	to want
nōlō, nōlle, nōluī	not to want
mālō, mālle, māluī	to prefer

Indicative

Present

	to be	to be able	to want	not to want	to prefer
1st sg.	sum	possum	volō	nōlō	mālō
2nd sg.	es	potes	vīs	nōn vīs	māvīs
3rd sg.	est	potest	vult	nōn vult	māvult
1st pl.	sumus	possumus	volumus	nōlumus	mālumus
2nd pl.	estis	potestis	vultis	nōn vultis	māvultis
3rd pl.	sunt	possunt	volunt	nōlunt	mālunt

Imperfect [*only* **sum** *and* **possum** *have irregular forms here*]

	to be	to be able	to want	not to want	to prefer
1st sg.	eram	poteram	volēbam	nōlēbam	mālēbam
2nd sg.	erās	poterās	volēbās	nōlēbās	mālēbās
3rd sg.	erat	poterat	volēbat	nōlēbat	mālēbat
1st pl.	erāmus	poterāmus	volēbāmus	nōlēbāmus	mālēbāmus
2nd pl.	erātis	poterātis	volēbātis	nōlēbātis	mālēbātis
3rd pl.	erant	poterant	volēbant	nōlēbant	mālēbant

Future [*only* **sum** *and* **possum** *have irregular forms here*]

	to be	to be able	to want	not to want	to prefer
1st sg.	erō	poterō	volam	nōlam	mālam
2nd sg.	eris	poteris	volēs	nōlēs	mālēs
3rd sg.	erit	poterit	volet	nōlet	mālet
1st pl.	erimus	poterimus	volēmus	nōlēmus	mālēmus
2nd pl.	eritis	poteritis	volētis	nōlētis	mālētis
3rd pl.	erunt	poterunt	volent	nōlent	mālent

Perfect [*these are all regular forms*]

	to be	to be able	to want	not to want	to prefer
1st sg.	fuī	potuī	voluī	nōluī	māluī
2nd sg.	fuistī	potuistī	voluistī	nōluistī	māluistī
3rd sg.	fuit	potuit	voluit	nōluit	māluit
1st pl.	fuimus	potuimus	voluimus	nōluimus	māluimus
2nd pl.	fuistis	potuistis	voluistis	nōluistis	māluistis
3rd pl.	fuērunt	potuērunt	voluērunt	nōluērunt	māluērunt

Pluperfect [*these are all regular forms*]

	to be	to be able	to want	not to want	to prefer
1st sg.	fueram	potueram	volueram	nōlueram	mālueram
2nd sg.	fuerās	potuerās	voluerās	nōluerās	māluerās
3rd sg.	fuerat	potuerat	voluerat	nōluerat	māluerat
1st pl.	fuerāmus	potuerāmus	voluerāmus	nōluerāmus	māluerāmus
2nd pl.	fuerātis	potuerātis	voluerātis	nōluerātis	māluerātis
3rd pl.	fuerant	potuerant	voluerant	nōluerant	māluerant

Future Perfect [*these are all regular forms*]

	to be	to be able	to want	not to want	to prefer
1st sg.	fuerō	potuerō	voluerō	nōluerō	māluerō
2nd sg.	fueris	potueris	volueris	nōlueris	mālueris
3rd sg.	fuerit	potuerit	voluerit	nōluerit	māluerit
1st pl.	fuerimus	potuerimus	voluerimus	nōluerimus	māluerimus
2nd pl.	fueritis	potueritis	volueritis	nōlueritis	mālueritis
3rd pl.	fuerint	potuerint	voluerint	nōluerint	māluerint

Subjunctive
Present

	to be	to be able	to want	not to want	to prefer
1st sg.	sim	possim	velim	nōlim	mālim
2nd sg.	sīs	possīs	velīs	nōlīs	mālīs
3rd sg.	sit	possit	velit	nōlit	mālit
1st pl.	sīmus	possīmus	velīmus	nōlīmus	mālīmus
2nd pl.	sītis	possītis	velītis	nōlītis	mālītis
3rd pl.	sint	possint	velint	nōlint	mālint

Imperfect [*these are all regular forms*]

	to be	to be able	to want	not to want	to prefer
1st sg.	essem	possem	vellem	nōllem	māllem
2nd sg.	essēs	possēs	vellēs	nōllēs	māllēs
3rd sg.	esset	posset	vellet	nōllet	māllet
1st pl.	essēmus	possēmus	vellēmus	nōllēmus	māllēmus
2nd pl.	essētis	possētis	vellētis	nōllētis	māllētis
3rd pl.	essent	possent	vellent	nōllent	māllent

Perfect [*these are all regular forms*]

	to be	to be able	to want	not to want	to prefer
1st sg.	fuerim	potuerim	voluerim	nōluerim	māluerim
2nd sg.	fuerīs	potuerīs	voluerīs	nōluerīs	māluerīs
3rd sg.	fuerit	potuerit	voluerit	nōluerit	māluerit
1st pl.	fuerīmus	potuerīmus	voluerīmus	nōluerīmus	māluerīmus
2nd pl.	fuerītis	potuerītis	voluerītis	nōluerītis	māluerītis
3rd pl.	fuerint	potuerint	voluerint	nōluerint	māluerint

Pluperfect [*these are all regular forms*]

	to be	to be able	to want	not to want	to prefer
1st sg.	fuissem	potuissem	voluissem	nōluissem	māluissem
2nd sg.	fuissēs	potuissēs	voluissēs	nōluissēs	māluissēs
3rd sg.	fuisset	potuisset	voluisset	nōluisset	māluisset
1st pl.	fuissēmus	potuissēmus	voluissēmus	nōluissēmus	māluissēmus
2nd pl.	fuissētis	potuissētis	voluissētis	nōluissētis	māluissētis
3rd pl.	fuissent	potuissent	voluissent	nōluissent	māluissent

Imperative
Present

	to be	to be able	to want	not to want	to prefer
2nd sg.	es	-------	-------	nōlī	-------
2nd pl.	este	-------	-------	nōlīte	-------

Infinitive

	to be	to be able	to want	not to want	to prefer
Present	esse	posse	velle	nōlle	mālle
Perfect	fuisse	potuisse	voluisse	nōluisse	māluisse
Future	futūrus esse *or* fore	-------	-------	-------	-------

Participle

	to be	to be able	to want	not to want	to prefer
Present	-------	potēns, -ntis	volēns, -ntis	nōlēns, -ntis	-------
Perfect	-------	-------	-------	-------	-------
Future	futūrus, -a, -um	-------	-------	-------	-------

eō, īre, iī (īvī), itūrus   to go
Indicative

	Present	Imperfect	Future	Perfect	Pluperfect	Future Perfect
1st sg.	eō	ībam	ībō	iī, (īvī)	ieram	ierō
2nd sg.	īs	ībās	ībis	iistī > īstī	ierās	ieris
3rd sg.	it	ībat	ībit	iit	ierat	ierit
1st pl.	īmus	ībāmus	ībimus	iimus	ierāmus	ierimus
2nd pl.	ītis	ībātis	ībitis	iistis > īstis	ierātis	ieritis
3rd pl.	eunt	ībant	ībunt	iērunt	ierant	ierint

Subjunctive

	Present	Imperfect	Perfect	Pluperfect
1st sg.	eam	īrem	ierim	īssem
2nd sg.	eās	īrēs	ierīs	īssēs
3rd sg.	eat	īret	ierit	īsset
1st pl.	eāmus	īrēmus	ierīmus	īssēmus
2nd pl.	eātis	īrētis	ierītis	īssētis
3rd pl.	eant	īrent	ierint	īssent

Infinitive   **Imperative**
Present	īre	*2nd sg.*	ī
Perfect	īsse	*2nd pl.*	īte
Future	itūrus esse		

Participle
Present	iēns, euntis
Future	itūrus, -a, -um
Gerundive	eundum

ferō, ferre, tulī, lātus   to bear
Indicative

	Present	Active Imperfect	Future	Present	Passive Imperfect	Future
1st sg.	ferō	ferēbam	feram	feror	ferēbar	ferar
2nd sg.	fers	ferēbās	ferēs	ferris	ferēbāris	ferēris
3rd sg.	fert	ferēbat	feret	fertur	ferēbātur	ferētur
1st pl.	ferimus	ferēbāmus	ferēmus	ferimur	ferēbāmur	ferēmur
2nd pl.	fertis	ferēbātis	ferētis	feriminī	ferēbāminī	ferēminī
3rd pl.	ferunt	ferēbant	ferent	feruntur	ferēbantur	ferentur

	Active Perfect	Passive Perfect
1st sg.	tulī	lātus sum
2nd sg.	tulistī	lātus es
3rd sg.	tulit	lātus est
1st pl.	tulimus	lātī sumus
2nd pl.	tulistis	lātī estis
3rd pl.	tulērunt	lātī sunt

the pluperfect and future perfect active and passive forms are all regular

Subjunctive

	Active		**Passive**	
	Present	**Imperfect**	**Present**	**Imperfect**
1st sg.	feram	ferrem	ferar	ferrer
2nd sg.	ferās	ferrēs	ferāris	ferrēris
3rd sg.	ferat	ferret	ferātur	ferretur
1st pl.	ferāmus	ferrēmus	ferāmur	ferrēmur
2nd pl.	ferātis	ferrētis	ferāminī	ferrēminī
3rd pl.	ferant	ferrent	ferantur	ferrentur

	Perfect		**Pluperfect**	
1st sg.	tulerim	tulissem	lātus sim	lātus essem
2nd sg.	tulerīs	tulissēs	lātus sīs	lātus essēs
3rd sg.	tulerit	tulisset	lātus sit	lātus esset
1st pl.	tulerīmus	tulissēmus	lātī sīmus	lātī essēmus
2nd pl.	tulerītis	tulissētis	lātī sītis	lātī essētis
3rd pl.	tulerint	tulissent	lātī sint	lātī essent

Imperative

2nd sg.	fer
2nd pl.	ferte

Infinitive

Present	ferre	ferrī
Perfect	tulisse	lātus esse
Future	lātūrus esse	-------

Participle

Present	ferēns, ferentis	-------
Perfect	-------	lātus, -a, -um
Future	lātūrus, -a, -um	ferendus, -a, -um

fiō, fierī, factus sum

	Indicative			**Subjunctive**	
	Present	**Imperfect**	**Future**	**Present**	**Imperfect**
1st sg.	fīō	fīēbam	fīam	fīam	fierem
2nd sg.	fīs	fīēbās	fīēs	fīās	fierēs
3rd sg.	fit	fīēbat	fīet	fīat	fieret
1st pl.	fīmus	fīēbāmus	fīēmus	fīāmus	fierēmus
2nd pl.	fītis	fīēbātis	fīētis	fīātis	fierētis
3rd pl.	fīunt	fīēbant	fīent	fīant	fierent

Vocabulary by Chapter

Chapter 1
Nouns
agricola, agricolae *m.*	farmer
aqua, aquae *f.*	water
fēmina, fēminae *f.*	woman
fortūna, fortūnae *f.*	chance, luck, fortune
nauta, nautae *m.*	sailor
pecūnia, pecūniae *f.*	money, property
rosa, rosae *f.*	rose

Verbs
amō, amāre, amāvī, amātus	to love
dēbeō, dēbēre, dēbuī, dēbitus	"ought to, should"; to owe; to be obligated to
habeō, habēre, habuī, habitus	to have, consider
iaceō, iacēre, iacuī, iacitūrus	to lie (*e.g.* on the ground), lie dead
iuvō, iuvāre, iūvī, iūtus	to help; please
labōrō, labōrāre, labōrāvī, labōrātus	to work, strive
laudō, laudāre, laudāvī, laudātus	to praise
moneō, monēre, monuī, monitus	to advise, warn, remind
optō, optāre, optāvī, optātus	to choose, desire, wish for
superō, superāre, superāvī, superātus	to overcome, conquer, surpass
taceō, tacēre, tacuī, tacitūrus	to be silent ("I am silent")
terreō, terrēre, terruī, territus	to terrify, scare
timeō, timēre, timuī	to fear, be afraid (of)
videō, vidēre, vīdī, vīsus	to see
vocō, vocāre, vocāvī, vocātus	to call, summon

Other
-ne *(attached to the end of the first word in the sentence, usually the most important word in the question)*	signals a yes-no question *(no English translation)*

Chapter 2
Nouns
ager, agrī *m.*	(cultivated) field; countryside
amīcus, amīcī *m.*	friend
animus, animī *m.*	mind, spirit, courage; soul
bellum, bellī *n.*	war
casa, casae *f.*	house, hut
cōnsilium, cōnsiliī *n.*	plan, advice
dominus, dominī *m.*	master, lord
dōnum, dōnī *n.*	gift, present
locus, locī *m.* *(in pl. sometimes also neuter)*	place, position
lūna, lūnae *f.*	moon
nātūra, nātūrae *f.*	nature
puer, puerī *m.*	boy
puella, puellae *f.*	girl

rēgnum, rēgnī *n.*	kingdom, royal power
vir, virī *m.*	man; *occasionally* "husband"

Verbs

audeō, audēre, ausus sum	to dare
clāmō, clāmāre, clāmāvī, clāmātus	to shout
dubitō, dubitāre, dubitāvī, dubitātus	to hesitate, doubt
rīdeō, rīdēre, rīsī, rīsus	to laugh, laugh at
soleō, solēre, solitus sum	to be accustomed

Coordinating Conjunctions

et	and
et ... et	both ... and
-que	and
sed	but

Chapter 3
Nouns

arma, armōrum *n.* (pl.)	arms, weapons
caelum, caelī *n.*	sky, heavens
cēna, cēnae *f.*	dinner
dea, deae *f.*	goddess
dat. pl. and abl. pl. = deābus	
deus, deī *m.*	god
nom. pl. = dī; *dat. pl. and abl. pl.* = dīs	
fābula, fābulae *f.*	story
filius, filiī *m. (voc. sg.* = filī)	son
imperium, imperiī *n.*	command, (military) power
liber, librī *m.*	book
nēmō *m.; acc. sg.* = nēminem	no one
pontus, pontī *m.*	sea, ocean
Rōmulus, Rōmulī *m.*	Romulus (legendary founder of Rome)
silva, silvae *f.*	forest, wood
templum, templī *n.*	temple, shrine
turba, turbae *f.*	crowd
ventus, ventī *m.*	wind, breeze

Verbs

aedificō, aedificāre, aedificāvī, aedificātus	to build
dō, dare, dedī, datus	to give
impleō, implēre, implēvī, implētus	to fill up; complete
mōnstrō, mōnstrāre, mōnstrāvī, mōnstrātus	to show, demonstrate
nārrō, nārrāre, nārrāvī, nārrātus	to tell (a story)
parō, parāre, parāvī, parātus	to prepare
portō, portāre, portāvī, portātus	to carry, bring
pugnō, pugnāre, pugnāvī, pugnātus	to fight

Chapter 4
Nouns

factum, factī *n.*	deed, act, exploit, achievement
oculus, oculī *m.*	eye
saxum, saxī *n.*	rock, stone; cliff
verbum, verbī *n.*	word
via, viae *f.*	road; way

Verbs

ambulō, ambulāre, ambulāvī, ambulātūrus	to walk
errō, errāre, errāvī, errātus	to wander; err
festīnō, festīnāre, festīnāvī, festīnātus	to hurry, hasten

nāvigō, nāvigāre, nāvigāvī, nāvigātus	to sail, sail over (across), navigate
sedeō, sedēre, sēdī, sessūrus	to sit

Adverbs

facile	easily
nōn not	
saepe	often
semper	always
tandem	finally
tum then, at that time; next	

Prepositions

ā, ab (+ abl.)	away from
ad (+ acc.)	to, toward
ē, ex (+ abl.)	out of, from
in (+ abl.)	in, on
in (+ acc.)	into, onto, against
post (+ acc.)	after, behind
prō (+ abl.)	in front of; on behalf of; instead of
trāns (+ acc.)	across, beyond

Chapter 5

Nouns

cūra, cūrae *f.*	care, anxiety
exemplum, exemplī *n.*	example, model
sapientia, sapientiae *f.*	wisdom
terra, terrae *f.*	land, earth, soil; country

Verbs

iactō, iactāre, iactāvī, iactātus	to throw
sum, esse, fuī, futūrus	to be, exist

Adjectives

aeger, aegra, aegrum	sick, weak
altus, alta, altum	high, deep
bonus, bona, bonum	good
dīvīnus, dīvīna, dīvīnum	divine, of the gods; prophetic
līber, lībera, līberum	free
longus, longa, longum	long
magnus, magna, magnum	large, great; important
malus, mala, malum	bad
meus, mea, meum	my, mine
multus, multa, multum	much; many (pl.)
noster, nostra, nostrum	our, ours
parvus, parva, parvum	small
prīmus, prīma, prīmum	first
pulcher, pulchra, pulchrum	beautiful, handsome; fine
tuus, tua, tuum	your, yours, your own (sg.)
vester, vestra, vestrum	your, yours (pl.)

Prepositions

cum (+ abl.)	with
sub (+ abl.)	under, beneath
sub (+ acc.)	to the foot/base of, along under *(implying motion)*

Chapter 6

Nouns

fāma, fāmae *f.*	fame, report, reputation; rumor
fīlia, fīliae *f.*	daughter
dat. pl. and abl. pl. = fīliābus	

īra, īrae *f.*	anger
Ītalia, Ītaliae *f.*	Italy
populus, populī *m.*	the people, a people, nation
rēgīna, rēgīnae *f.*	queen
vīta, vītae *f.*	life

Verbs

doleō, dolēre, doluī, dolitūrus	to grieve, mourn, suffer pain
maneō, manēre, mānsī, mansūrus	to remain, stay
moveō, movēre, mōvī, mōtus	to move; excite; affect
nūntiō, nūntiāre, nūntiāvī, nūntiātus	to announce, report
ōrō, ōrāre, ōrāvī, ōrātus	to pray, beg, beg for (*often with 2 accusatives, one of the person, the other of the thing*)
teneō, tenēre, tenuī, tentus	to hold, possess, keep; restrain

Adjectives

laetus, laeta, laetum	happy; fertile
miser, misera, miserum	miserable, unhappy
novus, nova, novum	new; strange
Rōmānus, Rōmāna, Rōmānum; Rōmānī, Rōmānōrum *m.* (pl.) *(as a noun)*	Roman the Romans

Adverbs

diū	for a long time
nunc	now, at present
tunc	then

Prepositions

dē (+ abl.)	down from; about, concerning
propter (+ acc.)	because of, on account of
sine (+ abl.)	without

Coordinating Conjunction

enim *(never appears as the first word in a sentence - "postpositive")*	for; in fact; yes, truly

Chapter 7
Nouns

caput, capitis *n.*	head; summit
cīvitās, cīvitātis *f.*	state; citizenship
cōnsul, cōnsulis *m.*	consul (one of two supreme magistrates elected annually in the Roman Republic)
corpus, corporis *n.*	body, corpse
dux, ducis *m.*	(military) leader, commander
frāter, frātris *m.*	brother
homō, hominis *m.*	human being, man
iūs, iūris *n.*	right, law; justice
lex, lēgis *f.*	law
lībertās, lībertātis *f.*	freedom, liberty
lūx, lūcis *f.*	light
māter, mātris *f.*	mother
nōmen, nōminis *n.*	name
pater, patris *m.*	father; senator
pāx, pācis *f.*	peace
rēx, rēgis *m.*	king
virtūs, virtūtis *f.*	courage, excellence, virtue

Pronouns

ego, nōs	I, we
tū, vōs	you, you (pl.)

Verbs

careō, carēre, caruī, caritūrus (+ abl.)

to be without, free from; need, miss
(*the ablative case originally indicated
separation*)

noceō, nocēre, nocuī, nocitūrus (+ dat.)

to harm, be harmful to

pāreō, pārēre, pāruī, paritūrus (+ dat.)

to obey, be obedient to

placeō, placēre, placuī, placitūrus (+ dat.)

to please, be pleasing to

possum, posse, potuī

to be able, "I can"

Chapter 8
Nouns

moenia, moenium *n.* (pl.)

walls; fortifications

littera, litterae *f.*

letter (of the alphabet); (pl.) letter,
literature

nihil *n. (indeclinable)*
   nīl *(contracted form)*

nothing

vēritās, vēritātis *f.*

truth

Verbs

agō, agere, ēgī, actus
   quid agis?

to do, perform; drive
how are you (doing)?

audiō, audīre, audīvī, audītus

to hear, listen (to)

capiō, capere, cēpī, captus

to take, seize, capture

creō, creāre, creāvī, creātus

to create; elect, choose

dīcō, dīcere, dīxī, dictus

to say, speak, tell

doceō, docēre, docuī, doctus

to teach (*often with 2 accusatives,
one of the person, the other of the
thing taught*)

dormiō, dormīre, dormīvī, dormitūrus

to sleep

dūcō, dūcere, dūxī, ductus

to lead

faciō, facere, fēcī, factus

to do; make

iūdicō, iūdicāre, iūdicāvī, iūdicātus

to judge; to decide

legō, legere, lēgī, lēctus

to read; choose, select

mittō, mittere, mīsī, missus

to send

regō, regere, rēxī, rēctus

to rule

scrībō, scrībere, scrīpsī, scrīptus

to write

sentiō, sentīre, sēnsī, sēnsus

to feel, perceive

valeō, valēre, valuī, valitūrus
   valē, valēte (*imperative*)

to be well, healthy; to be strong
goodbye, farewell

veniō, venīre, vēnī, ventūrus

to come

Adjectives

īrātus, īrāta, īrātum

angry

plēnus, plēna, plēnum (+ gen. *or* abl.)

full (of), filled (with)

Pronoun

is, ea, id

he, she, it, they; this, that

Chapter 9
Nouns

carmen, carminis *n.*

song, poem

coniūnx, coniugis *m.* or *f.*

wife; husband; spouse

lacrima, lacrimae *f.*

tear

mīles, mīlitis *m.*

soldier

patria, patriae *f.*

country, fatherland

poēta, poētae *m.*

poet

timor, timōris *m.*

fear, terror

Verbs

crēdō, crēdere, crēdidī, crēditus	to believe, trust (+ dat. of *person believed*; + acc. *of thing believed*)
fīniō, fīnīre, fīnīvī, fīnītus	to end, finish; limit; die
fugiō, fugere, fūgī, fugitūrus	to flee (from), escape, avoid
incipiō, incipere, incēpī, inceptus	to begin
petō, petere, petīvī *or* petiī, petītus	to seek, go after; ask; attack
praebeō, praebēre, praebuī, praebitus	to show; offer, provide
relinquō, relinquere, relīquī, relictus	to leave, abandon
serviō, servīre, servīvī *or* servii, servītūrus (+ dat.)	to serve

Adjectives

clārus, clāra, clārum	clear, bright; famous; loud
dexter, dextra, dextrum	right (side); right hand; pledge (of friendship)

Pronouns

hic, haec, hoc	this
ille, illa, illud	that

Adverbs

ōlim	once (upon a time), one day (in the future)
tamen	however, nevertheless, yet
et	even; also

Prepositions

ante (+ acc.)	before, in front of
inter (+ acc.)	between, among

Coordinating Conjunction

aut	or
aut ... aut	either ... or

Chapter 10
Nouns

*ars, artis *f.*	skill, art
causa, causae *f.*	cause, reason
causā (+ gen.)	for the sake of, because of
grātia, grātiae *f.*	grace; favor, kindness; gratitude
grātiā (+ gen.)	for the sake of, because of
grātiās agere (+ dat.)	to thank
*ignis, ignis *m.*	fire
*mare, maris *n.*	sea
abl. sg. = mare *and* marī	
*mēns, mentis *f.*	mind, judgment, reason
*mors, mortis *f.*	death
*pars, partis *f.*	part, share, direction
*urbs, urbis *f.*	city

Adjectives

ācer, ācris, ācre	sharp, fierce; eager
brevis, breve	brief, short
celer, celeris, celere	swift, quick, rapid
difficilis, difficile	difficult
dulcis, dulce	sweet; pleasant
facilis, facile	easy
fēlīx, fēlīcis	fortunate, lucky
fortis, forte	brave; strong
ingēns, ingentis	huge; mighty
omnis, omne	all, every
potēns, potentis	powerful; able

Prepositions

ob (+ acc.)	because of
per (+ acc.)	through, along; because of; by (in oaths and prayers)

Coordinating Conjunctions

atque, ac	and
nec *or* neque	and not, and … not
nec … nec; neque … neque	neither … nor

Chapter 11
Nouns

aetās, aetātis *f.*	age, life
annus, annī *m.*	year
hōra, hōrae *f.*	hour, season
*nox, noctis *f.*	night
nūmen, nūminis *n.*	divine will, divine power
ratiō, ratiōnis *f.*	reason, judgment; method
tempus, temporis *n.*	time, period of time (*e.g.* a season); opportunity

Verbs

discēdō, discēdere, discessī, discessūrus	to depart, go away; separate
misceō, miscēre, miscuī, mixtus	to mix, mingle; stir up, disturb

Adjectives

alius, alia, aliud	other, another
(alterīus *is commonly used for gen. sg.*)	
aliud … aliud	one thing … another (thing)
aliī … aliī	some … others
alter, altera, alterum	the one, the other (of two); next, second
neuter, neutra, neutrum	neither (of two)
nūllus, nūlla, nūllum	not any, no
secundus, secunda, secundum	second; favorable
sōlus, sōla, sōlum	alone, only
nōn sōlum … sed etiam	not only … but also
tōtus, tōta, tōtum	whole, entire
ūllus, ūlla, ūllum	any
ūnus, ūna, ūnum	one
uter, utra, utrum	which? (of two)
numerals in §58 as assigned by your instructor	

Adverbs

etiam	also; even
iam	now; already
sīc	thus, so
subitō	suddenly

Chapter 12
Nouns

arbor, arboris *f.*	tree
flūmen, flūminis *n.*	river
*gēns, gentis *f.*	clan, tribe, family; nation; people
iter, itineris *n.*	journey, path, route; a day's march
pēs, pedis *m.*	foot

Verbs

absum, abesse, āfuī, āfutūrus	to be absent, away, distant
gerō, gerere, gessī, gestus	to bear, carry on; wear
bellum gerō	to wage war

Adjectives

amīcus, amīca, amīcum	friendly (to)
aptus, apta, aptum	fit, suitable (for)
cārus, cāra, cārum	dear (to)
fidēlis, fidēle	faithful, loyal (to)
inimīcus, inimīca, inimīcum	unfriendly, hostile (to)
pār, paris	equal (to)
similis, simile	similar (to), like

Adverb

forte	by chance

Coordinating Conjunction

itaque	and so, therefore

Subordinating Conjunctions

antequam	before
cum	when
dum	while, as long as
postquam	after; when
quia	because
quod	because; since
sī	if
ubi	when; where

Chapter 13

Nouns

epistula, epistulae *f.*	letter
*fīnis, fīnis *m.*	end; border; (pl.) boundary, territory
*mōns, montis *m.*	mountain
*nāvis, nāvis *f.*	ship
Rōma, Rōmae *f.*	Rome
uxor, uxōris *f.*	wife

Verbs

accipiō, accipere, accēpī, acceptus	to receive
currō, currere, cucurrī, cursūrus	to run
concurrō, concurrere, concucurrī, concursūrus	to charge, rush together, clash
discō, discere, didicī	to learn
incolō, incolere, incoluī	to inhabit, to live in
inveniō, invenīre, invēnī, inventus	to find; discover, invent
pōnō, pōnere, posuī, positus	to put, place
spectō, spectāre, spectāvī, spectātus	to watch, look at
vertō, vertere, vertī, versus	to turn, turn around; destroy; change
vincō, vincere, vīcī, victus	to conquer; win

Adjectives

fessus, fessa, fessum	tired
medius, media, medium	middle; middle of (medium mare = "the middle of the sea")
paucī, paucae, pauca (pl.)	few
reliquus, reliqua, reliquum	remaining, rest (of)

Adverbs

hodiē	today
ita	thus, so, in this way

Pronouns

quī, quae, quod	who, which, that *also a subordinating conjunction*
suī, sibi, sē	himself, herself, itself, themselves

Coordinating Conjunction

nam *(sometimes used as a particle)* — for (= because); indeed, truly

Chapter 14
Nouns

genus, generis *n.*	birth, origin; kind; race
honor, honōris *m.*	honor, respect; public office
*hostis, hostis *m.* (usually in pl.)*	enemy
	n.b. hostis *is an enemy of the state;* inimīcus *(Ch. 12) is a personal enemy*
iūdicium, iūdiciī *n.*	court; trial; judgment
lēgātus, lēgātī *m.*	delegate, envoy, ambassador; legion commander
lītus, lītoris *n.*	shore, beach, coast
nūbēs, nūbis *f.*	cloud
ops, opis *f.*	power, help; (pl.) wealth, resources
Trōia, Trōiae, *f.*	Troy
unda, undae *f.*	wave, waters; sea

Verbs

āmittō, āmittere, āmīsī, āmissus	to lose
cōnstituō, cōnstituere, cōnstituī, cōnstitūtus	to decide, appoint, establish
rapiō, rapere, rapuī, raptus	to seize, snatch, carry off
stō, stāre, stetī, statūrus	to stand
surgō, surgere, surrēxī, surrēctus	to get up, (a)rise
trahō, trahere, trāxī, tractus	to drag, pull; derive
videor, vidērī, vīsus sum *(often with dative of the person)*	to seem (*see* Ch. 15); be seen "it seems best to _____" ?
vīvō, vīvere, vīxī	to live, be alive
volvō, volvere, volvī, volūtus	to roll, turn/twist around

Adjectives

tantus, tanta, tantum	so much, so great
tantum	only
uterque, utraque, utrumque	both, each (of two)

Adverb

vērō *(postpositive)*	in fact, truly, indeed

Prepositions

ā, ab (+ *animate noun, in a passive sentence*)	by
contrā (+ acc.)	opposite; against
contrā (adv.)	in reply; face to face

Chapter 15
Nouns

*cīvis, cīvis *m.* or *f.*	citizen
dolor, dolōris *m.*	pain, sorrow
equus, equī *m.*	horse
humus, humī *f.*	ground, earth
Gallia, Galliae *f.*	Gaul
labor, labōris *m.*	work, labor, effort; hardship
laus, laudis *f.*	praise
pectus, pectoris *n.*	breast, chest; heart
perīculum, perīculī *n.*	danger
proelium, proeliī *n.*	battle
prōvincia, prōvinciae *f.*	province
rūs, rūris *n.*	the country(side)

Verbs

condō, condere, condidī, conditus	to found, build, establish
frangō, frangere, frēgī, frāctus	break, shatter, wreck
incendō, incendere, incendī, incēnsus	to set fire to, burn; inflame
prohibeō, prohibēre, prohibuī, prohibitus	to prohibit, keep from; to keep someone (acc.) from something (abl. – *separation*)
vītō, vītāre, vītāvī, vītātus	to avoid

Adjectives

aequus, aequa, aequum	even, calm, equal
cēterī, cēterae, cētera	the rest, the others
dignus, digna, dignum	worthy; worth, fitting
indignus, indigna, indignum	unworthy; undeserved; shameful
suus, sua, suum	his, her, its, their own

Prepositions

circum / circā (+ acc.)	around
super (+ acc.)	over, above, on (top of)

Chapter 16

Nouns

aciēs, aciēī *f.*	battle line
cāsus, cāsūs *m.*	fall; misfortune, destruction; chance, accident
cornū, cornūs *n.*	horn; wing (of an army)
diēs, diēī *m.* or *f.*	day; *fem. used when it is an appointed or set day*
domus, domūs *f.*	house(hold), home
exercitus, exercitūs *m.*	army
faciēs, faciēī *f.*	face; appearance
fidēs, fideī *f.*	faith, trust; loyalty, trustworthiness
flūctus, flūctūs *m.*	wave; commotion
genū, genūs *n.*	knee
impetus, impetūs *m.*	attack; charge; impulse
manus, manūs *f.*	hand; band (of men)
metus, metūs *m.*	fear, dread; anxiety
passus, passūs *m.*	pace, footstep
mille passūs; mīlia passuum (pl.)	mile (*lit.* "1000 paces"); miles
rēs, reī *f.*	thing, matter, business; court case
rēs pūblica, reī pūblicae *f.*	state, republic
senātus, senātūs *m.*	senate
spēs, speī *f.*	hope
vultus, vultūs *m.*	expression; face

Verbs

ardeō, ardēre, arsī, arsūrus	to burn, be on fire, glow
cadō, cadere, cecidī, cāsūrus	to fall

Adverbs

igitur (*postpositive*)	therefore
inde	from there; then, from that time forth
tam	so, to such a degree

Chapter 17

Nouns

amor, amōris *m.*	love
Caesar, Caesaris *m.*	Julius Caesar (a Roman general)
castra, castrōrum *n.* (pl.)	camp
castra ponere	to pitch camp

clāmor, clāmōris *m.*	shout; cheer
crīmen, crīminis *n.*	crime; accusation, charge
fātum, fātī *n.*	fate, destiny
ferrum, ferrī *n.*	iron; sword
gaudium, gaudiī *n.*	joy, delight
nūntius, nūntiī *m.*	messenger; message
prīnceps, prīncipis *m.*	leader, chief; first citizen, emperor
servus, servī *m.*	slave, servant
signum, signī *n.*	sign, token, signal; (military) standard
vīnum, vīnī *n.*	wine
vulnus, vulneris *n.*	wound

Verbs

interficiō, interficere, interfēcī, interfectus	to kill, destroy
canō, canere, cecinī, cantus	to sing
pateō, patēre, patuī	to be open, stand open
persuādeō, persuādēre, persuāsī, persuāsus (+ dat.)	to persuade
vulnerō, vulnerāre, vulnerāvī, vulnerātus	to wound
temptō, temptāre, temptāvī, temptātus	to try, attempt; test, prove

Subordinating Conjunction

quamquam	although

Chapter 18

Nouns

adventus, adventūs *m.*	arrival
aestus, aestūs *m.*	heat; tide
*arx, arcis *f.*	citadel, summit
aurum, aurī *n.*	gold
auxilium, auxiliī *n.*	aid, help; *in* pl. *often* auxiliary troops
mōs, mōris *m.*	custom, tradition
*orbis, orbis *m.*	circle; universe
orbis terrārum	the world
scelus, sceleris *n.*	crime, wicked deed, wickedness
senex, senis *m.*	old man
vōx, vōcis *f.*	voice

Verbs

cognōscō, cognōscere, cognōvī, cognitus	to learn, recognize, understand
efficiō, efficere, effēcī, effectus	to bring about, produce

Adjectives

aureus, aurea, aureum	golden, of gold
Graecus, Graeca, Graecum	Greek
levis, leve	light, easy; swift
quī, quae, quod	which _____?, what _____?
tot	so many, as many

Pronouns

īdem, eadem, idem	the same
ipse, ipsa, ipsum	_____self; himself, herself, itself, themselves; very
quis, quid	who?, what?

Chapter 19

Nouns

*caedēs, caedis *f.*	slaughter, murder
cōpia, cōpiae *f.*	abundance, plenty, resources, wealth; (pl.) troops

dolus, dolī *m.*	trick, deceit
līberī, līberōrum *m.* (pl.)	children

Verbs

ait, aiunt; āiō	he says, they say; I say
caedō, caedere, cecīdī, caesus	to kill, cut; sacrifice (of animals)
cernō, cernere, crēvī, crētus	to see, discern, perceive, decide
cōgitō, cōgitāre, cōgitāvī, cōgitātus	to think, consider
gaudeō, gaudēre, gāvīsus sum	to rejoice, be glad; delight in (+ abl.)
inquit	he said *(introduces a direct quotation)*
negō, negāre, negāvī, negātus	to deny, say that … not
nesciō, nescīre, nescīvī, nescītus	not to know
ostendō, ostendere, ostendī, ostentus/ostēnsus	to show, reveal
putō, putāre, putāvī, putātus	to think, consider; suppose
respondeō, respondēre, respondī, respōnsus	to answer, reply; correspond to
sciō, scīre, scīvī, scītus	to know; know how to (+ inf.)
spērō, spērāre, spērāvī, spērātus	to hope, hope for *(+ acc. and* future inf.*)*
trādō, trādere, trādidī, trāditus	to hand over, surrender; hand down, report

Adverbs

ante	before *(of space or time)*, in front; previously
bene	well
ibi	there

Chapter 20

Nouns

multitūdō, multitūdinis *f.*	multitude, great number, crowd
Graecia, Graeciae *f.*	Greece

Verbs

cōgō, cōgere, coēgī, coāctus	to force, compel; collect
cupiō, cupere, cupīvī *or* cupiī, cupītus	to want, desire
iubeō, iubēre, iūssī, iūssus	to order, command
mālō, mālle, māluī	to prefer, want (something) more
necesse est	it is necessary
nōlō, nōlle, nōluī	to be unwilling, not want
postulō, postulāre, postulāvī, postulātus	to demand, claim; prosecute
sinō, sinere, sīvī, sītus	to allow, permit
vetō, vetāre, vetuī, vetitus	to forbid; order … not
volō, velle, voluī	to wish, want, be willing

Adjectives

mortālis, mortāle	mortal, transient; human
sacer, sacra, sacrum	sacred
sapiēns, sapientis	wise, sensible
superus, supera, superum superī, superōrum *m.* (pl.)	upper, higher, above gods
tālis, tāle	such, of such a kind
tristis, triste	sad; gloomy

Adverbs

celeriter	quickly
fortiter	bravely, forcefully
numquam	never

Chapter 21
Noun

plūs, plūris *n. (often* + gen.)   more

Verbs

adveniō, advenīre, advēnī, adventūrus   to arrive, come to; happen
cōnficiō, cōnficere, cōnfēcī, cōnfectus   to finish, accomplish; weaken, kill
cūrō, cūrāre, cūrāvī, cūrātus   to care for/about, pay attention to; cure
dēleō, dēlēre, dēlēvī, dēlētus   to destroy; blot out
intellegō, intellegere, intellēxī, intellēctus   to understand
quaerō, quaerere, quaesīvī(-iī), quaesītus   to look for, seek; ask
resistō, resistere, restitī *(often* + dat.*)*   to resist, oppose, make a stand

Adjectives

commūnis, commūne   shared, common; public
gravis, grave   heavy; serious, important; difficult
iūstus, iusta, iūstum   just, fair
quīdam, quaedam, quoddam   a certain _____, a sort of _____
turpis, turpe   shameful, base; ugly, foul
** *irregular comparatives and superlatives in* §99

Pronoun

quīdam, quaedam, quoddam   a certain _____, a sort of _____
        **can also be used as an adjectival modifier*

Coordinating Conjunction

quam   (rather) than, as *(in comparison)*

Subordinating Conjunction

quoniam   since, seeing that

Chapter 22
Nouns

cibus, cibī *m.*   food
culpa, culpae *f.*   fault, blame
mora, morae *f.*   delay
pōtus, pōtūs *m.*   drink

Verbs

arbitror, arbitrārī, arbitrātus sum   to think, judge
cōnor, cōnārī, conātus sum   to try
fīdō, fīdere, fīsus sum (+ dat.)   to trust, confide in
fruor, fruī, frūctus sum (+ abl.)   to enjoy
fungor, fungī, fūnctus sum (+ abl.)   to perform, do
ingredior, ingredī, ingressus sum   to enter; march, walk
loquor, loquī, locūtus sum   to speak, talk, say
mīror, mīrārī, mīrātus sum   to wonder (at), be surprised at; admire
moror, morārī, morātus sum   to delay
patior, patī, passus sum   to suffer, allow
potior, potīrī, potītus sum (+ abl.)   to get hold of, acquire
proficīscor, proficīscī, profectus sum   to set out, depart
sequor, sequī, secūtus sum   to follow, accompany; pursue
ūtor, ūtī, ūsus sum (+ abl.)   to use
vescor, vescī (+ abl.)   to eat, feed on

Adjective

propinquus, propinqua, propinquum   near (to), neighboring; near, not far off *(of time)*
        propinquus, propinquī *m.*   relative, kinsman

Adverb

quam   how, how much;
                                                       as _____ as possible *(with superlatives)*

Chapter 23
Noun
vīs, vīs *f.*	power, force, violence;
vīrēs, vīrium (pl.)	strength

Verbs
eō, īre, iī *or* -īvī, itūrus	to go
abeō, abīre, abiī *or* -īvī, abitūrus	to go away, depart
adeō, adīre, adiī *or* -īvī, aditūrus	to go towards, approach
exeō, exīre, exiī *or* -īvī, exitūrus	to go out, exit
ineō, inīre, iniī *or* -īvī, initūrus	to enter; begin
pereō, perīre, periī *or* -īvī, peritūrus	to perish, die
redeō, redīre, rediī *or* -īvī, reditūrus	to go back, return
subeō, subīre, subiī *or* -īvī, subitūrus	to go up; to undergo; to approach
trānseō, trānsīre, trānsiī *or* -īvī, trānsitūrus	to go across, cross
ferō, ferre, tulī, lātus	to carry, bear, endure; report, say
adferō, adferre, attulī, adlātus	to bring to; cause
auferō, auferre, abstulī, ablātus	to carry away, take away
cōnferō, cōnferre, contulī, collātus	to bring together, collect; compare; contribute
sē cōnferre	to proceed, go
īnferō, īnferre, intulī, illātus	to bring in, introduce; inflict
offerō, offerre, obtulī, oblātus	to offer, bring forward
referō, referre, rettulī, relātus	to carry back, bring back, report
tollō, tollere, sustulī, sublātus	to lift up, raise; remove, carry off, steal

Adjectives
īnfēlix, īnfēlīcis	unhappy, unlucky
cunctus, cuncta, cunctum	the whole, all (collectively)

Chapter 24
Nouns
frūctus, frūctūs *m.*	fruit, enjoyment; profit
glōria, glōriae *f.*	glory, fame; ambition, boasting
memoria, memoriae *f.*	memory, recollection; history
mōtus, mōtūs *m.*	emotion, impulse; movement

Verbs
accidō, accidere, accidī	to fall at *or* near; happen
adsum, adesse, adfuī, adfutūrus	to be present, be near
appellō, appellāre, appellāvī, appellātus	to name, call upon, address
bibō, bibere, bibī, bibitūrus	to drink
dēspērō, dēspērāre, dēspērāvī, dēspērātus	to despair
dīmittō, dīmittere, dīmīsī, dīmissus	to send away, send forth; dismiss; abandon
flōreō, flōrēre, flōruī	to bloom; prosper, flourish
hortor, hortārī, hortātus sum	to urge, encourage
neglegō, neglegere, neglēxī, neglēctus	to ignore, neglect

Adjectives
beātus, beāta, beātum	happy, blessed; prosperous
rēctus, rēcta, rēctum	straight, upright; right; virtuous, honest

Adverbs
dēnique	finally, at last; in short; in fact
equidem	truly, indeed
forsitan	perhaps
utinam	*signals a wish;* if only, would that

Coordinating Conjunction
an	or

Chapter 25
Nouns
cupiditās, cupiditātis *f.*	desire, wish, longing, eagerness
cupīdō, cupīdinis *f.*	desire, wish, longing, eagerness
ingenium, ingeniī, *n.*	talent, (innate) nature, character
iniūria, iniūriae *f.*	injury, harm; insult; wrong
opus, operis *n.*	work, labor, task
opus est (+ dat.)	there is a need / use (for)
mūrus, mūrī *m.*	wall; fortification wall for a city
*pons, pontis *m.*	bridge

Verbs
iungō, iungere, iūnxī, iūnctus	to join, unite, connect; yoke
mentior, mentīrī, mentītus sum	to lie, speak *or* say falsely
morior, morī, mortuus sum	to die

Adjectives
certus, certa, certum	fixed, established, certain; specified; reliable, sure
certē (adv.)	certainly, surely, of course; at least
quantus, quanta, quantum	how much

Adverbs
autem (*postpositive*)	however; on the contrary
cūr	why?
nē	not (*used with imperative & perfect subjunctive*)
quidem (*postpositive*)	indeed, certainly, in fact
nē ... quidem	not ... even
totiēns	so often

Coordinating Conjunction
at	but; at least; then

Subordinating Conjunctions
nē	in order that ... not (*used with subjunctive*)
ut	in order that; so that

Chapter 26
Nouns
nefās *n. (indeclinable)*	sin, crime (against divine law), wrong
poena, poenae *f.*	penalty
poenam dare	to pay the penalty
sōl, sōlis *m.*	sun

Verbs
appropinquō, appropinquāre, appropinquāvī, appropinquātūrus	to approach, draw near
exspectō, exspectāre, exspectāvī, exspectātus	to wait for, expect; hope for
tremō, tremere, tremuī	to tremble, shake

Adjectives
dīrus, dīra, dīrum	awful, horrible
lātus, lāta, lātum	wide, broad
maestus, maesta, maestum	sad, mournful

Adverbs
posteā	afterwards
quoque	also
unde	from where, whence

Pronouns
aliquis, aliquid	someone, something, anyone, anything
quisquis, quicquid (quidquid)	whoever, whatever; everyone who

Subordinating Conjunctions

cum	when; because, since; although
dum	until *(with the subjunctive)*

Chapter 27
Nouns

amīcitia, amīcitiae *f.*	friendship
imperātor, imperātōris *m.*	general; emperor
iūdex, iūdicis *m.*	judge
odium, odiī *n.*	hatred, unpopularity
philosophia, philosophiae *f.*	philosophy
sēnsus, sēnsūs *m.*	sense, perception; emotion; idea
socius, sociī *m.*	companion, comrade, ally
victōria, victōriae *f.*	victory

Verbs

concēdō, concēdere, concessī, concessūrus	to go away, withdraw; yield to, submit; allow; forgive
cōnservō, cōnservāre, cōnservāvī, cōnservātus	to save, preserve, keep
cōnspiciō, cōnspicere, cōnspexī, cōnspectus	to observe, catch sight of, look at
metuō, metuere, metuī, metūtus	to fear, dread
ōdī, ōdisse	to hate; dislike
vereor, verērī, veritus sum	to fear, be afraid; respect

Adverb

num	*signals a question which expects the answer "no"*; whether *(in indirect question §126)*

Subordinating Conjunctions

nisi = nī	unless, if ... not
sīn	but if, if however

Chapter 28
Nouns

canis, canis *m.* or *f.*	dog
gladius, gladiī *m.*	sword
oppidum, oppidī *n.*	town
tēlum, tēlī *n.*	weapon; spear
tempestās, tempestātis *f.*	storm; weather

Verbs

ēripiō, ēripere, ēripuī, ēreptus	to snatch away; rescue, free
fīō, fierī, factus sum	to happen, occur; be done, be made
imperō, imperāre, imperāvī, imperātus (+ dat)	to command, order; rule (over)
mōs est	it is the custom, habit, way
requīrō, requīrere, requīsīvī *or*-iī, requīsītus	to search for; ask, inquire after; demand
rogō, rogāre, rogāvī, rogātus	to ask, ask for

Adjective

quot *(indeclinable)*	how many?

Adverbs

quōmodo	how
quotiēns	how often?
statim	immediately, at once
undique	on all sides

Preposition

apud (+ acc.)   among, with, near, at (the house of)

Chapter 29

Nouns

occāsiō, occāsiōnis *f.*   occasion, opportunity

studium, studiī *n.*   eagerness, zeal; study

voluptās, voluptātis *f.*   pleasure, delight

Verbs

committō, committere, commīsī,   to join, unite, engage in
     commissus

conveniō, convenīre, convēnī   to assemble, gather; meet; agree
     conventūrus

probō, probāre, probāvī, probātus   to approve (of); prove, show

Adjectives

cīvīlis, cīvīle   civil, public, political

perītus, perīta, perītum   experienced, skilful

ūtilis, ūtile   useful, profitable

vērus, vēra, vērum   true

vērum, vērī *n.*   truth, what is true

Adverbs

male   badly

tamquam   as, just as, just like

Chapter 30

Nouns

Aenēās, Aenēae *m.*   Aeneas, leader of the Trojans
     Aenēan (acc.)

aura, aurae *f.*   breeze; air

Verbs

coepī, coepisse, coeptus   began (*a "defective" verb with no present system*)

nāscor, nāscī, natus sum   to be born

nātus, nātī *m.*   son

Adjectives

celsus, celsa, celsum   high

Trōiānus, Trōiāna, Trōiānum   Trojan

Adverbs

circiter   about, near

deinde   then, next

iterum   again, a second time

prīmum   first, in the first place, for the first time

prius   before, sooner

Coordinating Conjunction

-ve   or

Chapter 31

Nouns

fās *n. (indeclinable)*   right; divine law

fās est   it is right

nefās est   it is wrong

impedimentum, impedimentī *n.*   hindrance, obstacle

īnsidiae, īnsidiārum *f.* (pl.)   ambush, plot; treachery

lūmen, lūminis *n.*   light, lamp, torch; eye

tellūs, tellūris *f.*   the earth; land, ground

Verbs

licet, licēre, licuit (*impersonal* + dat.)   it is allowed, it is lawful

oportet, oportēre, oportuit (*impersonal* + acc.)	it is right, one should; it is necessary

Adjectives

dūrus, dūra, dūrum	hard, harsh, rough
honestus, honesta, honestum	honest, worthy, honorable
ignārus, ignāra, ignārum	ignorant (of), unaware (of)

Adverbs

hīc	here
hinc	from this place; hence

Chapter 32

Verb

recipiō, recipere, recēpī receptus	to receive, accept; take back regain

Adjectives

asper, aspera, asperum	rough, harsh; cruel
ferōx, ferōcis	fierce, bold; wild, savage
ferus, fera, ferum	wild, fierce; cruel; uncivilized
mīrābilis, mīrābile	wonderful, extraordinary
paulus, paula, paulum	little, small

Adverb

prīmō	at first

Coordinating Conjunction

ut	as, when

ENGLISH TO LATIN VOCABULARY

abandon	relinquō, relinquere, relīquī, relictus
able, to be	possum, posse, potuī
about	dē (+ abl.)
accident	cāsus, cāsūs *m.*
accomplish	cōnficiō, cōnficere, cōnfēcī, cōnfectus
accustomed	soleō, solēre, solitus sum
achievement	factum, factī *n.*
acquire	potior, potīrī, potītus sum (+ abl.)
across	trāns (+ acc.)
act	agō, agere, ēgī, actus
admire	mīror, mīrārī, mīrātus sum
afraid, be	timeō, timēre, timuī; vereor, verērī, veritus sum
after	post (+ acc.); postquam
against	in (+ acc.)
aid	auxilium, auxiliī *n.*
alive, be	vīvō, vīvere, vīxī
all	omnis, omne
allow	sinō, sinere, sīvī, sītus
ally	socius, sociī *m.*
alone	sōlus, sōla, sōlum
although	quamquam; cum (+ subjunctive)
always	semper
among	inter (+ acc.)
and	et; -que
anger	īra, īrae *f.*
angry	īrātus, īrāta, īrātum
announce	nūntiō, nūntiāre, nūntiāvī, nūntiātus
another	alius, alia, aliud
answer	respondeō, respondēre, respondī, respōnsus
any	ūllus, ūlla, ūllum
appearance	faciēs, faciēī *f.*
appoint	cōnstituō, cōnstituere, cōnstituī, cōnstitūtus
approach	adeō, adīre, adiī *or* -īvī, aditūrus
arms	arma, armōrum *n.* (pl.)
army	exercitus, exercitūs *m.*
around	circum / circā (+ acc.)
arrival	adventus, adventūs *m.*
arrive	adveniō, advenīre, advēnī, adventūrus
as _____ as possible	quam (+ superlative)
ask	rogō, rogāre, rogāvī, rogātus; quaerō, quaerere, quaesīvī (-iī), quaesītus; requīrō, requīrere, requīsīvī (-iī), requīsītus
at that time	tum
attack	impetus, impetūs *m.*
attack (v.)	petō, petere, petīvī *or* petiī, petītus

avoid	fugiō, fugere, fūgī, fugitūrus; vītō, vītāre, vītāvī, vītātus;
away, be	absum, abesse, āfuī, āfutūrus
away from	ā, ab (+ abl.)
bad	malus, mala, malum
band (of men)	manus, manūs f.
battle	proelium, proeliī n.
be	sum, esse, fuī, futūrus
be pleasing to	placeō, placēre, placuī, placitūrus (+ dat.)
bear	ferō, ferre, tulī, lātus
beautiful	pulcher, pulchra, pulchrum
because	quia; quod; cum (+ subjunctive)
because of	ob (+ acc.); propter (+ acc.); per (+ acc.); causā (+ gen.); grātiā (+ gen.)
before	antequam
beg (for)	ōrō, ōrāre, ōrāvī, ōrātus
begin	incipiō, incipere, incēpī, inceptus; ineō, inīre, iniī or -īvī, initūrus
believe	crēdō, crēdere, crēdidī, crēditus (+ dat.)
between	inter (+ acc.)
big	magnus, magna, magnum
body	corpus, corporis n.
book	liber, librī m.
both	uterque, utraque, utrumque
boy	puer, puerī m.
brave	fortis, forte
bravely	fortiter
bridge	*pons, pontis m.
bring	portō, portāre, portāvī, portātus; ferō, ferre, tulī, lātus
bring about	efficiō, efficere, effēcī, effectus
brother	frāter, frātris m.
build	aedificō, aedificāre, aedificāvī, aedificātus
burn	ardeō, ardēre, arsī, arsūrus (intrans.); incendō, incendere, incendī, incēnsus (trans.)
but	sed
by	ā/ab (+ *animate noun, in a passive sentence*)
Caesar	Caesar, Caesaris m.
call	vocō, vocāre, vocāvī, vocātus
calm	aequus, aequa, aequum
camp	castra, castrōrum n. (pl.)
can	possum, posse, potuī
capture	capiō, capere, cēpī, captus
care	cūra, cūrae f.
carry	portō, portāre, portāvī, portātus; ferō, ferre, tulī, lātus
carry away	auferō, auferre, abstulī, ablātus
carry off	rapiō, rapere, rapuī, raptus; tollō, tollere, sustulī, sublātus
cause	faciō, facere, fēcī, factus; efficiō, efficere, effēcī, effectus
certain	quīdam, quaedam, quoddam
children	līberī, līberōrum m. (pl.)
choose	creō, creāre, creāvī, creātus; legō, legere, lēgī, lēctus
citadel	*arx, arcis f.
citizen	*cīvis, cīvis m. or f.
city	*urbs, urbis f.
collect	cōnferō, cōnferre, contulī, collātus
come	veniō, venīre, vēnī, ventūrus

command	iubeō, iubēre, iūssī, iūssus; imperō, imperāre, imperāvī, imperātus (+ dat)
companion	socius, sociī *m.*
compare	cōnferō, cōnferre, contulī, collātus
conquer	superō, superāre, superāvī, superātus; vincō, vincere, vīcī, victus
consider	habeō, habēre, habuī, habitus
consul	cōnsul, cōnsulis *m.*
contribute	cōnferō, cōnferre, contulī, collātus
country	patria, patriae *f.*
country(side)	rūs, rūris *n.*
courage	animus, animī *m.*; virtūs, virtūtis *f.*
cross	trānseō, trānsīre, trānsiī *or* -īvī, trānsitūrus
crowd	turba, turbae *f.*; multitūdō, multitūdinis *f.*
custom	mōs, mōris *m.*
danger	perīculum, perīculī *n.*
dare	audeō, audēre, ausus sum
daughter	fīlia, fīliae *f.*
dawn	prīma lūx
day	diēs, diēī *m.* or *f.*
dear (to)	cārus, cāra, cārum
death	*mors, mortis *f.*
deceit	dolus, dolī *m.*
deed	factum, factī *n.*
deep	altus, alta, altum
defeat	vincō, vincere, vīcī, victus
delay	mora, morae *f.*
delay (v.)	moror, morārī, morātus sum
delegate	lēgātus, lēgātī *m.*
deny	negō, negāre, negāvī, negātus
depart	abeō, abīre, abiī *or* -īvī, abitūrus; proficiscor, proficiscī, profectus sum; discēdō, discēdere, discessī, discessūrus
desire	optō, optāre, optāvī, optātus
despair	dēspērō, dēspērāre, dēspērāvī, dēspērātus
destroy	dēleō, dēlēre, dēlēvī, dēlētus
destruction	cāsus, cāsūs *m.*
difficult	difficilis, difficile
dinner	cēna, cēnae *f.*
discover	inveniō, invenīre, invēnī, inventus
divine	dīvīnus, dīvīna, dīvīnum
do	agō, agere, ēgī, actus; faciō, facere, fēcī, factus
dog	canis, canis *m.* or *f.*
doubt	dubitō, dubitāre, dubitāvī, dubitātus
drink	bibō, bibere, bibī, bibitūrus
eagerness	cupiditās, cupiditātis *f.*; cupīdō, cupīdinis *f.*
easy	facilis, facile
eat	vescor, vescī (+ abl.)
eight	octō
either ... or	aut ... aut
elect	creō, creāre, creāvī, creātus
emperor	prīnceps, prīncipis *m.*
encourage	hortor, hortārī, hortātus sum
enemy	*hostis, hostis *m. (usually in* pl.)

enjoy	fruor, fruī, frūctus sum (+ abl.)
enter	ingredior, ingredī, ingressus sum; ineō, inīre, iniī *or* -īvī, initūrus
envoy	lēgātus, lēgātī *m.*
equal (to)	pār, paris
escape	fugiō, fugere, fūgī, fugitūrus
every	omnis, omne
everyone	omnes, omnium
example	exemplum, exemplī *n.*
eye	oculus, oculī *m.*;
face	vultus, vultūs *m.*; faciēs, faciēī *f.*
fair	iūstus, iūsta, iūstum
faithful	fidēlis, fidēle
fall	cadō, cadere, cecidī, cāsūrus
fame	fāma, fāmae *f.*
family	*gēns, gentis *f.*
famous	clārus, clāra, clārum
farmer	agricola, agricolae *m.*
father	pater, patris *m.*
fatherland	patria, patriae *f.*
fault	culpa, culpae *f.*
fear	timor, timōris *m.*; metus, metūs *m.*
fear (v.)	timeō, timēre, timuī; vereor, verērī, veritus sum; metuō, metuere, metuī, metūtus
fertile	laetus, laeta, laetum
few	paucī, paucae, pauca (pl.)
field	ager, agrī *m.*
fierce	ācer, ācris, ācre
fight	pugnō, pugnāre, pugnāvī, pugnātus
fill (up)	impleō, implēre, implēvī, implētus
finally	tandem; dēnique
find	inveniō, invenīre, invēnī, inventus
finish	fīniō, fīnīre, fīnīvī, fīnītus
fire	*ignis, ignis *m.*
five	quīnque
flee	fugiō, fugere, fūgī, fugitūrus
follow	sequor, sequī, secūtus sum
food	cibus, cibī *m.*
foot	pēs, pedis *m.*
for	enim (*never appears as the first word in a sentence - "postpositive"*); nam
for a long time	diū
for the sake of	causā (+ gen.)
forbid	vetō, vetāre, vetuī, vetitus
force	vīs, vīs *f.*
force (v.)	cōgō, cōgere, coēgī, coāctus
forest	silva, silvae *f.*
fortunate	fēlīx, fēlīcis
fortune	fortūna, fortūnae *f.*
found	condō, condere, condidī, conditus
free	līber, lībera, līberum
free (v.)	ēripiō, ēripere, ēripuī, ēreptus
free from (v.)	careō, carēre, caruī, caritūrus (+ abl.)
freedom	lībertās, lībertātis *f.*

friend	amīcus, amīcī *m.*
friendly (to)	amīcus, amīca, amīcum
from	ab (+ abl.); ex (+ abl.); dē (+ abl.)
full (of)	plēnus, plēna, plēnum (+ gen. *or* abl.)
Gaul	Gallia, Galliae *f.*
general	imperātor, imperātōris *m.*
gift	dōnum, dōnī *n.*
girl	puella, puellae *f.*
give	dō, dare, dedī, datus
go	eō, īre, iī *or* īvī, itūrus
go away	abeō, abīre, abiī *or* -īvī, abitūrus
go out	exeō, exīre, exiī *or* -īvī, exitūrus
god	deus, deī *m.*
goddess	dea, deae *f.*
gold	aurum, aurī *n.*
good	bonus, bona, bonum
great	magnus, magna, magnum
Greek	Graecus, Graeca, Graecum
grieve	doleō, dolēre, doluī, dolitūrus
hand	manus, manūs *f.*
happen	accidō, accidere, accidī; fīō, fierī, factus sum
happy	laetus, laeta, laetum
hardship	labor, labōris *m.*
harm	noceō, nocēre, nocuī, nocitūrus (+ dat.)
have	habeō, habēre, habuī, habitus
head	caput, capitis *n.*
hear	audiō, audīre, audīvī, audītus
heat	aestus, aestūs *m.*
help	auxilium, auxiliī *n.*; ops, opis *f.*
help (v.)	iuvō, iuvāre, iūvī, iūtus
her	is, ea, id
hesitate	dubitō, dubitāre, dubitāvī, dubitātus
high	altus, alta, altum
him	is, ea, id
his	is, ea, id (gen.); suus, sua, suum
hold	teneō, tenēre, tenuī, tentus
home	domus, domūs *f.*
honor	honor, honōris *m.*
hope	spēs, speī *f.*
horse	equus, equī *m.*
hostile	inimīcus, inimīca, inimīcum
hour	hōra, hōrae *f.*
house	casa, casae *f.*; domus, domūs *f.*
how	quōmodo
how many?	quot (*indeclinable*)
how often?	quotiēns
huge	ingēns, ingentis
human being	homō, hominis *m.*
hurry	festīnō, festīnāre, festīnāvī, festīnātus
I	ego
if	sī

immediately	statim
in	in (+ abl.)
in front of	prō (+ abl.); ante (+ acc.)
in order (that)	ut
in order (that) ... not	nē
into	in (+ acc.)
introduce	īnferō, īnferre, intulī, illātus
iron	ferrum, ferrī *n.*
it	is, ea, id
Italy	Ītalia, Ītaliae *f.*
journey	iter, itineris *n.*
joy	gaudium, gaudiī *n.*
judge	iūdex, iūdicis *m.*
judge (v.)	iūdicō, iūdicāre, iūdicāvī, iūdicātus; arbitror, arbitrārī, arbitrātus sum
justice	iūs, iūris *n.*
keep	teneō, tenēre, tenuī, tentus
kill	interficiō, interficere, interfēcī, interfectus; caedō, caedere, cecīdī, caesus
king	rēx, rēgis *m.*
kingdom	rēgnum, rēgnī *n.*
knee	genū, genūs *n.*
know	sciō, scīre, scīvī, scītus
land	terra, terrae *f.*
large	magnus, magna, magnum
laugh (at)	rīdeō, rīdēre, rīsī, rīsus
law	lex, lēgis *f.*; iūs, iūris *n.*
lead	dūcō, dūcere, dūxī, ductus
leader	dux, ducis *m.*
learn	discō, discere, didicī
leave	relinquō, relinquere, relīquī, relictus
letter	epistula, epistulae *f.*
lie (e.g. on the ground)	iaceō, iacēre, iacuī, iacitūrus
lie (say falsely)	mentior, mentīrī, mentītus sum
life	vīta, vītae *f.*
light	lūx, lūcis *f.*
listen (to)	audiō, audīre, audīvī, audītus
live	vīvō, vīvere, vīxī
long	longus, longa, longum
look for	petō, petere, petīvī *or* petiī, petītus
lord	dominus, dominī *m.*
lose	āmittō, āmittere, āmīsī, āmissus
a lot of	= *much*
loud	clārus, clāra, clārum
love	amor, amōris *m.*
love (v.)	amō, amāre, amāvī, amātus
loyalty	fidēs, fideī *f.*
lucky	fēlīx, fēlīcis
make	faciō, facere, fēcī, factus
man	homō, hominis *m.*; vir, virī *m.*
many	multus, multa, multum *(pl.)*
march	ingredior, ingredī, ingressus sum
master	dominus, dominī *m.*

me	mē
memory	memoria, memoriae *f.*
message	nūntius, nūntiī, *m.*
messenger	nūntius, nūntiī, *m.*
middle (of)	medius, media, medium (medium mare = "the middle of the sea")
mighty	ingēns, ingentis
mile	mille passūs
miles	mīlia passuum (pl.)
mind	*mēns, mentis *f.;* animus, animī *m.*
mine	meus, mea, meum
miss	careō, carēre, caruī, caritūrus (+ abl.)
money	pecūnia, pecūniae *f.*
more	plūs, plūris *n.* (*often* + gen.); magis (adv.)
mortal	mortālis, mortāle
mother	māter, mātris *f.*
mountain	*mōns, montis *m.*
mourn	doleō, dolēre, doluī, dolitūrus
much	multus, multa, multum
multitude	multitūdō, multitūdinis *f.*
must	*see* §130
my	meus, mea, meum
name	nōmen, nōminis *n.*
nation	*gēns, gentis *f.*
navigate	nāvigō, nāvigāre, nāvigāvī, nāvigātus
near	propinquus, propinqua, propinquum
necessary, it is	necesse est
need	careō, carēre, caruī, caritūrus (+ abl.)
nevertheless	tamen
new	novus, nova, novum
night	*nox, noctis *f.*
nine	novem
no	nūllus, nūlla, nūllum
no one	nēmō *m.,* acc. sg. = nēminem
noon (= the sixth hour)	sexta hōra
not	nōn; nē
nothing	nihil *n.*
now	nunc;
obey	pāreō, pārēre, pāruī, paritūrus (+ dat.)
ocean	pontus, pontī *m.*
offer	offerō, offerre, obtulī, oblātus
often	saepe
old man	senex, senis *m.*
on	in (+ abl.)
on behalf of	prō (+ abl.)
one	ūnus, ūna, ūnum
one day	ōlim
one hundred	centum
opposite	contrā (+ acc.)
other	alius, alia, aliud
ought	dēbeō, dēbēre, dēbuī, dēbitus; see §130
our	noster, nostra, nostrum

out of	ē, ex (+ abl.)
overcome	superō, superāre, superāvī, superātus
owe	dēbeō, dēbēre, dēbuī, dēbitus
own (his, her, their)	suus, sua, suum
part	*pars, partis *f.*
peace	pāx, pācis *f.*
people	populus, populī *m.*
perception	sēnsus, sēnsūs *m.*
perhaps	forsitan
pitch camp	castra ponere
place	locus, locī *m. (in pl. sometimes also neuter)*
place (v.)	pōnō, pōnere, posuī, positus
plan	cōnsilium, cōnsiliī *n.*
pleasant	dulcis, dulce
please	iuvō, iuvāre, iūvī, iūtus; placeō, placēre, placuī, placitūrus (+ dat.)
poet	poēta, poētae *m.*
possess	teneō, tenēre, tenuī, tentus
power	vīs, vīs *f.*
powerful	potēns, potentis
praise	laudō, laudāre, laudāvī, laudātus
prefer	mālō, mālle, māluī
prepare	parō, parāre, parāvī, parātus
profit	frūctus, frūctūs *m.*
province	prōvincia, prōvinciae *f.*
public	commūnis, commūne; cīvīlis, cīvīle
pull	trahō, trahere, trāxī, tractus
put	pōnō, pōnere, posuī, positus
queen	rēgīna, rēgīnae *f.*
quick	celer, celeris, celere
quickly	celeriter
quiet, be	taceō, tacēre, tacuī, tacitūrus
quite	*use comparative*
race	genus, generis *n.*
read	legō, legere, lēgī, lēctus
receive	accipiō, accipere, accēpī, acceptus
rejoice	gaudeō, gaudēre, gāvīsus sum
remain	maneō, manēre, mānsī, mansūrus
report	nūntiō, nūntiāre, nūntiāvī, nūntiātus; trādō, trādere, trādidī, trāditus; ferō, ferre, tulī, lātus; referō, referre, rettulī, relātus
reputation	fāma, fāmae *f.*
rescue	ēripiō, ēripere, ēripuī, ēreptus
respect	honor, honōris *m.*
restrain	teneō, tenēre, tenuī, tentus
return	redeō, redīre, rediī *or* -īvī, reditūrus
reveal	ostendō, ostendere, ostendī, ostentus/ostēnsus
right	iūs, iūris *n.*
right (adj.)	dexter, dextra, dextrum
river	flūmen, flūminis *n.*
road	via, viae *f.*
rock	saxum, saxī *n.*
roll	volvō, volvere, volvī, volūtus

Roman	Rōmānus, Rōmāna, Rōmānum;
Rome	Rōma, Rōmae *f.*
Romulus	Rōmulus, Rōmulī *m.*
rose	rosa, rosae *f.*
rule	regō, regere, rēxī, rēctus
run	currō, currere, cucurrī
sacred	sacer, sacra, sacrum
sad	tristis, triste
sail	nāvigō, nāvigāre, nāvigāvī, nāvigātus
sailor	nauta, nautae *m.*
same	īdem, eadem, idem
save	cōnservō, cōnservāre, cōnservāvī, cōnservātus
say	dīcō, dīcere, dīxī, dictus
scare	terreō, terrēre, terruī, territus
sea	pontus, pontī *m.*; *mare, maris *n.*
second	secundus, secunda, secundum
see	videō, vidēre, vīdī, vīsus
seek	petō, petere, petīvī *or* petiī, petītus; quaerō, quaerere, quaesīvī (-iī), quaesītus;
seem	videor, vidērī, vīsus sum
seize	capiō, capere, cēpī, captus; rapiō, rapere, rapuī, raptus
_____self	ipse, ipsa, ipsum
senate	senātus, senātūs *m.*
send	mittō, mittere, mīsī, missus
send away	dīmittō, dīmittere, dīmīsī, dīmissus
serious	gravis, grave
servant	servus, servī *m.*
set out	proficiscor, proficiscī, profectus sum
seven	septem
seventh	septimus, septima, septimum
shameful	turpis, turpe
ship	*nāvis, nāvis *f.*
short	brevis, breve
shout	clāmor, clāmōris *m.*
shout (v.)	clāmō, clāmāre, clāmāvī, clāmātus
show	mōnstrō, mōnstrāre, mōnstrāvī, mōnstrātus; ostendō, ostendere, ostendī, ostentus/ostēnsus
should	dēbeō, dēbēre, dēbuī, dēbitus; *or use subjunctive mood*
sick	aeger, aegra, aegrum
silent ("I am silent")	taceō, tacēre, tacuī, tacitūrus
since	quod; quoniam; cum *(+ subjunctive)*
sing	canō, canere, cecinī, cantus
sit	sedeō, sedēre, sēdī, sessūrus
six	sex
skill	*ars, artis *f.*
sky	caelum, caelī *n.*
slave	servus, servī *m.*
sleep	dormiō, dormīre, dormīvī, dormitūrus
small	parvus, parva, parvum
so	tam
so (such) great	tantus, tanta, tantum
soldier	mīlēs, mīlitis *m.*

some	alius, alia, aliud
someone	aliquis, aliquid
son	fīlius, fīliī *m.* (*voc. sg.* = fīlī)
song	carmen, carminis *n.*
sorrow	dolor, dolōris *m.*
speak	dīcō, dīcere, dīxī, dictus; loquor, loquī, locūtus sum
specified	certus, certa, certum
stand	stō, stāre, stetī, statūrus
state	cīvitās, cīvitātis *f.*; rēs pūblica, reī pūblicae *f.*
stay	maneō, manēre, mānsī, mansūrus
step	passus, passūs *m.*
stone	saxum, saxī *n.*
story	fābula, fābulae *f.*
strange	novus, nova, novum
strong	fortis, forte
strong, be	valeō, valēre, valuī, valitūrus
such	tālis, tāle
suddenly	subitō
summit	caput, capitis *n.*
surprised, be	mīror, mīrārī, mīrātus sum
surrender	trādō, trādere, trādidī, trāditus
sweet	dulcis, dulce
swift	celer, celeris, celere; levis, leve
sword	gladius, gladiī *m.*
take	capiō, capere, cēpī, captus
talent	ingenium, ingeniī, *n.*
tall	altus, alta, altum
teach	doceō, docēre, docuī, doctus
tear	lacrima, lacrimae *f.*
tell	nārrō, nārrāre, nārrāvī, nārrātus; dīcō, dīcere, dīxī, dictus
temple	templum, templī *n.*
ten	decem
tenth	decimus, decima, decimum
than (rather)	quam
thank	grātiās agere (+ dat.)
that	ille, illa, illud
that (*subord. conjunction*)	quī, quae, quod
their; their own	is, ea, id (gen.); suus, sua, suum
there	ibi
these	hic, haec, hoc (pl.)
they	is, ea, id (pl.)
think	putō, putāre, putāvī, putātus; cōgitō, cōgitāre, cōgitāvī, cōgitātus; arbitror, arbitrārī, arbitrātus sum
third	tertius, tertia, tertium
this	hic, haec, hoc
those	ille, illa, illud (pl.)
three	trēs, tria
through	per (+ acc.)
throw	iactō, iactāre, iactāvī, iactātus
time	tempus, temporis *n.*
tired	fessus, fessa, fessum

today	hodiē
toward	ad (+ acc.)
town	oppidum, oppidī *n.*
tradition	mōs, mōris *m.*
tree	arbor, arboris *f.*
trial	iūdicium, iūdiciī *n.*
tribe	*gēns, gentis *f.*
troops	cōpia, cōpiae, *f.* (pl.)
Troy	Trōia, Trōiae, *f.*
trust	crēdō, crēdere, crēdidī, crēditus (+ dat.)
truth	vēritās, vēritātis *f.*
try	cōnor, cōnārī, cōnātus sum; temptō, temptāre, temptāvī, temptātus
two	duo, duae, duo
ugly	turpis, turpe
under	sub (+ abl.)
undergo	subeō, subīre, subiī *or* -īvī, subitūrus
understand	cognōscō, cognōscere, cognōvi, cognitus; intellegō, intellegere, intellēxī, intellēctus
unfriendly	inimīcus, inimīca, inimīcum
unhappy	miser, misera, miserum; īnfēlix, īnfēlīcis
unlucky	īnfēlix, īnfēlīcis
until	dum (+ subjunctive)
unwilling, be	nōlō, nōlle, nōluī
us	nōs
use	ūtor, ūtī, ūsus sum (+ abl.)
useful	ūtilis, ūtile
very	ipse, ipsa, ipsum; *use superlative*
victory	victōria, victōriae *f.*
virtue	virtūs, virtūtis *f.*
voice	vōx, vōcis *f.*
wage	gerō, gerere, gessī, gestus
wait (for)	exspectō, exspectāre, exspectāvī, exspectātus
walk	ambulō, ambulāre, ambulāvī, ambulātūrus
wall	mūrus, mūrī *m.;* moenia, moenium *n.* (pl.)
wander	errō, errāre, errāvī, errātus
want	cupiō, cupere, cupīvī *or* cupiī, cupītus; volō, velle, voluī
war	bellum, bellī *n.*
warn	moneō, monēre, monuī, monitus
watch	spectō, spectāre, spectāvī, spectātus
water	aqua, aquae *f.*
wealth	ops, opis *f.*
weapon(s)	arma, armōrum *n.* (pl.); tēlum, tēlī *n.*
well	bene
when	cum; ubi
where	ubi
whether	num
while	dum
who, which / what	quī, quae, quod; quis, quid?
whole	tōtus, tōta, tōtum; cunctus, cuncta, cunctum
why?	cūr
wife	coniūnx, coniugis *f.;* uxor, uxōris *f.*

willing, be	volō, velle, voluī
wind	ventus, ventī *m.*
wine	vīnum, vīnī *n.*
wing (of an army)	cornū, cornūs *n.*
wisdom	sapientia, sapientiae *f.*
wise	sapiēns, sapientis
wish	optō, optāre, optāvī, optātus; volō, velle, voluī
with	cum (+ abl.); *but sometimes ablative without a preposition*
without	sine (+ abl.)
woman	fēmina, fēminae *f.*
word	verbum, verbī *n.*
work	labōrō, labōrāre, labōrāvī, labōrātus
world	orbis terrārum
worthy	dignus, digna, dignum
wound	vulnerō, vulnerāre, vulnerāvī, vulnerātus
wreck	frangō, frangere, frēgī, frāctus
write	scrībō, scrībere, scrīpsī, scrīptus
year	annus, annī *m.*
you, you (pl.)	tū, vōs
your (sg.)	tuus, tua, tuum
your (pl.)	vester, vestra, vestrum

LATIN TO ENGLISH VOCABULARY

Numbers refer to the chapter in which the word first appears in the chapter vocabulary.

ā, ab (+ abl.)	away from	4
ā, ab (+ *animate noun, in a passive sentence*)	by	14
abeō, abīre, abiī *or* -īvī, abitūrus	to go away, depart	23
absum, abesse, āfuī, āfutūrus	to be absent, away, distant	12
ac, atque	and	10
accidō, accidere, accidī	to fall at *or* near; happen	24
accipiō, accipere, accēpī, acceptus	to receive	13
ācer, ācris, ācre	sharp, fierce; eager	10
aciēs, aciēī *f.*	battle line	16
ad (+ acc.)	to, toward	4
adeō, adīre, adiī *or* -īvī, aditūrus	to go towards, approach	23
adferō, adferre, attulī, adlātus	to bring to; cause	23
adsum, adesse, adfuī, adfutūrus	to be present, be near	24
adveniō, advenīre, advēnī, adventūrus	to arrive, come to; happen	21
adventus, adventūs *m.*	arrival	18
aedificō, aedificāre, aedificāvī, aedificātus	to build	3
aeger, aegra, aegrum	sick, weak	5
Aenēās, Aenēae *m.* Aenēan (acc.)	Aeneas, leader of the Trojans	30
aequus, aequa, aequum	even, calm, equal	15
aestus, aestūs *m.*	heat; tide	18
aetās, aetātis *f.*	age, life	11
ager, agrī *m.*	(cultivated) field; countryside	2
agō, agere, ēgī, actus	to do, perform; drive	8
quid agis?	how are you (doing)?	
grātiās agere (+ dat.)	to thank	10
agricola, agricolae *m.*	farmer	1
ait, aiunt; āiō	he says, they say; I say	19
aliquis, aliquid	someone, something, anyone, anything	26
alius, alia, aliud	other, another	11
(alterīus *is commonly used for gen. sg.*)		
aliud ... aliud	one thing ... another (thing)	
aliī ... aliī	some ... others	
alter, altera, alterum	the one, the other (of two); next, second	11
altus, alta, altum	high, deep	5
ambulō, ambulāre, ambulāvī, ambulātūrus	to walk	4
amīcitia, amīcitiae *f.*	friendship	27
amīcus, amīca, amīcum	friendly (to)	12
amīcus, amīcī *m.*	friend	2
āmittō, āmittere, āmīsī, āmissus	to lose	14
amō, amāre, amāvī, amātus	to love	1
amor, amōris *m.*	love	17
an	or	24
animus, animī *m.*	mind, spirit, courage; soul	2
annus, annī *m.*	year	11

ante (prep.) (+ acc.)	before, in front of	9
ante (adv.)	before *(of space or time)*, in front; previously	19
antequam	before	12
appellō, appellāre, appellāvī, appellātus	to name, call upon, address	24
appropinquō, appropinquāre, appropinquāvī, appropinquātūrus	to approach, draw near	26
aptus, apta, aptum	fit, suitable (for)	12
apud (+ acc.)	among, with, near, at (the house of)	28
aqua, aquae *f.*	water	1
arbitror, arbitrārī, arbitrātus sum	to think, judge	22
arbor, arboris *f.*	tree	12
ardeō, ardēre, arsī, arsūrus	to burn, be on fire, glow	16
arma, armōrum *n.* (pl.)	arms, weapons	3
*ars, artis *f.*	skill, art	10
*arx, arcis *f.*	citadel, summit	18
asper, aspera, asperum	rough, harsh; cruel	32
at	but; at least; then	25
atque, ac	and	10
audeō, audēre, ausus sum	to dare	2
audiō, audīre, audīvī, audītus	to hear, listen (to)	8
auferō, auferre, abstulī, ablātus	to carry away, take away	23
aura, aurae *f.*	breeze; air	30
aureus, aurea, aureum	golden, of gold	18
aurum, aurī *n.*	gold	18
aut	or	9
aut ... aut	either ... or	
autem (*postpositive*)	however; on the contrary	25
auxilium, auxiliī *n.*	aid, help; *in* pl. *often* auxiliary troops	18
beātus, beāta, beātum	happy, blessed; prosperous	24
bellum, bellī *n.*	war	2
bene	well	19
bibō, bibere, bibī, bibitūrus	to drink	24
bonus, bona, bonum	good	5
brevis, breve	brief, short	10
cadō, cadere, cecidī, cāsūrus	to fall	16
*caedēs, caedis *f.*	slaughter, murder	19
caedō, caedere, cecīdī, caesus	to kill, cut; sacrifice (of animals)	19
caelum, caelī *n.*	sky, heavens	3
Caesar, Caesaris *m.*	Julius Caesar (a Roman general)	17
canis, canis *m.* or *f.*	dog	28
canō, canere, cecinī, cantus	to sing	17
capiō, capere, cēpī, captus	to take, seize, capture	8
caput, capitis *n.*	head; summit	7
careō, carēre, caruī, caritūrus (+ abl.)	to be without, free from; need, miss (*the ablative case originally indicated separation*)	7
carmen, carminis *n.*	song, poem	9
cārus, cāra, cārum	dear (to)	12
casa, casae *f.*	house, hut	2
castra, castrōrum *n.* (pl.)	camp	17
castra ponere	to pitch camp	
cāsus, cāsūs *m.*	fall; misfortune, destruction; chance, accident	16
causa, causae *f.*	cause, reason	10
causā (+ gen.)	for the sake of, because of	

celer, celeris, celere	swift, quick, rapid	10
celeriter	quickly	20
celsus, celsa, celsum	high	30
cēna, cēnae *f.*	dinner	3
cernō, cernere, crēvī, crētus	to see, discern, perceive, decide	19
certus, certa, certum	fixed, established, certain; specified; reliable, sure	25
certē (adv.)	certainly, surely, of course; at least	
cēterī, cēterae, cētera	the rest, the others	15
cibus, cibī *m.*	food	22
circiter	about, near	30
circum / circā (+ acc.)	around	15
cīvīlis, cīvīle	civil, public, political	29
*cīvis, cīvis *m.* or *f.*	citizen	15
cīvitās, cīvitātis *f.*	state ; citizenship	7
clāmō, clāmāre, clāmāvī, clāmātus	to shout	2
clāmor, clāmōris *m.*	shout; cheer	17
clārus, clāra, clārum	clear, bright; famous; loud	9
coepī, coepisse, coeptus	began – *a "defective" verb with no present system*	30
cōgitō, cōgitāre, cōgitāvī, cōgitātus	to think, consider	19
cognōscō, cognōscere, cognōvī, cognitus	to learn, recognize, understand	18
cōgō, cōgere, coēgī, coāctus	to force, compel; collect	20
committō, committere, commīsī, commissus	to join, unite, engage in	29
commūnis, commūne	shared, common; public	21
concēdō, concēdere, concessī, concessūrus	to go away, withdraw; yield to, submit; allow; forgive	27
condō, condere, condidī, conditus	to found, build, establish	15
cōnferō, cōnferre, contulī, collātus	to bring together, collect; compare; contribute	23
sē cōnferre	to proceed, go	
cōnficiō, cōnficere, cōnfēcī, cōnfectus	to finish, accomplish; weaken, kill	21
coniūnx, coniugis *m.* or *f.*	wife; husband; spouse	9
cōnor, cōnārī, cōnātus sum	to try	22
cōnservō, cōnservāre, cōnservāvī, cōnservātus	to save, preserve, keep	27
cōnsilium, cōnsiliī *n.*	plan, advice	2
cōnspiciō, cōnspicere, cōnspexī, cōnspectus	to observe, catch sight of, look at	27
cōnstituō, cōnstituere, cōnstituī, cōnstitūtus	to decide, appoint, establish	14
cōnsul, cōnsulis *m.*	consul (one of two supreme magistrates elected annually in the Roman Republic)	7
contrā (prep.) (+ acc.)	opposite; against	14
contrā (adv.)	in reply; face to face	
conveniō, convenīre, convēnī, conventūrus	to assemble, gather; meet; agree	29
cōpia, cōpiae *f.*	abundance, plenty, resources, wealth; (pl.) troops	19
cornū, cornūs *n.*	horn; wing (of an army)	16
corpus, corporis *n.*	body, corpse	7
crēdō, crēdere, crēdidī, crēditus	to believe, trust (+ dat. *of a person believed*; + acc. *of a thing believed*)	9
creō, creāre, creāvī, creātus	to create; elect, choose	8
crīmen, crīminis *n.*	crime; accusation, charge	17
culpa, culpae *f.*	fault, blame	22
cum (prep.) (+ abl.)	with	5
cum (+ indicative)	when	12
(+ subjunctive)	when; because, since; although	26
cunctus, cuncta, cunctum	the whole, all (*collectively*)	23
cupiditās, cupiditātis *f.*	desire, wish, longing, eagerness	25

cupīdō, cupīdinis *f.*	desire, wish, longing, eagerness	25
cupiō, cupere, cupīvī *or* cupiī, cupītus	to want, desire	20
cūr	why?	25
cūra, cūrae *f.*	care, anxiety	5
cūrō, cūrāre, cūrāvī, cūrātus	to care for/about, pay attention to; cure	21
currō, currere, cucurrī, cursūrus	to run	13
concurrō, concurrere, concucurrī, concursūrus	to charge, rush together, clash	13
dē (+ abl.)	down from; about, concerning	6
dea, deae *f.*	goddess	3
dat. pl. and abl. pl. = deābus		
dēbeō, dēbēre, dēbuī, dēbitus	"ought to, should"; to owe; to be obligated to	1
deinde	then, next	30
dēleō, dēlēre, dēlēvī, dēlētus	to destroy; blot out	21
dēnique	finally, at last; in short; in fact	24
dēspērō, dēspērāre, dēspērāvī, dēspērātus	to despair	24
deus, deī *m.*	god	3
nom. pl. = dī; *dat. pl. and abl. pl.* = dīs		
dexter, dextra, dextrum	right (side); right hand; pledge (of friendship)	9
dīcō, dīcere, dīxī, dictus	to say, speak, tell	8
diēs, diēī *m. or f.*	day; *fem. used when it is an appointed or set day*	16
difficilis, difficile	difficult	10
dignus, digna, dignum	worthy; worth, fitting	15
dīmittō, dīmittere, dīmīsī, dīmissus	to send away, send forth; dismiss; abandon	24
dīrus, dīra, dīrum	awful, horrible	26
discēdō, discēdere, discessī, discessūrus	to depart, go away; separate	11
discō, discere, didicī	to learn	13
diū	for a long time	6
dīvīnus, dīvīna, dīvīnum	divine, of the gods; prophetic	5
dō, dare, dedī, datus	to give	3
doceō, docēre, docuī, doctus	to teach (*often with 2 accusatives, one of the person, the other of the thing taught*)	8
doleō, dolēre, doluī, dolitūrus	to grieve, mourn, suffer pain	6
dolor, dolōris *m.*	pain, sorrow	15
dolus, dolī *m.*	trick, deceit	19
dominus, dominī *m.*	master, lord	2
domus, domūs *f.*	house(hold), home	16
dōnum, dōnī *n.*	gift, present	2
dormiō, dormīre, dormīvī, dormitūrus	to sleep	8
dubitō, dubitāre, dubitāvī, dubitātus	to hesitate, doubt	2
dūcō, dūcere, dūxī, ductus	to lead	8
dulcis, dulce	sweet; pleasant	10
dum (+ indicative)	while, as long as	12
(+ subjunctive)	until	26
dūrus, dūra, dūrum	hard, harsh, rough	31
dux, ducis *m.*	(military) leader, commander	7
ē, ex (+ abl.)	out of, from	4
efficiō, efficere, effēcī, effectus	to bring about, produce	18
ego, nōs	I, we	7
enim (*never appears as the first word in a sentence - "postpositive"*)	for; in fact; yes, truly	6
eō, īre, iī *or* īvī, itūrus	to go	23
epistula, epistulae *f.*	letter	13
equidem	truly, indeed	24

equus, equī *m.*	horse	15
ēripiō, ēripere, ēripuī, ēreptus	to snatch away; rescue, free	28
errō, errāre, errāvī, errātus	to wander; err	4
et (*coord. conj.*)	and	2
et ... et	both ... and	
et (*adv.*)	even; also	9
etiam	also; even	11
exemplum, exemplī *n.*	example, model	5
exeō, exīre, exiī *or* -īvī, exitūrus	to go out, exit	23
exercitus, exercitūs *m.*	army	16
exspectō, exspectāre, exspectāvī, exspectātus	to wait for, expect; hope for	26
fābula, fābulae *f.*	story	3
faciēs, faciēī *f.*	face; appearance	16
facile	easily	4
facilis, facile	easy	10
faciō, facere, fēcī, factus	to do; make	8
factum, factī *n.*	deed, act, exploit, achievement	4
fāma, fāmae *f.*	fame, report, reputation; rumor	6
fās *n. (indeclinable)*	right; divine law	31
fās est	it is right	
nefās est	it is wrong	
fātum, fātī *n.*	fate, destiny	17
fēlīx, fēlīcis	fortunate, lucky	10
fēmina, fēminae *f.*	woman	1
ferō, ferre, tulī, lātus	to carry, bear, endure; report, say	23
ferōx, ferōcis	fierce, bold; wild, savage	32
ferrum, ferrī *n.*	iron; sword	17
ferus, fera, ferum	wild, fierce; cruel; uncivilized	32
fessus, fessa, fessum	tired	13
festīnō, festīnāre, festīnāvī, festīnātus	to hurry, hasten	4
fidēlis, fidēle	faithful, loyal (to)	12
fidēs, fideī *f.*	faith, trust; loyalty, trustworthiness	16
fīdō, fīdere, fīsus sum (+ dat.)	to trust, confide in	22
filia, filiae *f.*	daughter	6
dat. pl. and abl. pl. = filiābus		
filius, filiī *m. (voc. sg.* = filī)	son	3
finiō, finīre, finīvī, finītus	to end, finish; limit; die	9
*finis, finis *m.*	end; border; (pl.) boundary, territory	13
fīō, fierī, factus sum	to happen, occur; be done, be made	28
flōreō, flōrēre, flōruī	to bloom; prosper, flourish	24
flūctus, flūctūs *m.*	wave; commotion	16
flūmen, flūminis *n.*	river	12
forsitan	perhaps	24
forte	by chance	12
fortis, forte	brave; strong	10
fortiter	bravely, forcefully	20
fortūna, fortūnae *f.*	chance, luck, fortune	1
frangō, frangere, frēgī, frāctus	break, shatter, wreck	15
frāter, frātris *m.*	brother	7
frūctus, frūctūs *m.*	fruit, enjoyment; profit	24
fruor, fruī, frūctus sum (+ abl.)	to enjoy	22
fugiō, fugere, fūgī, fugitūrus	to flee (from), escape, avoid	9
fungor, fungī, fūnctus sum (+ abl.)	to perform, do	22
Gallia, Galliae *f.*	Gaul	15

gaudeō, gaudēre, gāvīsus sum	to rejoice, be glad; delight in (+ abl.)	19
gaudium, gaudiī *n.*	joy, delight	17
*gēns, gentis *f.*	clan, tribe, family; nation; people	12
genū, genūs *n.*	knee	16
genus, generis *n.*	birth, origin; kind; race	14
gerō, gerere, gessī, gestus	to bear, carry on; wear	12
bellum gerō	to wage war	
gladius, gladiī *m.*	sword	28
glōria, glōriae *f.*	glory, fame; ambition, boasting	24
Graecia, Graeciae *f.*	Greece	20
Graecus, Graeca, Graecum	Greek	18
grātia, grātiae *f.*	grace; favor, kindness; gratitude	10
grātiā (+ gen.)	for the sake of, because of	
grātiās agere (+ dat.)	to thank	
gravis, grave	heavy; serious, important; difficult	21
habeō, habēre, habuī, habitus	to have, consider	1
hīc	here	31
hic, haec, hoc	this	9
hinc	from this place; hence	31
hodiē	today	13
homō, hominis *m.*	human being, man	7
honestus, honesta, honestum	honest, worthy, honorable	31
honor, honōris *m.*	honor, respect; public office	14
hōra, hōrae *f.*	hour, season	11
hortor, hortārī, hortātus sum	to urge, encourage	24
*hostis, hostis *m.* *(usually in* pl.*)*	enemy (*n.b.* hostis *is an enemy of the state;* inimīcus *(Ch. 12) is a personal enemy*)	14
humus, humī *f.*	ground, earth	15
iaceō, iacēre, iacuī, iacitūrus	to lie (*e.g.* on the ground), lie dead	1
iactō, iactāre, iactāvī, iactātus	to throw	5
iam	now; already	11
ibi	there	19
īdem, eadem, idem	the same	18
igitur (*postpositive*)	therefore	16
ignārus, ignāra, ignārum	ignorant (of), unaware (of)	31
*ignis, ignis *m.*	fire	10
ille, illa, illud	that	9
impedimentum, impedimentī *n.*	hindrance, obstacle	31
imperātor, imperātōris *m.*	general; emperor	27
imperium, imperiī *n.*	command, (military) power	3
imperō, imperāre, imperāvī, imperātus (+ dat)	to command, order; rule (over)	28
impetus, impetūs *m.*	attack; charge; impulse	16
impleō, implēre, implēvī, implētus	to fill up; complete	3
in (+ abl.)	in, on	4
in (+ acc.)	into, onto, against	4
incendō, incendere, incendī, incēnsus	to set fire to, burn; inflame	15
incipiō, incipere, incēpī, inceptus	to begin	9
incolō, incolere, incoluī	to inhabit, to live in	13
inde	from there; then, from that time forth	16
indignus, indigna, indignum	unworthy; undeserved; shameful	15
ineō, inīre, iniī *or* -īvī, initūrus	to enter; begin	23
īnfēlix, īnfēlīcis	unhappy, unlucky	23
īnferō, īnferre, intulī, illātus	to bring in, introduce; inflict	23
ingenium, ingeniī, *n.*	talent, (innate) nature, character	25

ingēns, ingentis	huge; mighty	10
ingredior, ingredī, ingressus sum	to enter; march, walk	22
inimīcus, inimīca, inimīcum	unfriendly, hostile (to)	12
iniūria, iniūriae f.	injury, harm; insult; wrong	25
inquit	he said (introduces a direct quotation)	19
īnsidiae, īnsidiārum f. (pl.)	ambush, plot; treachery	31
intellegō, intellegere, intellēxī, intellēctus	to understand	21
inter (+ acc.)	between, among	9
interficiō, interficere, interfēcī, interfectus	to kill, destroy	17
inveniō, invenīre, invēnī, inventus	to find; discover, invent	13
ipse, ipsa, ipsum	____self; himself, herself, itself, themselves; very	18
īra, īrae f.	anger	6
īrātus, īrāta, īrātum	angry	8
is, ea, id	he, she, it, they; this, that	8
ita	thus, so, in this way	13
Ītalia, Ītaliae f.	Italy	6
itaque	and so, therefore	12
iter, itineris n.	journey, path, route; a day's march	12
iterum	again, a second time	30
iubeō, iubēre, iūssī, iūssus	to order, command	20
iūdex, iūdicis m.	judge	27
iūdicium, iūdiciī n.	court; trial; judgment	14
iūdicō, iūdicāre, iūdicāvī, iūdicātus	to judge; to decide	8
iungō, iungere, iūnxī, iūnctus	to join, unite, connect; yoke	25
iūs, iūris n.	right, law; justice	7
iūstus, iūsta, iūstum	just, fair	21
iuvō, iuvāre, iūvī, iūtus	to help; please	1
labor, labōris m.	work, labor, effort; hardship	15
labōrō, labōrāre, labōrāvī, labōrātus	to work, strive	1
lacrima, lacrimae f.	tear	9
laetus, laeta, laetum	happy; fertile	6
lātus, lāta, lātum	wide, broad	26
laudō, laudāre, laudāvī, laudātus	to praise	1
laus, laudis f.	praise	15
lēgātus, lēgātī m.	delegate, envoy, ambassador; legion commander	14
legō, legere, lēgī, lēctus	to read; choose, select	8
levis, leve	light, easy; swift	18
lex, lēgis f.	law	7
līber, lībera, līberum	free	5
liber, librī m.	book	3
līberī, līberōrum m. (pl.)	children	19
lībertās, lībertātis f.	freedom, liberty	7
licet, licēre, licuit (impersonal + dat.)	it is allowed, it is lawful	31
littera, litterae f.	letter (of the alphabet); (pl.) letter, literature	8
lītus, lītoris n.	shore, beach, coast	14
locus, locī m. (in pl. sometimes also neuter)	place, position	2
longus, longa, longum	long	5
loquor, loquī, locūtus sum	to speak, talk, say	22
lūmen, lūminis n.	light, lamp, torch; eye	31
lūna, lūnae f.	moon	2
lūx, lūcis f.	light	7
maestus, maesta, maestum	sad, mournful	26
magnus, magna, magnum	large, great; important	5
male	badly	29

mālō, mālle, māluī	to prefer, want (something) more	20
malus, mala, malum	bad	5
maneō, manēre, mānsī, mansūrus	to remain, stay	6
manus, manūs *f.*	hand; band (of men)	16
*mare, maris *n.*	sea	10
abl. sg. = mare *and* marī		
māter, mātris *f.*	mother	7
medius, media, medium	middle; middle of (medium mare = "the middle of the sea")	13
memoria, memoriae *f.*	memory, recollection; history	24
*mēns, mentis *f.*	mind, judgment, reason	10
mentior, mentīrī, mentītus sum	to lie, speak *or* say falsely	25
metuō, metuere, metuī, metūtus	to fear, dread	27
metus, metūs *m.*	fear, dread; anxiety	16
meus, mea, meum	my, mine	5
mīles, mīlitis *m.*	soldier	9
mīrābilis, mīrābile	wonderful, extraordinary	32
mīror, mīrārī, mīrātus sum	to wonder (at), be surprised at; admire	22
misceō, miscēre, miscuī, mixtus	to mix, mingle; stir up, disturb	11
miser, misera, miserum	miserable, unhappy	6
mittō, mittere, mīsī, missus	to send	8
moenia, moenium *n.* (pl.)	walls; fortifications	8
moneō, monēre, monuī, monitus	to advise, warn, remind	1
*mōns, montis *m.*	mountain	13
mōnstrō, mōnstrāre, mōnstrāvī, mōnstrātus	to show, demonstrate	3
mora, morae *f.*	delay	22
morior, morī, mortuus sum	to die	25
moror, morārī, morātus sum	to delay	22
*mors, mortis *f.*	death	10
mortālis, mortāle	mortal, transient; human	20
mōs est	it is the custom, habit, way	28
mōs, mōris *m.*	custom, tradition	18
mōtus, mōtūs *m.*	emotion, impulse; movement	24
moveō, movēre, mōvī, mōtus	to move; excite; affect	6
multitūdō, multitūdinis *f.*	multitude, great number, crowd	20
multus, multa, multum	much; many (pl.)	5
mūrus, mūrī *m.*	wall; fortification wall for a city	25
nam *(sometimes used as a particle)*	for (= because); indeed, truly	13
nārrō, nārrāre, nārrāvī, nārrātus	to tell (a story)	3
nāscor, nāscī, nātus sum	to be born	30
nātūra, nātūrae *f.*	nature	2
nātus, nātī *m.*	son	30
nauta, nautae *m.*	sailor	1
nāvigō, nāvigāre, nāvigāvī, nāvigātus	to sail, sail over (across); navigate	4
*nāvis, nāvis *f.*	ship	13
nē (adv.)	not *(used with imperative & perfect subjunctive)*	25
nē	in order that … not *(used with subjunctive)*	25
nec *or* neque	and not, and … not	10
nec … nec; neque … neque	neither … nor	
necesse est	it is necessary	20
nefās *n. (indeclinable)*	sin, crime (against divine law), wrong	26
neglegō, neglegere, neglēxī, neglēctus	to ignore, neglect	24
negō, negāre, negāvī, negātus	to deny, say that … not	19
nēmō *m.; acc. sg.* = nēminem	no one	3

nesciō, nescīre, nescīvī, nescītus	not to know	19
neuter, neutra, neutrum	neither (of two)	11
nihil *n. (indeclinable)*	nothing	8
nīl *(contracted form)*		
nisi = nī	unless, if … not	27
noceō, nocēre, nocuī, nocitūrus (+ dat.)	to harm, be harmful to	7
nōlō, nōlle, nōluī	to be unwilling, not want	20
nōmen, nōminis *n.*	name	7
nōn	not	4
nōs	we	7
noster, nostra, nostrum	our, ours	5
novus, nova, novum	new; strange	6
*nox, noctis *f.*	night	11
nūbēs, nūbis *f.*	cloud	14
nūllus, nūlla, nūllum	not any, no	11
num	*signals a question which expects the answer "no";*	27
	whether *(in indirect question* §126)	
nūmen, nūminis *n.*	divine will, divine power	11
numquam	never	20
nunc	now, at present	6
nūntiō, nūntiāre, nūntiāvī, nūntiātus	to announce, report	6
nūntius, nūntiī, *m.*	messenger; message	17
ob (+ acc.)	because of	10
occāsiō, occāsiōnis *f.*	occasion, opportunity	29
oculus, oculī *m.*	eye	4
ōdī, ōdisse	to hate; dislike	27
odium, odiī *n.*	hatred, unpopularity	27
offerō, offerre, obtulī, oblātus	to offer, bring forward	23
ōlim	once (upon a time), one day (in the future)	9
omnis, omne	all, every	10
oportet, oportēre, oportuit *(impersonal* + acc.)	it is right, one should; it is necessary	31
oppidum, oppidī *n.*	town	28
ops, opis *f.*	power, help; (pl.) wealth, resources	14
optō, optāre, optāvī, optātus	to choose, desire, wish for	1
opus, operis *n.*	work, labor, task	25
opus est (+ dat.)	there is a need / use (for)	
*orbis, orbis *m.*	circle; universe	18
orbis terrārum	the world	
ōrō, ōrāre, ōrāvī, ōrātus	to pray, beg, beg for *(often with 2 accusatives,*	6
	one of the person, the other of the thing)	
ostendō, ostendere, ostendī, ostentus/ostēnsus	to show, reveal	19
pār, paris	equal (to)	12
pāreō, pārēre, pāruī, paritūrus (+ dat.)	to obey, be obedient to	7
parō, parāre, parāvī, parātus	to prepare	3
*pars, partis *f.*	part, share, direction	10
parvus, parva, parvum	small	5
passus, passūs *m.*	pace, footstep	16
mille passūs; mīlia passuum (pl.)	mile *(lit.* "1000 paces"); miles	
pateō, patēre, patuī	to be open, stand open	17
pater, patris *m.*	father; senator	7
patior, patī, passus sum	to suffer, allow	22
patria, patriae *f.*	country, fatherland	9
paucī, paucae, pauca (pl.)	few	13
paulus, paula, paulum	little, small	32

pāx, pācis *f.*	peace	7
pectus, pectoris *n.*	breast, chest; heart	15
pecūnia, pecūniae *f.*	money, property	1
per (+ acc.)	through, along; because of; by (*in oaths and prayers*)	10
pereō, perīre, periī *or* -īvī, peritūrus	to perish, die	23
perīculum, perīculī *n.*	danger	15
perītus, perīta, perītum	experienced, skilful	29
persuādeō, persuādēre, persuāsī, persuāsus (+ dat.)	to persuade	17
pēs, pedis *m.*	foot	12
petō, petere, petīvī *or* petiī, petītus	to seek, go after; ask; attack	9
philosophia, philosophiae *f.*	philosophy	27
placeō, placēre, placuī, placitūrus (+ dat.)	to please, be pleasing to	7
plēnus, plēna, plēnum (+ gen. *or* abl.)	full (of), filled (with)	8
plūs, plūris *n.* (*often* + gen.)	more	21
poena, poenae *f.*	penalty	26
poenam dare	to pay the penalty	
poēta, poētae *m.*	poet	9
pōnō, pōnere, posuī, positus	to put, place	13
*pons, pontis *m.*	bridge	25
pontus, pontī *m.*	sea, ocean	3
populus, populī *m.*	the people, a people, nation	6
portō, portāre, portāvī, portātus	to carry, bring	3
possum, posse, potuī	to be able, "I can"	7
post (+ acc.)	after, behind	4
posteā	afterwards	26
postquam	after; when	12
postulō, postulāre, postulāvī, postulātus	to demand, claim; prosecute	20
potēns, potentis	powerful; able	10
potior, potīrī, potītus sum (+ abl.)	to get hold of, acquire	22
pōtus, pōtūs *m.*	drink	22
praebeō, praebēre, praebuī, praebitus	to show; offer, provide	9
prīmō	at first	32
prīmum	first, in the first place, for the first time	30
prīmus, prīma, prīmum	first	5
prīnceps, prīncipis *m.*	leader, chief; first citizen, emperor	17
prius	before, sooner	30
prō (+ abl.)	in front of; on behalf of; instead of	4
probō, probāre, probāvī, probātus	to approve (of); prove, show	29
proelium, proeliī *n.*	battle	15
proficiscor, proficiscī, profectus sum	to set out, depart	22
prohibeō, prohibēre, prohibuī, prohibitus	to prohibit, keep from – to keep someone (acc.) from something (abl. – *separation*)	15
propinquus, propinqua, propinquum	near (to), neighboring; near, not far off (of time)	22
propinquus, propinquī *m.*	relative, kinsman	
propter (+ acc.)	because of, on account of	6
prōvincia, prōvinciae *f.*	province	15
puella, puellae *f.*	girl	2
puer, puerī *m.*	boy	2
pugnō, pugnāre, pugnāvī, pugnātus	to fight	3
pulcher, pulchra, pulchrum	beautiful, handsome; fine	5
putō, putāre, putāvī, putātus	to think, consider; suppose	19
quaerō, quaerere, quaesīvī (*or* -iī), quaesītus	to look for, seek; ask	21

quam	(rather) than, as (*in comparison*)	21
quam (adv.)	how, how much; as _____ as possible (*with superlative*)	22
quamquam	although	17
quantus, quanta, quantum	how much	25
-que	and	2
quī, quae, quod (rel. pron.)	who, which, that *also a subordinating conjunction*	13
quī, quae, quod (interrog. adj.)	which _____?, what _____?	18
quia	because	12
quīdam, quaedam, quoddam	a certain _____, a sort of _____	21
quidem (*postpositive*)	indeed, certainly, in fact	25
nē ... quidem	not ... even	
quis, quid	who?, what?	18
quisquis, quicquid (quidquid)	whoever, whatever; everyone who	26
quod	because; since	12
quōmodo	how	28
quoniam	since, seeing that	21
quoque	also	26
quot (*indeclinable*)	how many?	28
quotiēns	how often?	28
rapiō, rapere, rapuī, raptus	to seize, snatch, carry off	14
ratiō, ratiōnis *f.*	reason, judgment; method	11
recipiō, recipere, recēpī, receptus	to receive, accept; take back, regain	32
rēctus, rēcta, rēctum	straight, upright; right; virtuous, honest	24
redeō, redīre, rediī *or* -īvī, reditūrus	to go back, return	23
referō, referre, rettulī, relātus	to carry back, bring back, report	23
rēgīna, rēgīnae *f.*	queen	6
rēgnum, rēgnī *n.*	kingdom, royal power	2
regō, regere, rēxī, rēctus	to rule	8
relinquō, relinquere, relīquī, relictus	to leave, abandon	9
reliquus, reliqua, reliquum	remaining, rest (of)	13
requīrō, requīrere, requīsīvī (*or* -iī), requīsītus	to search for; ask, inquire after; demand	28
rēs, reī *f.*	thing, matter, business; court case	16
rēs pūblica, reī pūblicae *f.*	state, republic	16
resistō, resistere, restitī (*often* + dat.)	to resist, oppose, make a stand	21
respondeō, respondēre, respondī, respōnsus	to answer, reply; correspond to	19
rēx, rēgis *m.*	king	7
rīdeō, rīdēre, rīsī, rīsus	to laugh, laugh at	2
rogō, rogāre, rogāvī, rogātus	to ask, ask for	28
Rōma, Rōmae *f.*	Rome	13
Rōmānus, Rōmāna, Rōmānum;	Roman	6
Rōmānī, Rōmānōrum *m.* (pl.) (*as a noun*)	the Romans	6
Rōmulus, Rōmulī *m.*	Romulus (legendary founder of Rome)	3
rosa, rosae *f.*	rose	1
rūs, rūris *n.*	the country(side)	15
sacer, sacra, sacrum	sacred	20
saepe	often	4
sapiēns, sapientis	wise, sensible	20
sapientia, sapientiae *f.*	wisdom	5
saxum, saxī *n.*	rock; cliff	4
scelus, sceleris *n.*	crime, wicked deed, wickedness	18
sciō, scīre, scīvī, scītus	to know; know how to (+ inf.)	19
scrībō, scrībere, scrīpsī, scrīptus	to write	8

secundus, secunda, secundum	second; favorable	11
sed	but	2
sedeō, sedēre, sēdī, sessūrus	to sit	4
semper	always	4
senātus, senātūs *m.*	senate	16
senex, senis *m.*	old man	18
sēnsus, sēnsūs *m.*	sense, perception; emotion; idea	27
sentiō, sentīre, sēnsī, sēnsus	to feel, perceive	8
sequor, sequī, secūtus sum	to follow, accompany; pursue	22
serviō, servīre, servīvī *or* serviī, servītūrus (+ dat.)	to serve	9
servus, servī *m.*	slave, servant	17
sī	if	12
sīc	thus, so	11
signum, signī *n.*	sign, token, signal; (military) standard	17
silva, silvae *f.*	forest, wood	3
similis, simile	similar (to), like	12
sīn	but if, if however	27
sine (+ abl.)	without	6
sinō, sinere, sīvī, sītus	to allow, permit	20
socius, sociī *m.*	companion, comrade, ally	27
sōl, sōlis *m.*	sun	26
soleō, solēre, solitus sum	to be accustomed	2
sōlus, sōla, sōlum	alone, only	11
nōn sōlum ... sed etiam	not only ... but also	11
spectō, spectāre, spectāvī, spectātus	to watch, look at	13
spērō, spērāre, spērāvī, spērātus	to hope, hope for *(+ acc. and future inf.)*	19
spēs, speī *f.*	hope	16
statim	immediately, at once	28
stō, stāre, stetī, statūrus	to stand	14
studium, studiī *n.*	eagerness, zeal; study	29
sub (+ abl.)	under, beneath	5
sub (+ acc.)	to the foot/base of, along under *(implying motion)*	5
subeō, subīre, subiī *or* -īvī, subitūrus	to go up; to undergo; to approach	23
subitō	suddenly	11
suī, sibi, sē	himself, herself, itself, themselves	13
sum, esse, fuī, futūrus	to be, exist	5
super (+ acc.)	over, above, on (top of)	15
superō, superāre, superāvī, superātus	to overcome, conquer, surpass	1
superus, supera, superum	upper, higher, above	20
superī, superōrum *m.* (pl.)	gods	20
surgō, surgere, surrēxī, surrēctus	to get up, (a)rise	14
suus, sua, suum	his, her, its, their own	15
taceō, tacēre, tacuī, tacitūrus	to be silent ("I am silent")	1
tālis, tāle	such, of such a kind	20
tam	so, to such a degree	16
tamen	however, nevertheless, yet	9
tamquam	as, just as, just like	29
tandem	finally	4
tantus, tanta, tantum	so much, so great	14
tantum	only	14
tellūs, tellūris *f.*	the earth; land, ground	31
tēlum, tēlī *n.*	weapon; spear, sword	28
tempestās, tempestātis *f.*	storm; weather	28
templum, templī *n.*	temple, shrine	3

temptō, temptāre, temptāvī, temptātus	to try, attempt; test, prove	17
tempus, temporis *n.*	time, period of time (*e.g.* a season); opportunity	11
teneō, tenēre, tenuī, tentus	to hold, possess, keep; restrain	6
terra, terrae *f.*	land, earth, soil; country	5
terreō, terrēre, terruī, territus	to terrify, scare	1
timeō, timēre, timuī	to fear, be afraid (of)	1
timor, timōris *m.*	fear, terror	9
tollō, tollere, sustulī, sublātus	to lift up, raise; remove, carry off, steal	23
tot	so many, as many	18
totiēns	so often	25
tōtus, tōta, tōtum	whole, entire	11
trādō, trādere, trādidī, trāditus	to hand over, surrender; hand down, report	19
trahō, trahere, trāxī, tractus	to drag, pull; derive	14
trāns (+ acc.)	across, beyond	4
trānseō, trānsīre, trānsiī *or* -īvī, trānsitūrus	to go across, cross	23
tremō, tremere, tremuī	to tremble, shake	26
tristis, triste	sad; gloomy	20
Trōia, Trōiae, *f.*	Troy	14
Trōiānus, Trōiāna, Trōiānum	Trojan	30
tū, vōs	you, you (pl.)	7
tum	then, at that time; next	4
tunc	then	6
turba, turbae *f.*	crowd	3
turpis, turpe	shameful, base; ugly, foul	21
tuus, tua, tuum	your, yours, your own (sg.)	5
ubi	when; where	12
ūllus, ūlla, ūllum	any	11
unda, undae *f.*	wave, waters; sea	14
unde	from where, whence	26
undique	on all sides	28
ūnus, ūna, ūnum	one	11
*urbs, urbis *f.*	city	10
ut	in order that; so that;	25
	as	32
uter, utra, utrum	which? (of two)	11
uterque, utraque, utrumque	both, each (of two)	14
ūtilis, ūtile	useful, profitable	29
utinam	*signals a wish;* if only, would that	24
ūtor, ūtī, ūsus sum (+ abl.)	to use	22
uxor, uxōris *f.*	wife	13
valeō, valēre, valuī, valitūrus	to be well, healthy; to be strong	8
valē, valēte *(imperative)*	goodbye, farewell	8
-ve	or	30
veniō, venīre, vēnī, ventūrus	to come	8
ventus, ventī *m.*	wind, breeze	3
verbum, verbī *n.*	word	4
vereor, verērī, veritus sum	to fear, be afraid; respect	27
vēritās, vēritātis *f.*	truth	8
vērō *(postpositive)*	in fact, truly, indeed	14
vertō, vertere, vertī, versus	to turn, turn around; destroy; change	13
vērus, vēra, vērum	true	29
vērum, vērī *n.*	truth, what is true	29
vescor, vescī (+ abl.)	to eat, feed on	22
vester, vestra, vestrum	your, yours (pl.)	5

vetō, vetāre, vetuī, vetitus	to forbid; order ... not	20
via, viae f.	road; way	4
victōria, victōriae f.	victory	27
videō, vidēre, vīdī, vīsus	to see	1
videor, vidērī, vīsus sum (*often with dative of the person*)	to seem (see Ch. 15); be seen; "it seems best to _____" ?	14
vincō, vincere, vīcī, victus	to conquer; win	13
vīnum, vīnī n.	wine	17
vir, virī m.	man; occasionally "husband"	2
virtūs, virtūtis f.	courage, excellence, virtue	7
vīs, vīs f.	power, force, violence;	23
vīrēs, vīrium (pl.)	strength	23
vīta, vītae f.	life	6
vītō, vītāre, vītāvī, vītātus	to avoid	15
vīvō, vīvere, vīxī	to live, be alive	14
vocō, vocāre, vocāvī, vocātus	to call, summon	1
volō, velle, voluī	to wish, want, be willing	20
voluptās, voluptātis f.	pleasure, delight	29
volvō, volvere, volvī, volūtus	to roll, turn/twist around	14
vōs	you (pl.)	7
vōx, vōcis f.	voice	18
vulnerō, vulnerāre, vulnerāvī, vulnerātus	to wound	17
vulnus, vulneris n.	wound	17
vultus, vultūs m.	expression; face	16

Intransitive Verbs with the Future Active Participle in the fourth principal part slot

absum, abesse, āfuī, āfutūrus	to be absent, away, distant	12
adsum, adesse, adfuī, adfutūrus	to be present, be near	24
adveniō, advenīre, advēnī, adventūrus	to arrive, come to; happen	21
ambulō, ambulāre, ambulāvī, ambulātūrus	to walk	4
appropinquō, appropinquāre, appropinquāvī, appropinquātūrus	to approach, draw near	26
ardeō, ardēre, arsī, arsūrus	to burn, be on fire, glow; be eager	16
bibō, bibere, bibī, bibitūrus	to drink	24
cadō, cadere, cecidī, cāsūrus	to fall	16
careō, carēre, caruī, caritūrus (+ abl.)	to be without, free from; need, miss	7
concēdō, concēdere, concessī, concessūrus	to go away, withdraw; yield to, submit; allow; forgive	27
concurrō, concurrere, concucurrī, concursūrus	to charge, rush together	13
conveniō, convenīre, convēnī, conventūrus	to assemble, gather; meet; agree	29
currō, currere, cucurrī, cursūrus	to run	13
discēdō, discēdere, discessī, discessūrus	to depart, go away; separate	11
doleō, dolēre, doluī, dolitūrus	to grieve, mourn, suffer pain	6
dormiō, dormīre, dormīvī, dormitūrus	to sleep	8
eō, īre, iī *or* ivī, itūrus	to go	23
abeō, abīre, abiī, *or* -īvī, abitūrus	to go away, depart	
adeō, adīre, adiī, *or* -īvī, aditūrus	to go towards, approach	
exeō, exīre, exiī, *or* -īvī, exitūrus	to go out, exit	
ineō, inīre, iniī, *or* -īvī, initūrus	to enter; begin	
pereō, perīre, periī, *or* -īvī, peritūrus	to perish, die	
redeō, redīre, rediī *or* -īvī, reditūrus	to go back, return	
subeō, subīre, subiī *or* -īvī, subitūrus	to go up; to undergo; to approach	
trānseō, trānsīre, trānsiī, *or* -īvī, trānsitūrus	to go across, cross	
fugiō, fugere, fūgī, fugitūrus	to flee (from), escape, avoid	9
iaceō, iacēre, iacuī, iacitūrus	to lie (e.g. on the ground), lie dead	1
maneō, manēre, mānsī, mansūrus	to remain, stay	6
noceō, nocēre, nocuī, nocitūrus (+ dat.)	to harm, be harmful to	7
pāreō, pārēre, pāruī, paritūrus (+ dat.)	to obey, be obedient to	7
placeō, placēre, placuī, placitūrus (+ dat.)	to please, be pleasing to	7
sedeō, sedēre, sēdī, sessūrus	to sit	4
serviō, servīre, sērvīvī *or* serviī, servītūrus (+ dat.)	to serve	9
stō, stāre, stetī, statūrus	to stand	14
sum, esse, fuī, futūrus	to be, exist	5
taceō, tacēre, tacuī, tacitūrus	to be silent ("I am silent")	1
valeō, valēre, valuī, valitūrus	to be well, healthy; to be strong	8
veniō, venīre, vēnī, ventūrus	to come	8

Verbs which lack the participial stem

accidō, accidere, accidī	to fall at *or* near; happen	24

discō, discere, didicī	to learn	13
flōreō, flōrēre, flōruī	to bloom; prosper, flourish	24
incolō, incolere, incoluī	to live (in), inhabit	13
pateō, patēre, patuī	to be open, stand open	17
possum, posse, potuī	to be able, "I can"	7
resistō, resistere, restitī *(often* + dat.*)*	to resist, oppose, make a stand	21
timeō, timēre, timuī	to fear, be afraid (of)	1
tremō, tremere, tremuī	to tremble	26

Index

References are to page numbers.

Ablative case
  forms of   15, 16, 17, 30, 59-60, 85, 143, 144
  review of   294
  uses of
    absolute   159-160
    accompaniment   42
    agent   129-130
    cause   89
    comparison   192
    degree of difference   293
    description (quality)   293
    manner   42-43
    means (instrument)   30, 129, 263
    object of verb   63-64, 206
    place from which (motion away)   30
    place where   30
    separation / source   142, 294, 327
    specification (respect)   139, 291
    time when   103
    time within which   104
Accent   3
Accusative case
  forms of   15, 16, 17, 59-60, 85, 143, 144
  review of   274
  uses of
    degree   111-112
    direct object   13-14
    extent (of space)   111-112
    object complement   71-72
    place to which (motion towards)   30
    purpose (ad + gerund)   262
    subject of infinitive   175, 184
    time – length (duration)   92
    two accusatives   57, 72, 75
Adjective
  agreement of   39
  comparison of   189-191
  declension of
    first and second   38
    third   86-88
    genitive in -ius   101
    comparative   189-191
    superlative   189-191
  definition of   6, 29
  interrogative   166

possessive	138
relative clause, adjectival use	117-118, 272
substantive	40
verbal – see gerundive; participle	
Adverb	
comparative	203-204
definition of	6, 29
superlative	203-204
Agent	
ablative	129-130
dative	265
subject	6, 125
Agreement	
noun & adjective	39
subject & verb	17, 18
Alphabet	1
Antecedent	118, 165
Case	
definition of	13
review & common uses	273-274, 285, 294
see specific uses under case names – ablative, accusative, dative, genitive, locative, nominative, vocative	
Cause, expressions of	89
Chunk	32-33, 104
Clause marker (subordinating conjunction)	109-110, 117, 228-229, 239, 246-247, 255-256, 292
Clauses, dependent (subordinate)	
adjectival	117-118, 132-133, 200, 272, 281-282
adverbial	109-110, 159-160, 200, 228-229, 239, 246-247, 273, 281-282, 292
causal	110, 159-160, 239
characteristic	272
circumstantial	159-160, 239
comparison	292
concessive	159-160, 239
conditions	110, 159-160, 246-247
definition of	109
fearing	256
indirect command	255
indirect question	254-255
indirect statement	175
noun	175, 184, 200, 253-256, 282
place	110
purpose (final)	228-229, 273
relative	117, 165, 272-273
result (consecutive)	229, 254
temporal	110, 159-160, 239
Commands	
direct – with imperative	23
direct – with subjunctive	221
indirect	255
negative	183, 222, 237
prohibition	222, 237
Comparative	
of adjectives	189-191

of adverbs	203-204
Comparison	
ablative of	192
definition of	189
of adjectives	189-191
of adverbs	203-204
with quam	192
Conditions	
with indicative	109-110, 246-247
with subjunctive	246-247
Conjugation	
definition of	7
first	8
second	8
third and third -iō	69-70
fourth	69-70
Conjunctions	
coordinating	18, 271-272
definition of	6, 18, 109
subordinating (clause marker)	109-110, 117, 228-229, 239, 246-247, 255-256, 292
Consonants	1-2, 154
Core items	6, 23, 32, 41, 48, 63, 95, 153
Dative case	
forms of	15, 16, 17, 25, 59-60, 85, 143, 144
review of	285
uses of	
agent	265
double	284
indirect object	25
(indirect) object of compound verbs	283
object of intransitive verb	63-64
possession	54
purpose	284
reference (interest)	25
with adjectives	112, 262
Declension	
definition of	14
first	15
second	16-17
third (consonant stem)	59-61
third (i-stem)	85-86
fourth	143
fifth	144
Deponent & semi-deponent verbs	204-205
Dictionary entry	9, 15, 30, 37
Dictionary Practice / Form Identification	48, 94, 152, 200, 274, 286, 295
Diphthongs	1
Eius to show possession	138
English abbreviations & phrases	50, 96, 154, 202
Eō, īre and compounds	211-212
Expectations	6, 9, 10, 18-19, 25-26, 30-32, 63, 175, 192, 238, 247, 254, 255, 282
Factitive (sentence pattern)	71
Ferō, ferre and compounds	212-213

Fīō, fierī   253
Gap   53-54
Gender   14-15, 61, 86
Genitive case
   forms of   14, 15, 16-17, 24, 59-60, 85, 143, 144
   review of   285
   uses of
      after causā & grātiā   89, 262
      explanatory   40-41, 262
      objective   40-41, 262
      of the whole (partitive) 24
      possession   24
      purpose   262
      subjective   40-41
Gerund   261-263
Gerundive   263-265
Hic, haec, hoc   78-79
Īdem, eadem, idem   168
Ille, illa, illud   78-79
Imperative
   forms of
      deponent verbs   205
      first and second conjugation 23
      third and fourth conjugation 70
      irregular   70
   use of   23
Impersonal constructions   254
Indicative
   forms of
      first and second conjugation 8, 51-52, 97-100, 126-127, 135-136
      third and fourth conjugation 69, 97-100, 126-127, 135-136
   uses of   9
Indirect command   255
Indirect question   254-255
Indirect statement   175-177
Infinitive
   definition of   8
   forms of
      first and second conjugation 8, 128, 137, 173
      third and fourth conjugation 70, 128, 137, 173
      review of forms   174
   uses of
      complementary   9
      indirect statement   175-177
      noun, as a (subjective) 54
      objective   184
Ipse, ipsa, ipsum   167
Is, ea, id   71, 79
Linking (sentence pattern)   41-42
Locative case   13, 145, 294
Mālō, mālle   183, 221, 228
Modification / Modifier
   Adjectival   41, 48, 95, 153, 200

Adverbial	31-32 , 48, 95, 153, 200
Mood, definition of	7
see specific uses under mood names – imperative, indicative, subjunctive	
Nōlō, nōlle	183, 221, 228
Nominative case	
forms of	15, 16-17, 59-60, 85, 143, 144
review of	273
uses of	
subject	13
subject complement (predicate nominative)	42
Noun	
definition of	5, 14
declension of	
first	15
second	16-17
third	59-61
fourth	143
fifth	144
infinitive as	54
Number, definition of	7, 14
Numerals	102-103
Object	
ablative	63-64, 206
complement	71-72
dative	63-64
direct (accusative)	6, 13-14
indirect	25
Parts of speech, overview	5-6
Participles	
definition of	155
forms of	156-157
uses of	
adjectival	155, 158
ablative absolute	159-160
tenses of	157-158
Passive Periphrastic	265
Person, definition of	7
Place, expressions of	28, 30, 145
Possession	
adjective, possessive	138
dative of	54
eius	138
genitive of	24
Possum, posse	
indicative and infinitive	63, 174
subjunctive	221, 228, 236
Postpositive	57
Predicate nominative	42
Preposition, definition of	6, 29-30
Principal parts, definition of	9
Pronouns	
definition of	6, 62

demonstrative	78-80
indefinite	192
intensive	167-168
interrogative	166
personal	62, 71
reflexive	119-120
relative	117, 165, 271-273
Pronunciation	1-3
Purpose, expressions of	
dative	284
gerund	262
gerundive	262
relative clauses	273
supine	291
ut clauses	228-229
Question words	48-49, 95, 153, 200-201
Questions	
direct	9
indirect	254-255
Quīdam, quaedam, quodam	192
Reading skills	18-19, 25-26, 32-33
Roots	95
Sentence, definition of	5
Sentence patterns	
definition of	6-7
factitive	71-72
intransitive	7
linking	41-42
passive	129
special intransitive	63-64, 206
transitive	7
Sentence, review & parts	5-7, 48, 95, 153
Sequence of Tenses	238
Statements	9
Syllables	2-3
Subject, definition of	6
Subject complement (predicate nominative)	42
Subjunctive	
definition of	219
forms of	
imperfect active, passive	227-228
present active, passive	219-220
perfect active, passive	235, 245
pluperfect active, passive	235, 245
uses of	
characteristic	272
circumstance, cause, concession (cum clauses)	239
conditions	246-247
deliberative	222, 237
doubt	222
fearing clauses	256
hortatory (exhortation)	221, 237
indirect command	255

indirect question	254-255
jussive (command)	221, 237
optative (wish)	222, 237
potential	222, 237
prohibitions (negative commands)	222, 237
purpose clauses	228-229, 273
result clauses	
adverbial	229
noun	254
subordinate clauses in indirect speech	281
time, with anticipation	239
uses of tenses	237, 238
Substantive use of adjective	40
Sum	
future and imperfect indicative	53-54
infinitives	41, 174
participle	156
present indicative	41
perfect indicative	98
pluperfect indicative	99
future perfect indicative	100
subjunctive	221, 228, 236
Superlative	
of adjectives	189-191
of adverbs	203-204
Supine	291
Syllables	2-3
Tenses (indicative of regular conjugations)	
definition of	7
future	52, 77-78, 127
future perfect	100, 137-138
imperfect	51-52, 77, 127
perfect	97-98, 135
pluperfect	99, 136
present	8, 69, 126
primary, secondary (definition of)	238
Time, expressions of	103-104
Ut	
with indicative	292
with subjunctive	228-229, 254, 255
Verbs	
defective	9
definition of	5, 6, 7
deponent	205
finite	7
infinitive	
definition of	8
see specific forms and uses under infinitive	
intransitive	7
mood	
definition of	7
see specific uses under mood names –	
imperative, indicative, subjunctive	
non-finite	8, 155

participle
  definition of   155
  see specific forms and uses under
    participles
principal parts   9
special intransitive   63-64, 206
stem   8
tense
  definition of   7
  primary   238
  secondary   238
  see specific tenses under tenses
transitive   7
voice, definition of   7, 125
Vīs, vīs, f.   213
Vocative case, direct address   13, 24, 59, 273
Voice
  active   7
  passive   125, 135
Volō, velle   183, 221, 228
Vowels   1, 96
Word building   95-96, 153-154, 201
Word derivations   49; chapter vocabulary 1-29
Word group (= chunk)   32-33, 104
Word order   5, 9, 13, 18-19, 25, 32, 109, 111